# Old South,

# New South,

# or

# Down South?

# OLD SOUTH,

# NEW SOUTH,

# OR

EDITED BY
## IRVIN D. S. WINSBORO

# DOWN SOUTH?

## FLORIDA AND THE MODERN
## CIVIL RIGHTS MOVEMENT

WEST VIRGINIA UNIVERSITY PRESS
WWW.WVUPRESS.COM

West Virginia University Press, Morgantown 2009

© 2009 by West Virginia University Press

First edition published 2009 by West Virginia Press

Printed in the United States of America

15 14 13 12 11 10 09          9 8 7 6 5 4 3 2 1

ISBN-10: 1-933202-44-0

ISBN-13: 978-1-933202-44-0

(alk. paper)

Library of Congress Cataloguing-in-Publication Data

Old South, New South, or Down South? : Florida and the modern civil rights movement / edited by Irvin D.S. Winsboro.

   p.     cm.

Includes index.

1. Florida--Race relations--History--20th century. 2. African Americans--Civil rights--Florida--History--20th century. 3. Civil rights--Florida--History--20th century. I. Winsboro, Irvin D. S.

E185.93.F5O43 2009

323.11960730759--dc22

Library of Congress Control Number: 2009019223

Cover Design by Than Saffel

Book Design by Than Saffel; layout by Michael Rabjohns

Cover Photograph: *NAACP members marching to the Capitol during legislative session, Tallahassee, Florida*; Photographer unknown; used by permission of the State Library and Archives of Florida. Image call number RC12405.

# CONTENTS

# Preface and Acknowledgments

The subject of these essays has long intrigued me. For over twenty years I have explored, taught, and written about Florida's complex history, and throughout that time the "big question" addressed in this volume has loomed over my collective work: How did a state with such a profoundly racist and violent past emerge in the modern civil rights era with a "moderate" reputation among its one-time Confederate peers? Certainly, Florida's history of race relations was sometimes at variance with those of its neighbors, but just as assuredly, the Sunshine State embraced, manifested, and perpetuated all the insidious practices associated with white supremacy. Indeed, it even surpassed other southern states in expressions of Negrophobia such as lynching.

How, then, I asked, did the proverbial Sunshine State surmount this burden of history following the Supreme Court's *Brown v. Board of Education* decision in 1954? As this drive began to consume my intellectual endeavors, I came to realize that a comprehensive re-contextualizing of Florida's racial "images, illusions, and realities" demanded a collective rather than individual effort. While I could produce a volume testing and rethinking the model, I could not alone imbue that study with the richly textured local and state experiences needed to produce both macro- and micro-examinations of the subject. As a result, this book brings together the musings of a group of scholars on selected locales and actions. The contributors present findings that transcend the ability of a single historian to discuss Florida's remarkable geographic focus. Admittedly, there are more settings and issues (gender, for example) of the expansive Sunshine State that need to be discussed.

The Introduction establishes the theoretical framework for this volume and briefly traces some of the significant events and interpretations contributing to Florida's often presumed exceptionalism (in both the relevant scholarship, and vernacular and journalism of the state). It is not my intention to reinforce or debunk conventional understanding, but rather to establish a fresh and richer perspective of the Sunshine State's racial legacy. I propose that a people's memories of past events may sometimes be at odds with the conventional narratives of those events. Readers of this anthology must be aware that image, illusion, and reality work both individually and collectively to influence memories and the recording of events.

Building on this foundation, Professor Marvin Dunn traces the Sunshine State's Old South racial habits and violence through the post-World War II era. Dunn, author of *Black Miami in the Twentieth Century*, presents an important and sometimes provocative perspective on the indelible role that white supremacy and black agency played in molding Florida's racial character, even as the transforming events of modern civil rights swept the rest of the nation. In Dunn's words, "In this light, the sweeping generalization that Florida was a 'moderate' state, notably dissimilar from the other states of the region in the era of civil rights, is problematic and invites reassessment."

Abel A. Bartley, a scholar of Pan-African studies, documents and describes the same sort of subjugation, violence, and stonewalling of the civil rights agenda on a local level in Jacksonville. In particular, Bartley probes Florida's propensity towards racial violence by exploring the 1960 and 1964 race riots in Jacksonville, disturbing events that heretofore have largely escaped analysis within the context of the civil rights struggle. Bartley concludes, "Florida's African Americans suffered the same racial prejudice [and violence] that other black southerners faced."

"It changed it all," a black teacher in Lee County proclaimed when recalling the new federal powers growing out of the Civil Rights Act of 1964. My essay puts under a microscope the little-discussed "brotherhood of defiance" exercised by the state leaders in Tallahassee and the local jurisdictions across the state regarding the desegregation of public schools. Using Lee County as a case study, I provide a window on the depth and breadth of the state-local interaction in efforts to prevent desegregation of the county's public schools. Indeed, Lee County did not implement total and meaningful desegregation until 1969, and then only under federal court order. The ruses that Tallahassee fashioned and Lee County adopted worked all too well for all too long. While this type of event played out in many localities of the Sunshine State, Lee County provides one felicitous example of just how effective the Down South brotherhood of stonewalling was. The "hidden" tragedy of this is the fact that black settlers of Lee County had struggled for quality education for their children since the first black family moved there in 1867.

In his study of "Toms and Bombs," Professor Leonard R. Lempel offers an engaging and sometimes chilling exposé of the black struggle for dignity and rights at the "world's most famous beach." Often described as a "good place" for blacks because of the influence of northern tourists and Bethune-Cookman College, in reality Daytona Beach manifested the same types of political, economic, and social divisiveness as perhaps any city of Dixie. As Lempel demonstrates, the struggle to desegregate Daytona Beach proved long and arduous, and its New South stature remained problematic even by the late 1960s. Lempel describes, for possibly the first time in the literature, how the stonewalling of civil rights advocates after *Brown* fomented an almost predictable militancy among young, disenchanted blacks whose actions came to be characterized nationally in the mid-to-late-1960s as Black Power. The rise of black militancy and street actions in Daytona Beach similarly resulted in a reactionary movement against black agency often termed the "white backlash." Lempel reminds us that Florida mirrored many of the disappointments and defeats of the civil rights crusade that swept both the region and nation.

In the ensuing essay, legal scholar Amy Sasscer provides important insight into Florida's nationally reported desegregation case, *Hawkins v. Board of Control*, in the 1950s. In his persistent attempt to become the first African American admitted to the University of Florida's Law School, Virgil Hawkins directly and dramatically clashed with Florida's racial codes and legal roadblocks, and in the process demonstrated just how painful "promises made and promises betrayed" could be for a black person in the state. Warning that "public mischief" would ensue if a black person were admitted to a white university, the Florida Supreme Court, the board controlling state universities, and many of Florida's elected officials effectively prevented Hawkins from pursuing his dream of attending the University of Florida's law school. Sasscer's piece discloses the critical connections between Florida's subtle legal/educational processes and the radical defiance of states like Mississippi and Alabama. In all these cases, Old South white supremacy and Down South foot-dragging continued to deny court redress, including "exceptional" Florida. Sasscer provides a penetrating perspective on the anatomy of "legal mischief" in Florida's prolonged defiance of desegregation.

In an innovative study of the peculiar aspects and history of black agency on farms, Connie L. Lester, student of agrarian social factors and editor of the *Florida Historical Quarterly*, provides insight into a forgotten corner of civil rights agency in the Sunshine State. In Florida, a state that rapidly transitioned from a frontier, agrarian-producer society to an urban, service-oriented society, civil rights narratives have characteristically focused on events in the largest cities—Miami, Tampa, Jacksonville, Orlando, Tallahassee, and Pensacola. The less-visible but highly nuanced history of the struggle by African Americans in the countryside needs more attention.

In "Planting the Seeds of Freedom," Lester argues that the necessity of dealing with the white political and economic hierarchy on a face-to-face basis forced a less confrontational, but a no less important, mechanism for gaining economic, social, and political rights. Focusing on land-owning black farmers from 1945–1960, Lester demonstrates that the African American social and agricultural organizations worked to develop strong communal ties that addressed the problems of poverty and education, and promoted black leadership among established farmers as well as younger men and women of promise. Although seldom reported as extensively as urban events, rural blacks also organized local branches of the NAACP, demanded voting rights, and pressed for an end to Jim Crow segregation—often with dire economic and violent consequences. Including the stories of African American farmers demonstrates the presence of intergenerational support among rural blacks for dignity and progress in an Old South milieu and richly complicates the civil rights narratives of the Sunshine State.

Using oral histories in much the same fashion that Lester mined farm family and farm agency records, graduate student and oral history practitioner Lise Steinhauer has titled her chapter "'Wait' Has Almost Always Meant 'Never.'" Drawing inspiration from the words uttered by Dr. Martin Luther King Jr. in 1963, Steinhauer captures many of the frustrations that blacks across Dixie experienced as they sought the promises inherent in *Brown* and the U.S. Constitution.

Steinhauer then focuses on the interrelationships of Florida's post-*Brown* stonewalling and the intolerable "wait" that black residents of Palm Beach County endured in their quest for federal rights and desegregated public schools. For years after *Brown*, state and local officials felt no compelling reason to desegregate. Not until two local black attorneys launched personal court battles did the school district consider the possibility of a racially unified school system. As with Lee County, the Civil Rights Act of 1964 ultimately provided everyday blacks in Palm Beach County with the confidence to become more aggressive in their demands for educational progress. And also like Lee County, Palm Beach County exhibited no demonstrable "exceptionalism" in its long and tortured movement toward desegregation. By the time the county finally desegregated in the early 1970s, the period of "wait" must have seemed like "never" to its black community. If this was moderation, it was moderation with a nineteen-year gestation period!

Abel A. Bartley further demonstrates how persistent racism and white domination proved to be in the booming Sunshine State of the 1950s and 1960s in his examination of the gubernatorial election of 1964. In his narrative-analysis of Florida in this time period, Bartley reveals a state with more than its share of stubborn racists at the helm of leadership. Tracing the career of race-baiter Mayor William "Haydon" Burns of Jacksonville, and later Governor Haydon Burns of Florida, the author illuminates how this machine politician served as a steward of white racial attitudes and stereotypes during the modern civil rights years.

Bartley challenges his readers to solve a riddle: if Florida was a racially moderate state during the 1950s and 1960s, how then do historians explain the landslide Democratic primary victory (in one-party Florida) of Haydon Burns, an unrepentant segregationist who opposed the Civil Rights Act of 1964 and ran against Robert King High, Miami's moderate mayor? As Professor Bartley points out, residents had a clear opportunity to collectively voice moderation and reconciliation in 1964, but instead they overwhelmingly supported a racial "business-as-usual" politician. In Bartley's words, "If Floridians wanted to tell the world they were not like the vicious racists in Alabama, Mississippi, and Georgia, they could not have had a better opportunity than the 1964 gubernatorial election."

Many of the essays herein point to continuity of protest by Florida's black community prior to and through the era of modern civil rights. In his study of the evolution of civil rights to preserve places of "special" public space in Dade County, Gregory W. Bush, a specialist in public and oral history at the University of Miami, traces these peculiar struggles and the changing constituencies they have created from the post-World War II years right through present times. His study is significant for showing how blacks in Florida fought for both the right to enjoy public spaces of leisure and recreation and how they had to fight once again decades later to convince income-oriented public agencies of the "special significance" that some public spaces have for African Americans. Focusing on the historically black Virginia Key Beach site in South Florida, Bush constructs a complex and compelling story of how blacks fought for the beach in one of the first protests in pre-*Brown* Florida.

Bush also demonstrates how local black leaders and groups had to fight continually through the end of the century to redefine and preserve Virginia Key Beach's "special" association and memory for the black community. Only through concerted efforts by the black community and local professionals did the government change its plans to convert the space into a high-end eco-resort. Professor Bush sounds a warning for the South in general to be aware that the struggle to preserve special spaces of leisure, protest, and memory for the black community is unfinished business.

In the final essay in this volume, Paul Ortiz, recognized scholar of African American protest and praxis, and author of the award-winning *Emancipation Betrayed: The Hidden History of Black Organizing and White Violence in Florida from Reconstruction to the Bloody Election of 1920*, provides a recapitulation of the purpose of this book and its suggested place in the historiography of civil rights and race in Florida. Subtitled "Towards a New Civil Rights History in Florida," Professor Ortiz's essay speaks powerfully to the manner in which the contributors to this book have challenged conventions through "historical rather than anecdotal" recounting of the Sunshine State's burdensome racial history. Ortiz frames his discourse with these provocative assumptions: the fallacy of Florida's often presumed exceptionalism and the possibly misguided view that Yankee immigrants and progressive leaders like LeRoy Collins converted Florida into a more enlightened (i.e., moderate) southern state than its peers. As a corollary to the these positions, Ortiz finds that the "record" of black submission to injustices in the Sunshine State is also faulty inasmuch as an accurate historical recording places black agency in the middle of any era in the state's history and central to any experiences of the black community around the state, whether urban or rural.

In his conclusion, Ortiz pushes the significance of this work past a mundane review of the moderation/exceptionalism thesis. He observes that this book challenges readers to expand their understandings of the dynamic tensions between image and reality to encompass other defining issues of the state, such as "tensions between organizations and activists across lines of class and gender especially." He also promotes the historian's closer look at the role of everyday, working-class people as agents of change as opposed to the often-accepted model of middle-class organizers fomenting and achieving change. Finally, Ortiz reminds readers that the story of how African Americans incorporated historical memory into their motivations for protest and preserving public spaces is incomplete. In Paul Ortiz's words: "The field of civil rights studies in Florida is on the verge of a revolution. *Old South, New South, or Down South?* gives us a solid foundation on which to build. We are now better placed to understand how African Americans and their allies created social movements for justice and dignity in the face of what seemed like impossible odds. At the same time, however, there is much new work to be done."

Ortiz, as with other contributors, reminds readers that this anthology on Florida may also suggest broader application to major themes in U.S./southern history. For example, is Florida's often presumed exceptionalism simply a variation of the so-called Border South exceptionalism, the idea that the states of the Border South were more progressive than their Deep South counterparts? George Wright, among others, has challenged this notion in *Racial Violence in Kentucky*, noting that Kentucky generally was strikingly similar to the Deep South in its racial behavior toward African Americans.[1] Wright has forced scholars to rethink the exceptionalism of Border States that, like Kentucky, routinely perpetrated horrific acts against and placed institutional roadblocks in front of their African American residents.

It can also be argued that, perhaps with the notable exception of Mississippi, a number of southern states attempted to self-promote an image of moderation. Even before the modern civil rights era, the "New South Gospel" promised southern-style progressivism to attract northern investment, tourism, and political advantage. Atlanta became the "city too busy to hate," Memphis became the city "known for a better way of doing business," and North Carolina, as historian William H. Chafe demonstrates, was a state caught up in its own illusory progressive mystique. Chafe notes in *Civilities and Civil Rights* that civility "was what white progressivism was all about—a way of dealing with people and problems that made good manners more important than substantial actions . . . [it] encompassed all of the other themes of the progressive mystique."[2] Indeed, the Sunshine State had its leader with "good manners" in the person of Governor LeRoy Collins, whose years produced little if any "substantial" change in Florida's color line. If one accepts Alexis De Tocqueville's enduring image of American egalitarianism—what historian Edward Pessen has so provocatively characterized as "the egalitarian myth and the American social reality"—readers would do well to extrapolate lessons from these essays to a broader theater than Florida.[3]

The authors herein have produced an array of nuanced studies of Florida and the modern civil rights movement that will speak to the issues of moderation and more. These works inform readers of the varied interpretations of a given event, and, perhaps more importantly, of Florida's "hidden story" of racism, violence, and racial stonewalling right down to present times. With no hubris intended, I anticipate that this anthology will stimulate discussions about a "moderate" and "exceptional" Florida in new and useful ways and help illuminate the state's racial odyssey in all its complexity. We welcome critical feedback and trust that the multiplicity of interpretations will move the understanding of Florida's complex historical record forward.

## NOTES

1. George Wright, *Racial Violence in Kentucky, 1865 to 1940: Lynchings, Mob Rule, and "Legal Lynchings"* (Baton Rouge: Louisiana State Press, 1990).

2. William H. Chafe, *Civilities and Civil Rights: Greensboro, North Carolina, and the Black Struggle for Freedom* (New York: Oxford University Press, 1980), 8.

3. Edward Pessen, "The Egalitarian Myth and the American Social Reality: Wealth, Mobility, and Equality in the 'Era of the Common Man,'" *American Historical Review* 76 (October 1971): 989–1035.

## ACKNOWLEDGMENTS

I have incurred many debts over the long journey of conceptualizing and completing this book. Special thanks go to my mentors, Robert L. Zangrando and the late Sheldon B. Liss, who instilled in me the necessity for a historian's deep, critical, and sometimes contentious use of evidence and argumentation. As for the conceptual approach to and the possible criticism of the "big question" (i.e., moderation/exceptionalism) of this book, I am deeply grateful for the intellectual guidance, extensive manuscript review, and substantial editorial and other profound advice of a number of scholars, academics, and professionals. None were more helpful and forthcoming with their support, constructive criticism, and professional time in fleshing out the "big question" of this book than Abel A. Bartley, director of the Pan-African Studies Department at Clemson University; Leonard R. Lempel, formerly of Bethune-Cookman College and now of Daytona Beach State College and a director of the Florida Historical Society; Connie L. Lester of the University of Central Florida and editor of the *Florida Historical Quarterly*; and, especially, Professor Paul Ortiz of the University of Florida. Ortiz's fine work on black organizing in Florida informed many of the chapters in this book, particularly my Preface, Introduction, and chapter on Lee County.

As I grappled with the issue of "Old South, New South, or Down South?," scholars of greater achievement and intellect than I crafted approaches and challenges to my musings (many in endless streams of email) that dramatically shaped the theoretical, practical, and argumentative approach to my "big question." Ronald L. Lewis, former Stuart and Joyce Robbins Chair in History at West Virginia University, and John Boles of Rice University and editor of the *Journal of Southern History* generously shared their editorial probings with me, as did author and educator David B. Mock, and Donald K. Routh, longtime editor of three national journals and now professor emeritus at the University of Miami. Those contributors to this book who helped me develop a more mature thinking of the issues at hand are Marvin Dunn, formerly of Florida International University, and Gregory Bush of the University of Miami. Jean McNary, educator and a past director of the Florida Historical Society, helped shape the book into a work of both scholarly and general interest as did Florida scholar Joe Knetsch. Those many special collections librarians and archivists who work all the way from the Library of Congress and National Archives in Washington, D.C.; to Florida archives, repositories, and special collections; to the Lee County (Florida) Black History society deserve my praise and appreciation for their professional assistance in this project. Daisy Sapp Benjamin, a retired teacher in Lee County, and Nina Rodgers, both formerly of the Lee County Black History Society, proved most helpful in my research. My student research assistant, Alex Jordan, delivered all that I asked of him and more over the past years. There are others too numerous to list who deserve my appreciation, as well. Finally, no one deserves more gratitude and admiration for her keen editorial eye and intellectual perspicacity than the joy of my life for the last thirty-one years, Betsy L. Winsboro.

# INTRODUCTION

## IMAGE, ILLUSION, AND REALITY: FLORIDA AND THE MODERN CIVIL RIGHTS MOVEMENT IN HISTORICAL PERSPECTIVE

### IRVIN D. S. WINSBORO

A thing moderately good is not so good as it ought to be. Moderation in temper is always a virtue; but moderation in principle is always a vice.

—Thomas Paine, *The Rights of Man*, 1791

This book adds insight into the complexities of the modern civil rights movement in Florida. The contributors have produced a stimulating discussion of the prevailing narratives of the Sunshine State's role and place in civil rights. Echoing a trend in recent literature on the civil rights movement, the authors challenge readers to rethink the traditional periodization of black activism in the Sunshine State (from *Brown* in 1954 to the Voting Rights Act in 1965), and related conventions regarding Florida's "exceptionalism" relative to the other "more radical and violent" states of Dixie. In its effort to dust off the Florida file, this volume elevates from obscurity many of the critical events, protagonists, and themes of the Sunshine State's complicated racial past. This work thus presents new visions of Florida's racial past and encourages new ideas about what civil rights meant to constituencies around the state and, possibly, around the nation.

The studies here also address a generally recurring assumption in both academic as well as popular discourse that Florida has always been more progressive in race relations than its southern neighbors. Such finite views are no longer justified. In addition to violence, the essays here demonstrate that white Floridians fought as hard as their Dixie neighbors to maintain segregated schools, communities, and unequal political and employment opportunities. Although Florida often escaped the ugly national images of die-hard segregationists, the state was little more accepting of racial progress than the more rabid states so ingrained in the popular mind of the 1950s and 1960s. Indeed, the list of violent acts against civil rights activists in Florida is pervasive once one pierces the state's veneer of genteel progressivism and regional exceptionalism.

Many advocates of the moderation hypothesis trace its roots to the post-*Brown* years of the 1950s. In fact, the theory of Florida as a state at variance with its cohorts has deeper roots. For much of the early twentieth century, the national media often portrayed the state as more temperate on race relations than its cohorts. That image, however, sidestepped the Sunshine State's history of racial exploitation and such white patterns of subjugation and violence as debt peonage, convict labor and convict lease systems (only Alabama perpetuated the convict lease system longer than Florida), race riots, and Florida's leading the nation in the rate of per capita lynchings for a number of decades. As historian David R. Colburn reminds us, Florida's passage from simple Cracker to complex Sun Belt lifestyle did little to change the centrality of conservatism and status quo politics in what is now one of the nation's most diverse entities. In its journey from typically southern "yellow dog Democrats" to modern "red state Republicans," and from a state defined by race and a reluctance to come to terms with civil rights, Colburn argues that "conservative Florida's story is more complex than those that unfolded in other southern states."[1]

As the Sunshine State embarked on its transformative journey in the post-World War II years, the image of its exceptionalism sprang palpably from V. O. Key Jr.'s enduring study, *Southern Politics in State and Nation*. Primarily based on its "incredibly complex [political] factors" and unusually divisive demographic and geographic characteristics, Key found the Sunshine State to be "scarcely part of the South." While Florida occasionally emitted "a faint tropical rebel yell," for the most part it was "a world of its own." Key and others, notably Ulrich B. Phillips and the later works of Hugh Douglas Price, Donald Matthews and James Prothro, and Manning J. Dauer, concluded in similar fashion that the lack of Deep South racial characteristics stemmed from the state's urbanization and the influence of its northern population which set Florida apart from bordering states like Georgia and Alabama.[2]

In reality, historical Florida reflected the economic predation, political exclusion, spiritual oppression, and endemic violence indicative of its Old South roots and its regional neighbors. Moreover, "Yankee"-influenced Florida also echoed its radical brethren in its institutional and prolonged defiance of *Brown* and local activism. Some scholars have theorized that the northern transplants (mostly seniors) in Florida, what leading state politician Bob Graham has termed the "Cincinnati factor," worked quietly to mitigate the color line and to elect moderates. But in respective studies, Raymond A. Mohl and Gary R. Mormino, and David R. Colburn have questioned this theory by establishing that most *condo commandos* remained focused on "back-home" or national issues rather than on statewide realities. A recent generation of historians, to include Jason Soros, Joseph Crespino, and Matthew D. Lassiter, has added insight to the issue by establishing that the economic boom of the post-World War II South brought both fiscally and socially conservative corporations and traditional suburban Republicans to Dixie—by relocating their segregated communities and schools with them, they actually contributed to a tide of neo-conservatism in southern states like Florida. These findings undermine the conventional wisdom that northerners heavily contributed to the Sunshine State's presumed moderation.[3]

Northern migrants sometimes imbued Florida with a degree of progressivism, yet that social progressivism did not necessarily translate to racial progressivism in a state characterized by a sizable black population and a sizable number of new immigrants of color from the Bahamas and Caribbean. More analysis is needed to determine why meaningful desegregation and enfranchisement did not occur after *Brown* and a concurrent massive Yankee influx. Rather, what did occur was an open and submerged defiance to integration and a painful deferment of the inevitable—what this work newly defines as Florida's "Down South" strategy of delay and stonewalling.

It was not until Reubin O'Donovan Askew entered office in 1971 as Florida's first post-*Brown* "reform" governor that the state undertook meaningful progress on the civil rights front. Finally responding to the black community's, and such leading edge organizations as CORE's and the NAACP's, long years of struggle, a Florida governor enacted and not simply enunciated racial progressivism despite ongoing opposition from conservative elements across the state.

During the run up to Askew's election, 76 percent of Florida's counties operated their school districts under federal court-ordered desegregation or Health, Education, and Welfare (HEW) plans of compliance. By 1966, over 90 percent of students still attended segregated schools, and many of the 2- and 4-year colleges of the state had not integrated. Black voter registration had bumped up somewhat but nevertheless lagged woefully behind white voter registration, and blacks remained locked out of state-level public office and positions of authority. As Florida eased out of the 1960s, its congressional representation voted 12 to 2 against passage of the Open Housing Bill (Fair Housing Act), the last major civil rights action of the era. While the federal Fair Housing Act barred most forms of housing discrimination, in ensuing years housing segregation continued to be an issue in the Sunshine State. Perhaps as tellingly, Alabama's George "segregation forever" Wallace garnered almost 30 percent of the presidential vote as a third-party candidate in Florida in 1968. Wallace's tally, combined with the reactionary Richard M. Nixon's 40.5 percent of the vote, certainly could be interpreted as a victory for conservatism in the Sunshine State. To punctuate Wallace's own popularity in the state, he won every county when he ran in the Democratic primary in 1972.[4] Despite its popular reputation, Florida's racial protocol marched boldly forward into the 1970s.

The essays in this book should encourage laypersons and scholars alike to reconsider Florida's reputation for moderation and a place that gave only "a faint tropical rebel yell" during its trek to and through the modern civil rights years. Thanks to these studies, we now know that racism in Florida has been far more complicated than the "rebel yell" or redneck stereotype would suggest. Blacks and whites might well have viewed these historical trends and moderation in Florida from a different vantage point. The absence of extreme action and inflammatory rhetoric cannot be the only measure of moderation for different racial groups in a complex state, and the concept of moderation cannot be the purview of only one group in such an entity. After all, for the black community of Florida, like the black communities across Dixie, civil rights was never to be a limited pursuit arising Phoenix-like from the ashes of muted rhetoric and white subterfuge, but rather the imminent and total death of a painful epoch in their history. Readers will find these essays useful in thinking about the meaning of such lines of inquiry not just in Florida but throughout the South, and by extension, the entire nation.

Within this context, Florida's experiment with civil rights can be interpreted (or reinterpreted) through a historical examination of three significant factors: image, illusion, and reality. Although these factors may be conjoined elements of the same historical moment, they may also mature independently of each other and signify different results to different constituencies. Through this approach, readers can define (or redefine) Florida's rightful place in modern civil rights by moving beyond hypothesis and convention to the sociohistorical complexities that the term moderation actually held for the era's broad range of players.

## OLD SOUTH FLORIDA

By the time of *Brown* in 1954, Florida's record on race did not bode well for a course of moderation. Like other sons of the Confederacy, Florida was wedded to the Old South, both in ideal and practice. Historians have theorized that Florida's racial norms were tempered by political infighting and northern influences, but in reality the state instituted the same Jim Crow laws and practices (e.g., anti-labor laws, vagrancy acts, and debt peonage) characteristic of the region in general. As with all former Confederate states, Florida constructed a hostile and largely impregnable "for whites only" infrastructure.

During Reconstruction, black Floridians envisioned new hope and opportunity. Instead, post-Reconstruction witnessed a rigid re-segregation once the white plutocrats, the Bourbons, consolidated their control over the state. Thus, by the early 1880s, the Sunshine State had essentially recodified its plantation-based concept of racial protocols. When social mandates, legal sanctions, and deceit did not satisfy whites, they often turned to Klan renegades, characterized by Michael Newton in *The Invisible Empire: The Ku Klux Klan in Florida* as a "130-year history as one of the Klan's strongest and most violent realms . . ."[5]

By the turn of the century, the state's white leaders had embraced a spate of new priorities, all with a "for whites only" mandate. When authorities in Tallahassee planned for growth in the railroad, cattle, lumber, and citrus industries, they simultaneously enacted laws designed to terminate or erode many of the rights blacks had cherished under Reconstruction. Not only did the era witness a resurgence in social discrimination, it also ushered in new Jim Crow laws and practices that effectively segregated and disfranchised African Americans well into the years of the modern civil rights movement.

Many historians trace the explosion of these measures to the nadir of race relations following the *Plessy* decision of 1896. Yet, Tallahassee had set in motion "separate and unequal" treatment of blacks well before the ruling. For example, the Florida Constitution of 1885 stated that "White and colored children shall not be taught in the same school, . . ." That same document provided for a poll tax, and in the late 1880s Florida became the first state to adopt this measure, one clearly designed to disfranchise blacks. With the stroke of a pen, Tallahassee had nullified the spirit and practices of Reconstruction and in other statutes in 1905, 1913, and 1939 reinforced subordinate treatment and status for people of color. Not content with mere separation of the races, Florida wrote racial disparity and brutulization into its criminal and penal systems, which included a race-based convict lease system by 1915 and a death penalty that routinely executed twice as many blacks as whites.[6] By 1900, the Democratic primary and lagging black voter registration rates in one-party, "Yellow Dog Democrats" Florida differed little from those of the "more radical" states of Dixie.

In his groundbreaking study, *Emancipation Betrayed: The Hidden History of Black Organizing and White Violence in Florida from Reconstruction to the Bloody Election of 1920*, social historian Paul Ortiz has encapsulated the black spirit of protest by concluding that "African American resistance . . . was continuous over time, but its effectiveness varied with changes in regional and national economic, political, and legal structures."[7] Although Ortiz restricted his analysis to the decades leading up to "the bloody election of 1920," he could have extrapolated his proposition through the next half-century of racial experiences in the Sunshine State.

Most troubling for blacks was the state's propensity to use violence to enforce its code of white supremacy. Throughout the former Confederacy, as Robert L. Zangrando and others have noted, the principal means of enforcing white domination and social control remained the extralegal practice of lynching, and this practice of mob murder in Florida differed little from its one-time Confederate allies. Between 1880 and the 1930s, white mobs had lynched 3,220 blacks in the South. For much of that time, Florida led the nation in the per capita rates of extralegal deaths, and as Phillip Dray has observed in his work on lynchings, Florida exited the 1930s with "the last of the big American spectacle lynchings." Even into the World War II years, Florida practiced lynchings. As one recent study, titled "'Hitler is Here': Lynching in Florida During the Era of World War II," has noted, wartime Florida extended its record of bloody lynchings by four.[8]

Lynch-prone Florida had hanged, beaten, or otherwise mutilated and killed 256 persons by the time of World War II. One researcher found that Florida's lynching fever reached a per capita rate twice that of Mississippi, three times that of Alabama, and six times that of South Carolina for comparable time periods. Not content to simply lynch selected blacks, white Floridians attempted pogroms against black communities in Ocoee in 1920 and Rosewood in 1923, when the Klan boasted of almost 400,000 members in Florida. These hooded terrorists extended their mayhem to the post-World War II years by practicing numerous "legally sanctioned" lynchings, most notably those carried out by Lake County Sheriff (and Klansman) Willis V. McCall in the notorious Groveland shootings. In 1951, whites undertook terror bombings in Miami and Orlando, and on Christmas night white supremacists killed black civil rights activist and McCall critic Harry T. Moore and his wife Harriette. Even as the Supreme Court of the United States agreed to hear the five cases leading up to *Brown*, many reactionary whites believed, as Klan infiltrator Stetson Kennedy of Jacksonville has noted, "it was a civic duty to lynch."[9]

In the decade preceding *Brown*, the federal courts had rendered decisions meant to broaden the franchise and educational opportunities for African Americans. Even so, as David R. Colburn and Lance deHaven-Smith have concluded in *Government in the Sunshine State*, Florida governors Millard Fillmore Caldwell, Fuller Warren, and Daniel Thomas McCarty "stonewalled implementation of the decisions at every turn."[10] Thus, contextualized historically, the Down South strategies of the Sunshine State well preceded *Brown*, and, as demonstrated in this book, these strategies and their proponents seldom buckled under federal pressures in the years following *Brown*. A full decade after the historic decision, Florida remained almost as racially divided as it had since the collapse of Reconstruction. From the wake of *Brown* during the years of reactionary Acting Governor Charley Johns to the inauguration of progressive Governor Reubin Askew in 1971, Florida found itself mired in both the apartheid of the past and the intransigence of the present.

## NEW SOUTH FLORIDA

Scholars and journalists have often found Florida's civil rights journey to be a metaphor for a state "scarcely part of the South." Originating largely in the work of V. O. Key Jr. and perpetuated in media coverage of the 1950s and 1960s, notions of exceptional Florida promoted an image of a Deep South state that had reinvented itself in the image of a New South progressive. The image also maintained the fiction that Florida's power brokers and racist diehards eschewed the public demagoguery and sensational actions of other Dixie extremists (e.g., the denigrating public outcries, school closings, and mob attacks on black protesters) in their attempt to portray Florida as a national unity state. The desire for northern tourists and dollars meant Florida wanted to be seen as an integral part of the nation and not as an extreme appendage of it. Thus, although not always enunciated as such, the Sunshine State's leaders often emphasized the rhetoric of moderation during the post–World War II era in an effort to present an image of national unity rather than domestic discord. But the image was an illusion.

While there may be a kernel of truth in the image of non-radical Florida, at the same time this characterization sidesteps the continued marginalization of blacks and the key role of regional variation within this complicated state. Subjugation occurred not only through Down South delay and stonewalling but, as demonstrated in this book, through typical Deep South intimidation, violence, or white backlashes in both North and South Florida. In reality, New South Florida stubbornly clung to its racist baggage throughout most of the 1950s and 1960s.

White supremacy did not disappear after *Brown*. Instead, it reappeared in measured policies of state government, back-room scheming, and in the guise of the "all-American" Klan and White Citizens Councils (the genteel Klan). Concurrently, other state-sanctioned measures of defiance arose, including public and secretive investigative bodies, which reinforced Florida's historical intimidation and coercion of blacks. The state's congressional representation reflected this reactionary sentiment as well. Florida's two U.S. Senators (Spessard Holland and George Smathers) and six of its eight House representatives supported the "Southern Manifesto" condemning *Brown*. In the same year, a Gallup poll found that 90 percent of whites in the South, including Florida, opposed desegregation.

Even as gubernatorial candidate Sumter Lowry matched or surpassed the most racially inflammatory rhetoric of any demagogue of Dixie, the *New York Times* stood by its moderation thesis by reporting to the nation that segregation yet "reigns in Florida . . . but even so, its human and climatic temperatures remain mild."[11]

Operating under this image and illusion, the Sunshine State subordinated civil rights progress to economic goals. While it was enjoying its post-war "Big Bang" growth period, as historian Gary R. Mormino has termed it, the Sunshine State became more concerned with selling itself as a tourist and business haven than establishing itself as a land of equal opportunity. While Old South denial continued, New South Florida sagely sold itself as a place of civil rights quiescence, a land rejecting racial turmoil on the one hand and offering a stable climate for economic growth and lucrative tourism on the other.[12]

The image and illusion brought good fortune to the Sunshine State. Exemplified by its luring the high-tech and business-promoting Kennedy Space Center and ultimately "the Mouse" (the Disney World empire), the Sunshine State embarked on an unprecedented demographic and economic makeover. In the midst of the Big Bang, the nation seemed blithely unaware of the state's underlying white supremacy, often practiced through institutional delays and situational violence. By failing to acknowledge its past, Big Bang Florida and the nation overlooked its present.

Throughout much of this period, Governor LeRoy Collins perhaps exemplified for his detractors Florida's historical image of what Mormino has characterized as the state's long-held love affair with "enchanted reality and shattered dreams."[13] In retrospect, Collins, a decent and moral human being, nevertheless succumbed to the white majority's call for racial divisiveness. The governor, characterized by his two major biographers as "spokesman of the New South" and "Floridian of his century," stated in the wake of *Brown* that "I will do the right thing."[14] Thereafter, Collins persuaded the voters of the state that he had prevented the "noise and confusion" that had swept the more defiant states of Dixie. Even so, *Look* magazine ran an article quoting the governor as stating: "To listen to some reformers talk all the Negro needs in the South is to break down the lines of segregation. Nothing could be more ridiculous." Earl Black in *Southern Governors and Civil Rights* found that the governor achieved a national reputation as one of the South's leading racial moderates "despite his consistent opposition to school desegregation."[15]

Similar to Collins, former governor and then U.S. Senator Spessard Holland called for "patience and moderation," and "new breed" U.S. Senator George Smathers echoed the response. Yet, like Holland, Smathers sidestepped integration measures by simply looking the other way or quietly voting against civil rights bills.[16] Whereas Governor Collins had at least sought to mediate between public spheres, Florida's U.S. senators found *Brown* non-redemptive and did little for its spirit and practice. In retrospect, the *right thing* in the Sunshine State meant restrained rhetoric but not progress regarding the human condition. The national media and the chroniclers of the times, in turn, attributed the rhetorical restraint to a legacy of moderation and lack of racial turmoil in Florida, despite the state's ongoing commitment to the uncivil rights of racial disadvantage and violence. Arguably, Florida's sizable African American population might well have characterized the white leaders as politicians without a civil rights portfolio—simply stated, they were leaders willing to subordinate civil rights to the "old ways."

Indeed, modern Florida remained a bifurcated society in which its residents followed "white only" and "colored only" street signs. This racial demarcation did not change because the state's power brokers did not want it to change. If racism is learned behavior, then Florida's leaders did little or nothing to unlearn that behavior following the 1954 mandate. As the Sunshine State crept into the civil rights decade of the 1960s, only one school district had moved to desegregate, Dade County (in advance of a Court order), which technically desegregated Orchard Villa Elementary by enrolling four black students. Although the media touted the act as yet another instance of moderate action in Florida, by March 1960 Orchard Villa had become virtually an all-black school (a victim of "white flight"). At the same time, voter registration as a percentage of the total black population declined slightly from the early 1950s, as Florida's racial indicators continued to signal bleak times for African Americans.[17]

In keeping with this separate-but-unequal trend, Deep South rhetoric still proved key to Florida's statewide elections, with the gubernatorial elections of 1956, 1960, 1964, and 1968, and the U.S. Senate race of 1968, all being won by candidates who successfully fought, as Earl Black has concluded, to reinforce—rather than ease out of—segregation. Indeed, the successful candidates were those who managed to out-white their opponents, even in this peripheral state with demographics so atypical of the Deep South. While the historical record has been kind to Florida based in large part on the state's flattering national image and Governor LeRoy Collins's public pragmatism, there are scholars who dismiss this largess as presumptive fallacy and the governor's achievements as far less impressive than his aura. William R. Jones, Florida State University's first head of African American Studies, finds in "The Disguise of Discrimination: Under Closer Scrutiny, Gains Were Ephemeral," that Collins's administration "kept the system (Jim Crowism) rolling along in a changed form." Marvin Dunn, author of *Black Miami in the Twentieth Century*, argues that "history should not grant 'moderate' leaders like Gov. LeRoy Collins a 'get-out-of-jail-free card' merely because other southern leaders of the period were more extreme than he. Despite his image as a moderate and pioneer of the New South,

LeRoy Collins was, in retrospect, a part of the overriding problem of his time."[18] Such views from "the other side" deserve attention.

Governor LeRoy Collins left office in early 1961 as a respected leader of New South Florida who had, in fact, taken a temperate but abstruse stand on the legal and moral pitfalls of segregation. At times he bucked the racial excesses of his region as his stature grew with his years in office. And to be fair to Collins, his success as governor and promoter of New South imagery often pivoted on his ability to reach working agreements with the ultraconservative "Pork Chopper" elements of the state. As Charles U. Smith and Charles Grigg have found in *The Civil Rights Movement in Florida and the United States*, "[Collins's] posture brought attacks from both blacks and whites, segregationists and desegregationists, who accused him of doing virtually nothing in their desired direction."[19] In retrospect, his statements were often contradictory and ambiguous on the racial issues at hand, making it difficult for historians to decode Collins's record on civil rights. Perhaps like many decent politicians in the South, Governor Collins exemplified those leaders caught between old attitudes and new realities, those uncomfortable with the past and unsettled by the present. In the end, however, for many blacks and liberals, the governor's time in office possibly did little more than conceal to outsiders the Sunshine State's racial Potemkin Village.

The question for readers thus becomes: did Florida image-building intentionally or unintentionally disguise the state's stonewalling and sometimes violent reactions to the goals of modern civil rights? Perhaps the much-vaunted restraint did mitigate the sensational images of the benchmark radical states like Alabama and Georgia—yet that, too, is debatable based on the substance of this book. But was Florida's image of moderation itself deceiving, a construct of the white ruling class and an illusion for the African American underclass? If nothing else, an exploration into these issues helps integrate and refine the themes of the era.

## DOWN SOUTH FLORIDA

As an amalgam of the conventions of Old South, New South, and Down South, Florida was less on the frontier of the modern civil rights movement than on the ramparts of resistance to it. Past image, illusion, and reality in the Sunshine State may have represented separate visions to separate constituencies, but they did not represent within the larger scheme of things a commitment to mitigating patterns of life. Many of the state's New South leaders did avoid the provocative rhetoric of neighboring states of Dixie, but significant school, housing, public desegregation, voter registration, and other civil rights targets remained apparitions nonetheless. Wherein lies the reality of moderate and exceptional Florida?

Contributors to this volume have found that the State of Florida delayed substantive change in its racial codes and conduct for as many years as did its more radical cohorts. Almost immediately following *Brown*, state and local leaders adopted the mentality and actions of *all deliberate impede* as they sought massive and continuous preventive or control measures, some of which included secret investigative committees and debilitating attacks on statewide civil rights groups such as the NAACP. The practices in Florida often matched the patterns of other former Confederate states and, just as frequently, proved all too effective.[20] Perhaps the intent of white power brokers was to mollify civil rights advocates by creating a sort of Down South tunnel with a New South light at the end. But for modern protagonists of Paul Ortiz's generations of defiance, the dark tunnel and not the light defined the state's response to *Brown* and its progeny.

White resistance to the court mandate occurred almost immediately. Florida Supreme Court Chief Justice William Glenn Terrell, a LeRoy Collins mentor, concluded in an ensuing legal opinion that, "segregation . . . has always been the unvarying law of the animal kingdom," and, in a backhanded reference to *Brown*, he added that, "we are now advised that God's plan was in error and must be reversed." Popular U.S. Senator George Smathers, while professing restraint, told the media that *Brown* was a "clear abuse of judicial power." Acting Governor Charley E. Johns quickly repudiated the Court's ruling, suggested legislative action to stymie it, and participated in an anti-*Brown* conference on segregation in Virginia where he proclaimed that the vast majority of Florida's white and black citizens opposed integration. Johns then submitted a proposal to the Southern Governor's Conference calling for federal measures to grant southern states an option "to maintain separate but equal public schools for all races." Within short order, as *Brown* scholar Richard Kluger has noted, Florida submitted the "most extensive and spirited brief" challenging *Brown* in an attempt to "slow the desegregation process."[21]

Johns's stonewalling filtered down to other officials in Tallahassee as well as to local lawmakers and school board members across the state. While promoting a more controlled response to *Brown* than Johns, his successor in the governor's mansion, former State Senator LeRoy Collins, contributed to the delay and deferral framework: "In the quest for right, there are times when wisdom must restrain the pace of unfettered justice . . ."[22] Collins subsequently observed that in the wake of *Brown*, "the legislature passed many bills patterned after the most radical segregationist actions taken in other Southern states."[23] Tebeau and Marina, in the latest edition of *A History of Florida*, concluded that "it was Collins' moderation rather than the intransigence of the legislators that prevailed, and desegregation proceeded slowly but largely without violence."[24] The studies in this volume raise questions about this interpretation.

Florida, in fact, was in the vanguard of forestalling integration. Through such measures as the so-called Ervin (Gradualism) Brief to the Supreme Court, rejection of the *Hawkins* legal attempt to desegregate institutions of higher education, the Fabisinski Committee, legislative resolutions, Pupil Assignment, Freedom of Choice plans, Private School Corporation Acts, red-baiting, secret committees, and collateral actions, Tallahassee provided subordinate jurisdictions in the state with blueprints for maintaining Jim Crow. One present essayist has characterized this Florida-style gradualism as "the wait that almost always meant never."

Through it all, much of the nation failed to acknowledge Florida's racial underbelly. Perhaps this was a result of the state's juxtaposition with rabidly segregationist Alabama and Georgia, its seeming disdain for incendiary rhetoric and dramatic headlines, its unprecedented Big Bang image, or its much-touted northern and liberal influences (concentrated in South Florida). Whatever the case, the fact remains that during the modern civil rights years, Florida stubbornly perpetuated its Old South habits through an effective system of New South illusions and Down South delays. It is left to readers to determine whether the fifteen years of stalling after Brown constituted moderation or perhaps an opposing reality then that is now clouded by image and illusion.

## CONVENTION VERSUS EXCEPTION

The historiography of the modern civil rights movement is often overarched by two assumptions. First, as noted, the relevant literature reflects a strain of moderation and exceptionalism characterizing the Sunshine State both before and after the *Brown* decision. The literature also contains a corollary to that interpretation: that Florida's establishment practiced restraint and that black residents abstained from many of the mass- and direct-action protests found in other southern states.

While both arguments may hold elements of truth, this work raises questions about Florida's reputation for restraint and black quiescence in literature and media. Indeed, black Floridians—both male and female—have a deep history of finding ways to express their goals of equality and dignity in a racist society, although the full complexity of that story demands further study and refinement. The authors of *A History of Florida* have noted the "obvious need . . . for more studies of the cultural and social history of the people of Florida."[25] In this spirit, the contributors herein have sought to chart new and sometimes unconventional visions of the human and institutional drama that constitutes Florida's past.

Perhaps as important as the question of the Sunshine State's legacy of moderation is the inquiry into whether the state's African American population reinforced that image by generally eschewing direct actions. The thesis of relative black passivity conveniently reinforces Florida's reputation for moderation but equally begs the historical record. As many of the essays in this book demonstrate, *Brown* merely served as a catalyst for a long-simmering resentment against Florida's traditional Jim Crow practices. Following the decision, blacks quickly organized and carried out direct-action marches and militant protests, some of which were the earliest actions in the South and many of which met with the typical white virulence observed in other southern states. In brief, while *Brown* transformed the collective consciousness of blacks throughout the South, in Florida it simply stimulated the latest generation of local black activists to pursue protests with a new fervor. Moreover, as Connie L. Lester has underscored in her essay on black agrarians in Florida, they, too, "planted the seeds of racial equality" in their rural communities by taking actions peculiar and fitting for a non-urban way of life. In perhaps the first study of its focus, Lester identifies the personal and flexible responses of black agrarians, including strong-willed women, to the racial interactions and denials of a rural setting. As with the cities, the author finds that black agrarians' resistance to discrimination in backwater Florida were realistic responses to local conditions and therefore practical for their situational settings and times.

William H. Chafe has opined in *Civilities and Civil Rights* that this mode of analysis is significant on several levels. Although Chafe focused on black agency in North Carolina, many of the essays in this book confirm his findings that societal change occurred as a result of grassroots activism often isolated from the national movements. Moreover, Chafe finds that North Carolina, like Florida, sustained a non-monolithic protest milieu composed mainly of local-level movements and associated elements seeking common change.[26]

Chafe's work and others that have followed, for example Matthew D. Lassiter and Andrew B. Lewis's *The Moderates' Dilemma*, demonstrate that individual commitment can bring change, that sometimes the major impediments to change are not necessarily axe handle-wielding whites but the "better class" of whites, and that keeping schools open (done by Gov. Hodges in North Carolina and Gov. Collins in Florida) often resulted in the "moderate label" as an outgrowth of illusions. Historian David L. Chappell complicates the story by suggesting that moderates in the South actually outmaneuvered the die-hard segregationists and subsequently "could call the shots" in their respective state's reaction to movement and federal pressures. But what were the results of those "shots"? Merely token integration, as Chappell seems to suggest, or gradual movement towards dismantling generations of institutional bigotry and inequality? Matthew Dalb, writing from his vantage point at historically black Jackson State University, frames the controversy over perspectives on white moderation in southern Border States in the following manner: "the distinction between the massive resisters and the moderates is so minute as to make the moderates only slightly less awful than the conservatives." This perspective places in doubt not only the conventional wisdom on the place of moderates in the modern civil rights movement, but it also questions what is meant by the word moderation itself within the context of sustained resistance to integration.[27]

Historians would do well to reappraise Florida's mobilization within the groundwork of Lassiter and Lewis's findings that "through close scrutiny of grassroots activities within the black communities, scholars of the civil rights era have advanced a more expansive interpretation of the movement for racial equality. . ."[28] While serving to broaden our understanding of moderation versus mobilization, the evidence of localized black reactions to Florida's civil rights progress on the white timetable is congruent with Lassiter and Lewis's regional experiences. In the following pages are examples of all the convictions and sacrifices of black communities found elsewhere in Dixie. The evidence of black agency and the violent backlash of white reactionaries in the Sunshine State are clear and compelling. From the assassination of civil rights activist Harry T. "Doc" Moore (possibly the South's first civil rights martyr of the modern era) to the crosses burned on the lawns of Tallahassee bus boycotters, to the violent attacks on the blacks attempting to integrate the beaches of St. Augustine, to the axe handle assault on blacks in Jacksonville, to the alleged police brutalities and killing of black protesters, the intensity of white suppression in Florida not infrequently resembled that of Mississippi, Georgia, and Alabama.

In the Sunshine State, black agency did exist but was perhaps more closely planned and carried out by everyday blacks than in some of its regional cohorts. Defiant action by poor and working-class blacks in itself is not unusual, as Charles M. Payne, John Dittmer, and other scholars have established, but the lack of national attention and resources does render Florida's movement palpably different from many of the other one-time Confederate states, for instance, Mississippi, the subject of Payne's and Dittmer's research.[29] In essence, Florida's history of repression through such vehicles as the nine-year Florida Legislative Investigation Committee (the Johns Committee), charged with rooting out such "unconstitutional" groups as communists, liberals, and desegregationists, all too often intimidated and eviscerated the leadership and membership of such statewide organizations as the NAACP. Hence, the Sunshine State witnessed a civil rights movement often arising as a patchwork quilt of home-spun actions.

In the following chapters, readers will find that white repression of black protest occurred in both rural and urban settings and that white violence against local protests ranged from North Florida (home of the reactionary "Pork Choppers") to South Florida (home of the "liberal Yankees"). As readers will note, protests sparked white backlash and clashes that lasted right into the 1970s in conformity with other regional experiences, and that included situational violence. In St. Augustine, white segregationists "called for a bullet between the eyes" of a local black activist and later resorted to acid and an alligator to dissuade blacks from desegregating a swimming pool. When hundreds of blacks and dozens of whites marched in St. Augustine to protest the total segregation of the city, a mob of five-hundred whites attacked and beat them in a rabid action that Martin Luther King Jr. described, in his only major foray in Florida, as worse than the bloody events of Birmingham, Alabama, under the notorious Eugene "Bull" Connor.[30] More ominously, in North Florida, congruent with nearby states, white police officers allegedly killed a black youth, and a white rifleman murdered an unsuspecting black pedestrian, Johnnie Mae Chappell. No matter which repressive tactics surfaced, the determination by everyday blacks to counter oppression often paralleled that of their colleagues elsewhere in Dixie. In Florida, however, the everyday people caught up in these direct actions and reactionary backlashes often walked the line without the benefit of national and state-wide leadership.

Post-*Brown* Florida was at once dissimilar and similar to the regional trends. For instance, even though there were epic struggles in Florida such as the Tallahassee Bus Boycott, the St. Augustine Movement, the CORE Movement in Miami as well as its Gadsden and Dunnellon actions, not to mention the NAACP's post-World War II voter registration campaigns, Florida possibly witnessed as much movement activity as many states of Dixie. Nevertheless, the Sunshine State's actions seldom received the national prominence and media coverage that other states' sustained and sensational actions tended to attract. Perhaps the reason for this is that most often grassroots, rather than statewide, movements signified black agency in Florida.

As poor and working-class blacks sought to achieve their goals, they differed in another way from their counterparts in the South. From the time of *Brown* through the Civil Rights Act of 1964 and the Voting Rights Act of 1965, grassroots African Americans in Florida looked to local leaders and to the federal government and not to state and national race leaders and organizations to dispatch Ol' Jim Crow. Steven F. Lawson has written of this linkage between "pressure from below" and "assistance from above" as producing one of the cornerstones of black advances in the South. Certainly, other protesters in other states learned the same lessons of federal oversight and intervention, but in Florida, with its arguable absence of powerful statewide organizations (although the NAACP did maintain somewhat of a statewide presence in post-World War II Florida) and figures, the force of the federal government played an unusually critical role in inducing ground-level strategies and victories. While this paradigm may come as no surprise to experts in the field, Florida's black community's critical intersection of redress at the "below" and "above" levels goes far in explaining the localized nature of protest in this complicated state.[31]

The essays in this book underscore the notion that grassroots blacks actively and persistently protested Florida's "faint tropical rebel yell" and experienced the same sorts of resistance and violence so indicative of Dixie. If some scholars see Florida's image of moderation as a New South prototype for slow but steady progress, others may see black agency as an equally pragmatic, resourceful, and rational cry to arms. In either case, however, historians should gain from this debate a new appreciation of why a complex state might have an equally complex experience with the intersection of race and moderation.

History books often give scant attention to this subject. Indeed, during the movement itself most black agency continued, as in past eras, to be published in the black press and seldom reached white audiences. David R. Colburn's portrayal of an "ignorant" and therefore unobjective public barely aware of Florida's racial reality suggests further reasons why the memories of the state's racist baggage have become clouded or contrived. As W. Fitzhugh Brundage concluded in a recent work, this "clash of race and memory" has swept the entire South.[32] Both Colburn and Brundage submit that memory, or lack thereof, is inextricably linked to the ways that different constituencies interpret the modern civil rights movement. Simply put, the reality of Florida's past is more complex and racially ciphered than much of the historiography and journalism recognizes.

This paradox becomes even more confounding given the propensity of everyday black agency to almost leap from the pages of this work. With Florida's long history of segregation and racial mayhem, it is of little surprise that street-level and field-level blacks across the state protested Jim Crow in personal and flexible ways for generations. Therein lies another less-publicized analogy with the states comprising radical Dixie. In a recent work, Samuel C. Hyde Jr. has reminded historians that in the states bordering the Gulf of Mexico, this type of intergenerational protest has been "an on-going process that continues today." Vincent Harding's metaphor "there is a river" for this freedom struggle is also fitting and accurate, even for a Gulf state like Florida deemed by some to be "scarcely part of the South."[33]

In their effort to speak to these issues, the contributors and editor of this book do not intend to denigrate or devalue notable Floridians and scholars, nor demand a massive paradigm shift on the subject. Rather, they are suggesting that a rethinking of moderation, exceptionalism, and lack of black agency in Florida's civil rights experiences is an appropriate inquiry for the next generation of historians of the Sunshine State. As the eminent historian John Lewis Gaddis has argued, the first generation of historiography—that written closest to the actual time period of the event under review—often overlooks an opposing view of causation and transformation in favor of giving "one sided disproportionate attention" to prevailing ideas.[34] While *Old South, New South, or Down South?* may not produce a wholesale revision of "one sided notions" regarding Florida and the modern civil rights movement, it can do no less than stimulate fresh conversations on the subject.

By carefully tracing and analyzing the thoughts and actions of racial Florida in its pre- and post-*Brown* phases, the authors herein have taken a major stride toward promoting and diversifying an understanding of image, illusion, and reality in traditions and behaviors of Old South, New South, and Down South Florida. In the end, the chapters in this book provide both conventional and exceptional views on the big question of Florida and the modern civil rights movement, and by implication, perhaps for the South at large.

## NOTES

1. Margaret Vandiver, *Lethal Punishment: Lynchings and Legal Executions in the South* (New Brunswick, N.J.: Rutgers University Press, 2006), 22; David R. Colburn, *From Yellow Dog Democrats to Red State Republicans: Florida and Its Politics Since 1940* (Gainesville: University Press of Florida, 2007) 4, 8. For background studies on the historiography of civil rights and the periodization issue, see Steven F. Lawson, "Freedom Then, Freedom Now: The Historiography of the Civil Rights Movement," *American Historical Review* 96 (April 1991): 456–71; Kathryn L. Nasstrom, "Beginnings and Endings: Life Stories and the Periodization of the Civil Rights Movement," *Journal of American History* 86 (September 1999): 700–711; and Jerrell H. Shofner, "The Legacy of Racial Slavery: Free Enterprise and Forced Labor in Florida in the 1940s," *Journal of Southern History* 47 (August 1981): 411–26.

2. V. O. Key Jr., *Southern Politics in State and Nation* (New York: Alfred A. Knopf, 1949 [1950]), 83–84; Ulrich B. Phillips, "The Central Theme of Southern History," *American Historical Review* 34 (1928): 30; see Hugh Douglas Price, *The Negro and Southern Politics: A Chapter of Florida History* (New York: New York University Press, 1957); Donald Matthews and James Prothro, *Negroes and the New Southern Politics* (New York: Harcourt, Brace and World, 1966); Manning J. Dauer, "Florida: The Different State," in *The Changing Politics of the South*, ed. William C. Havard (Baton Rouge: Louisiana State University Press, 1972), 92–164; Colburn, *Yellow Dog Democrats*, 13.

3. Raymond A. Mohl and Gary R. Mormino, "The Big Change in the Sunshine State: A Social History of Modern Florida," in *The New History of Florida*, ed. Michael Gannon (Gainesville: University Press of Florida, 1996), 441; David R. Colburn and Lance deHaven-Smith, *Government in the Sunshine State: Florida Since Statehood* (Gainesville: University Press of Florida, 1999), 33; David R. Colburn, "Florida Politics in the Twentieth Century," in *The New History of Florida*, 361; Colburn, *Yellow Dog Democrats*, 23; Jason Sokol, *There Goes My Everything: White Southerners in the Age of Civil Rights, 1945–1975* (New York: Alfred A. Knopf, 2006); Joseph Crespino, *In Search of Another Country: Mississippi and the Conservative Counterrevolution* (Princeton, N.J.: Princeton

University Press, 2007); Matthew D. Lassiter, *The Silent Majority: Suburban Politics in the Sunbelt South* (Princeton, N.J.: Princeton University Press, 2005). On the origins of studies characterizing "moderation," see Robert Howard Akerman, "The Triumph of Moderation In Florida Thought and Politics: A Study of the Race Issue from 1954 to 1960" (PhD diss., American University, 1967), especially ii-vi, 368–79.

4. Department of Education, Survey of Florida School Desegregation Compliance Status, September 11, 1970, Smathers Library, University of Florida, Gainesville, Fla.; Southern Education Reporting Service, *A Statistical Summary, State By State, of School Segregation-Desegregation in the Southern and Border Areas from 1954 to the Present* (Nashville, Tenn.: Southern Education Reporting Service, 1967), 11; Larry Johnson, Deirdre Cobb-Roberts, and Barbara Shircliffe, "African Americans and the Struggle for Opportunity in Florida Public Higher Education, 1947–1977," *History of Education Quarterly* 47 (August 2007): 328–58; Darryl Paulson, "Unfinished Journey: After 50 Years of Striving, The Destination Is Still Unclear," *Forum* (Spring 2004), 11; registration data compiled from Division of Elections, Bureau of Election Records, R.A. Gray Building, Room 316, Tallahassee, Fla.; *Congressional Quarterly: Almanac 90th Congress, Second Session. . . 1968*, 24-H,9–S; Stephen Lesher, *George Wallace: American Populist* (Reading, MA: Addison-Wesley, 1994), 470–75; George Corley Wallace "The Inaugural Address of Governor George C. Wallace, January 14, 1963," Alabama Department of Archives and History, Montgomery, Alabama; *The Florida Handbook, 1993–1994*, comp. Allen Morris (Tallahassee: Peninsular Publishing Co., 1993), 617.

5. Michael Newton, *The Invisible Empire: The Ku Klux Klan in Florida* (Gainesville: University Press of Florida, 2001), xv; see Jerrell H. Shofner, "Customs, Law, and History: The Enduring Influence of Florida's 'Black Codes,'" *Florida Historical Quarterly* 55 (Winter 1977): 277–98.

6. Florida Constitution (1885), Article 12, Section 12; Margaret Vandiver, "Race, Clemency, and Executions in Florida, 1924–1966" (Masters thesis, Florida State University, 1983), 1, 20; see J. Irving E. Scott, *The Education of Black People in Florida* (Philadelphia: Dorrance and Co., 1974), 5–12; Joseph Aaron Tomberlin, "The Negro and Florida's System of Education: The Aftermath of the Brown Case" (PhD diss., Florida State University, 1967), 1–16; Shofner, "Custom, Law, and History," 281–87; James Button, "Blacks," in *Florida's Politics and Government*, ed. Manning J. Dauer (Gainesville: University Presses of Florida, 1984), 286–89.

7. Paul Ortiz, *Emancipation Betrayed: The Hidden History of Black Organizing and White Violence in Florida from Reconstruction to the Bloody Election of 1920* (Berkley: University of California Press, 2005), xix; see Gary R. Mormino, "A History of Florida's White Primary," in *Sunbelt Revolution: The Historical Progression of the Civil Rights Struggle in the Gulf South, 1866–2000*, ed. Samuel C. Hayes Jr. (Gainesville: University Press of Florida, 2003), 133–50; and Robert Cassanello, "Avoiding 'Jim Crow': Negotiating Separate and Equal on Florida's Railroads and Streetcars and the Progressive Era Origins of the Modern Civil Rights Movement," *Journal of Urban History* 34 (March 2008): 435–57.

8. Robert L. Zangrando, *The NAACP Crusade Against Lynching, 1909–1950* (Philadelphia: Temple University Press, 1980), 3–21; W. Fitzhugh Brundage, "Introduction," in *Under Sentence of*

*Death: Lynching in the South*, ed. W. Fitzhugh Brundage (Chapel Hill: University of North Carolina Press, 1997), 4; Stewart E. Tolnay and E.M. Beck, *A Festival of Violence: An Analysis of Southern Lynching, 1883–1930* (Chicago: University of Illinois Press, 1995), 37–38; Phillip Dray, *At the Hands of Persons Unknown; The Lynching of Black Americans* (New York: Random House, 2002), 344; Tameka Bradley Hobbs, "'Hitler is Here': Lynching in Florida During the Era of World War II" (PhD diss., Florida State University, 2004).

9. Molefi K. Asante and Mark T. Mattson, *The Historical and Cultural Atlas of African Americans* (New York: MacMillan, 1992), 95, 101; Arthur F. Raper, *The Tragedy of Lynching* (Chapel Hill: University of North Carolina Press, 1933), 28; Vandiver, *Lynching and Legal Executions in the South*, 22–27; see Gary R. Mormino, "GI Joe Meets Jim Crow: Racial Violence and Reform in World War II Florida," *Florida Historical Quarterly* 73 (July 1994): 230–42; Jeffrey S. Adler, "Black Violence in the New South: Patterns of Conflict in Late-Nineteenth Century Tampa," in *The African American Heritage of Florida*, eds. David R. Colburn and Jane L. Landers (Gainesville: University Press of Florida, 1995), 207–39; Robert P. Ingalls, "Lynching and Established Violence in Tampa, 1858–1935," *Journal of Southern History* 53 (November 1987): 613–44; Steven F. Lawson, David R. Colburn, and Darryl Paulson, "Groveland: Florida's Little Scottsboro," in *The African American Heritage of Florida*, 289; Maxine D. Jones and Kevin M. McCarthy, *African Americans in Florida* (Sarasota: Pineapple Press, 1993), 81–84, 106–07; Maxine D. Jones, Larry E. Rivers, David R. Colburn, R. Tom Dye, and William R. Rogers, "A Documented History of the Incident Which Occurred at Rosewood, Florida, in January 1923," submitted to the Florida Board of Regents, Tallahassee, December 22, 1993; Caroline Emmons, "'Somebody Has Got to Do That Work': Harry T. Moore and the Struggle for African-American Voting in Florida," *Journal of Negro History* 82 (Spring 1997): 232–43; Jake C. Miller, "Harry T. Moore's Campaign for Racial Equality," *Journal of Black Studies* 31 (November 2000): 214–31; Ben Green, *Before His Time: The Untold Story of Harry T. Moore, America's First Civil Rights Martyr* (New York: Free Press, 1999), 193–95; Kennedy quoted in Martin A. Dyckman, *Floridian of His Century: The Courage of Governor LeRoy Collins* (Gainesville: University Press of Florida, 2006), 9.

10. Colburn and deHaven-Smith, *Government in the Sunshine State*, 36.

11. "Report on the South: The Integration Issue: Florida," *New York Times*, March 13, 1956; see Helen L. Jacobstein, *The Segregation Factor in the Florida Democratic Gubernatorial Primary of 1956* (Gainesville: University of Florida Press, 1972), 27, 40, 84; David R. Colburn, "Florida's Governors Confront the Brown Decision: A Case Study of the Constitutional Politics of School Desegregation, 1954–1970," in *An Unknown Tradition: Constitutionalism and the History of the South*, eds. Kermit L. Hall and James W. Ely Jr. (Athens: University of Georgia Press, 1989), 326–55; Joseph Tomberlin, "Florida Whites and the Brown Decision," *Florida Historical Quarterly* 51 (1972): 22–36; Charlton W. Tebeau and William Marina, *A History of Florida* (Coral Gables: University of Miami Press, 1999), 428.

12. Gary R. Mormino, *Land of Sunshine, State of Dreams: A Social History of Modern Florida* (Gainesville: University Press of Florida, 2005), 2.

13. Mormino, *Land of Sunshine*, 3.

14. Tom Wagy, *Governor LeRoy Collins of Florida: Spokesman of the New South* (Tuscaloosa: University of Alabama Press, 1985), see 59–103, 120–43; Dyckman, *Floridian of His Century*, 1–4.

15. *Miami Herald*, February 3, 1956; LeRoy Collins, "How It Looks from the South," *Look*, May 27, 1958, 92, 95–97; Earl Black, *Southern Governors and Civil Rights: Racial Segregation as a Campaign Issue in the Second Reconstruction* (Cambridge, Mass.: Harvard University, 1976), 93.

16. Holland quoted in the *Palm Beach Post*, May 18, 1954; "Former Sen. Smathers Dies at 93," *Fort Myers News-Press*, January 21, 2007.

17. Southern Education Reporting Service, *A Statistical Summary*, 11; Tomberlin, "The Negro and Florida's System of Education," 196–98; *Tampa Tribune*, September 9, 1959; *Tallahassee Democrat*, September 10, 1959; Registration data compiled from Division of Elections, Bureau of Election Records, R.A. Gray Building, Room 316, Tallahassee, Fla.

18. See David R. Colburn and Richard K. Scher, "Race Relations and Florida Gubernatorial Politics Since the *Brown* Decision," *Florida Historical Quarterly* 53 (October 1976): 153–69; William R. Jones, "The Disguise of Discrimination: Under Closer Scrutiny, Gains Were Ephemeral," *Forum*, Summer (1995), 27; Earl Black, *Southern Governors and Civil Rights*, 90–98; and Marvin Dunn in the first essay of this book.

19. Charles U. Smith and Charles Grigg, "School Desegregation in Florida," in *The Civil Rights Movement in Florida and the United States*, ed. Charles U. Smith (Tallahassee: Father and Sons Publishing, 1989), 194.

20. See Don Shoemaker, ed., *With All Deliberate Speed: Segregation-Desegregation in Southern Schools* (Westport, Conn.: Negro University Press, 1957), table, 225.

21. "Terrell Says Mix Mandate Reverses God," *Orlando Sentinel*, October 20, 1955; Wagy, *Governor LeRoy Collins of Florida*, 14, 42; Dyckman, *Floridian of His Century*, 106; "Former Sen. Smathers Dies at 93," *Fort Myers News-Press*, January 21, 2007; *Tallahassee Democrat*, May 18, 1954; "Johns Considers Special Session of Legislature," *Fort Myers News-Press*, May 18, 1954; *Jacksonville Florida Times-Union*, May 19, May 20, June 9, June 11, and June 16, 1954; *St. Petersburg Times*, June 12, 1954; "Johns Suggests Governors Act on Segregation," *Fort Myers News-Press*, November 12, 1954; Richard Kluger, *Simple Justice: The History of Brown v. Board of Education and Black America's Struggle for Equality* (New York: Vintage, 1975), 724.

22. LeRoy Collins, "How It Looks from the South," *Look*, May 15, 1958, 95–97.

23. LeRoy Collins, "Past Struggles, Present Changes, and the Future Promise for Civil Rights in Florida and the Nation," in *The Civil Rights Movement in Florida*, 16.

24. Charlton W. Tebeau and William Marina, *A History of Florida* (Coral Gables: University of Miami Press, 1999), 427.

25. Tebeau and Marina, *A History of Florida*, xiii.

26. William H. Chafe, *Civilities and Civil Rights: Greensboro, North Carolina, and the Black Struggle for Freedom* (New York: Oxford University Press, 1980), see especially 67–97, 337–55.

27. Matthew D. Lassiter and Andrew B. Lewis, eds. *The Moderates' Dilemma: Massive Resistance*

*to School Desegregation in Virginia* (Charlottesville: University of Virginia Press, 1998); David L. Chappell, *Inside Agitators: White Southerners in the Civil Rights Movement* (Baltimore: Johns Hopkins University Press, 1994), 195; Matthew Dalb, "Review of *The Moderates' Dilemma: Massive Resistance to School Desegregation in Virginia*," in *Journal of Negro History* 85 (2000): 128.

28. Matthew D. Lassiter and Andrew B. Lewis, "Massive Resistance Revisited: Virginia's White Moderates and the Byrd Organization," in *The Moderates' Dilemma*, 2.

29. Charles M. Payne, *I've Got the Light of Freedom: The Organizing Tradition and the Mississippi Freedom Struggle* (Berkley: University of California Press, 1995); John Ditmer, *Local People: The Struggle for Civil Rights in Mississippi* (Urbana: University of Illinois Press, 1994), especially 19–388.

30. See William C. Havard and Loren P. Balch, *The Politics of Mis-Representation: Rural-Urban Conflict in the Florida Legislature* (Baton Rouge: Louisiana State University Press, 1962), 50, 62; David R. Colburn and Richard K. Scher, *Florida's Gubernatorial Politics in the Twentieth Century* (Gainesville: University Presses of Florida, 1980), 173–77; David R. Colburn, *Racial Change and Community Crisis: St. Augustine, Florida, 1877–1980* (Gainesville: University of Florida Press, 1991), 61–115; Jones and McCarthy, *African Americans in Florida*, 113–15; quoted in Patsy Sims, *The Klan* (New York: Stein and Day, 1978), 154.

31. Steven F. Lawson, *Running for Freedom: Civil Rights and Black Politics in America Since 1941* (Philadelphia: Temple University Press, 1991), 65. For an early historiographical perspective on the significance of federal responses, or lack thereof, to the protest and organizing activities of grassroots blacks, see Robert L. Zangrando, "Black Initiative, The Vote, and Federal Responses," *Reviews in American History* 5 (December 1977): 560–65; Steven F. Lawson, "The Role of the National Government," in *Debating The Civil Rights Movement, 1945–1968*, eds. Steven F. Lawson and Charles Payne (Lanham, Md: Rowman and Littlefield, 2006), 40–42.

32. David Colburn, "Introduction," in *The African American Heritage of Florida*, 14; W. Fitzhugh Brundage, *The Southern Past: A Clash of Race and Memory* (Cambridge, Mass.: Belknap Press of Harvard University Press, 2005), 1–11.

33. Samuel C. Hyde Jr., "Introduction: The Challenge and Expectations of Social Change in The Gulf South, 1866–2000," in *Sunbelt Revolution*, 5; Vincent Harding, *There Is a River: The Black Struggle for Freedom in America* (New York: Vintage, 1983), especially Chapter 16.

34. John Lewis Gaddis, "The New Cold War History: First Impressions," in *We Now Know: Rethinking Cold War History* (New York: Oxford University Press, 1997), 281–95.

# CHAPTER ONE

# THE ILLUSION OF MODERATION

## A RECOUNTING AND REASSESSING OF FLORIDA'S RACIAL PAST

### MARVIN DUNN

Scholars and laypersons alike have argued that the civil rights movement in Florida was neither as violent nor as attenuated as it was in other states of the Old South. It is also generally accepted that the "Yankee factor" and the leadership of Governor LeRoy Collins (1955–1961) were major factors in the "relatively minor" white resistance to racial integration in the Sunshine State. What most people often overlook, however, is that blacks actually died in the Sunshine State as a consequence of white resistance to racial progress and that Florida's state and local leadership may not have been as moderate as is generally recorded in the literature. Perhaps the civil rights struggle in Florida did not produce sustained headlines in the national media, but it did, nevertheless, reflect pioneering black actions and troubling racial issues that scarred neighboring Deep South states in the 1950s and 1960s. Thus, a premise of this recounting of Florida's racial past is that white resistance to desegregation, often including violence and stalling tactics, ran deep and long in Florida's past and that blacks largely overcame that burden through homegrown leadership and grassroots movements.

A further premise of this study is that white reactionaries in the Sunshine State seldom "saw the light," as has been often portrayed in the histories of the era. Rather, civil rights momentum characteristically resulted from black activism and resistance arising within the state, particularly in the period after the Second World War. The movements were often stimulated by both local issues and external forces, such as decisions from federal courts, national civil rights measures, and, possibly, the arrival of northern whites (the "Yankee factor") from more progressive regions of the country, especially to the central and southern sections of the peninsula. However, even as Florida became less Old South in habits and, presumably, more New South in values, Jim Crow patterns persisted in the state. In this light, the sweeping generalization that Florida was a "moderate" state, notably dissimilar from the other states of the region in the era of civil rights, is problematic and invites a reassessment.

North Florida politicians, who controlled the state political machine during the Jim Crow era, kept the Sunshine State a true son of the Confederacy. Indeed, they opposed racial integration in any form until compelled to yield by homegrown activism or by federal authority. Although far removed from the other population regions and assumed segregation centers of the state, North Florida typified the full range of Jim Crow mentality and measures that rang throughout Florida. It is often presumed that Florida's regionalism (Pensacola is almost as far from Key West as it is from Chicago) and its particular brand of constitutional government, combined with the presumed Yankee factor, worked historically to temper the Sunshine State's endemic racism. The actual historical record of this former Confederate state and its much-vaunted "moderate" leaders like LeRoy Collins may well belie that notion.

As civil rights protests swept the country in the 1950s, Governor LeRoy Collins walked a tightrope between the North Florida conservatives, often-reactionary politicians termed "Pork Choppers," and the growing regional internal and external pressures to move Florida into a more progressive profile. Collins must have recognized the looming death of Jim Crow in the state. In his first race for governor in 1954, against the archetypical racist Charley Johns, Collins declared his own commitment to segregation. He triumphed over Johns in the "lily-white" Democratic primary, and then trounced his Republican opponent with nearly 80 percent of the vote, most likely because of his image as a progressive candidate calling for a modernization of his state.[1] For Collins, modernization was a complex subject, but it did not include dismantling Florida's racial divides. Consequently, from the Panhandle to Tampa Bay through Central Florida and into the rapidly growing Miami-Fort Lauderdale regions, the national civil rights movement found few public partisans in the Sunshine State, including high-profile, "progressive" Gov. Leroy Collins.

In the aftermath of the 1954 *Brown v. Board of Education* decision, in which the Supreme Court ordered the desegregation of public schools, most public officials in Florida either ignored the Court mandate or openly defied it. In Tallahassee, Collins himself declared that, "Florida was just as determined as any other Southern state to maintain segregation." He labeled *Brown* "a cruel hoax on the people."[2] At one point, in an apparent act of defiance, Collins vowed to use the powers of his office to maintain racial separation in the Sunshine State. As the dean of Florida historians, Charlton W. Tebeau, has noted, "Governor Collins accepted segregation as a part of Florida custom and law and promised to use the lawful processes of his office to maintain it."[3]

On March 21, 1956, the governor, the cabinet, and other high-ranking state officials joined in recommending a committee of legalists to promulgate legal means to avoid integration. As black-led civil rights demonstrations sprouted locally around the state, Collins ultimately ordered sheriffs to suppress all KKK parades or other "disorderly" acts, but was careful to note that, "the ban would also cover demonstrations by the NAACP."[4] It was a shallow and ineffective step, if not a cynical one, since Collins must have known at the time that members of the Ku Klux Klan had infiltrated many Florida law enforcement agencies. Moreover, the ban rhetorically placed civil rights demonstrators in the same lawless category as racial bigots and thugs.

In a real sense, Collins embodied the vital issues of the burgeoning civil rights movement: would Florida remain firmly entrenched in the bigoted politics of the past or would the state progress into a more moderate image of what was increasingly being called the "New South"? Collins's response, like the actions of other political leaders who followed him into the 1960s, was one of equivocation, defiance, and Florida's peculiar Down South-style of delaying and stonewalling racial advancement.

As local black students demonstrated for civil rights in Tallahassee in 1960, Collins made public remarks that seemed to accept the fact that blacks were now demanding freedom as never before. But according to one of the state's most active civil rights advocates, Patricia Stephens Due, who was among those blacks arrested for demonstrating in Tallahassee, Collins did little to impress her. In her view, "While many Negroes were hailing Gov. Collins as courageous and heroic for his remarks (which, admittedly, were unusual for a Southern governor during that time), they still rang hollow to me. For one thing, we were still in jail. Words have never meant anything to me without action to back them up."[5]

University of Florida historian David R. Colburn also has expressed the view that Collins accepted racial segregation: "Collins was not an extremist . . . he sought to create an environment that would help the state diversify economically and understood that racial militancy would crush his modernization program . . . Still, he was not prepared at this point to accept desegregation, and he joined with other southern leaders in opposing the Court's [Brown] decision."[6] Facing stiff opposition from the Pork Choppers of North Florida, Collins seems to have adopted a politically expedient, but not necessarily progressive, policy regarding the debate in the state over the implementation of Brown and desegregation of Florida's public institutions. In Colburn's words, "Collins pursued a variety of measures that were designed to preserve school segregation but also sought to avoid racial extremism."[7]

Although Collins is often credited as being the state's first moderate governor, Florida's first truly moderate governor did not emerge until a decade after Collins had left office. He was Reubin O'Donovan Askew (1971–1979). Askew made the first appointment of a black, Miami's M. Athalie Range, to the state cabinet as secretary of Community Affairs in 1971, a decade after Collins had left office. For Askew, unlike Collins, moderation was not a rhetorical device but rather an actual point of policy. Even so, meaningful changes in the Sunshine State's age-old patterns of race relations did not take place until well after such unsettling events as Birmingham and even the implementation of unprecedented federal actions such as the Civil Rights Act of 1964 and the Voting Rights Act of 1965. "Moderate" Florida simply could not easily shed the racial time warp that had engulfed it for so many generations of bigotry and violence.

Thus, it may be a misnomer to portray Florida in the civil rights era as a state of "moderation," and regional "exceptionalism." At best, the Sunshine State projected a contrived image of moderation, and at worst, Florida simply continued its color line under the guise of New South progress. As Colburn concluded, "Although Florida was only one of four southern states with virtually no integration by 1960, the national press continued to portray Florida as a progressive state because of the leadership provided by Collins and because his counterparts in Arkansas, Mississippi and Alabama pursued extremist policies."[8] Within this context, the only significance "moderation" assumes is that it characterizes a state that did not pursue the ultra-extreme policies of Arkansas, Mississippi, and Alabama.

To further contextualize this phenomenon, one must recognize that Florida, since becoming a U.S. territory in 1821, has been an especially dangerous place for black people. Before the in-migration of English-speaking whites from the United States, Florida was a wilderness where Native Americans and possibly thousands of armed and proud escaped slaves lived as liberated people. Free blacks averaged 10 percent or more of the black population, most of whom lived in Spanish communities such as St. Augustine in the east and Pensacola in the west of the Panhandle. By 1814, colonial figures showed that blacks numbered about 57 percent of the total population of Spanish Florida. As whites moved into Florida in the pre-Civil War period (many with their slaves), they demanded suppression of this unruly amalgamation of reds and blacks. As a result, some of the harshest anti-black legislation in the history of the United States was ushered forth from the early territorial assemblies of Florida. The laws were notably hard on free blacks, who were seen as threats to the institution of slavery by enticing (by their mere existence) enslaved blacks to seek freedom.[9]

As the American Civil War approached, Florida was the third state to leave the Union after the two most radical Southern states, South Carolina and Mississippi. Florida's Black Codes, laws passed after Reconstruction by southern legislatures to oppress people of color, were as stridently oppressive as those in other former Confederate states. Conservative white Democrats, who controlled the state politically since the end of Reconstruction, excluded blacks from one-party rule until the mid-1940s when the Supreme Court struck down the practice in *Smith v. Allwright*, a case that originated in Texas.[10] Yet the reality of one-party rule still reigned in Florida, as it did in many of the former Confederate states.

Even worse, Florida was a physically dangerous place for blacks. As Michael Newton has noted in his book on KKK violence, the number of blacks lynched in Florida lagged behind the body counts in neighboring states, but Florida's smaller population made it the per capita leader in the national "lynching bee." Florida's tally of four lynchings per ten thousand blacks tripled Alabama's rate and doubled the rates of Mississippi, Georgia, and Louisiana. Some of the last lynchings in the United States took place in the Sunshine State even as the practice had been virtually halted in other parts of the South.[11] The most infamous of Florida late-era lynchings took place in the Panhandle in Marianna in 1934. It involved the hanging of Claude Neal, a black man whose murder created a firestorm of protest in the North because the lynching had actually been predicted days before it took place.[12] Notwithstanding northern eyes, and even an influx of northerners to the state, Florida doggedly continued on its racist path.

The brutal lynching of Emmett Till, a fourteen-year-old black boy in Mississippi in 1955, riled black America and refocused northern attention on the bloody practices of the Old South. But when Till was a toddler, what would happen to him in Mississippi had already happened to a black child in Florida—though the event escaped the national news. Fifteen-year-old Willie James Howard was lynched in Live Oak, Florida, by three white men in 1944. His offense: writing a note to a white girl. The killing was a reflection of the protracted lynching of blacks in Florida until the very eve of the modern civil rights movement. Additionally, Howard's murder demonstrates that while the similar murder of Emmett Till in "reactionary" Mississippi caused a national furor a decade later, the murder of a black child in "moderate" Florida, although shocking the black citizens of the state itself, did not rise to the level of the national press.[13]

However, Brevard County black activist Harry T. Moore openly condemned the crime. Moore would subsequently become the leader of black resistance to racial hate crimes in the state. He led the active resistance to anti-black violence in Florida, writing articles for national black newspapers, advising the national NAACP to enter Florida to help end bigotry and mayhem, and challenging liberal whites in the North and in the nation's capital to support his efforts. After a Suwannee County grand jury refused to indict the accused white men, Moore still persisted in his pursuit of justice for Howard's murderers. He wrote to the governor asking for an official investigation into the matter. He organized chapters of the NAACP in many small towns across the state. Tellingly, it was the working-class blacks—laborers, maids, agricultural workers, and the like—who rose to Moore's challenge and supported him and the NAACP at the local level.[14] This would be a pattern of local black commitment that would last right through the post-*Brown* movement in Florida itself.

In 1945, a year after Moore's organizing, the bullet-riddled body of a thirty-year-old black man was found on a lonely stretch of a highway south of Madison in North Florida. Jesse James Payne had been dragged out of the county jail by a lynch mob, reportedly because he had once complained about being cheated by a white man. The raid on the jail was expedited by the local sheriff, who lived next door and left the jail keys in his unlocked police car. Apparently, the mob was able to secure the keys while the sheriff (presumably) slept.[15] Payne vehemently denied the charges, yet the frenzied white crowd proceeded to lynch him. The killing came just weeks after V-J Day, which ended the Second World War. It was the only lynching reported in the nation that year.[16] While America rejoiced in its vanquishing of the international fascists, the image of brutal and oppressive Florida fell by the wayside.

In the fight for justice for Jesse James Payne, it was Harry T. Moore who once again stepped forward. As in the Howard case, he arose as the link between the local chapters of the NAACP and black protesters and other interested state and national figures. And, as in the Howard affair, he boldly implicated the local sheriff in the lynching and called for his suspension from office.[17] By challenging the rigid social code of the state, Moore led the way into the modern civil rights era in Florida and, in the process, perhaps sealed his own fate in this racist state.

Moore expanded his efforts to obtain justice for Jesse James Payne, but even the national NAACP could offer little support, citing the weakness of the civil rights laws and the lack of Florida's official interest in the case. But Moore had emerged as a legitimate race leader with connections to the federal government's Department of Justice, various white liberal groups in the North, the NAACP, and the national press. As a result of his activism, Moore was seen as a dangerous black man by many racists in a state with a moderate image but an Old South proclivity.

Moore also worked actively for grassroots causes like equal pay for black teachers in Florida. During this period, white public school boards in Florida paid black teachers on a lower scale than white teachers. For example, the average yearly salary in 1936 was $495 for black teachers and $1,039 for white teachers.[18] But when Moore gained support from the NAACP's national office to file a test case in Mims to challenge the pay differences, he could not find a black teacher who would agree to file a discrimination charge. The hard facts were that any black teacher who filed such a suit in Florida was certain to be fired.[19]

For weeks, no one came forward to represent black teachers in this cutting-edge issue in traditionalist Florida. Finally, Moore's friend, John Gilbert, volunteered. Gilbert was, at the time, principal of Cocoa Junior High School in Brevard County. In New York, the NAACP issued a glowing press release, predicting that this first case in the Deep South would be "watched keenly by other southern states" and, if successful, "would have a profound effect upon the fortunes of negro [sic] teachers in the South."[20] Predictably, John Gilbert lost his job. Brevard Circuit judge M. B. Smith dismissed Gilbert's subsequent petition for redress. Thurgood Marshall (later the first black justice of the U.S. Supreme Court) and his assistants in the NAACP's legal office filed an immediate appeal with the Florida Supreme Court.[21] While not actually capturing the national headlines, the course of the NAACP's actions further dispelled the myth of Florida as a moderate state on race issues. Even so, the image, or illusion, of Florida's moderation would persist through this and numerous spin-off actions at both the local and state level of the proverbial Sunshine State.

In June 1939, the Florida Supreme Court heard arguments in the case. The Florida Court's reactionary position proved worse than Marshall had feared. According to Dr. Gilbert Porter, a black educator from Miami and an eyewitness to the suit, several justices actually turned their backs on the plaintiffs when they stood up to present oral argument. Consequently, no one was surprised when the Florida Supreme Court unanimously denied the plaintiffs' petition on July 25, 1939.[22] The case proved that Florida's Old South heritage was not about to die at the hands of in-state, black protesters or even national intervention at this point.

In the following decade, Florida's most notorious civil rights case of the modern period took place in rapidly growing Central Florida. In 1949 when a black person in Lake County pondered the word "cracker," a dry biscuit did not come to mind—rather, Lake County sheriff Willis V. McCall did. Just before the start of the contemporary civil rights movement in Florida, the sensational killing of a black man by the white Lake County sheriff, while the man was in his custody, both terrified and energized black Floridians. Public outrage reached new proportions as the national media finally began to cover social injustice in the Sunshine State. The "Groveland Incident" produced for blacks one of the state's most hated racists, Willis McCall, whom Harry T. Moore openly accused of killing the victim. The incident at Groveland nudged blacks closer to overt activism and support for organizations like the NAACP. Florida's illusions of racial tolerance were now on the verge of unprecedented state and national challenges.

On Christmas night 1951, Harry T. Moore and his wife, Harriette, perished as a result of a bomb exploding under the floorboards of their Central Florida home. The device had been placed below the Moores' bedroom, where they slept after celebrating both the holiday and their twenty-fifth wedding anniversary. Within hours, the soft-spoken former NAACP state coordinator and civil rights activist lay dead, tragically ending his seventeen-year battle for racial justice in Florida. Harriette died several weeks later.

The FBI subsequently focused its investigation on five suspects. Several of them had attended a Klan barbecue at which agents believed the murder plot emerged. However, agents were unable to pierce the Klan's wall of silence to confirm a report that one of the suspects displayed a floor plan of the Moores' home at the meeting. The FBI ultimately found that there was a widespread network of local officials, police, and militant whites operating throughout Central Florida seeking to intimidate and bully blacks into obsequience.[23] No convictions resulted, but the Moores' case was reopened in 1991 after a woman claimed that her Klansman ex-husband had once boasted of participating in their killings.[24]

Klan membership in Florida has waxed and waned, but the Klan has always played a role in enforcing the racial codes of the Sunshine State. Not surprisingly, the Klan opposed post-*Brown* desegregation in Florida and participated in rallies and demonstrations to publicize its position and to intimidate would-be civil rights activists. The Klan frequently resorted to violence in its sustained efforts to suppress local black political movements, such as voting marches and registration attempts. The Klan attacked civil rights activists with little fear of retribution. Indeed, white law enforcement officers in Florida often held Klan membership over the years. Nevertheless, Florida blacks historically resisted Klan and other forms of white oppression in all locales and regions of the state; while some history books trace local black agency to the post-*Brown* era in Florida, this is not technically accurate.

Like black men, black women too risked their lives in racist Florida to secure and exercise their rights. Resistance by black women in Florida during the 1920s and beyond was led by Mary McLeod Bethune, the founder of Daytona's Bethune-Cookman College. When Klansmen appeared before Bethune's home seeking to intimidate her, they were intercepted by local blacks who stood their ground. Although only one example of similar actions by committed blacks in the state, Mary McLeod Bethune's face-off with the Klan in Daytona Beach reflects how black women throughout Florida drew on their inner strengths and convictions to "stand up to the man." Indeed, histories of Florida need to more fully explore this theme and build on the pioneering studies of black women produced by such scholars as Maxine D. Jones of Florida State University.[25]

The historical example of blacks demanding and demonstrating for voting rights, in particular, offers a felicitous example of black agency in the Sunshine State. This primarily local movement began in earnest on April 3, 1944, following the Supreme Court's ruling in *Smith v. Allwright* that blacks must be allowed to register as Democrats and vote in Deep South primary elections. The Court ruling marked a new entry of blacks onto the political stage of every state of Dixie. Now, Old South politicians, much to their dismay, had to reckon with black ballots. This was possibly the true birthing moment of the modern civil rights movement because it was an act of great empowerment of southern blacks with far-reaching consequences in American political life.[26]

Supervisors of registration in Florida generally ignored the decision. For instance, in Brevard County, the supervisor of elections refused to register blacks as Democrats or change their registration from Republican to Democrat despite the ruling. "Before I register any niggers as Democrats, I will get out of politics altogether," he declared. After repeated challenges originating from within the local black communities of the state, many such cases were subsequently overturned by circuit courts, which ordered that blacks could be admitted to party rolls.[27] In a historical sense, this action by blacks in Florida broke new ground, because it added to their unrelenting demands that force of the federal government now be exercised to redress grievances—grievances that traditionalist Florida, left to its own habits, had long refused to even acknowledge. The growing shadow of the federal government thereafter offered a powerful stimulant to blacks in their long search for dignity and rights in the Sunshine State.

It was against this historical backdrop of Old South-style racism, violence, and stonewalling that the Sunshine State moved into the burgeoning civil rights era of the 1950s and 1960s. With such a legacy, it would be hard to believe that Florida and its leaders now readily adopted a "moderate," New South approach to racial equality and opportunity. Many of the lessons of Florida during the heightened civil rights movement of mid-century, analyzed in retrospect, would challenge the post-*Brown* notion of the Sunshine State adopting a sincere mindset and policy of moderation. Certainly, if such black leaders as Harry T. Moore had lived through the post-*Brown* legal and racial permutations, it would be an impossible leap of faith to presume that they would have characterized the era and its leaders as moderate. A review of modern civil rights events in Florida (some of the earliest and most successful examples of local black activism in the nation) from the black perspective sheds light on this proposition.

By the mid-1950s, many of the state's local NAACP chapters and other civil rights groups began to organize for political change as the state entered a period of heightened activism and danger. The most active of the civil rights organizations, the Congress on Racial Equality (CORE), held its first Southern Interracial Institute in Miami in mid-1959. About seventy-five people attended the session on theories of nonviolent, direct action. During the event, CORE went beyond theory and actually held a sit-in at a seg-regated Miami lunch counter. This was six months prior to the famous student sit-ins at Greensboro, North Carolina, which are generally credited by historians with originating the sit-in movement. CORE in South Florida succeeded only in closing the lunch coun-ter temporarily. The first sustained lunch counter demonstrations in the Sunshine State would follow in North Florida in November of that year.[28]

Rev. C. K. Steele led the new fight for dignity and equality in Tallahassee. Hundreds of students from Florida Agricultural and Mechanical University (FAMU), the state's institution of higher education for people of color, participated in a boycott to end the requirement for blacks to sit at the back of the city-operated buses.[29] On May 27, 1956, two black female students, Wilhemina Jakes and Carrie Patterson, tested the rule. They took seats in the white section of the bus and refused to move when asked to do so by the driver. They were immediately arrested.[30]

Steele organized the subsequent protest and kept it nonviolent, although he received many threats from whites, including the installation of a fiery cross at the entrance to his church. The Ku Klux Klan marched in front of his home and threw bottles through its windows. But Steele held steady and continued to organize carpools similar to the ones that had been used in similar boycotts in Montgomery and Baton Rouge. Protest-ers held mass meetings despite intimidation and threats from the police. In a show of local black solidarity, an estimated 90 percent of the city's black population refused to ride the busses.[31]

The boycott, and Steele's leadership of it, lasted more than a year. Rev. Steele organized voter registration drives, lectured around the country to raise money for the fight, and mentored many area freedom fighters. When the protest organizers ultimately demanded total integration of the city-operated busses, the *Tallahassee Democrat* editorialized that they were being "unreasonable." The Tallahassee City Commission tried desperately to quell the protest. True to its heritage, the KKK held is own meetings and cross-burnings. A city judge called the arrested students "fly-by-night martyrs" and sentenced them to sixty days in jail and fined each $500.[32]

After losing thousands of black riders, the Tallahassee bus boycott, the third bus boy-cott in the Old South, ended successfully on January 7, 1957, when the City Commission replaced segregated seating with a new plan based on "maximum health and safety" for passengers. The plan allowed bus drivers to determine where passengers could sit based upon his assessment of the situation.[33] Even with this minor victory, however, moderate Florida seemed but an abstract notion rather than a reality to most of the state's black residents.

Shortly after Tallahassee, the struggle turned to the desegregation of public accom-modations in the city. FAMU student-leader Patricia Stephens Due had attended CORE training in South Florida in 1959, and returned, much energized, to the Panhandle cam-pus. Due canvassed the dormitories for volunteers and recruited other emerging student protesters. In October, she and about thirty student leaders, including some white stu-dent supporters from nearby Florida State University, met with Rev. Steele to plan their strategy for the state's next direct, nonviolent action.[34]

That effort came quickly. Although there had been the brief and little-heralded CORE lunch counter sit-in in Miami in 1959, it was the February 1, 1960, sit-in by four black college students in Greensboro, North Carolina, that sparked the sit-in movement across the South. The new spirit of protest quickly spread across Florida as well, with similar lunchroom counter demonstrations breaking out in many corners of the state, such as Miami, Tampa, and Tallahassee. The demonstrations in the state capital are especially instructive regarding the new confrontations between would-be New South Florida and its leaders and persistent Old South Florida and its proponents. Two weeks after Greens-boro, FAMU students and CORE activists organized their first sit-in at the local Wool-worth's lunch counter.[35]

Patricia Stephens Due and Richard Haley, a FAMU music instructor, emerged as the two leaders of the Tallahassee chapter of CORE. They groomed students for the next sit-in on February 20, again at Woolworth's. At the demonstration that day, the mayor arrived and asked them to leave. Six left and eleven others were arrested and marched to jail as a jeering crowd of whites harassed them. Whites brandishing knives, baseball bats, and axe handles (a particularly common form of white "moderation" in Florida) went unchecked by the police, some of whom even called the white students in the demonstration "white niggers."[36] Hundreds of FAMU students planned to attend the trial of the "Tallahassee Eleven," but when authorities learned of the plan, they postponed the trial. A biographer of LeRoy Collins has found that the governor "strongly disapproved, saying at his March 3 press conference that the tactic was unlawful and dangerous. He said he understood how the black students felt but that the merchants had the law on their side."[37]

On March 12, after a three-week preparation period, Due and others marched downtown for another demonstration. This time large numbers of students joined the effort. According to Patricia Stephens Due, "I witnessed twelve FAMU students and FSU students arrested that day at the Woolworth lunch counter and taken to jail. They were marched down the street in interracial pairs, escorted by police on all sides, with police and onlookers branding the whites as nigger lovers."[38] At the appearance of armed members of the segregationist White Citizens Council, the decision was made for the other students to return to campus. Once back on campus, over a thousand FAMU and FSU students began massing to march on the downtown. They were met by the police, who began firing teargas and pushing the students back onto the campus. A white police officer singled out Due and fired a teargas canister into her face at point-blank range.[39] There were mass arrests, among them the editor of the FSU school newspaper and three of its reporters. Governor Collins responded by restricting FAMU students to their campus.[40]

The governor and other political leaders placed heavy pressure on university officials to rein in students and faculty members. Richard Haley, a CORE leader and music professor at FAMU, was denied a new contract.[41] Miami black educator Dr. Raymond Dunn was then a student at the university and among those arrested. He and many others were taken to cattle holding pens on the Tallahassee fairgrounds, where they remained incarcerated like animals for days. All this occurred in the shadow of the governor's mansion, and Collins did little or nothing to protect expelled students and those faculty members who lost their jobs, or to relieve the conditions under which the students were being held.[42]

The trial of the "Tallahassee Eleven" gained national attention, the results of which seriously undermined Florida's moderate image across the land. The judge, John Rudd, told the students that their lawyers from the ACLU in Miami, Tobias Simon and Howard Dixon, were "closely affiliated with the Communist Party in the United States." Eight of the eleven chose jail over bail and refused to pay their fines and go free. They were the first students in the modern civil rights era in all of Dixie to choose jail over freedom. Eventually, CORE's leadership was suspended from the campus and angry students responded by demonstrating in front of the home of FAMU's president. The picketing continued throughout the fall.[43]

This nonviolent action brought unwanted attention to the local struggle in Tallahassee, the capital of "moderate" Florida. Demonstrations and marches continued, one of the largest in front of the state capital building. The city responded by quietly desegregating its lunch counters in 1963. Even so, the community muddled through the slow, Down South process of delay and stonewalling for several more years before blacks in Leon County could finally consider the struggle for equal accommodations a success.[44]

At essentially the same time, four Klansmen were acquitted of beating four members of the NAACP in St. Augustine. Not long thereafter, President Kennedy's sweeping civil rights bill became law and St. Augustine—the ancient gem of moderate Florida—took center stage in the nation as one of the most racist and violent white reactionary cities in the modern era. As with the initial voter registration drives in Florida, it would once again take the full force of the federal government to turn the Sunshine State away from its firmly entrenched racist habits.

Dr. Robert Hayling, a dentist from the black section of the city called Lincolnville, arose as the leading civil rights activist of the period. Given the violence in St. Augustine, and the insidious activities of the Klan in North Florida, Hayling's courage equaled that of any state or national civil rights leader of the day. In 1963, Dr. Hayling had organized a campaign against segregated public facilities. The local chapter of the NAACP urged the White House not to recognize the 400th anniversary of the city of St. Augustine, given the pervasive and historical discrimination blacks faced there. When both efforts failed, St. Augustine's black leadership turned to Martin Luther King Jr.'s Southern Christian Leadership Conference (SCLC) for assistance.[45]

By that spring, King had rented a St. Augustine cabin, which was fired upon on May 28 (King was away at a meeting). It then took armed bodyguards to protect him in St. Augustine. Dr. King called the city lawless and prone to violence. As demonstrations proceeded, police arrested hundreds of protestors. Included was Mrs. Malcolm Peabody, the seventy-two year-old mother of the governor of Massachusetts when, at the Ponce de Leon Motor Lodge, she tried to be served a meal while a member of an integrated group. Her arrest led to national media coverage, including a front-page photograph in the *New York Times*.[46] The event gave national focus to St. Augustine, Florida, as a racially violent rather than a progressive place.

In June, Rev. King and Rev. Ralph David Abernathy of the SCLC participated in a sit-in at the Monson Motor Lodge. The manager of the lodge, James Brock, captured national headlines as he berated black and white protestors in the lodge's swimming pool. When the protesters did not get out, Brock doused the pool with hydrochloric acid. Still, blacks did not leave the water. Out-doing himself the next day, Brock deposited a live alligator in the pool in an attempt to panic activists. When the alligator stunt failed, Brock resorted to the police.[47]

King and Abernathy suffered arrest along with other protesters as St. Augustine assumed the dubious title of one of the ugliest racist reprisals anywhere in the Deep South. Later, Abernathy wrote, "St. Augustine put us on notice that the violence we experienced during our marches in Birmingham was by no means the worst we could expect."[48] In

St. Augustine in 1964, it was apparent that the Old South lived on in rather violent, strange, and unparalleled ways. Certainly, for those watching the events on national television, the word "moderation" seemed totally out of place in regard to this Florida city.

By the end of 1964, the SCLC, licking its wounds, had left St. Augustine and Dr. Hayling to their own resources and moved on to other higher-priority targets like Selma, Alabama. Abernathy, the SCLC, and King had failed in St. Augustine. Their time-tested nonviolent, direct activism was ineffective in desegregating Florida's legendary tourist attraction. Only the passage of the national civil rights legislation of the mid-1960s settled public access issues in Florida's, and the nation's oldest European-rooted city.

It should be noted, though, that the civil rights movement had also begun a nonviolent, activist period in the presumed more progressive and Yankee-influenced southeast region of the state well before the demonstrations in Tallahassee and St. Augustine. Blacks had conducted or threatened wade-ins at public beaches in the South Florida since the end of the Second World War. Their first efforts focused on Virginia Key Beach, where the navy had trained black seamen to swim since Crandon Park, a Dade County beach where white sailors trained, remained off-limits to sailors of color. When the county attempted to close the beach after the war, blacks threatened a direct-action "swim-in" at Crandon Park. The county relented and dropped the color line at Virginia Key Beach. Thus ended a civil rights, direct-action campaign in South Florida, occurring almost a decade prior to similar, yet better publicized, actions that swept Dixie.[49]

There was also white resistance to desegregated housing in Dade County. On September 23, 1951, 100 pounds of dynamite exploded under an unoccupied apartment building in what had been an all-white neighborhood. The bomb was meant to discourage blacks from moving into the community. The culprits were never caught. Indeed, desegregation of housing in all of Dade County met with widespread white resistance. In Coconut Grove, whites had a concrete wall built to divide the affluent white section of the Grove from the adjacent, largely black Bahamian section. The same happened as blacks moved from Overtown, the historically black section near downtown, into an area northwest dubbed Liberty City. Parts of both walls remain today as silent testimony to Florida's segregationist ways in what was rapidly becoming a northern-influenced enclave of the Sunshine State.[50]

Despite the presumed liberal influence of this "Yankee factor" in South Florida, the historical record reflects little actual change in local racial patterns. White and black populations remained physically apart, and Jim Crow still ruled over most of the other institutions in this section of the state that often has been seen as the antithesis of Old South Florida. Was post-World War II South Florida actually a part of the larger Old South Florida itself? After separating reality from image and illusion, the answer may not be as simple as some historians would have us believe. An exploration into some of the key black activism of South Florida helps underscore this point.

The most dynamic civil rights organization in Miami was the local chapter of CORE, led by black ophthalmologist Dr. John O. Brown. He moved to Miami from Wewoka, Oklahoma, after mustering out of the army at the end of World War II. Brown was quickly appalled by the stark racial fault lines of Miami. He soon joined the nascent local movement by becoming one of twelve black parents to sue the Dade County School Board to admit their children to all-white schools. He thereafter organized numerous integration demonstrations and became a mainstay of grassroots activism in South Florida.[51]

Brown credited sympathetic white supporters and "the little man" for keeping the movement fueled with money and volunteers. "You couldn't get black professional people involved. They were afraid of losing their jobs. It was the janitor, the maid, the bus driver, the yardman, who gave us the 5 and 10 dollar contributions that got us through."[52] Brown specifically mentioned white attorneys Howard Dixon and Tobias Simon. He also praised some transplanted northerners and local Jews, such as Jack Gordon (later a powerful member of the State Senate) and his wife, Barbara. Other white supporters he mentioned were Ruth Perry, a librarian from Miami Beach who served CORE for many years as its secretary. Yet, while acknowledging some white support, Brown readily noted the persistence of Jim Crow practices and mentality throughout the entire white power structure of South Florida.

Miami produced other notable black activists such as the Reverend Theodore Gibson. The Miami leadership also included A. D. Moore, a leader of the Miami chapter of CORE. He led a boycott of one of the city's largest department stores, Shell City, for refusing to serve blacks at its lunch counter. In August 1960, eighteen blacks were arrested in their attempt to desegregate the lunch counter. Howard Dixon and Tobias Simon defended the CORE demonstrators.[53]

In Miami, black activism and white intransigence landed the NAACP and the state of Florida before the United States Supreme Court in 1963. The Gibson case gained national recognition, because white conservatives had charged that the movement was under the influence of communists who had infiltrated civil rights organizations such as the NAACP.[54] As in so many other troubling attacks on civil rights across Dixie, Florida too found itself embroiled in the odious red-baiting phase of the movement. In a real sense, the Sunshine State may have even led the entire South, save Mississippi, in the most un-American and immoral attacks on street-level, civil rights activists.

In the late 1950s, a fight over the membership list of the Miami's NAACP sent two black ministers to jail. Rev. Theodore R. Gibson, the organization's leader through the turbulent 1960s, estimated the local group to have a membership of one thousand in 1963.[55] The demand for the chapter's membership list came from Tallahassee and was a reflection of the nation's preoccupation with communists in the 1950s and the argument of many conservatives that "Reds" had infiltrated the civil rights movement. At the national level, this phenomenon played out before the brutalizing McCarthy Committee (the House Committee on Un-American Activities), under the leadership of "red-baiter" Joseph R. McCarthy. Many unwilling and innocent citizens were dragged into hearings before the committee in its unfounded search for communists in the government.

Florida's version of the McCarthy Committee was the Johns Committee of the Florida Senate, named after reactionary state senator and one-time acting governor Charley E. Johns. It operated in much the same way as the McCarthy Committee and the notorious Mississippi Sovereign Commission—by secrecy, innuendo, ridicule, red-baiting, and similar harassments of those targeted as subversives. Yet, as previously noted, the "communist card" was not only played out in the state legislature; Governor Collins himself had even used it against the student protesters in Tallahassee.[56]

In 1959, the Johns Committee demanded that the Miami Chapter of the NAACP submit its membership list to allow the committee to decide if communists operated inside the organization. Gibson and the Rev. Edward T. Graham, the organization's former president, refused. They agreed to testify from memory but declared that they would not give up the organization's records. They were arrested and charged with contempt of the legislature.[57] In their refusal to turn over the membership list, Gibson and Graham cited the First and Fourteenth Amendments to the U.S. Constitution, which pertain to the rights of free speech, assembly, association, and the equal protection of all citizens. But Dade Circuit Court Judge W. May Walker pronounced the two ministers guilty, sentenced them to six months in jail, and fined them each $1,200. Gibson and Graham appealed the decision to a Federal Court.[58]

Miami blacks closed ranks behind the two ministers. On September 15, 1963, a major rally and fundraiser took place at Overtown's Mount Zion Baptist Church. The city's black newspaper, the *Miami Times,* exhorted blacks to fill the church to overflowing: "Their stand for freedom is not only a personal one with them it is a thing which includes all of us in this area."[59] A divided U.S. Supreme Court issued one of its most important decisions of the modern civil rights era in February 1963; in a five-four decision in favor of the two ministers from South Florida, the Court concluded that the Johns Committee had no inherent right to probe for communists in the membership rolls of non-subversive organizations like Miami's local NAACP chapter.[60] Once again Florida captured national headlines, but certainly not for its racial moderation.

As more sensational civil rights actions swept the Sunshine State in the 1960s, Mayor Haydon Burns of Jacksonville, as part of his North Florida-based campaign for governor, condemned the demonstrations. As if to mock him, a series of demonstrations began in that city, and one black woman, Johnnie Mae Chappell, the mother of ten children, died at the hands of a white supremacist assassin. By the time it was all over, Jacksonville's era of civil rights activism had included not only a death, but also the same sort of police neglect and mob violence so characteristic of the Deep South as a whole. As Abel Bartley has found in *Keeping the Faith: Race Politics, and Social Development in Jacksonville, Florida, 1940–1970*, the reactionary leadership of Mayor Haydon Burns played perhaps the most important role in moving Florida's leading economic center to what Bartley found to be "[a] new and restive spirit [in] the Black Community, as those who had once silently accepted second-class citizenship [now] militantly expressed their desire for change."[61] As with other corners of the state, some scholars seem to find little moderation in North Florida's racial experiences.

Farther to the south, Fort Lauderdale, Florida's fastest-growing city of the 1960s due to a massive Yankee influx, began local protests over access to whites-only places of public space in Broward County. In 1956, the year that marked the rise of Dr. King as a national figure during the Montgomery, Alabama, bus boycott, local blacks in Florida marched on the county courthouse demanding a beach of their own. In response, Broward County bought land for a Jim Crow beach where John U. Lloyd State Park is currently located. However, blacks had to use an inconvenient ferry to reach "their" beach.[62]

Dissatisfied black leaders later marched to the white beaches near Las Olas Boulevard and staged a wade-in on July 4, 1961. Dr. Von D. Mizell, one of the black leaders of the demonstration, later recalled, "I was scared that day. I had to walk through a little corridor there with a human wall on both sides. It was so tense, and one little spark could have started a riot. I had to look straight ahead, and I was not at ease at all." The police arrested several black leaders, but the City Commission later agreed to build a road to the black beach.[63]

But local blacks wanted more from "moderate" Florida; they wanted an end to segregated beaches. Eula Johnson, a widowed mother of three and past president of the Broward County NAACP, led seven carloads of young people to the white beaches in late July 1961. The Ku Klux Klan, often thought to be weak and ineffective in Yankee-influenced South Florida, destroyed her car, and the Fort Lauderdale police tried to convince her to call off wade-ins because her actions would keep away tourists—but she persisted. When officials took Johnson to court, a federal judge ruled that blacks had a right to swim at the public beaches.[64] As with the other regions of Florida, it was local black activism and determination to secure dignity and rights that eventually turned cities like Miami and Ft. Lauderdale away from their persistent Jim Crow practices and policies. Indeed, in the early throes of the civil rights movement in Florida, from Pensacola to Miami and from Jacksonville to Tampa, it was local black agency and determination that stood up to the persistent and pervasive Old South practices of the Sunshine State.

As much as reactionary whites across Florida resisted an attempt to delay the desegregation of public facilities—what this work is defining as the Down South brand of civil rights delaying and stonewalling—it was the movement to desegregate public schools that most riled Florida's white reactionaries. When the 1954 *Brown* decision ended the separate–but–equal doctrine in public education, the Florida legislature immediately sought ways to nullify or enact obfuscation or stonewalling of the edict. Even so, the *Brown* decision changed Florida forever. By the 1960s, it had helped to produce numerous foot soldiers and leaders for the civil rights movement in all locales and regions of the state.

The Sunshine State's first response was a Down South ploy to give local school boards the authority to assign students to public schools based upon the maintenance of law and order, which essentially meant "keep everybody where they are." Later, during his second inaugural address, Gov. Collins said that Florida would accept bus desegregation but he saw "no hope of integrated classrooms in the foreseeable future." In 1956, *Time* magazine seemed to have second thoughts about Collins's presumed moderation: "LeRoy Collins' moderation has begun to look more and more like the protective coloring of a good politician who has discovered the magic combination for winning friends in the North and offending precious few in the South."[65] Most Florida congressmen at the time joined several other southern delegations in signing the Southern Manifesto in 1956, a resolution decrying the advent of integration. These and other delaying tactics were rejected repeatedly as black parents across the state sued in federal courts, demanding enforcement of the desegregation decision.[66]

When the Dade County Public School Board finally desegregated its first public school, Orchard Villa Elementary (1959), the school opened with space for hundreds of students, but by the end of the first holiday break, only a handful of white children remained. The school quickly became all-black.[67] Like other states of the Deep South, Florida thereafter witnessed the explosion of private and parochial schools as a result of white flight from public schools across the state. The experience did change the Sunshine State, but essentially it moved Florida from a dedicated Old South state to a pragmatic Down South state. That is to say, Florida moved from being a state with open defiance of racial progress to one of more subtle and sustained denial of federally ordered measures.

Even before the historic *Brown* decision, Florida and several other southern states were pressured to provide higher educational opportunities for blacks. However, the reactionary separate-but-equal doctrine refused to die. Accordingly, the Florida State Cabinet voted in October 1946 to provide scholarships for qualified black students so that they might attend out-of-state colleges, which provided courses not offered at Florida A&M College, the state's publicly supported college for blacks.[68]

In 1949, five black students, Virgil Hawkins, William T. Lewis, Oliver Moxey, Benjamin Finley, and Rose Boyd, challenged the state's longtime law prohibiting blacks from enrolling in graduate programs at the University of Florida.[69] On June 18, 1958, Federal District Court Judge Dozier DeVane found in favor of the remaining plaintiff, Virgil Hawkins. The university countered, declaring that Hawkins did not meet its admission requirements and that it would not enroll him. Despite his long-delayed court victory, Hawkins never did attend the University of Florida Law School.[70]

Like its system of lower education, Florida's undergraduate private universities and colleges were typically segregated. For example, the University of Miami practiced racial segregation from its birth in the 1920s. The university even resisted playing northern sports teams with black players. The University of Miami did not admit its first black students until several years after *Brown*. In 1967, Ray Bellamy became the university's first black varsity athlete—well after the "Yankee factor" had swollen South Florida's population and presumably made it a more racially progressive corner of the Sunshine State.[71]

Rather than admit black students to its junior colleges, Florida officials sought to delay the inevitable, authorizing the establishment of twelve black junior colleges following the *Brown* decision in 1954.[72] But court challenges and other pressures from blacks led to the phasing out of the black campuses and the acceptance of black students on the main campuses of the state's community colleges. By the time the University of Miami had elected to fully integrate, all of the black junior colleges were gone as well.[73] But, that did not occur until many years after *Brown* and many local actions by black and white supporters who were determined to transform a stubbornly racist state to one of contemporary values and norms.

The demise of Old South values and politicians in Florida was long delayed by the unequal distribution of political power in the state as the civil rights movement dawned. As noted, state politics and money were ruled by a handful of politicians (the Pork Choppers) from rural counties primarily stretched from Pensacola to Jacksonville. But as white northerners flowed into Florida, settling especially in South Florida, the political power base should have shifted in that direction. Still, the Pork Choppers prevailed long into the 1970s after which reapportionment, which they had resisted so fiercely, finally redistributed political representation more equitably across the Sunshine State. However, as the cracks in the wall of segregation began to appear and expand in the southern region of the state, the northern panhandle region, under the control of reactionary white politicians, marked the last bastion of resistance in Florida.

More homogeneous than Yankee-influenced South Florida, the northern panhandle would emerge as the final section of the Sunshine State to embrace the civil rights changes sweeping the nation and the lower-peninsula by the mid-to-late 1960s. If Florida were a "moderate" state in the contemporary civil rights movement, its moderate progress was painfully slow for those who wished to enjoy and practice full citizenship rights in what transpired from Old South, to Down South, to New South Florida.

Moreover, history should not grant "moderate" leaders like Gov. LeRoy Collins a "get-out-of-jail-free card" merely because other southern leaders of the period were more extreme than he. Despite his image as a moderate pioneer of the New South, LeRoy Collins was, in retrospect, a part of the overriding problem of his time. Collins conferred with bigots and he supported racial segregation as a part of Florida custom and law. He did nothing tangible to empower blacks in state government, which remained a bastion of segregation during his tenure as governor. Collins generally refused or failed to use the powers of his office to protect civil rights demonstrators and activists, who had been unjustly treated by the courts and subjected to racial violence during his tenure as governor. Though he conceded that blacks were being bullied out of registering to vote in five Florida counties cited by the U.S. Civil Rights Commission, he objected strongly to the proposed appointment of federal voting registrars. Instead, Collins joined the chorus of Florida conservatives and bigots who placed property rights (states' rights) above human rights and who unfairly assailed local freedom demonstrators as communist-influenced dupes.[74]

The governor of Florida had other motives for appearing to be a moderate, despite his own moral views about segregation. He was a realist, even if the Pork Choppers were not. The state's political powerbase was shifting to more politically progressive South Florida and eventually the reapportionment of the legislature would spell doom for the reactionary Pork Choppers. Concurrently, Florida was trying to attract new businesses to the state. Much of this success was dependent upon the state being portrayed to outsiders as a stable economic environment (i.e., the New South). Thus, when he began his second term in 1957 by declaring, to the abject horror of racists in northern counties, that the word of the United States Supreme Court was the law of the land, Collins may have been speaking more to outside economic interests than to oppressed blacks in his own backyard.

To his credit, Collins did declare in a timely statewide television address that although segregation was legally right, it was morally wrong. He was the first southern governor to do so. But this is a low standard for moderation, the very meaning of which implies movement, in this instance movement towards an integrated society in Florida. However his views may have changed after he left office, Collins was openly opposed to integration in his state during his years as governor.[75]

By the time Collins left office, conservatives and racist whites in Florida were now facing a new challenge: increasing migration into the state by liberal (mostly liberal on social issues and not necessarily racial issues) northerners, particularly to South Florida. When the civil rights movement began in the state, the white population, relative to other southern states, was often considered to be more open to social change. Still, Florida was a son of the Confederacy and, as witnessed in this recounting, racial change came at a dear and often bloody price, as well as at a painfully slow pace. In order to fully understand and appreciate the complexities of this phenomenon, scholars must now probe deeply into the recognized and perhaps hidden aspects of the racial heritage and associated social/political intricacies of the Sunshine State. Indeed, this study is but a glimpse of the historical and often painful nature of race relations in Florida, yet the examples herein of southern intransigence and leadership waffling on the race issue offer testimony to the Old South character of Florida and the possibility for reconsidering that story in a new light. Certainly, in a state as physically and demographically diversified as Florida, it is problematic to characterize the modern civil rights movement as springing from a "moderate" racial heritage and climate there. Much work needs to be done in that regard, including probing analyses of regions like Tampa Bay and Pensacola in the Panhandle that, because of publishing constraints, have not been thoroughly addressed here.

Back agency had always existed in Florida and race relations underwent new changes in the 1950s with the decision in *Brown* and the arrival of thousands of migrants, white and black. But, as history notes, the reactionary forces of the state tenaciously clung to the old way of life while seeking to attract more business investments to a stable and tourist-friendly Sunshine State. In the midst of it all, Florida persisted in its post-Reconstruction mores and folkways, and, when that lifestyle appeared doomed, shifted tactics to delaying and stonewalling the inevitable. Consequently, for many students of history, the record may reflect notably less than a "moderate" Sunshine State in the modern civil rights movement. While many readers of this essay may take exception to that notion, others may well find deep historical and moral causes to both reassess and reconsider Florida's conventional place in civil rights lore.

## Notes

1. See Martin A. Dyckman, *Floridian of His Century: The Courage of Governor LeRoy Collins* (Gainesville: University Press of Florida, 2006), 54–71; Tom Wagy, *Governor LeRoy Collins: Spokesman of the New South* (Tuscaloosa: University of Alabama Press, 1985), 35–45; David R. Colburn and Lance de Haven-Smith, *Government in the Sunshine State: Florida Since Statehood* (Gainesville: University Press of Florida, 1999), 51; Charlton W. Tebeau and William Marina, *A History of Florida* (Coral Gables: University of Miami Press, 1999), 425; David R. Colburn, "Florida Politics in the Twentieth Century," in *The New History of Florida*, ed. Michael Gannon (Gainesville: University Press of Florida, 1996), 361.

2. Quoted in Michael Newton, *The Invisible Empire: The Ku Klux Klan in Florida* (Gainesville: University Press of Florida, 2001), 143–44.

3. Charlton W. Tebeau, *A History of Florida* (Miami: University of Miami Press, 1971), 441.

4. Newton, *The Ku Klux Klan in Florida*, 33, 150.

5. Tananarieve Due and Patricia Stephens Due, *Freedom in the Family: A Mother-Daughter Memoir of the Fight for Civil Rights* (New York: One World Book, 2003), 78.

6. Colburn, "Florida Politics in the Twentieth Century," 361.

7. Colburn, "Florida Politics in the Twentieth Century," 362.

8. See David R. Colburn, "Florida Governors Confront the *Brown* Decision: A Case Study of the Constitutional Politics of School Desegregation, 1954–1970," in *An Uncertain Tradition: Constitutionalism and the History of the South*, ed. Kermit L. Hall and James W. Ely Jr. (Athens: University of Georgia Press, 1989), 326–55; quoted in Colburn, "Florida Politics in the Twentieth Century," 362.

9. Jane L. Landers, "Traditions of African American Freedom and Community in Spanish Colonial Florida," in *The African American Heritage of Florida*, ed. David R. Colburn and Jane L. Landers (Gainesville: University Press of Florida, 1995), 20; Larry Eugene Rivers, *Slavery in Florida: Territorial Days to Emancipation* (Gainesville: Viking Press of Florida, 2000), 1–64, 125–44.

10. *Smith v. Allwright*, 321 U.S. 649 (1944).

11. Newton, *The Ku Klux Klan in Florida*, 33; Philip Dray, *At The Hands of Person Unknown: The Lynching of Black Americans* (New York: Random House, 2002), 344–53.

12. See Stewart E. Tolnay and E. M. Beck, *A Festival of Violence: An Analysis of Southern Lynchings, 1882–1930* (Urbana: University of Illinois Press, 1995), 239.

13. Mamie Perry, interview with author, Orlando, Fla., October 2006; Douglas Udell, interview with author, Live Oak, Fla., October 2006; Samuel Beasley, interview with author, Live Oak, Fla., October 2006; James McCullers, interview with author, Live Oak, Fla., October 2006; Steve Mitchell, "Murder Way Down Upon the Suwannee River" (unpublished paper, Brunswick, Me., 2004), 1; Ben Green, *Before His Time: The Untold Story of Harry T. Moore, America's First Civil Rights Martyr* (New York: Free Press, 1999), 46–57.

14. Green, *Before His Time*, 46–51; see Caroline Emmons, "'Somebody Has got to Do That Work': Harry T. Moore and the Struggle for African-American Voting in Florida," *Journal of Negro*

*History* 82 (Spring 1997), 232–43; Jake C. Miller, "Harry T. Moore's Campaign for Racial Equality," *Journal of Black Studies* 31 (November 2000), 214–31.

15. Green, *Before His Time*, 55–58.

16. Gary R. Mormino, "World War II," in *The New History of Florida*, 337.

17. Emmons, "'Somebody Has Got to Do That Work,'" 232–43; Miller, "Harry T. Moore's Campaign For Racial Equality," 214–31; Green, *Before His Time*, 55–57.

18. William W. Rogers, "The Great Depression," in Gannon, *The New History of Florida*, 313.

19. Green, *Before His Time*, 39–42.

20. Quoted in, Green, *Before His Time*, 40.

21. Green, *Before His Time*, 40, 46–51; see Emmons, "'Somebody Has Got to Do That Work,'" 232–43; Miller, "Harry T. Moore's Campaign for Racial Equality," 214–31.

22. Green, *Before His Time*, 40.

23. Colburn, "Florida Politics in the Twentieth Century," 359.

24. *Miami Herald*, May 13, 1999.

25. See Malu Halasa, *Mary McLeod Bethune: Educator* (New York: Chelsea House, 1989); Maxine D. Jones, "No Longer Denied: Black Women in Florida, 1920–1950," in *The African American Heritage of Florida*, 240–74.

26. Maxine D. Jones, "The African-American Experience in Twentieth-Century Florida," in *The New History of Florida*, 376–90.

27. Quoted in Green, *Before His Time*, 54.

28. Due and Due, *Freedom in the Family*, 38–43.

29. Charles Kenzie Steele, "The Tallahassee Bus Protest Story," in *Go Sound the Trumpet!: Selections in Florida's African American History*, ed. David H. Jackson Jr. and Canter Brown Jr. (Tampa: University of Tampa Press, 2005), 323–29; Maxine D. Jones and Kevin M. McCarthy, *African Americans in Florida* (Sarasota, Fla.: Pineapple Press, 1993), 111–12; Due and Due, *Freedom in The Family*, 45; Gregory B. Padgett, "The Tallahassee Bus Boycott," in *Sunbelt Revolution: The Historical Progression of the Civil Rights Struggle in the Gulf South, 1866–2006*, ed. Samuel C. Hyde Jr. (Gainesville: University Press of Florida, 2003), 190–209.

30. Steele, "The Tallahassee Bus Protest Story," 323–29; Dyckman, *Floridian of His Century*, 126.

31. Due and Due, *Freedom in the Family*, 45.

32. Clayborne Carson, *Civil Rights Chronicle: The African-American Struggle for Freedom* (Lincolnwood, Ill.: Legacy Publishing, 2003), 88; Steele, "The Tallahassee Bus Protest Story," 323–29; Jones and McCarthy, *African Americans in Florida*, 111–12; see Glenda A. Rabby, "Out of the Past: The Civil Rights Movement in Tallahassee, Florida" (PhD diss., Florida State University, 1984); Gregory B. Padgett, "C.K. Steele and the Tallahassee Bus Boycott" (Master's thesis, Florida State University, 1977); and Gregory B. Padgett, "C. K. Steele, A Biography" (PhD diss., Florida State University, 1994).

33. Carson, *Civil Rights Chronicle*, 88.

34. Due and Due, *Freedom in the Family*, 44.

35. Marvin Dunn, *Black Miami in the Twentieth Century* (Gainesville: University Press of Florida, 1997), 217; Mormino, *Land of Sunshine*, 257; Dyckman, *Floridian of His Century*, 191.

36. Due and Due, *Freedom in the Family*, 49–50.

37. Dyckman, *Floridian of His Century*, 191.

38. Due and Due, *Freedom in the Family*, 53.

39. Due and Due, *Freedom in the Family*, 54–55.

40. Dyckman, *Floridian of His Century*, 192.

41. Due and Due, *Freedom in the Family*, 100–105.

42. Raymond Dunn, interview with author, Miami, Fla., September 4, 2006.

43. Due and Due, *Freedom in the Family*, 70.

44. Due and Due, *Freedom in the Family*, 166.

45. Newton, *The Ku Klux Klan in Florida*, 164; Jones and McCarthy, *African Americans in Florida*, 113–15; David R. Colburn, *Racial Change and Community Crisis: St. Augustine, Florida, 1877–1980* (Gainesville: University of Florida Press, 1991), 29–175.

46. Colburn, *Racial Change and Community Crisis*, 66–67; Robert K. Massie, "Don't Tread on Grandmother Peabody," *Saturday Evening Post*, May 16, 1964, 76; *New York Times*, April 1, April 2, 1964.

47. In Carson, *Civil Rights Chronicle*, 264–65; Colburn, *Racial Change and Community Crisis*, 99.

48. Quoted in Carson, *Civil Rights Chronicle*, 264–65.

49. *Miami Herald*, May 10, 1945. Dunn, *Black Miami*, 160–61; Mormino, *Land of Sunshine*, 311–12; see Gregory Bush, "Politicized Memories in the Struggle for Miami's Virginia Key Beach," in *"To Love the Wind and the Rain": African-Americans and Environmental History*, ed. Dianne D. Glave and Mark Stoll (Pittsburgh: University of Pittsburgh Press, 2005), 164–88.

50. Marvin Dunn, "Blacks in Miami," in *Miami Now: Integration, Ethnicity, and Social Change*, ed. Guillermo J. Grenier and Alex Stepick III (Gainesville: University Press of Florida, 1992), 41–56; Dunn, *Black Miami*, 210–11.

51. Dr. John O. Brown, interview with author, Miami, Fla., October 1996.

52. Dr. John O. Brown interview.

53. Dunn, *Black Miami*, 219–20.

54. *Gibson v. Florida Legislative Investigative Committee* 372 U.S. 539 (1963); Dunn, *Black Miami*, 220–23; *Miami News*, December 13, 1959; *Miami Times*, September 15, 1963; *Miami Herald*, February 26, 1963.

55. Dunn, *Black Miami*, 220–23.

56. Dunn, *Black Miami*, 221; Mormino, *Land of Sunshine*, 316.

57. Dunn, *Black Miami*, 221.

58. Dunn, *Black Miami*, 221.

59. *Miami Times*, September 15, 1965; Dunn, *Black Miami*, 223.

60. *Gibson v. Florida Legislative Investigative Committee*, 372 U.S. 539 (1963); Dunn, *Black Miami*, 223.

61. Abel Bartley, *Keeping the Faith: Race, Politics, and Social Development in Jacksonville, Florida, 1940–1970* (Westport, Conn.: Greenwood, 2000), 97; see James B. Crooks, *Jacksonville: The Consolidation Story, from Civil Rights to the Jaguars* (Gainesville: University Press of Florida, 2004), 1–36.

62. Vivian Reissland Rouson-Gossett and C. Spenser Pompey, eds. "Like a Mighty Banyan: Contributions of Black People to the History of Palm Beach County" (Palm Beach, Fla.: Palm Beach Junior College, 1982), 26–53.

63. Quoted in Rouson-Gossett and Pompey, eds. "Like a Mighty Banyan," 26–53.

64. Quoted in Rouson-Gossett and Pompey, eds. "Like a Mighty Banyan," 26–53.

65. Quoted in Dyckman, *Floridian of His Century*, 177.

66. Dunn, *Black Miami*, 225–26; see Dyckman, *Floridian of His Century*, 75, 107; Tebeau, *A History of Florida*, 442.

67. Dunn, *Black Miami*, 230; see Dyckman, *Floridian of His Century*, 184–85, 190, 199–200.

68. Edward D. Davis, *A Half Century of Struggle for Freedom in Florida* (Orlando, Fla.: Drake's Publishing, 1981), 198–99.

69. See Jones, "The African American Experience in the Twentieth Century Florida," 385–86; Jones and McCarthy, *African Americans in Florida*, 103–105; Algia R. Cooper, "*Brown v. Board of Education* and Virgil Darnell Hawkins: Twenty-Eight Years and Six Petitions to Justice," *Journal of Negro History* 64 (Winter 1979): 1–20; Samuel Selkow, "Hawkins, the United States Supreme Court and Justice," *Journal of Negro Education* 31 (Winter 1962): 97.

70. Cooper, "*Brown v. Board of Education*," 1–20; Dunn, *Black Miami*, 386; see Harley Herman, "Anatomy of a Bar Resignation: The Virgil Hawkins Story: An Idealist Faces the Pragmatic Challenges of the Practice of Law," *Florida Coastal Law Journal* 2 (Fall 2002): 77–81.

71. Dunn, *Black Miami*, 238.

72. Walter L. Smith, *The Magnificent Twelve: Florida's Black Junior Colleges* (Tallahassee: FOUR-G Publishers, 1994), xix–xxiv.

73. See Dunn, *Black Miami*, 238–39; Smith, *The Magnificent Twelve*, xix-xxiv.

74. See Dyckman, *Floridian of His Century*, 190–97; Robert Howard Akerman, "The Triumph of Moderation in Florida Thought and Politics: A Study of the Race Issue From 1954 to 1960" (PhD diss., The American University, 1967), 72–199; Wagy, *Governor LeRoy Collin*, 59–143; Dunn, *Black Miami*, 225–26.

75. Dyckman, *Floridian of His Century*, 190–97.

# CHAPTER TWO

# FROM OLD SOUTH TO NEW SOUTH, OR WAS IT?

## JACKSONVILLE AND THE MODERN CIVIL RIGHTS MOVEMENT IN FLORIDA

### ABEL A. BARTLEY

Behind Florida's carefully cultivated image of a racially moderate paradise with year-round sunshine, sandy beaches, and scenic palm trees is the reality of its ugly racial heritage. African American residents know that Florida's history is not quite as pristine and alluring as its beaches and sunny images. In reality, much of the state's past, like its numerous gated communities today, is hidden from public view.

Florida of yesteryear, like the rest of Dixie, was a totally segregated milieu in which the social, political, and economic institutions were designed to maintain and preserve white supremacy. Florida's African Americans suffered the same racial prejudice that other black southerners faced. Civil rights protestors met with the same violence and resistance that activists experienced in other "more radical" states. Remarkably, much of this Old South history remains concealed from those who reside in what has long been cast by state and business leaders as a progressive, New South Florida.

By focusing on the struggle for civil rights in Jacksonville, students of these issues can gain a useful understanding of the complexities of the contemporary civil rights struggle in a city and state in major transition. In essence, Jacksonville's struggle mirrored the statewide struggle to open society to full African American participation. Jacksonville, a city often politically and culturally associated with southern Georgia, is in many aspects a microcosm of "New South" Florida, a place where African Americans were tolerated but civil rights progress was resisted. Jacksonville's long-time mayor, Haydon Burns, served as a sort of warden locking the door to racially progressive initiatives until he moved to Tallahassee as governor in 1964. The leading proponent for civil rights in Jacksonville, Rutledge Pearson, served as local and then state president of the NAACP. Pearson, whose own career had been cut short by racism, became a determined opponent of segregation. These two men carried on a real and symbolic localized battle over civil rights, a poignant contest that ultimately captured the attention of the state and nation. By uncovering the Burns-Pearson confrontation in Jacksonville, and the key role that "everyday people" played in the destruction of Jim Crow institutions in that key Florida city, this and future generations will better understand the Sunshine State's painfully racist past and its African American community's resistance to inequality in a state characterized by complex changes as it faced the modern civil rights movement.

As one of Florida's largest and most complicated mixes of natives, immigrants, South Georgia transplants, Yankee newcomers, and African American populations, Jacksonville reflected well the demographic, social, and racial diversity that was sweeping most of peninsular Florida in the post-*Brown* era. In that regard, Jacksonville at once maintained the status of reflecting and shaping the nature of race relations in the proverbial Sunshine State. Indeed, as the city grew over the years, so did its prestige and racial problems. Between 1920 and 1960, the city's population had increased from 25,000 to 388,000. The 105,700 African Americans who resided in the city became concentrated in Jacksonville's urban core. As this process occurred, whites left the city for the more affluent suburbs. This population shift created new racial tensions as the decreasing numbers of whites sought to maintain their hegemony over the city. These white leaders were not only opposed to civil rights, but they also demonstrated a hostile attitude towards public education and open government in general. Thus, in order for Jacksonville to transcend from an Old South mindset to a New South profile, painful and sustained changes would have to occur from the bottom to the top of city affairs. Predictably, Jacksonville's rendezvous with modern civil rights would not be tranquil.[1]

After the May 17, 1954, Supreme Court decision in *Brown v. Board of Education*, most whites foresaw the demise of segregation; the only issues still in question were how long would it take and how much resistance would the South manifest? Both of these questions were quickly answered as the Supreme Court issued its ruling in the so-called *Brown II* case on May 31, 1955. It did not mention segregation or desegregation; nevertheless, it did reaffirm the High Court's commitment to seeing the process of public school desegregation begin immediately. Although the Court did not force any radical timetable for integration, it did order that officials open up public schools to children of all races "with all deliberate speed."[2]

The modern civil rights struggle in Jacksonville is traced to the post-*Brown II* era and involved several key and troubling events. In 1956, Ernest Jackson, a local African American attorney, successfully challenged Sarah Bryan in the Democratic primary for her Ward 3 Justice of the Peace position. This produced the first African American Democratic Party primary victory in Jacksonville, and one of the first in the Sunshine State. Though Jackson won the primary, the Democratic Party successfully challenged his victory, arguing that the voting districts were not the same as the districts used for the rest of the city. Party leaders then nullified the results and named white supremacist Sarah Bryan their candidate for the general election. Jackson ran in the general election as a write-in candidate, but lost. Despite this setback, the die had been cast; Jacksonville's civil rights movement had begun in earnest.[3]

Throughout the South, whites recognized their future and immediately organized to delay or stall the challenges to their way of life. On April 27, 1957, James Weldon Johnson Middle School and the Jacksonville Jewish Center—both representative of the changing demographics of this Georgia-border city—were the targets of bombs. These bombings were not unique but part of a growing violent trend. From January through early May 1957, there were forty-six bombings in southern cities. This was a clear sign that the South's march toward equality would not be a peaceful journey. The bombings in Jacksonville were designed to warn residents of their "proper place" more so than to cause damage. The bombs were placed in such a way as to minimize property damage and loss of life. Like most of the bombings in other southern cities, Jacksonville's terror was aimed at the city's new constituents and what were called "centers of integration" and were carried out by a group openly sympathetic to the "Confederate way." Southern mayors, including Jacksonville's Mayor Haydon Burns, came together to denounce the bombings. These mayors even raised $55,700 in reward money to help find the perpetrators. On the face of it, their actions indicated concern for social and ethnic well-being in their cities, but in reality mayors like Jacksonville's Haydon Burns were more interested in prioritizing images of business-friendly "Sun Cities" than in actually squelching Old South habits.[4]

Because of its burgeoning population, drive for national economic recognition, demographic transitions, and, perhaps above all, its Old South racial heritage, Jacksonville would prove a difficult city to integrate. Like much of Florida, Jacksonville at mid-century reflected a complex system of population factors, economic ideals, and social bylaws, all of which did not bode well for a smooth transition into a racially progressive city and state. Since 1949, segregationist Mayor Haydon Burns, who for political purposes made intermittent overtures to Jacksonville's sizable African American community, had run the city. He formed alliances with powerful African American figures, who sometimes helped secure votes for him during elections. In return, Burns offered a sort of segregation with a pragmatic face. For example, he hired a few black police officers, giving them policing powers only in African American neighborhoods. He also had helped organize the southern mayor's conference to denounce bombings of Jewish and African American institutions. Even so, Burns was always careful not to threaten the conservative, white power base that maintained a stronghold in the city's politics even as Jacksonville grew into a complex urban milieu in the post-*Brown* years.[5]

Even so, the Jackson election convinced African Americans that they could use collective action to challenge Burns's white power structure. Jackson was able to build a coalition of everyday citizens who voted for him, pulling off the stunning political upset. In retrospect, this move emboldened other African Americans to challenge injustices in and around the city. It also signaled the determination of a newly motivated African American community to challenge the Burns machine and to demand an end to the dual school system of the city.

On December 6, 1960, Earl Johnson, now attorney for Jacksonville's branch of the NAACP, filed a lawsuit challenging school segregation in the Duval County Public School system on behalf of a group of African American students. The plaintiffs were Daly N. Braxton, an eighth grader at James Weldon Johnson Junior High School, and Sharon Braxton, a tenth grader at New Stanton High School. They were named under sanction of their mother, Sadie Braxton, the spouse of an enlisted sailor away at sea. The plaintiffs were represented by Earl Johnson and NAACP lead lawyers and later federal jurists, Constance Motley Baker and Thurgood Marshall. The parents who filed the suits paid a heavy cost for their activities. Braxton was forced out of the city after receiving numerous threatening phone calls, and two of the original families involved in the suit were forced to drop out of the case over fears of reprisals from employers and other white power brokers in the community.[6] Despite its promoted image of a New South economic mecca, the Braxton case signaled that Jacksonville was still not ready to address the social complexities of its past and present.

The NAACP lawyers proceeded, nevertheless, accusing the Duval County Public School Board of operating a segregated school system, a clear violation of the Supreme Court's mandate in *Brown*. Johnson argued that the school system operated eighty-nine schools attended and staffed exclusively by whites and twenty-nine schools attended and staffed only by African Americans.[7] Like so many other districts in Florida, Jacksonville all but ignored the order.

The school board attempted a number of Down South delay tactics hoping to avert the inevitable. The first tactic involved arguing that the board could not desegregate until the state amended its constitution to allow integrated education. When this tactic failed, the board wrote an integration plan, which offered limited desegregation over time. When this tactic also failed, the board resorted to further legal maneuvers.[8]

To underscore their Old South heritage, school officials named a newly built school after the notorious Civil War Confederate officer and a presumed founder of the KKK, Nathan Bedford Forrest. The school desegregation issue now spawned several other protest movements within the city. At the same time, Rutledge Pearson, a teacher and leader of Jacksonville's NAACP branch, began his civil rights career. He volunteered his daughter to serve as one of the initial students to integrate Ribault high school. Like the Rev. C. K. Steele in the Tallahassee movement before him and Dr. Robert B. Hayling in the notoriously violent actions in St. Augustine after him, Pearson arose from the realm of the black community to become the single most important factor in the mobilizing efforts to force the issue of delayed civil rights to the fore in the post-*Brown* era.[9]

Rutledge Henry Pearson was born September 6, 1929, in Jacksonville. His father, Lloyd Pearson, worked as a postal worker, insurance salesman, and political activist, while his mother, Hattie Ruth McGee, worked as a day laborer and homemaker. They created a relatively comfortable home environment, despite the economic chaos of the 1930s. In 1947, he graduated from Stanton High School, one of Florida's oldest and most successful African American public schools.[10]

After graduation, Pearson attended Huston-Tillotson College in Austin, Texas, where he continued to hone his organizing skills, serving as senior class president, a star baseball player, and a tenor in the college choir. When his mother became ill, Pearson returned to his hometown to assist her and to play baseball for the Jacksonville Beach Seabirds in the segregated Class C Florida State League.[11]

However, Pearson's date with destiny was postponed when city officials, to prevent Pearson from playing, closed the park on the day before spring practice began. This event traumatized the young Pearson. He later described the insult as the "turning point in [his] life." He responded to the affront by joining the NAACP and promoting protests against segregation. With his baseball career denied, Pearson, like other educated blacks in Old South Florida, essentially had three employment choices: the post office, railroad, or school system. He chose to teach and accepted a job in social studies at Darnell-Cookman Junior High School, where he eventually rose to head of the Social Studies Department and vice president of the Social Studies Teacher's Council in Duval County.[12]

The stage in traditionally non-inclusive Jacksonville, Florida, was now set for a classic showdown between Old South segregationists like Haydon Burns and New South integrationists like Rutledge Pearson. Most whites strongly opposed integration and some had even threatened violence to maintain their Jim Crow system; but this did not deter Pearson and his new followers in the black community.[13] Pearson, who described himself as a "man in a hurry" to integrate, squared off with Burns, who certainly was in no hurry to desegregate anything. Burns refused to compromise on segregation, partly because he did not want to alienate the entrenched white power base of his city and partly out of fear of a white backlash on his planned run for governor.

Pearson used his teaching and NAACP Youth Council advisor positions to educate black children about the evils of segregation and racism while coordinating local protest activities. During the late 1950s he assumed the leadership of the local NAACP chapter, a typical Florida local branch that was not aggressive on the civil rights front. During the mid-1950s, while Tallahassee and other cities were experiencing civil rights protests, Jacksonville remained fairly quiet as local black leadership chose to work for change within the existing order. Mayor Haydon Burns used his influence with influential African American leaders to keep the city free from loud protest. Most people believed that Jacksonville, an area so close to southern Georgia, populated with Klansmen, Sons of the Confederacy, and White Citizens Council members, could never have a viable (or safe) NAACP chapter. Others said that North Florida's palpable Old South heritage, coupled with Pearson's quiet personality and teaching positions, limited his ability to build a sound chapter. Pearson proved his detractors wrong by creating a strong local NAACP organization in Jacksonville.[14]

Although he faced dismissal for active participation in NAACP activities, Pearson used his position to appeal to minority teachers for their help in leading civil rights protests. He also enlisted adults to work with the NAACP Youth Council in protest activities. For example, the adults and teachers made the signs that the students used in protest activities. Pearson also required students to memorize the Declaration of Independence, challenging them to show how the United States followed or betrayed its principles.[15] Such lectures and lessons had the effect of inspiring students to fight for social justice and racial equality.

In late 1959, Rodney Hurst, a sixteen-year-old high school student, assumed the presidency of the NAACP's Youth Council. Hurst, an ambitious young man with a quick mind and a restless spirit, symbolized Pearson's new generation of black youth in Jacksonville. A few years earlier, he had sat in Pearson's class listening to lessons about the evils of racism. Hurst remembers Pearson saying, "The way to hurt segregation is to hit segregationists in their pockets." By 1960 he believed that Jacksonville was ready for this sort of challenge. It had been five years since the *Brown* decisions, and yet very little in this emerging sun city had changed. As Frank Priestly, a teacher recruited by Pearson, said of the era, "Not only could we not sit and eat at some lunch counters, but at Stand and Snack, they would not even allow us to stand and eat next to whites."[16] Hurst believed that it was the time to end this type of humiliation.

After observing the success of sit-in campaigns in North Carolina in 1960, Pearson and Hurst organized sessions at local churches to train students to lead sit-in demonstrations. He enlisted the aid of prominent black attorneys like Earl Johnson and Ernest Jackson to counsel the students on the law and their rights during sit-in campaigns. By law, all persons had the right to sit at a lunch counter, but the storeowner did not have to serve them. The legal advice was followed by lectures from prominent, local black ministers on the principles of nonviolence. Like Dr. Martin Luther King Jr., these ministers encouraged the students to remain nonviolent no matter what the provocation.[17]

After the initial training sessions, NAACP leaders organized a series of sit-in demonstrations that failed because city officials refused to negotiate. These demonstrations ended, but as summer approached, the NAACP promised renewed direct actions. After a series of meetings, the NAACP Youth Council decided to reopen its sit-in campaign. Its leaders began the demonstrations on Saturday, August 13, 1960, and planned to continue them until storeowners desegregated their lunch counters. The students first targeted the downtown Woolworth's.[18]

Typical of the Sunshine State, Jacksonville's Woolworth's had a white lunch counter with many seats in the front of the store and a few seats for African Americans at an ancillary lunch counter in the rear of the store, hidden behind garden plants and tools. Rodney Hurst led eighty-two students in the first demonstration as they made small purchases in the store and then sat at the white counter and attempted to order lunch. The store's manager promptly closed the lunch counter, the demonstrators' goal. They wanted to close the counter during the busy lunch period, costing the store crucial business. Pearson and the others believed that if the lunch counters remained closed long enough, storeowners would feel the pain in their pocketbooks.[19]

After a week of demonstrations, tensions escalated. In an August 24 editorial, Eric Simpson, editor of the *Florida Star*, Jacksonville's predominant African American newspaper, warned, "Despite the relative calm that exists here the Negroe [sic] people in Florida, and particularly Jacksonville are faced with many . . . problems that have led to unrest in other parts of the country." He further warned that unless city officials joined with business owners and met African American leaders, violence would be unavoidable.[20]

Simpson's words rang true. The next day, two young demonstrators, running from the police, unintentionally knocked a white woman through a plate glass window. Then, on August 26, a scuffle broke out between a white and black female in front of a store where the latter was picketing. The two women knocked several nearby white women to the pavement during their confrontation. This incensed the white community; many whites drove to Sears and Roebuck to purchase axe handles. At one point, Sears sold over fifty axe handles in one fifteen-minute period. The incident proved so troubling for Florida that both the *New York Times* newspaper and *Time* magazine provided national coverage of the events. The articles did not seem to substantiate Florida's carefully crafted New South image of economic stability and social moderation.[21]

On August 27, a group of Klansmen and reactionary White Citizens Council members from south Georgia and north Florida, armed with axe handles, baseball bats, golf clubs, and heavy walking sticks held a rally in downtown Jacksonville. They warned merchants and others not to violate Florida's segregation laws. Police officers patrolling the area did nothing as the Klansmen passed out leaflets, signed the "Segregation Forces of Duval County," and threatened downtown businesses with citywide boycotts if they met African American demands. Once again, the national media provided coverage of these events, which must have seemed at the time to further contradict Florida's "moderate" image.[22]

Pearson and a group of NAACP Youth Council members drove through downtown Jacksonville just before 9:00 a.m. and saw men in Confederate uniforms handing out axe handles at Hemming Park. The NAACP held a somber meeting at the Laura Street Presbyterian Church and decided to proceed with a scheduled sit-in. However, protesters switched their target from Woolworth's to Grant's, another general store located three blocks away. At 11:00 a.m., about twenty-five students met at Grant's, entered, made small purchases, and took seats at the white lunch counter. At 11:37 a.m., the manager closed the counter and ejected the students. As the students left, they observed between 150 and 200 white men armed with axe handles and baseball bats running towards them. The frightened teenagers ran for cover, but nearby storeowners locked their doors to bar the panic-stricken demonstrators. The Klansmen then pummeled the students. As if to punctuate the Old South-type action, Jacksonville's police officers were missing, leaving jeering whites to watch with obvious satisfaction.[23] Throughout it all, Mayor Burns remained conspicuously on the sidelines.[24]

The Klansmen chased the teens through the city and into African American neighborhoods. When the attackers raced into the black neighborhood, a group of black youth assembled and counter-attacked the Klansmen, chasing them out of the area. Arnett Girardeau, a former activist and politician, later referred to the event as, "Axe handle Day." In a painful period of transition from Old South to New South, or at best an era of "new" race realities in Jacksonville, blacks met violence with violence in a poignant prelude to the defensive violence platform of the mid-decade Black Power movement.[25] In a real sense, Florida's social heritage coalesced in Jacksonville in both a historic and tragic way—the burden of legal and violent racism of the state moved, indeed forced, the civil rights movement in Jacksonville from nonviolence to defensive violence.[26]

A *Florida Times-Union* reporter estimated that at least fifty people suffered wounds in the melee. By the time the police appeared, many African Americans had sustained serious head injuries from the baseball bats and axe handles. As noted in such national newspapers as the *New York Times*, the city used more than 200 police officers to quell the violence. By nightfall the police had the situation under control, although sporadic violence continued. Jacksonville, Florida, had now irretrievably confronted its Old South heritage and embarked on a new era. Yet, the question remained: what would the new epoch's racial divide, or lack thereof, look like?[27]

A good portion of the blame for the rioting must fall on the Burns administration. His recalcitrant attitude and political posturing contributed palpably to the rioting. As Eric Simpson wrote, "It is clear that the disinterested attitude that our city fathers [Burns and his administration] have shown to the Negro citizens' problems has brought on this terrible catastrophe. . ." Simpson quoted from an article written in the *Tampa Tribune*, in an attempt to place his city within the context of less than a racially moderate state, "Sadly for Florida's reputation, Jacksonville could have had it this way [nonviolent] but Mayor Haydon Burns turned it down. He revealed that a variety of store operators came to him several weeks ago to open their lunch counters to Negroes, but he told them not to do so." Ruby Hurley, a lawyer working with the NAACP in Atlanta, predicted that "Jacksonville will be another Little Rock if the Mayor keeps up his recent attitude."[28]

Local NAACP officials asked Burns to create a biracial committee to discuss the problems. He refused, arguing that biracial meant integrated, and he would not foster integration. Florida Governor LeRoy Collins placed the National Guard on alert and Burns ordered all 400 of his police officers, along with Naval Shore Patrol units, to patrol the city. On August 28, as reported in the *New York Times*, local NAACP officials announced a citywide boycott of all places that practiced segregation. They also advised blacks against purchasing the local *Florida Times-Union*, because it slanted stories towards Burns's talking points and ignored news about Jacksonville's racial scene.[29]

Ever mindful of the economic benefits of a New South Jacksonville, members of the Chamber of Commerce met with local NAACP leaders to seek a solution. Chamber leaders particularly feared the economic impact of a prolonged boycott and adverse national attention. Later, black and white advisory groups crafted an agreement that desegregated some lunch counters and promised better jobs for African Americans, along with token desegregation in other areas. Jacksonville's two major racial communities now continued on their rendezvous with destiny; that destiny would, however, be shaped dramatically by both the energized black community of the city and new federal actions forcing Sunbelt Florida to confront its color line. The options of Old South, New South, or "half a loaf" Down South delays had never seemed so befuddling to the city's white political and economic power structure.[30]

After the tumultuous week of late August, lunch counter segregation in Jacksonville's downtown stores officially ended. Segregation in restaurants continued, but storeowners gave vague promises about revisiting the issue at a later date. In typical Down South fashion, the delay stretched to almost three painful years for the black community. Not surprisingly, the delay of the agreement led to renewed demonstrations.[31]

Not willing to accept the stonewalling, NAACP officials again met with Chamber of Commerce representatives in 1963. The African American negotiating team included Earl Johnson, Leander Shaw (later to rise to the position of Chief Justice of the Florida Supreme Court), Eric Simpson, W. W. Schell, and others. They negotiated with some of the city's most respected businesspeople, who were interested in devising ways to improve opportunities for blacks without negatively affecting the white-controlled business climate of Jacksonville. But the price the city would have to pay for a manufactured New South image would be steep.[32]

African Americans became increasingly militant in their response to delays. They grew impatient with the slow pace of the civil rights movement and leery of the nonviolent policy advocated by Dr. Martin Luther King Jr. and his Jacksonville disciple, Rutledge Pearson. As more inner-city blacks nationally moved toward a confrontational strategy emphasizing immediacy and self-defense, as opposed to seemingly endless nonviolent negotiations, so did a similar cohort in Jacksonville, Florida. As 1964 unfolded, the city again found itself in the midst of a violent and angry clash between whites and African Americans over the slow pace of civil rights. Meanwhile, Jacksonville's NAACP officials remained committed to King-style nonviolence and continued to protest peacefully for civil rights, although young black militancy there, reflective of the nation at large, seethed beneath the surface of the working-class black neighborhoods.[33]

In 1964, Pearson led the NAACP in a revived five-week direct action campaign against businesses and organizations that continued to practice segregation. Also that year, Burns made his second run for governor. He feared Pearson and his NAACP backers would use the civil rights movement to undermine his campaign. He knew that the Florida branch of the NAACP backed his opponent, Miami Mayor Robert King High. A direct-action campaign, and even worse, a Black Power action, in Jacksonville could bring Mayor Burns's white supremacist record into focus and possibly wreck his campaign.[34]

Almost immediately the controversy evolved into a bipolar battle between Burns and Pearson, resulting in yet another round of Jacksonville's prolonged and complex struggle to fit into an evolving New South. This time, however, the black community was determined to overcome the by-now standard tactic of delay, delay, and delay. Pearson wanted complete and immediate racial blending while Burns wanted complete and immediate political gratification. There were foreboding signs that the issue would not be settled without renewed turmoil. Extremist whites, clearly tied to the Burns machine, continued to threaten violence. Blacks became frustrated anew with the city's slow negotiation and the persisting neo-Confederate patterns. Those in the middle found little room for compromise: either the city made radical changes posthaste or it invited troubling protests. The standoff placed Jacksonville in the center of the ideological struggle in the Sunshine State, a place actively touting its own moderation.[35]

Simultaneously, the school issue continued to fester and reflect the mounting tensions. On February 16, 1964, at 3:00 a.m., a bomb exploded under the house of Iona Godfrey, an African American civil rights worker and mother of a six-year-old son, who had integrated the formerly all-white Lackawanna Elementary School. White parents threatened violence to protest Godfrey's presence at the school. The explosion alerted officials to the seriousness of the parents' threats. The Godfreys were not injured in the blast, but their home suffered massive damage. The Godfrey bombing signaled an end to the relative calm and truce that followed the earlier 1960 riots. The issue of white delay had now transposed into one of self-defense and agency for the black community.[36]

Pearson faced a tenuous situation. He wanted to maintain the pressure, but he did not want to resurrect the violence of 1960. He decided to lean heavily on the local Ministerial Alliance for guidance and support. Like so many other confrontations in Florida, the local clergymen stepped forward to offer their churches and support to the cause. A powerful force in the black community now re-energized Pearson and the movement he held so dear.[37]

Pearson preferred to let the Ministerial Alliance sponsor protests because, unlike the NAACP, it could not be sued. One black minister of the time described Pearson as the "pied piper," who played the music while the ministers marched behind him.[38] On February 17, 1964, four African American ministers were arrested for trying to register at the whites-only Robert Meyer Hotel. Four more black ministers then joined that group. While the ministers went inside the hotel to register, a group of African Americans protested in front of the structure. The entire affair had been carefully orchestrated by Pearson to showcase the hotel's racial drawbridge.[39]

On February 26, Pearson proclaimed that the direct-action campaign would continue until the city integrated. He demanded that a biracial committee be established to study racial problems in Jacksonville and promised to lead a group of disgruntled African Americans to a City Council meeting to air their complaints. The council rebuffed the attempt, which infuriated Pearson. "There were citizens who had come to voice support for their ideas." Pearson further stated, "This tends to indicate that the city government is failing to give direction and guidance to the community in the broad area of human relations." He promised to continue his direct-action campaign, even threatening to increase the pace and intensity of the demonstrations.[40] Mayor, and now statewide-candidate, Haydon Burns hoped to defuse the issue before it proliferated. He would find few black allies in his goal.[41]

On March 2, the Jacksonville Ministerial Alliance held a meeting attended by sixty-two ministers. They voted unanimously to draft a letter to Mayor Burns asking him to appoint a biracial committee to address racial problems in Jacksonville. The letter came on the heels of a similar recommendation forwarded by the Community Advisory Committee, an organization composed primarily of businesspeople and backed by the powerful Chamber of Commerce, to the City Council. The City Council, essentially composed of Burns's protégés, simply ignored the recommendations. The Ministerial Alliance thereafter hoped to force Burns, a candidate for governor of Florida, to take the lead in forging better race relations in Jacksonville and the state. By now, race relations in the city were rapidly deteriorating and only dramatic and effective leadership could reverse the tide. The ministers hoped that by appealing directly to candidate Burns, they could open a line of communication and foster racial reconciliation. They were sorely disappointed. In the midst of this drama, yet another significant factor came into play: the federal government.[42]

On March 5, the FBI announced that it had made an arrest in the Godfrey bombing. According to its intelligence, William Sterling Rosecrans, a thirty-year-old white laborer with a long criminal record, had planted the bomb. The suspect had been under FBI surveillance for some time, especially in regard to his connections with the long-active Duval County Ku Klux Klan, one of the many local KKK branches in the state.[43]

After Rosecrans's arrest, the FBI widened its investigation to identify other collaborators in Jacksonville's KKK. On March 15, agents arrested six white men associated with the Klan, charging them as accomplices in the Godfrey bombing. The national black press praised the FBI's handling of the case. Noting the significance of the action, a *Pittsburgh Courier* reporter wrote, "Seemingly, the arrests marked the first solid cases concerning the numerous bombings which have taken place in the South since post World War II days."[44] The arrests and subsequent convictions only strengthened the NAACP's resolve. By then Jacksonville's, and by implication Florida's, struggle to end the state's Jim Crow legacy had gained national attention. The *Pittsburgh Courier*, for example, praised the Jacksonville NAACP and specifically Pearson for having the courage and persistence to maintain the struggle.[45]

And Pearson did maintain the struggle. He even shifted tactics to a hit-and-run campaign to accelerate the pressure on Mayor "Jim Crow" Burns. He organized a mass march on City Hall to protest civil service hiring discrimination and to force the city's leaders to undertake negotiations. The march was peaceful, except for one ugly incident; a white female driver purposely tried to run over a young African American protester.[46]

The confrontation tactics came with a price. During one three-day period in March, thirty-seven black youths faced arrest. Judge John Santora, who presided over the cases, chastised the youths and their parents for causing the disturbances, "It is to say the least, in poor taste for teen-agers to become involved in something like this which might lead to racial strife . . . The parents of these children should be condemned." The situation intensified, but Burns still refused to move out of the Old South.[47]

African American frustrations mounted as they began to think that the Old South and its prodigy, the foot-dragging Down South, would never relent, though the racial disturbances were politically embarrassing to Burns. Burns's hopes for winning the governor's race were dependent in part on his ability to control Jacksonville's racial conflicts. He had to either placate the business community and progressives (by now many northern "Yankee" transplants), who wanted to solve the race problem, or the conservatives on whom his political strength depended. Now Jacksonville's Old South dilemma assumed a new statewide significance. At the very time that the Sunshine State itself was projecting a New South, business-friendly, inclusive agenda, Mayor Haydon Burns and Jacksonville seemed to be signaling to the nation that Florida, was, indeed, not the racially "moderate" state its business and political community had projected.

For Mayor Burns there was no dilemma. He responded with characteristic resistance and deputized 496 firefighters to back up his police force. The NAACP's state office warned Burns that increasing the size of the police force would increase racial tensions. Yet Burns knew the show of force played well with conservative voters across the state. He announced to his constituency a new "law-and-order" campaign, the same political message that would burst onto the national scene in 1968 in the reactionary presidential campaigns of Richard Nixon and racial demagogue George Wallace of Alabama. In words that would be echoed extensively, Burns told civil rights protesters, "You do not have such a legal or civil right." It had now been fully ten years since the decision of *Brown v. Board*, and Haydon Burns and his constituents still believed the post-*Brown* civil rights goals to be extralegal.[48]

Robert Saunders, serving in Tampa as state field secretary for the NAACP, sent telegrams to Burns, the Justice Department, and the U.S. Civil Rights Commission questioning Jacksonville's commitment to federal measures and the legality of Burns's action in deputizing the firefighters. He also notified the press that citizens of the United States had the inalienable right to hold peaceful protests against injustices. Saunders then took the key step of asking the federal courts to decide whether Burns had the right to halt Pearson's protests. Whether by design or default, Burns had now drawn the eyes of federal officials onto him and Jacksonville, Florida's racial brick wall.[49]

On March 21, Burns found it necessary to address Jacksonville's dilemma on television. He called for calm and argued that he did not need a biracial committee nor federal judges to help him solve Jacksonville's race problem. Instead, he felt that in his capacity as mayor and police and fire commissioner he should solve local problems himself, "I am the legally constituted head of government and the spokesman for this city . . . I refuse to delegate or relegate this responsibility to anyone or any bi-racial committee or any other group. It is my responsibility and I will face it."[50]

Monday, March 23, began peacefully. In the U.S. Senate, debate swirled over the landmark Civil Rights Bill, passed just days before in the House of Representatives. As discussion of the debate captured the national headlines, whites circulated a spurious report in Jacksonville that four black males had beaten, robbed, cut, and tied to a tree a twenty-five-year-old man named Billy James, who apparently fabricated the story. However, the tale created anger among already aroused Burns supporters. It was during this critical period that a person of character and leadership could have staved off the inevitable clash. Haydon Burns was not that leader. The mayor fiddled an Old South tune, while the federal government enacted a sweeping Civil Rights Bill and Jacksonville's racial fires exploded.[51]

That morning protests began at Hemming Park with about 350 people but soon spread to other venues. The crisis started when students entered the new Stanton High School and pulled a fire alarm. Students then poured into the streets where they could see NAACP officials protesting against local businesses. Many left the school grounds and joined other youth who had taken the day off to protest. Rather than submit to Burns's police force as usual, the students refused to be compliant in the face of white police violence.[52]

Rev. G. Vincent Lewis was a student at Matthew Gilbert High School during that period. According to Lewis, the police attacked students with nightsticks. "Any student who was standing up was hit. I noticed they were going after students who were standing so I fell to the ground." He remembered that many students tried to get arrested by the white police as a show of defiance. The *New York Times* noted that among the more than two hundred people arrested were seventy-five youths under the age of seventeen. The Johnson administration in Washington monitored the situation but issued no official response.[53]

Later that evening, Johnnie Mae Chappell, a thirty-six-year-old African American mother of ten, and Albert Smith, a friend, strolled up U.S. highway 1 searching for some lost property. Without warning, a white rifleman in a nearby car fired at the pair. The two pedestrians dived to the ground. Chappell shouted to her companion, "Help! I've been shot." Smith hurried to a nearby house to find help while Chappell lay on the side of the road clutching her wounds. Eventually, an ambulance rushed Chappell from the roadside to a hospital, but she died en route.[54] With this act, Jacksonville, Florida, and the nation, came to realize that the Sunshine State's New South image included a dark and vicious underside. For the black community, this was not a new incident for their generation but only the latest in a bloody string of events occurring in the Sunshine State.

During the nightlong protest by angry blacks over Chappell's assassination, rioters damaged four buildings with firebombs and torched a Burns-for-Governor campaign building. Roving bands of youth continued to harass the city throughout the night. Burns called in the Florida Highway Patrol when a group of youths began throwing rocks at passing cars on Interstates 295 and 95. The Highway Patrol sealed off exits on both roads and increased surveillance. Jacksonville's Old South heritage had led this Florida city to a veritable state of siege. The unsettling news made the pages of such national periodicals as the *U.S. News and World Report* and *Time* magazine. Tellingly, *Time* noted that the events might well set Florida's largest city on a course "Towards a Long, Hot Summer."[55]

Ironically, Burns now asked African American ministers to help restore calm to a city he argued had gone from good race relations to racial conflagration based on "outside agitation." Rev. J. S. Johnson, president of the local Interdenominational Alliance, offered to appear with Burns on his telecast to appeal for calm. However, Burns appeared alone on his paid telecast to blast his detractors in an attempt to deflect attention from his administration and to salvage his gubernatorial campaign. He told the television audience, "Its [sic] regrettable that men seeking the highest office, that of governor, would resort to disrupting the peace of a community and to involving the immature youth of either race in such a spectacle as today."[56] Burns's opponents reacted with scorn. Whether it was a failed Burns ploy or not, attention to the violence in Jacksonville and Burns's racial intransigence rose all the way to the White House.[57]

After consulting with his staff and top Justice Department officials, President Lyndon Johnson chose not to interfere in Florida's new racial crisis because he felt that the situation would soon resolve itself. The Florida press also kept the president focused by roasting Burns for his ongoing bad decisions. The *Miami News* editorialized, "We lament, too, the attitude of a candidate for the job of governor of Florida who proposes to outlaw the rights of Negroes to express their feelings in Jacksonville—or anywhere else [in the state]."[58]

On Tuesday, March 24, the second day of conflagration, forty-two teenagers were among the more than one hundred African Americans arrested. The rioting was not organized nor supported by Pearson, but was rather a spontaneous affair by street youth carrying out random acts of defiance. Later that evening Martin Luther King Jr. sent a telegram to Pearson offering his services. King praised Pearson for maintaining a nonviolent stance and ignoring the racial provocateurs. He wrote, "I join with you in calling on the leaders of Jacksonville to bend every effort to persuade the Negro community to remain nonviolent no matter how sorely provoked." Although Pearson appreciated King's offer, he declined it because he believed that a local disturbance demanded a local solution.[59] Had Pearson not politely declined King's offer, it is likely that the nation's, and perhaps the world's, number one civil rights advocate would have entered the fray in Jacksonville, Florida.

By Wednesday, March 25, much of the previous day's violence continued. Lester Phillips, a white man, suffered injuries after African American youth threw a brick that struck him in the head. Protesters also firebombed two cars. Police arrested a seventeen-year-old black youth and charged him with possession of an incendiary device. They also arrested seven other youths and charged them with unlawful assembly. It was during this critical juncture that Pearson interceded and asked the youth to end the violence. Speaking to a gathering during the night, he said, "This business of violence has got to stop. We've got downtown ready to negotiate, and we must stop this violence." After Pearson's appeal, destruction halted.[60]

This venting of frustration gave the nation an opportunity to see what the civil rights movement could turn into if white supremacist leaders were not held accountable for their stonewalling practices. According to Rev. Lewis, "Obviously, the city [leaders] had two choices after 1964. They could continue as they were going or they could open a line of communication and try to solve some of the problems." Even the *Florida Times-Union*, which had traditionally championed white hegemony, recognized the need for biracial communication to bring the city into an era of New South distinction, if only for media consumption. In an editorial titled "Inter-racial Talks Are City's First Need," the paper blamed the incidents on a breakdown in communications between leaders on both sides. Ruby Hurley said of Jacksonville's mayor, "Burns simply refuses to recognize the fact that there is a racial problem here. None of this [violence] would have happened if it had not been for Burns who is one of the most stupid men in the South."[61]

Finally on March 25, Burns reversed his position and suggested an end to the protest through biracial communication. He called on business and civic leaders to discuss the problems and promised to act on their recommendations.[62] However grudgingly, Burns had finally recognized the necessity of shedding his iconoclastic Old South stance. By establishing dialogue, Burns hoped to solve the city's racial dilemma and simultaneously reestablish his own political capital. Whether Burns and his reactionary constituents actually meant to move Jacksonville out of the shadow of Jim Crowism or simply quell the media coverage for political gain is a matter of historical debate.[63]

In the midst of his call for racial dialogue and healing, Burns nevertheless remained defiant in his segregationist stand. He openly attacked the demonstrations as an unwarranted presence and, in typical Down South fashion, accused the NAACP of trying to do away with segregation too quickly. He reiterated to his followers that he had not retreated from his promise, but instead had simply initiated dialogue between the races. As if to punctuate his segregationist image, he promised to never "force" their recommendations on the city.[64]

Seven people made up the new committee on dialogue, four whites and three blacks. With no official status, the committee never had a chance of instituting meaningful change in Florida's second-largest city. Eventually, its black representatives resigned over questions of issues and priorities. Black members wished to discuss the city's legendary discriminatory economic *and* social issues, while white representatives only wanted to discuss the immediate social and public relations issues. It was not until Haydon Burns left office, and Louis Ritter filled the role in late 1964, that a more cooperative agenda finally took root. Prejudice and discrimination did not disappear in Jacksonville, but the racial climate now inched toward New South expectations.[65]

Candidate Burns continued his segregationist gubernatorial campaign in Florida, eventually winning the race despite losing almost all support among the state's black voters. As he left the city, African Americans shed few tears. The new mayor, Louis Ritter, finally set about to create a desegregated Jacksonville. His integrationist stance was a dramatic but welcomed change to the Burns regime by a wide spate of city leaders and business executives intent on committing their increasingly diverse and changing city to a more realistic New South image, if not to equality between the races.

Burns's departure for a two-year stint as governor marked the rise of a new era in Jacksonville's Jim Crow heritage. While the city did not immediately experience a New South transformation, it did finally adopt a more realistic mid-twentieth-century position on race relations. Still, problems such as school desegregation and attendant protests occurred into the mid-to-late 1960s, but the stonewall, Old South/Down South attitude of Haydon Burns and his political allies no longer pre-determined the city's response to and subsequent outcome of those actions. When federal oversight did result in school desegregation in Jacksonville by the late 1960s, both whites and blacks held positions of authority in the city and both races worked to bridge racial gaps rather than widen them as had been the case under Burns.

As for Haydon Burns, he went on to serve an undistinguished two-year term as governor of Florida and then returned to his roots in Jacksonville. Not content with his work as a business consultant, Burns made yet another run for mayor in 1971, but was defeated. By the late 1960s, even Jacksonville had begun to reject his segregationist and divisive mode of leadership in favor of more progressive New South candidates like Louis Ritter. The Old South-to-New South transition of this "city on the move" simply left no room for reactionaries like Burns by the dawn of the 1970s.

As for Burns's nemesis, Rutledge Pearson continued his commitment to the cause through championing local actions and serving as president of the Jacksonville and state branches of the NAACP. In these efforts, Pearson became a vital force in bridging the gap between white and black communities, as he had in the Burns era, until his tragic death in a car accident in the late 1960s. Yet the racist culture of Jacksonville once more raised its ugly head; hate mail flowed into the Pearson home after his death. Just before the funeral, someone sent a letter to his home that read, "A dead nigger is a good nigger." Nevertheless, more than 5,000 white and black mourners crowded into the Shiloh Metropolitan Baptist Church to attend Pearson's funeral. The Old South show of contempt paled in comparison to the New South's show of support for Pearson's work and legacy.[66]

## NOTES

1. See *Duval County, Florida Public School, A Survey Report, Division of Surveys and Field Services* (Nashville, Tenn.: George Peabody College for Teachers, 1965), 5–6 (A report conducted by the Peabody College for Teacher's for the Duval County Public Schools); Abel Bartley, *Keeping the Faith: Race Politics and Social Development in Jacksonville, Florida, 1940–1970* (Westport, Conn.: Greenwood, 2000), 4–10; Hugh Price, *The Negro in Southern Politics* (New York: New York University Press, 1957), 23–24; Erick Dittus, "Jacksonville's Black Community Is Still Searching for the Promised Land," *Jacksonville Today*, January 1988; Barbara Walch, *New Black Voices: The Growth and Contributions of Sallye Mathis and Mary Singleton in Florida Government* (Jacksonville: Barbara Walch, 1990), for an understanding of the political changes the city underwent during the 1960s.

2. Richard Kluger, *Simple Justice: The History of Brown v. Board of Education and Black America's Struggle for Equality* (New York: Vintage Books, 2004), 657–778, and 779–87 for a text of the *Brown* decision; Charles Ogletree, *All Deliberate Speed: Reflections on the First Half Century of Brown v. Board of Education* (New York: W. W. Norton Company, 2004), 33, 124–25; Glen Feldman, ed.,

*Before Brown: Civil Rights and White Backlash in the Modern South* (Tuscaloosa: The University of Alabama Press, 2004), xi–20.

3. Bartley, *Keeping the Faith*, 49–51.

4. *New York Times* May 2, 1958; *New York Times* May 4, 1958.

5. Bartley, *Keeping the Faith*, 59–64; *New York Times* May 4, 1958; *New York Times* May 5, 1958.

6. *Daly N. Braxton, etc., et al. v. Board of Public Instruction of Duval County, Florida, etc., et al.*, 4598–Civ-J 1968, 6–11; *New York Times*, August 22, 1962; *Florida Times-Union*, August 4, 1970.

7. *Alveta Oveta Mims, etc., et al. v. The Duval County School Board*, 4598–Civ-J, June 23, 1971, 3–5; Kluger, *Simple Justice*, 742–50.

8. *Mims v. The Duval County School Board*, June 23, 1971, 3–5; Janet Johnson (School Board employee), interview by author, Jacksonville, January 3, 1990; see M. Stolee, *A Report to the Duval County Board of Public Instruction* (Miami: University of Miami Press, 1968).

9. Billy Parker (former Principal of Forrest High School), interview by author, Jacksonville, September 20, 2001; *Florida Times-Union*, December 10, 1964, February 20, 1999; Patricia Pearson, interview by author, Jacksonville, April 12, 2005.

10. Lloyd Pearson, telephone interview by author, Jacksonville, November 13, 1996; see Frederick T. Davis, *History of Jacksonville, Florida and Vicinity, 1513 to 1924* (Gainesville: University of Florida Press, 1964), 140; Carolyn Williams, "History of Jacksonville's Schools," *Jacksonville Historical Quarterly* (Fall 1993): 6–7; Barbara Richardson, *Decades of Disappointment: A History of Blacks in Jacksonville, Florida* (PhD diss., Carnegie-Mellon University, 1975), 164–65.

11. Lloyd Pearson interview; *Jacksonville Journal*, February 8, 1982; *Pearson Bio*, Jacksonville Public Library, Downtown Branch, Florida Room, Blacks in Jacksonville box, Pearson Folder, 5, 6; "Jacksonville's Native Son," *Jet*, April 30, 1964, 52; Mary Pearson, interview by author, Jacksonville, February 17, 1996, and personal papers in her file taken from Jacksonville NAACP records, Jacksonville, Fla.; *St. Petersburg Times*, March 27, 1964.

12. Lloyd Pearson, interview; *St. Petersburg Times*, March 27, 1964; *Jacksonville Journal*, February 8, 1982; *Pearson Bio*; Rodney Hurst, telephone interview by author, Jacksonville, August 26, 28, 1995.

13. "Promise of Trouble," *Time*, September 12, 1960, 27; quoted in *St. Petersburg Times*, March 27, 1964; Mary Ann Pearson (widow of Rutledge Pearson), interview by author, Jacksonville, December 29, 1994.

14. Mary Ann Pearson, interview; *Jacksonville Journal*, February 8, 1982; "Jacksonville's Native Son," 53.

15. Mary Ann Pearson, interview; Frank Priestly (former teacher, Isaiah Blocker school in Jacksonville), telephone interview by author, Jacksonville, August 20, 1995; Marvin Dawkins (former Jacksonville resident), interview by author, Tallahassee, February 17, 1996.

16. Hurst interview; *Florida Times-Union*, August 21, 1983.

17. Lloyd Pearson interview; Mary Ann Pearson interview.

18. Hurst interview; *Florida Times-Union*, October 23, 1993; Lloyd Pearson interview; Mary Ann Pearson, interview; *Jacksonville Journal*, August 29, 1960; "Racial Fury Over Sit-Ins," *Life*, September 21, 1960; *Florida Star*, September 3, 1960.

19. Rodney Hurst, interview.

20. *Florida Star*, August 24, 1960, January 15–21, 1994.

21. *New York Times*, August 28, 1960; "Florida Promise of Trouble," *Time*, September 12, 1960, 27.

22. "Racial Fury Over Sit-ins," *Life*, September 12, 1960, 37.

23. Hurst interview; *New York Times*, August 28, 1960; "Florida Promise of Trouble," 27.

24. See *Washington Post*, September 3, 1960.

25. Calvin Lang (participant in the protest), interview by author, Tallahassee, July 29, 1993; *Florida Times-Union*, August 28, 1960, August 21, 1983; Walch, *Black Voices*, 74.

26. See *Washington Post*, September 5, 1960.

27. See *New York Times*, August, 28 1960, March 26, 1964; *Florida Times-Union*, August 28, 1960; *Jacksonville Journal*, August 28, 1960.

28. *Florida Star*, September 3, 1960; quoted in *Washington Post*, September 5, 1960.

29. *Florida Star*, September 3, 1960; *Time*, September 12, 1960; *New York Times*, August 28, 1960.

30. Hurst interview; *New York Times*, November 5, 1964; *Florida Times-Union*, August 28, 1960; *Jacksonville Journal*, August 28, 1960.

31. Walch, *Black Voices*, 75; Mary Ann Pearson interview; Hurst interview; Bartley, *Keeping the Faith*, 103–16.

32. *Florida Star*, February 9, 1963; Bartley, *Keeping the Faith*, 103–06.

33. *Florida Times-Union*, March 26, 1964.

34. Joshua Williams (political activist in Jacksonville in the 1950s and 1960s), interview by author, Tallahassee, September 24, 1992, Tallahassee, Fla.; *Florida Times-Union*, February 17, March 24, May 23, and May 24, 1964.

35. Joshua Williams, interview.

36. Joshua Williams, interview; see *Florida Times-Union*, February 10, 2003.

37. Mary Ann Pearson interview; Charles Dailey (pastor of the Oakland Street Baptist Church and Head of the Jacksonville Branch Interdenominational Ministerial Alliance), telephone interview by author, Jacksonville, January 5, 1995; Lloyd Pearson interview; *Jacksonville Journal*, March 16, 1964.

38. Dailey interview.

39. Dailey interview; *Florida Times-Union*, February 18, 1964.

40. Quoted in *Florida Times-Union*, February 27, 1964.

41. Williams interview; *Florida Star*, March 14, 1964; David R. Colburn, "Florida Politics in the Twentieth Century," in *The New History of Florida*, ed. Michael Gannon (Gainesville: University Press of Florida, 1996), 363.

42. *Florida Times-Union*, March 3, 1964.

43. *Florida Times-Union*, March 5, 1964, February 10, 2003; *Washington Post*, March 5, 1964.

44. *Pittsburgh Courier*, March 24, 1964; *Washington Post*, July 5, 1964.

45. *Pittsburgh Courier*, March 28, 1964.

46. *Florida Times-Union*, March 24, 1964; *Jacksonville Journal*, March 25, 1964.

47. Quoted in *Pittsburgh Courier*, March 28, 1964; *Jacksonville Journal*, March 19, 1964.

48. *Florida Times-Union*, March 23, 1964; *Pittsburgh Courier*, March 24, 1964; quoted in *Florida Times-Union*, March 24,1964.

49. *Florida Times-Union*, March 24, 1964; *Miami News*, March 24, 1964.

50. Quoted in *Florida Times-Union*, March 24, 1964; Williams interview.

51. *Florida Times-Union*, March 24, 1964; see *New York Times*, November 5, 1964.

52. *Florida Times-Union*, March 24, 1964; *Washington Post*, March 29, 1964.

53. G. Vincent Lewis (assistant pastor of the Bethel Baptist Institutional Church of Jacksonville), interview by author, Tallahassee, September 29, 1993.

54. *Florida Times-Union*, March 24, 1964, and March 24, 1969; *St. Petersburg Times*, March 24, 1964. Much has been written about the Johnnie Mae Chappell murder in recent years as the family had pursued a lawsuit against the city and prosecution of the uncharged suspects; see *Florida Times-Union*, March 23, 2003, September 29, 2005, March 25, 2006, January 6, 2006, and January 7, 2006; *St. Petersburg Times*, October 12, 2005; *Associated Baptist Press*, July 25, 2005.

55. *Florida Times-Union*, March 26, 1964 "INTEGRATION: Long Day," *Newsweek*, April 4, 1964, 20–22; "A Summer of Race Violence on the Highway; Where Violence Has Started, Jacksonville Riots," *U.S. News and World Report*, April 6, 1964, 35–36; "Toward a Long, Hot Summer," *Time*, April 3, 1964, 28–29.

56. *Florida Times-Union*, March 24, 1964.

57. *Florida Times-Union*, March 24, March 26, 1964.

58. *Miami News*, March 24, 1964.

59. *Miami News*, March 24, 1964; *Florida Times-Union*, March 25, 1964; Martin Luther King Jr., telegram to Rutledge Pearson, March 24, 1964, in the Mary Ann Pearson Papers, copy in author's possession.

60. *Florida Times-Union*, March 25, 1964; quoted in "Jacksonville's Native Son," 52.

61. G. Vincent Lewis interview; quoted in *Washington Post*, March 29, 1964.

62. *Florida Times-Union*, March 25, 1964.

63. *Florida Times-Union*, March 25, March 26, 1964.

64. *Florida Star*, March 24, and March 28, 1964.

65. *Florida Times-Union*, March 26, 1964; Dailey interview; Lloyd Pearson interview; Mary Ann Pearson interview.

66. *Florida Times-Union*, May 2, 1967; see *Jacksonville Journal*, February 8, 1988; *Florida Times-Union*, February 3, 1991; Lloyd Pearson interview; Mary Ann Pearson interview.

# CHAPTER THREE

# BROTHERHOOD OF DEFIANCE

## THE STATE-LOCAL RELATIONSHIP IN THE DESEGREGATION OF LEE COUNTY PUBLIC SCHOOLS, 1954–1969

### IRVIN D. S. WINSBORO

At the start of the 1970–71 academic year, schools in Lee County, Florida, underwent a historic transformation. Sixteen years after the U.S. Supreme Court had declared racial segregation in public schools unconstitutional in *Brown v. Board of Education*, the Lee County School Board finally instituted countywide school desegregation. How Lee County had managed to delay this for so long is a story of local actions with state implications as well. As the convergence of state and local defiance swept the Lee County School Board away from allegiance to *Brown*, it eventually took federal actions to ensure compliance with the Court's mandate. In the end, the desegregation of Lee County Public Schools reflected an interconnected triumph of black agency and federal intervention over a state/local resistance of school desegregation. This is a story that played out in many of the communities of the Deep South following *Brown*, but seldom as long as it did in Lee County.[1]

Even though the literature on the subject has reflected a long-fashionable focus on the "moderation" of Florida's officials in the aftermath of *Brown*, in reality state leaders intuitively resisted desegregation in ways similar to that of other southern states, most notably in adopting or proposing racially based pupil assignment measures, granting extraordinary powers to the governor, probing and red-baiting desegregation groups, suggesting interposition and nullification acts, and using sovereign powers and legal counsel to prevent or delay desegregation—defined in this work as the "Down South" strategy.

Florida officials seldom, however, resorted to the sensational resistance of Virginia or the demagogic rhetoric of political leaders in Arkansas, Mississippi, and Alabama.[2]

While Orval Faubus, Ross Barnett, and George Wallace led their states into a bold defiance of *Brown*, more realistic segregationists positioned Florida to project a progressive "New South" image. Even so, leaders in Tallahassee stubbornly, and sometimes not so subtly, eschewed any meaningful measures to enact school desegregation in the Sunshine State. Some localities, Dade County (Miami), for example, initiated their own desegregation plans independent of state leadership and sanctions. Other school districts, following the lead of Tallahassee, steadfastly maintained their color lines. Representative of the latter, Lee County arose as one of the most defiant scofflaws of *Brown*; the county's actions are as much a story of state-orchestrated resistance to *Brown* as they are of sustained local defiance. Given the nature of that defiance, Lee County reflected but one extreme manifestation of state-promulgated policies and unofficial guidelines for orchestrating the rejection, crippling—or, most commonly, the Down South-style delay and stonewalling—*Brown*'s sweeping mandate. That account suggests important lessons for understanding the interplay of everyday politics and everyday protesters in the wake of *Brown* in the South.

Blacks in southwest Florida had viewed education as paramount to their improvement since they first settled there. Local lore has it that the Tillis family became the first black settlers in this region (then part of Monroe County) in 1867. After homesteading a small plot along the Caloosahatchee River, Nelson Tillis created a makeshift schoolhouse for the oldest of his eleven children. Tillis soon enticed J. Wesley Roberts away from Key West to preside over his small black academy. As other black families moved to the area, they continued the Tillis tradition of emphasizing education for their youth.[3]

Despite blacks initiating educational measures in the area, "separate but unequal" became the founding doctrine of the Lee County School District. In one of the first meetings of the Lee County Board of Public Instruction (LBPI), created in 1887 when Florida named the new county after Confederate icon Robert E. Lee, the Board moved that "colored people shall be encouraged to organize a [separate] school district . . . to the districts that served white students."[4] How that parallel district, subsequently known as "Sub-District No. 1," would be financed and staffed was left to the black community, since the governmental bodies of the new county provided no funding for minority schools.

Within two years of the creation of a public-funded white school district, black residents had opened their own (non-public funded) lower-level school in a church shared by Methodist and Baptist congregations. During the week, the church served as an academy for black children, with J. Wesley Roberts as its headmaster. Eventually, the LBPI acknowledged the school as part of its "Sub-District"; yet the board refused to equitably fund the separate school. It fell to the black community to pay the rent for the building and the salary of its teachers. By June 1896, the LBPI exercised jurisdiction over 654 white children and twenty-three black children, all of whom matriculated along dual academic and physical paths.[5] Thus, from its inception, Lee County offered education to blacks (whose families so valued education), but not under the public funding umbrella of the LBPI.

In 1896 the Old South applauded the Supreme Court's decision in *Plessy v. Ferguson*, which held that separate facilities for blacks and whites did not violate the Fourteenth Amendment's "due process" clause as long as those facilities were equal in services. Even before *Plessy* provided legal sanction to separation, Lee County had taken its segregationist cue from Tallahassee. The Florida Constitution of 1885 stipulated that, "White and colored children shall not be taught in the same school, . . ."[6] In that brief line, Florida had effectively contravened Reconstruction-era progress and legalized school segregation in Florida. *Plessy* in 1896, and other Florida statutes in 1905, 1913, and 1939 reinforced Florida's separate schools doctrine.[7]

The education of black students in Lee County remained limited to church and "colored" facilities until 1913, when the LBPI allocated meager funds to support the growing black school-age population in Lee County. The board subsequently created a segregated school in the "Safety Hill" section of Fort Myers. This new school, dubbed the Williams Academy, arose as the first government-funded black school in southwest Florida since the homesteading days of the Tillis family. In 1927, the board funded, with assistance from the national Julius Rosenwald Fund, the Paul Lawrence Dunbar School, which offered the first nine-month upper-level instruction to blacks in the region. Black students from nearby Collier, Hendry, Charlotte, and Glades Counties thereafter traveled to Fort Myers to attend the school. The black community of Fort Myers subsequently adopted Dunbar as its namesake.[8]

On May 18, 1954, Lee County awoke to find its historical practices under attack as a result of *Brown*. The ruling declared separate schools for white and black students to be inherently unequal and thus in violation of the Thirteenth and Fourteenth Amendments to the U.S. Constitution.[9] State officials immediately set in motion policies designed to repudiate the Court ruling. Acting Governor Charley E. Johns went so far as to suggest "a special legislative session on school segregation." Although Johns did not pursue the idea in his next cabinet meeting, he subsequently traveled to Richmond to attend a conference on segregation, proclaiming there that the vast majority of his state's black and white populations favored separation. As reported on the front page of the *Fort Myers News-Press*, Johns then proposed to the Southern Governors' Conference that the U.S. Constitution be amended to allow states "to maintain separate but equal public schools for the races."[10]

If the white leaders of Lee County feared *Brown* deconstructing their caste system, Johns's actions must have comforted them—the acting governor and his legislative supporters had certainly taken pains to assure localities like Lee that school desegregation would not sweep the state. Clearly, Tallahassee had signaled that *Brown* on its own merits would not contravene the state's long history of racial division.

Almost simultaneously, Johns's adversary in the Democratic primary for governor in 1954, pro-business State Senator LeRoy Collins of Tallahassee, assured his followers that he had never been a supporter of desegregation, that he "would support a continuance of... established customs in the South," and that *Brown* would not alter his views on that subject.[11] While promulgating a more measured response than Johns, Collins nevertheless chose a segregationist path. The most pensive, pragmatic, and flexible "New South" politician on the race issue, LeRoy Collins, had now set the ground rules for "moderation" in Florida: moderation would embrace pro-segregationist rather than pro-integrationist politics at the state level.

Although termed a moderate like Collins on the desegregation issue, Florida superintendent of Public Instruction, Thomas D. Bailey, also seemed to signal an intractability on the race issue when he stated in May 1954, "The greatest danger we have isn't just the segregation issue. We have a lot of people down here who hate to be pushed around, whether the state or federal government is doing the pushing."[12] The Republican candidate for governor shared common ground with Johns, Collins, and Bailey by declaring that *Brown* did not apply to Florida "in its present status." In 1970, a Florida State Department of Education report on the post-*Brown* years concluded that the decision had virtually "no effect on Florida" through the early 1960s, when federal authorities began serious enforcement of *Brown* as local activists filed suits in federal courts to force compliance.[13] In retrospect, Tallahassee's message to local boards was that of a firm, proactive stance against desegregation. The message worked well for many years.

Yet the message resonated even more profoundly at another level; for most leaders of Florida had also declined to lend any moral support to desegregation following the issuance of *Brown*. Without a significant stand on implementing *Brown*, Tallahassee ensured that segregation would remain a pillar of Florida's public education system. Compared to other states of Dixie, perhaps the public pronouncements of Florida's officials seemed less virulent than those of Faubus, Barnett, and Wallace and, subsequently, served to persuade scholars of the moderation factor in Florida. Even so, the business-friendly, image-minded Sunshine State prolonged segregation of its schools just as long, if not longer, than most of its more "radical" neighbors.

Lee County's white leaders took their cues from Tallahassee in this attenuated process. The county's immediate antipathy for *Brown* gained voice in the *Fort Myers News-Press*, which reported the story under a full banner headline. Both the front and second pages provided related articles. The *News-Press* also ran an editorial calling for rejection of the dictates of *Brown*, presumptively assuming that Tallahassee would effectively deflect or defer any action to implement the decision. Letters to the editor over the next few days from such writers as "A. Tom Bomb" reflected this sentiment. One letter cast the nine Justices of the Warren Court as ignorant monkeys, while another proposed that "Lee County officials simply take the *Brown* decision, put it on a platter and cast it out at the back door and dump it into the garbage can."[14]

School officials also made several statements based on anticipated state mandates to ensure that segregation would not become a legal dilemma. Apparently feeling empowered by state and local utterances on *Brown*, Lee County Superintendent of Schools Ray Tipton (1953–60) stated, "we will continue as we are" in regard to the district's segregated "zone" practices. In what would become an oft-repeated assertion by the white leaders of Lee County, Tipton claimed, "school boards are experienced by [state] law to fix boundaries . . . and we will continue as we are" on the dual racial attendance policy in Lee County.[15] At that time the segregated campus in Dunbar served virtually all of the 1,009 Lee County black students from grades one through twelve. It can be inferred that the superintendent thought Dunbar was the school best prepared to meet his definition of attendance zones, or, more accurately, racial enclaves.

School authorities sought to strengthen their hand by implying that blacks themselves were not interested in desegregating local schools. Dave Bull, chair of the school board, voiced the opinion that the State Education Department had forwarded a message suggesting that "Negro teachers don't want an end of segregation for fear of losing their jobs." Superintendent Tipton escalated the emotional fallout by declaring that he knew of no instances in the state where black parents had declared for district-wide integration.[16] Not only did this send a veiled threat to the local black community, but it equally sent a message that the school board intended to use state law and Down South presumptions to deflect *Brown*. Given the roots of segregation in Lee County, and the reinforcing anti-*Brown* messages coming out of Tallahassee, it is of little surprise that whites in Lee County moved so quickly to institute a stonewalling strategy.

Board minutes reveal that members believed segregation could continue under existing state laws regulating the attendance of children at county schools. The board's legal advisor, Attorney F. Ewing Barnes, reinforced that belief by proclaiming that the county could continue segregation on this basis. Barnes assured board members that state and local, and not federal, authorities would determine which school a student attended.[17] Thus, within days of the release of the 1954 ruling, both Tallahassee and Lee County had created a loosely constructed alliance demonstrating that neither entity had intentions of implementing the Court's decision, even to a moderate degree.

Florida's acting-governor, Charley Johns from rural Bradford County, strengthened this relationship by announcing his intentions to retain school segregation. Johns, one of the leaders of a coalition of gerrymandered reactionary legislators (known as the Pork Chop Gang) had opposed earlier measures in the legislature to break the white primary monopoly in Florida and to limit the excesses of the Ku Klux Klan. Cabinet members convinced the governor that legal and extralegal measures could be exercised, ensuring that desegregation would not be binding on the state.[18] In light of this, Johns decided not to call the legislature into special session. However, the following year Johns (now back in the State Senate) prompted the State Legislature to pass the Pupil Assignment Act, which allowed districts to assign students to schools on the basis of intelligence, scholastic aptitude, and background, but not on factors such as race. The revised pupil assignment bill subsequently passed both houses of the legislature with only one dissenting vote (Rep. John Orr of Miami); in response, the statewide NAACP promptly condemned the act as one designed only to "retard the advancement of Negroes" in Florida."[19] As a subterfuge to integration, the measure and a companion in the legislature to allow counties to abolish public schools (never enacted) essentially provided guidelines to pro-segregation school districts on how to nullify or delay *Brown*.

Governor LeRoy Collins, who succeeded Johns as governor in January 1955, later characterized the mood of the Florida State Legislature in the wake of *Brown*: "The legislature passed many bills patterned after the most radical segregationist actions taken in other states."[20] In an address to the legislature in 1955, Collins himself stated that "segregation in our public schools is a part of Florida's custom and law. I will use all the lawful power of the Governor's office to preserve this custom and law."[21] Collins also used his "lawful powers" to sign into law Johns's Pupil Assignment Bill.[22]

Although Collins saw no need for subsequent legislative action, other state officials felt differently. Florida's Superintendent of Public Instruction, Thomas D. Bailey, proposed that counties proceed with spending disproportionate amounts of money on new schools designed for segregation. The purpose, Bailey would later state, was to bring inferior black educational facilities in line with white ones, eliminating the need to desegregate the state's public school systems.[23]

To preempt a Court challenge to the anti-integration measures, Florida's Attorney General, Richard W. Ervin, desiring "a Constitutional method by which Florida could preserve segregation in its public schools," prepared legal arguments to show the federal bench why Florida would need an indefinite time period (defined as "gradualism") to desegregate its schools. The State Cabinet allocated $10,000 to prepare his argument. Ervin, later a chief justice of the Florida Supreme Court, purportedly undertook this action in response to a Court invitation to answer the ambiguous timeline of the *Brown* ruling. He completed his *Amicus Curiae Brief of the Attorney General of Florida* in October 1954. In his brief, Ervin argued that without a deadline, and by the Court granting "Broad Powers . . . in Local-School Authorities to Determine Administrative Procedures," Florida could eventually (no time period was given) embrace integration. While some historians have maintained that Ervin constructed his argument to "ease in" integration, in reality Ervin's actions resulted in yet another early roadblock to the implementation of *Brown* in the State of Florida.[24]

Ervin offered arguments as to why immediate desegregation was impractical, including studies purporting to document three-fourths of Florida's white population opposing desegregation. He declared a need to revise administrative procedures in the schools, and in a tacit rejection of the separate but unequal argument, Ervin cited the unfair competition between black and white students due to the inferiority of the black schools. In one of the first manifestations of Down South delaying tactics, Ervin asked the Court to consider that local communities needed time to adjust to the sociological and psychological shock of forced desegregation. In *Brown v. Board of Education II* (1955), the Court adopted a good portion of Ervin's brief.[25]

On May 31, 1955, the Supreme Court rendered its decision in *Brown II*. The judgment handed state and local officials the responsibility for ending school segregation under guidelines to be outlined by the respective federal district courts. The Court's ruling established neither timetables nor deadlines; it simply ordered desegregation as "soon as practicable." The *Fort Myers News-Press* responded by declaring that the $10,000 expended for Ervin's filing was the best money the state had ever spent.[26]

Now, without a Court-mandated deadline for desegregation, the State of Florida could encourage, and Lee County could continue, evasion and non-compliance. For Tallahassee, as with Lee County, the die had been cast. The reaction to *Brown* would be one of obfuscation, obstruction, and delay. The implications of this policy boded not only constitutional conflict but political and racial divisiveness as well. The interrelatedness of all these actions and policies made compliance with *Brown* unlikely in Florida localities such as Lee.

Lee County thereafter shifted its focus to the Pupil Assignment Act to solidify its policy of delay or denial. In an August 1956 meeting, the board sought to justify its actions by resolving, "said enactment of the Florida Legislature required that the Board . . . shall assign pupils to public schools so as to provide for the orderly and efficient administration of such public schools. . ."[27] The measure allowed students to petition for reassignment to a particular school, and since race was allegedly a non-factor in assignment decisions, the rule technically allowed for school integration. This stratagem proved all too effective. At the outset of the 1956–1957 school year, not one local district in Florida had moved to end its dual system of public education.[28]

Governor Collins swept back into office with 73.7 percent of the vote in 1956, claiming that he had squelched the "noise and confusion" of the region even while "no integration has occurred in our state." He continued his efforts to attract northern businesses to a "stable," New South Florida. The state itself all but ignored *Brown* until Collins left office.[29] As noted in a *Time* magazine piece, Collins's record in Tallahassee appeared one of ambivalence in shaping Florida into an egalitarian post-*Brown* society. Historians have noted that Collins attracted many black voters in the 1956 election, characterized by the *Miami News* as a contest of "I Love Segregation More Than You Do." Even so, scholars must concede that there was no other place for the black vote to go that year. Certainly, the record shows that Governor LeRoy Collins grew in his moral opposition to segregation during his years in power, yet as he left office the twisted face of Jim Crow itself remained a stubborn reality behind the image of smiling, New South Florida.[30]

In the year of Collins's re-election, he and other prominent officials in Tallahassee agreed to create a committee to review ways that the Sunshine State might address desegregation. Retired Circuit Judge L. L. Fabisinski headed the committee, which convened in March 1956. It subsequently recommended the strengthening of local school boards and the enhancement of the governor's powers of law enforcement, noting that the Pupil Assignment Act and any appeals thereto pertaining should be directed to the State Board of Education for "judicial review." The committee found that these measures were sufficient to maintain a separate public school system without resorting to school closures or inviting disruptive resistance. In the midst of Tallahassee's endorsement of the committee's stratagems, small-county champion, legislator Farris Bryant, undertook even more drastic actions by proposing a resolution giving the governor the power of "interposing" his and the state's authority between "hostile" federal actions and intra-state enforcement of them. Attorney General Richard Ervin observed that Bryant and the legislature that year "did almost all [they] could to prevent integration."[31] That anti-integration mood in Tallahassee characterized the following years, while Bryant won election as Florida's next pro-segregationist governor and the state continued to provide a rubric for local defiance of *Brown*.

As a result of the state-level attempts to derail the Court's order, Lee County's board pursued the evasive pupil assignment tactic and remained virtually unaffected by the school desegregation movement. A decade passed before the Lee County School Board even proposed a comprehensive desegregation plan. This effort finally came as a result of the federal Civil Rights Act of 1964, which effectively trumped the Sunshine State's de facto policy of segregation, or at least Tallahassee's guidelines for de facto segregation at the local level. Governor Bryant, and his immediate successors, Haydon Burns and Claude Kirk Jr., both staunch segregationists, felt little compulsion to make the Civil Rights Act of 1964 cornerstones of their policies. They moved instead to prioritize such measures as economic expansion, outdoor recreation, and increased executive powers.[32]

Titles IV and VI of the Civil Rights Act of 1964 provided the federal government and courts with the meaningful power of enforcement that they had heretofore lacked. The Department of Justice could act as a plaintiff to force school districts to comply with federal desegregation guidelines. Additionally, federal funds could be withheld by governmental agencies from school districts that practiced segregation. [33] Responding to the new federal mandate, which effectively defused gubernatorial and legislative pro-segregation policies, Lee County moved into a new level of reality.

After a decade of interplay between state and county, the school board of Lee County now realized that the federal government would supercede any combination of state and local segregationist policies and practices. In retrospect, the Civil Rights Act of 1964 underscored the doom of school segregation and strengthened the resolve of integrationists to finally, and permanently, tear down the wall of bigotry between dual and unequal schools. The act also coalesced grassroots black opponents of segregation and spurred them on to a new legal militancy. How the Lee County School Board would react to these new realities remained to be seen.

After the passage of the Civil Rights Act in July of 1964 (opposed by both U.S. senators from Florida), the school board proposed its initial "Plan for Desegregation." The plan, which ostensibly showed the board's "Assurance of Compliance" with the Department of Health, Education, and Welfare (HEW), called for gradual implementation, starting with the first grade in 1965. In an effort to forestall federal oversight, the board unanimously passed the plan in late 1964. Yet, the board's plan carried a rider allowing "Freedom of Choice" for all students, which effectively undermined desegregation. In reality, white students could choose *not* to desegregate under the rider—and they did.[34] Even though the board now faced the possibility of federal intervention for delaying school integration, they felt confident that an attenuated plan would both placate federal authorities and mollify the black community. The board miscalculated on both accounts.

In 1964, working-class blacks in Lee County took action to end separate schools, even before the county offered its piecemeal desegregation plan. It was no coincidence that the black community did not openly challenge segregation until the Civil Rights Act of 1964 undermined the ability of Tallahassee and the local board to perpetuate dual educational institutions. Put simply, educationally disfranchised, poor, and working-class blacks realized anew that federal authority both superceded and invalidated any state and local collusion to restrain *Brown*. As one local black educator recalled: "The Civil Rights Act of 1964 changed it all."[35]

On August 4, 1964, John H. Blalock from the black working-class community of Dunbar filed suit in the U.S. Circuit Court in Tampa. He petitioned for an injunction to enjoin the Lee County Board of Public Instruction from continuing "its policy, practice, custom, and usage of a biracial school system" for its 11,576 white students and its 2,583 black students. *Rosalind Blalock, et al. v. The Board of Public Instruction of Lee County, Florida, et al.*, filed directly on behalf of twenty-one school-age children and indirectly on behalf of the entire black community, argued that Lee County's dual system resulted in forced segregation by, "acting under *color of the authority . . . of the state of Florida. . .*" According to the lawsuit:

> This racially segregated public school system operated by defendants consists of 24 "white" schools which are limited to attendance by white students only and which are staffed by white teachers, white principals and other white professional personnel. Said racially segregated public school system . . . consists also of 4 "Negro" schools which are limited to attendance by Negro students only and which are staffed by Negro teachers, principals and other Negro professional personnel.[36]

The brief stated flatly that attendance at the various public "compulsory biracial school system" (or zones) of Lee County was determined solely "on the basis of race and color," a condition resulting directly from the Florida Pupil Assignment law.[37]

The suit prompted the school board to file a grade-a-year plan for desegregation one month later. The board initially asked Federal District Judge Joseph P. Lieb to cancel the case, saying its attenuated desegregation plan reflected the county's voluntary compliance with federal desegregation rules. Judge Lieb refused to dismiss the suit based on case law, however, and rejected the board's desegregation plan in the process, placing the onus on the board for explaining why an additional twelve years were needed to fully desegregate Lee County schools.[38]

On September 1, 1965, all parties reached a tentative accelerated plan, which presumably would satisfy the goals of *Blalock* and place the county in compliance with the Civil Rights Act of 1964.[39] Token staff and student integration was to begin in August 1965. The board assigned a white principal to historically black Dunbar High, and a white teacher to Dunbar Elementary, while sending four black staff members to the Central Administration Office rather than to white schools. Since no black teachers were assigned to white schools, Blalock and the NAACP challenged the county. The plaintiffs argued that Lee County continued to maintain a dual system through its attendance zones and practiced desegregation with a plan that, by 1966, affected the integration of only twenty-six children in a district with nearly 16,000 students.[40]

The current plan, the plaintiffs argued, still maintained an unacceptably slow pace of desegregation and allowed attendance zones (Pupil Assignment Zones) designed to minimize desegregation. The new suit argued that the county continued to sanction segregated facilities in the schools and administrative offices, as well. The school board's attorney argued for the county without addressing the issues raised in the motion, maintaining instead that all parties had approved the plan. The attorney also argued that the county's plan was voluntary, and its rejection would destroy incentives for the board to desegregate.[41]

By 1966, the United States government had entered the *Blalock* case. When the Department of Justice joined the suit at the behest of local blacks, the schools of Lee County reflected essentially the same racial footprint of the pre-*Blalock* days. In its motion on August 16, 1966, the Justice Department argued that Lee County had not in practice dismantled its historically dual school system and, thus, failed to be in compliance with the Civil Rights Act of 1964. U.S. Attorney General Nicholas Katzenbach approved the motion, marking the first time that the Justice Department joined a desegregation case in the Sunshine State. In a long editorial, the *Fort Myers News-Press* observed that the "climate has changed [; it] has been coerced by the federal civil rights legislation and the administrative actions of Washington."[42] The *News-Press* editorial all but delivered a eulogy for Lee County's stonewalling.

Judge Lieb approved the pending motion on September 7, 1966. The Justice Department continued, nevertheless, to focus on the county and the board continued to react with half-measures and more delays. Even so, the board's attorney now advised that Lee County stood without the benefit of state mandates and guidelines for this type of situation and he could not, in turn, reasonably prevent the county from becoming a federal test case for desegregation.[43]

On February 21, 1967, the board adopted an amendment to the February 1965 desegregation order. The measure called for a revised "Freedom of Choice" plan in school selection for all students, starting with the 1967–68 school year. By offering individual choice in selecting schools, the county hoped to satisfy the demands of the Justice Department while not instituting immediate district-wide integration. The board offered the plan to Judge Lieb as a substitute for the existing order. As it technically opened up all the twenty-seven schools to mixed-race assignments, Judge Lieb approved the county's new plan.[44]

The Freedom of Choice plan presumptively ended school assignments based on race. In actuality, the plan failed to achieve this. The burden of desegregation rested only on black students and families. Despite the years of court reviews and orders, board minutes confirmed that local schools still operated on the basis of "racial lines." By 1968, only a fraction of the black students in Lee County attended desegregated schools, and all those desegregated schools existed outside Dunbar, Fort Myers' black, working-class community.[45]

As with the previous plan, Freedom of Choice did not accelerate Lee County's school desegregation to the satisfaction of the Justice Department. Lee County still had identifiably all-black schools and all-black or all-white faculty, and only a small percentage of the county's black children attended integrated schools at a time when the state average for similar integration remained higher. Judge Lieb responded by threatening the board with a declaration of non-compliance. He then ordered the county to formulate a new desegregation plan.[46] Emmit Anderson, the board's new attorney, recommended that the directors commission the Florida School Desegregation Counseling Center at the University of Miami to create a "rapid desegregation plan that the courts and the school system can live with."[47]

At the end of the 1960s, school desegregation, not its delay, had finally become a priority for the Lee County School Board. The fact that the federal government had superceded the State of Florida's policies of denial or delay of desegregation, and that progressives on the race issue like Reubin Askew now moved to the center of political life in Tallahassee, played a major role in the county's decision to move towards integration. Once the state's pillars of segregation wavered under the weight of Washington's challenges, local officials had little choice but to comply with federal law.

In the face of these realities, the board ultimately accepted the center's plan, though much of it had been initially dismissed as too radical for Lee County. The designated director reporting on the plan at the board meeting began his report with the following statement: "Since the board finds itself caught between a legislative judiciary and a law-making executive branch of the government, we are compelled by the Federal Court to propose a plan to show that we are eliminating the dual school system."[48] The board filed the new plan with the Court on April 22, 1969, proposing the establishment of middle schools to replace the current junior high schools. Dunbar (862 students) and nearby Franklin Park Elementary School (903 students), until now all-black, would integrate grades 1–3.

Dunbar Junior and Senior High would become a countywide 9th grade facility—but the proposal still allowed choice for other schools.[49]

The U.S. Justice Department objected to this plan, noting that it smacked of "Attendance Zones" once again and it failed to remove all dual aspects of Lee County schools. The board amended the plan again, creating a system that called for a minimum attendance ratio of 20 percent black students in all schools and zones.[50] Lee County now adopted desegregation, but the level of integration was just enough to assure compliance with federal law. While this was not the level of integration that the plaintiffs in *Blalock* desired, it would serve to, at least partially, erase the color line in local public schools. On May 14, 1969, the Court ordered the county to accelerate the implementation of the new plan.[51] Even though moribund, the practice of segregation was dying a slow, tortuous death in Lee County, Florida.

The Lee County School Board would, however, make one last effort to retain its Freedom of Choice (now termed "Exercise of Choice" by the board) for its students. Superintendent Ray Williams (1965–1977) argued the legality of choice, since students could chose to attend black or white schools. The board filed a motion to amend the Court's findings, but the Court denied the appeal on June 9, 1969.[52] Higher court case precedent, in particular the 1968 *Alexander* and *Green* decisions (later validated in the *Holmes* case), in which the High Court not only struck down "freedom of choice" plans but also redefined the responsibility of local school boards to abolish dual attendance zones, now loomed over Lee County like the veritable sword of Damocles.[53] The board considered appealing the case, but its attorney counseled that, without state support or case precedent, such an appeal would fail. Moreover, the board's attorney warned that the county could face stiff financial penalties for a futile appeal.[54] The old *modus operandi* of state-local collusion in segregation now dissipated in the face of this new, but long unfolding, reality.

In August 1969, U.S. District Judge Ben Krentzman, to whom *Blalock* had been reassigned for disposition, rejected an eleventh-hour effort by Republican Governor Claude Kirk to intervene in the case and ordered the board to comply "forthwith" with the countywide desegregation mandates of the United States Fifth Circuit Court and the Supreme Court. With no options left, federal officials, now firmly intent on implementing and enforcing the law and spirit of *Brown*, and the state-local brotherhood of defiance now but a remembrance, the all-white District School Board of Lee County resubmitted a comprehensive "Plan of Desegregation" for "a unitary school district" on December 31, 1969.[55] After a decade and a half, the Lee County School Board had yielded to both the demands of its grassroots blacks and the overriding strength, if not the moral suasion, of federal authority. Neither state guidelines and delaying tactics nor local resistance and subterfuges could now prevent Lee County, Florida, from accepting the inevitable.

On the face of it, the eventual desegregation of the county's public school revealed a recalcitrant Down South scenario that persisted for fifteen years after *Brown*. Yet on a deeper level, the county's stonewalling tactics revealed a fundamental reality about the general delay of desegregation of public schools throughout the state—Tallahassee itself had actually sent out "blueprints" on how to resist *Brown* until Democrat Reubin Askew entered the governor's mansion in 1971. Indeed, in the year of Askew's election, a Florida Department of Education report noted that, of the state's sixty-seven counties, there were thirty-three operating under federal court orders and thirty-four operating desegregation plans under HEW guidelines.[56] Against this historical backdrop of state-county collusion and stonewalling, it is not surprising that Lee County, as well as other counties in the state, could protract their desegregation policies for so long after *Brown I* and *Brown II*.

## NOTES

1. *Brown v. Board of Education*, 347 U.S. 483 (1954). *Brown* represented the Court's view on five separate desegregation cases from South Carolina, Virginia, Delaware, the District of Columbia, and Kansas, the state in which *Brown* originated.

2. Don Shoemaker, ed., *With All Deliberate Speed: Segregation-Desegregation in Southern Schools* (Westport, Conn.: Negro University Press, 1957), table, 225; see J. Irving E. Scott, *The Education of Black People in Florida* (Philadelphia: Dorrance and Company, 1974), 91–141; Charles U. Smith and Charles Grigg, "School Desegregation in Florida," in *The Civil Rights Movement in Florida and the United States: Historical and Contemporary Perspectives*, ed. Charles U. Smith (Tallahassee: Father and Sons Publishing, 1989), 178–222; Joseph Aaron Tomberlin, "The Negro and Florida's System of Education: The Aftermath of the *Brown* Case" (PhD diss., Florida State University, 1967), 2–15; Darryl Paulson, "Unfinished Journey: After 50 Years of Striving, The Destination Is Still Unclear," *Forum* (Spring 2004), 9–11.

3. Nina Denson-Rogers, tape recording, April 10, 2001, Lee County Black History Society, Inc., Fort Myers, Fla.; "Black Pioneers Focus of Exhibit," *Fort Myers News-Press*, January 19, 2005; "History: Picturing the Past," *Fort Myers News-Press*, November 19, 2006.

4. Minutes, Lee County Board of Public Instruction (hereafter Minutes LCBPI), October 3, 1887; Donald O. Stone and Beth W. Carter, *The First 100 Years: Lee County Public Schools, 1887–1987* (Fort Myers, Fla.: The School Board of Lee County, n.d.), 25–27. The Lee County Board of Public Instruction changed its name to the Lee County School Board in 1970. For the sake of convenience, it will be referred to hereafter as School Board.

5. Minutes, LCBPI, October 8 and October 11, 1888, July 8, 1896, August 3 and August 29, 1896; Lee County Department of Community Development, Division of Planning, *Williams*

*Academy 1913 to 1995: The First Government-Funded Lee County School for African-Americans* (Lee County, Fla.: Lee County Department of Community Development, Division of Planning, 1995), 29; Denson-Rogers, tape recording.

6. Florida Constitution (1885), Article 12, Section 12.

7. See Scott, *The Education of Black People in Florida*, 5–13; Tomberlin, "The Negro and Florida's System of Education," 2–15.

8. Minutes, LCBPI, February 24, August 3, and December 7, 1927; Lee County Black History Society, Inc., boxed files, Fort Myers, Florida; Stone and Carter, *The First 100 Years*, 112–14, 153–56. The LCBPI sometimes referred to the Williams Academy as the Williams Institute.

9. *Brown v. Board of Education of Topeka, Kansas*, 347 U.S. 483 (1954).

10. "Johns Says He May Call Legislature," *Miami Herald*, May 18, 1954; "Johns Considers Special Session of Legislature," *Fort Myers News-Press*, May 18, 1954; "Johns Sees No Extra Session," *Tallahassee Democrat*, May 18, 1954; "Segregation Study Slated for Richmond," *Florida Times-Union (Jacksonville)*, June 10, 1954; "Governors Vote Closed Session Despite Protest Made by Johns," *Tallahassee Democrat*, June 10, 1954; "Fight Against Segregation Ban Indicated in 12 States," *Florida Times-Union (Jacksonville)*, June 11, 1954; "Johns Suggests Governors Act on Segregation," *Fort Myers News-Press*, November 12, 1954; see "Segregation Study Funds Given Ervin," *Florida Times-Union (Jacksonville)*, June 9, 1954.

11. Tomberlin, "Aftermath of the *Brown* Case," 36; Thomas R. Wagy, "A South to Save: The Administration of Governor LeRoy Collins of Florida" (PhD diss., Florida State University, 1980), 60, see, 57–102; LeRoy Collins, "Past Struggles, Present Changes, and the Future Promise for Civil Rights in Florida and the Nation," in *The Civil Rights Movement in Florida and the United States: Historical and Contemporary Perspectives*, 15; *Tallahassee Democrat*, May 16, May 18, 1954; "High Court Rules States Lack Right to Segregate Races in Public Schools," *The Florida Times-Union (Jacksonville)*, May 18, 1954; quoted in "Collins and Johns Caution on Ruling," *Miami Herald*, May 18, 1954; see "Collins Assails Foe; Johns Points Finger," *Miami Herald*, May 19, 1954.

12. Quoted in "Segregation Reaction," *The Florida Times-Union (Jacksonville)*, May 23, 1954. The crux of the conclusion that Florida's leaders followed a "moderate" approach to *Brown* rests on the assumption that pro-business advocates, such as Collins, recognized that Florida's urbanization, immigrant base, and dependence on tourism called for Florida to dissociate itself from the more rabid actions of other southern states. See, for example, Wagy, "A South To Save," 103–90; David R. Colburn and Richard K. Scher, "Race Relations of Florida Gubernatorial Politics Since the *Brown* Decision," *Florida Historical Quarterly*, 55 (October 1976), 154.

13. "Watson Cites State Rules on Segregation," *The Florida Times-Union (Jacksonville)*, May 19, 1954; Dan Cunningham, "School Desegregation in Florida, 1954–1970," Florida Department of Education, November 18, 1970 (five-page report, typed), Smathers Library, University of Florida, 1,4.

14. "Supreme Court Rules Unanimously Against Public School Segregation," and "The Segregation Ruling," *Fort Myers News-Press*, May 18, 1954; "A. Tom Bomb," Letter to the Editor, *Fort Myers News-Press*, May 19, and 20, 1954. It is easy to suspect some editorial slant in the selection

of these letters for publication. "A. Tom Bomb" was presumably a pseudonym. The byline occurred frequently in the editorial pages of the *News-Press* at that time, and one wonders how these letters reached the editor so soon after the *Brown* headlines. See James W. Jackson, "A History of School Desegregation in Lee County, Florida" (PhD diss., University of Miami, 1970), 81–156.

15. "Local Officials Adopt 'Wait and See' Policy," *Fort Myers News-Press*, May 18, 1954.

16. "Local Officials Adopt 'Wait and See' Policy," *Fort Myers News-Press*, May 18, 1954.

17. Minutes, LCBPI, May 18, 1954; Special Meeting Minutes, LCBPI, September 4, 1954.

18. "Florida Will Go Slowly in Shaping Segregation Policy," *Fort Myers News-Press*, May 19, 1954; see Kevin Norman Klein, "Guarding the Baggage: Florida's Pork Chop Gang and Its Defense of the Old South" (PhD diss., Florida State University, 1995), especially 364–412; David R. Colburn, "Florida Politics in the Twentieth Century," in *The New History of Florida*, ed. Michael Gannon (Gainesville: University Press of Florida, 1966), 361; Colburn and Scher, *Florida's Gubernatorial Politics*, 173–77. Those who favored redistricting in the legislature became known as "Lamb-Choppers."

19. "Takes Swift Action on Governor's Plan," *Fort Myers News-Press*, July 24, 1955; *Miami Herald*, April 12, 1955; "House Backs School Board Assignment Plan," *Fort Myers News-Press*, July 25, 1955; quoted in "Bill Would Help School Board Evade Desegregation," *Fort Myers News-Press*, May 18, 1955.

20. Collins, "Past Struggles," 16.

21. LeRoy Collins to the State Legislature, April 1955, Collins Papers, Special Collections, University of South Florida; Wagy, "A South to Save," 71, see 103–50.

22. Governor's Message, *Journal of the House*, Thirty-fifth Regular Session, 1955, Florida, 15.

23. "Bailey Sees No Push For Desegregation," *Fort Myers News-Press*, June 2, 1955.

24. "Says Plan Would Ban Integration, Be Constitutional," *Fort Myers News-Press*, March 17, 1955; Wagy, "A South to Save," 157–58; Charlton W. Tebeau and Ruby Leach Carlson, *Florida From Indian Trail to Space Age: A History* vol. 2 (Delray Beach, Fla.: The Southern Publishing Company, 1965), 103–04; "Florida Will Go Slowly In Shaping Segregation Policy," *Fort Myers News-Press* (Fla.), May 19, 1954; "Richard Ervin, 99, Ex-Attorney General," *Fort Myers News-Press,* August 27, 2004. Richard W. Ervin, *Amicus Curiae Brief of the Attorney General of Florida*, Supreme Court of the United States, 1954, quoted in Part One; Southern Education Reporting Service, *Southern School News* (Nashville: Southern Education Reporting Service, June 8, 1955), 18–19; see Manning J. Dauer, *Florida's Politics and Government* (Gainesville: University Presses of Florida, 1980), 504.

25. Florida, *Amicus Curiae Brief of the Attorney General of Florida,* September 1954, 18–24; *Brown v. Board of Education II* 349 U.S. 234 (1955).

26. "Justices Direct District Judges Guide Program," *Fort Myers News-Press*, June 1, 1955; *Brown v. Board of Education II*, 349 U.S. 294 (1955); "State Relieved," *Fort Myers News-Press*, June 1, 1955; "Desegregation Postponed Ervin Says," *Miami Herald*, June 3, 1955; see Joseph A. Tomberline, "Florida and the School Desegregation Issue, 1954–1959: A Summary View," *Journal of Negro Education* 43 (1974): 457–67; Kermit L. Hall and Eric W. Rise, *From Local Courts to National Tribunals:*

*The Federal District Courts of Florida* (Brooklyn: Carlson Publishing Company, 1991), 134.

27. Minutes, LCBPI, July 17, 1956, quoted in, Minutes, LCBPI, August 21, 1956; Tebeau and Carlson, *Florida,* 104; "House Approves Teacher Raise of $200 a Year," *Fort Myers News-Press,* March 18, 1955.

28. Southern Education Reporting Service, *A Statistical Summary, State By State, of School Segregation-Desegregation in the Southern and Border Area from 1954 to the Present* (Nashville, Tenn.: Southern Education Reporting Service, 1967), 11; Scott, *The Education of Black People in Florida,* 96; see Special Meeting Minutes, LCBPI, September 4, 1957.

29. "Collins Vows to Continue Battle Against Integration," *Miami Herald,* February 3, 1956.

30. "Words Against Deeds," *Time,* November, 25, 1957; "Segregation," *Miami News,* March 19, 1956.

31. Colburn and Scher, *Florida's Gubernatorial Politics in the Twentieth Century,* 224–26, see Appendix B for legislative measures taken by Florida and other southern states; Florida Advisory Commission on Race Relations, *Report of the Advisory Commission on Race Relations to Governor LeRoy Collins,* March 16, 1959, Smathers Library, University of Florida; Florida, *Acts and Resolutions of the Florida Legislature,* House Concurrent Bill 174, 1958; "Bill Would Fire Teachers Who Advocate Integration," *Tampa Morning Tribune,* April 28, 1959; "Ervin Says Legislature Did Almost All It Could to Prevent Integration," *St. Petersburg Times,* August 8, 1959; "Florida's School Assignment Law, Remarks of Hon. J. Lewis Hall, Member of the Fabisinski Committee on Florida's School Assignment Law and the Responsibilities of Local School Officials" (pamphlet), State Department of Education, Tallahassee, Florida, September 13, 1956, 4, Smathers Library, University of Florida.

32. Allen Morris, comp., *The Florida Handbook, 1933–1994* (Tallahassee, Peninsular Publishing, 1993), 342–45; see, for example, "I Conceive Our Goals To be As Simple to State As They Are Difficult to Achieve . . ." the Message of Governor Farris Bryant To The 1961 Florida Legislature, Tallahassee, April 4, 1961, Florida State Archives, Tallahassee, Fla., which remains silent on any aspect of integration and civil rights; Colburn, "Florida Politics in the Twentieth Century," 363; Colburn and Scher, *Florida's Gubernatorial Politics,* 227–29.

33. *United States Civil Rights Act of 1964* Title VI, 42 USC " 2000d B 2000d-7, available from http://www.dotcr.ost.dot.gov/Documents%5CYCR%5CCIVILR64.HTM (accessed June 9, 2004); see David R. Colburn, "Florida's Governors Confront the *Brown* Decision: A Case Study of the Constitutional Politics of School Desegregation," in *An Uncertain Tradition: Constitutionalism and the History of the South,* ed. Kermit L. Hall and James W. Ely (Athens: University of Georgia Press, 1989), 326–55.

34. "Assurance of Compliance with the Department of Health, Education, and Welfare Regulation Under Title VI of the Civil Rights Act of 1964," Special Meeting Minutes, LCBPI, March 2, 1965; "Plan of Desegregation Adopted By Board of Public Instruction of Lee County, Florida," Minutes, LCBPI, September 16, 1964; Stone and Carter, *The First One Hundred Years,* 77–321; "School Board Moves to Kill Integration Suit," *Fort Myers News-Press,* October 23, 1964; see Jackson "A

History of Desegregation," 139–56.

35. Daisy Sapp Benjamin, Lee Black History Society program chair (former teacher, Lee County Public Schools), interview by author, March 9, 2005.

36. *Rosalind Blalock et. al. v. The Board of Public Instruction of Lee County, Florida et. al.*, No. 64–168 (1964), copies of court case, decisions, court orders, and addenda in author's possession.

37. *Rosalind Blalock et. al. v. The Board of Public Instruction of Lee County, Florida et. al.*, No. 64–168 (1964).

38. "Ruling Delayed by Judge," *Fort Myers News-Press*, February 9, 1965; "Court Rejects Lee's Plan on Integration," *Fort Myers News-Press*, February 11, 1965; *Blalock*, Final Decree, filed on February 23, 1965; Special Meeting Minutes, LCBPI, March 2, 1965.

39. "Defendants Compliance With Final Decree, September 1, 1965," in *Blalock*; "Desegregation Plan," Minutes, LCBPI, September 16, 1965.

40. "District Court Suit Filed Asking Lee County School Desegregation Speed Up," *Fort Myers News-Press*, July 27, 1966; "Motion for Further Relief," July 25, 1966, in *Blalock*.

41. "Motion For Further Relief, July 25, 1966, " in *Blalock*; "District Court Urged to Drop Suit," *Fort Myers News-Press*, August 9, 1966; Minutes, LCBPI, July 26, 1966;

42. "The March of Desegregation," *Fort Myers News-Press*, August 18, 1966.

43. "Motion For Supplemental Relief, August 16, 1966" in *Blalock*; "Justice Department Enters Local Desegregation Case," *Fort Myers News-Press*, August 17, 1966; "U.S. Gets to Join Desegregation Suit," *Fort Myers News-Press*, September 8, 1966; Jackson, "A History of School Desegregation," 177–78; Minutes, LCBPI, August 16, 1966.

44. Special Meeting Minutes, LCBPI, January 30, 1967; Minutes, LCBPI, February 21, 1967; "15,000 Children Attend County School Classes," *Fort Myers News-Press*, February 21, 1967; "School Proposal for Integration Going to Court," *Fort Myers News-Press*, February 22, 1967; Judge Lieb Decrees, March 27, 1967, *Blalock*.

45. "Williams Sees Problems With Freedom Of Choice," *Fort Myers News-Press*, April 1, 1967; Jackson, "A History of School Desegregation," 184, 188; "Report of Lee County Board of Public Instruction," in *Blalock*; Minutes, LCBPI, May 16, 1967; quoted in Special Meeting Minutes, LCBPI, September 5, 1967.

46. "Switch in Integration Plan to Be Sought," *Fort Myers News-Press*, December 13, 1968; "Motion For Supplemental Relief," *Fort Myers News-Press*, December 16, 1968; Scott, *The Education of Black People in Florida*, 98; "Order by Judge Lieb, Feb 12, 1969," in *Blalock*; Minutes, LCBPI, February 18, 1969.

47. "Board Seeks Outside Help in Deseg Efforts," *Fort Myers News-Press*, December 13, 1968; Minutes, LCBPI, March 11, 1969.

48. Minutes, LCBPI, March 11, 1969; Dr. Robert Anderson, to the Board, Minutes, LCBPI, February 18, 1969.

49. "Integration Plan Poses Problem," *Fort Myers News-Press*, March 16, 1969; "A Comprehensive Plan For A Nondiscriminatory School System In Lee County," Lee County Board of Public

Institutions, Fort Myers, Florida, Plan Adopted April 16, 1969, Plan Amended April 21, 1969, Lee County, Florida Board of Education; "New Plan for Desegregation Is Adopted by School Board," *Fort Myers News-Press*, April 17, 1969; "Comprehensive Plan For Nondiscriminatory School System in Lee County, April 21, 1969," in *Blalock*; Special Meeting Minutes, LCBPI, April 21, 1969, data used from Table 10 and Table 11 on Percentage of White/Non-Whites from Dunbar and Franklin Park (both still 100 percent black by April 1969), 24–25.

50. "New Plan for Desegregation Is Adopted by School Board," *Fort Myers News-Press*, April 30, 1969; "Objection To Amended Desegregation Plan, May 1, 1969," in *Blalock*.

51. "Amended Comprehensive Plan, May 14, 1969," in *Blalock*; Minutes, LCBPI, June 6, 1969.

52. Special Meeting Minutes, LCBPI, May 19, 1969; Minutes, LCBPI, May 22, 1969; "Order Denying Defendants Motion For Amendment, June 9, 1969," in *Blalock*.

53. *Green v. School Board of New Kent County, Virginia*, 391 U.S. 430 (1968); *Alexander v. Holmes County Board of Education*, 396 U.S. 1218 (1969); see Rowland Young, "Review of Recent Supreme Court Decisions," *American Bar Association Journal* 54 (1968), 912–13; "'Desegregation Now': But How to Do It?," *U.S. News and World Report*, November 10, 1969, 45–46; "The Supreme Court: Integration Now," *Time*, November 7, 1969, 19–20.

54. Special Meeting Minutes, LCBPI, June 6, 1969; Minutes, LCBPI, June 16, 1969; Minutes, District School Board of Lee County (hereafter DSBLC), July 7, 1969, August 5, 1969; see "Integration Plan Poses Problems, *Fort Myers News-Press*, March 16, 1969; "District Court Suit Filed Asking Lee County School Desegregation Speed Up," *Fort Myers News-Press*, July 27, 1969; "Board Considers Appeal in Desegregation Case," *Fort Myers News-Press*, August 13, 1969; see "Desegregation Made Harder By Lee," *Miami Herald*, August 24, 1969. On July 2, 1969, the school regulating authority in Lee County changed its official designation from Board of Public Instruction to District School Board of Lee County, District School Board of Lee County Minutes.

55. "Order That Mandates Of The Court Be Carried Out" December 16, 1969," in *Blalock*; Minutes, DSBLC, December 19, 1969 and February 3, 1970; "Notice of Compliance, December 31, 1969," in *Blalock*.

56. Cunningham, "School Desegregation in Florida," 1–2.

# CHAPTER FOUR

# TOMS AND BOMBS

## THE CIVIL RIGHTS STRUGGLE IN DAYTONA BEACH

### LEONARD R. LEMPEL

By the time my wife and I moved to Daytona Beach in 1980, gone were the "white" and "colored" signs and other vestiges of enforced segregation that defined Florida's race relations during the Jim Crow era. Blacks and whites now attended the same public schools, shared the same restaurants, movie theaters, bathing beaches, and played together in the same municipal parks, playgrounds, and golf courses. Even some residential areas were integrated, and several white students attended the historically black Bethune-Cookman College (now Bethune-Cookman University), where I joined the history faculty.

Yet beyond these tangible signs of racial progress lay continued racial inequality, discrimination, and separation. It did not take long for me to realize that my new home's Old South past was not entirely dead. In Daytona Beach in 1980, the per capita income of African Americans was only 45 percent of whites', and the black poverty rate stood at nearly 39 percent while that of whites was 15 percent. The black business district adjacent to the college, which had thrived during the Jim Crow era, lay decimated.[1] A few days after my arrival, I entered the local hardware store seeking a household item and was told by the white attendant that the store did not carry it, but that I might be able to find the item "over in niggertown."

In 1981, my wife and I moved into Fairway Estates, a quiet, mostly white, middle-class development that bordered on Daytona's municipal golf course.[2] Adjacent to Fairway Estates was the black residential community formerly known as Waycross, one of three African American neighborhoods in Daytona that dated back to the early twentieth century.

Since our property bordered the golf course, my neighbors and I could walk directly onto the course, but the residents of old Waycross could not. A chain link fence, topped with barbed wire, stood between the course and Waycross residents. Furthermore, there were no through streets connecting old Waycross and Fairway Estates. In essence, these two adjacent neighborhoods symbolized Daytona's racial divide in 1981. Much of Daytona's segregationist lifestyle remained intact during the post-civil rights era.

A quarter century later, many of these Old South patterns remain in place. My wife and I yet live in Fairway Estates, and still no roads connect our development with old Waycross; the chain linked fence remains, topped with barbed wire in sections. And while Fairway Estates today is more integrated than in 1981, overall, Daytona Beach neighborhoods remain racially segregated. Out of the seventy-six Florida cities with populations of over 25,000, Daytona Beach ranks as the sixteenth most residentially segregated. Equally telling, the poverty rate for Daytona's blacks, who comprise almost one-third of the city's population, is over twice that of whites.[3]

The continued divisions along the conventional Old South fault lines demonstrate the limitations of change wrought by the struggle for civil rights in Daytona Beach. The following pages will explore that struggle by examining its evolution and impact, thereby providing clues as to the origins of Daytona's contemporary pattern of race relations. Arguably, Daytona Beach shares many Old South, New South, and Down South attributes with other communities in Florida. Therefore, an analysis of its civil rights struggles will help place into context the evolution of race relations elsewhere in the Sunshine State.

Compared to other communities in the South, Daytona Beach enjoyed a reputation for racial moderation, and its black community possessed a relatively high level of self-confidence and political activism during the decades preceding the modern civil rights movement. This reputation originated during the Reconstruction era, when Daytona was founded. Most pioneering white residents came from former abolitionist strongholds of the North, including Ohio, New York, Michigan, and Massachusetts. White abolitionist John Milton Hawks, a New Hampshire native who spearheaded a colony of several hundred freedmen just south of Daytona after the Civil War, remarked in 1887 that "the spirit of the white citizens of East Florida toward colored people in general, is so much more just and fair, that for such citizens to emigrate from South Carolina to this region is like escaping from slavery to a land of freedom."[4] Well into the 1890s, several of Daytona's more prominent African Americans owned homes and shops alongside whites in the center of town.[5]

African Americans played an integral part in developing this frontier community from its inception in 1870. Two black men, John Tolliver and Thaddeus Gooden, were among Daytona's twenty-six electors who voted to incorporate the town in 1876. Tolliver played an important role in Daytona's early development, receiving several contracts from the town council to build roads, including a large section of Ridgewood Avenue, which later became the Dixie Highway (U.S. Route 1). Gooden worked at the Palmetto House, Daytona's first tourist hotel, and was one of two black delegates elected to the Republican Party's county convention in 1884. Northern influence in Daytona continued with the arrival of Flagler's East Coast Railroad in 1888, which made the town accessible to afflu-ent winter visitors. Howard Thurman, the renowned black theologian who was raised in Waycross during the early twentieth century, concluded that the moderating influence of these turn-of-the-century snowbirds "made contact between the races less abrasive than it might have been otherwise."[6]

The presence of Mary McLeod Bethune and her school also helped temper racial discord. In 1904, Bethune founded the Daytona Educational and Industrial Training School for Negro Girls in Midway, the most business-oriented and progressive of Day-tona's three black neighborhoods. The school appealed to moderate elements in the white community by stressing domestic and industrial training and "Negro uplift," a formula successfully employed at Booker T. Washington's Tuskegee Institute. Bethune won over many whites who were suspicious of black education by inviting them to come to her school and see "The Booker T. Washington Idea of Education Demonstrated." She even procured the blessings of the city council. After receiving a letter from Bet-hune in 1905, the council unanimously approved a resolution endorsing Midway's new educational institution.[7]

In 1923 the school merged with Cookman Institute of Jacksonville to form the co-educational Bethune-Cookman College (B-CC). The college became "an oasis in the des-ert of segregation" during the first half of the twentieth century. In addition to acquiring support from Daytona's white moderates, Bethune provided leadership and inspiration to the town's black community. Howard Thurman noted that, "the very presence of the school, and the inner strength and authority of Mrs. Bethune, gave boys like me a view of the possibilities to be realized in some distant future."[8]

Although continued northern influence and the positive impact of Bethune and her school caused Daytona's racial climate to remain milder than most Florida cities during the early twentieth century, its color line nevertheless hardened during those years. Almost all African Americans were relegated to three adjacent neighborhoods, all located west of the Florida East Coast Railroad and running south to north: Waycross, Newtown, and Midway. Also, blacks were limited to minor roles in town politics, and spasms of violence occasionally pierced the city's veneer of racial civility. In 1907, a black man was lynched in Daytona and his body paraded through the streets as a warning to "uppity darkies." During the early 1920s, the Ku Klux Klan routinely strove to intimidate potential black voters in Daytona, marching on Bethune's school the night before the 1920 elections after discovering that she was instructing her students on how to vote. On March 3, 1922, just four days before municipal elections, 106 Klansmen in full regalia paraded down Daytona's main thoroughfare as thousands lined the route. In testimony to the bravery of Daytona's African American community and to the influence of the city's more moderate white element, Bethune's students and substantial numbers of blacks continued to vote in spite of the Klan intimidation. Apparently, the ongoing influx of northerners imparted a measure of racial toleration in Daytona. Thus, contrary to what transpired in most Florida communities during the Jim Crow era, Daytona's politicians continued to solicit black voters, especially in close elections.[9]

The political clout of Daytona Beach's African American community burgeoned with the election of Mayor Edward Armstrong in 1927. A white grocer originally from St. Louis, Armstrong was elected mayor of the newly consolidated Daytona Beach by establishing a biracial coalition of voters. In all but two of the years between 1927 and 1937, Armstrong and his allies on the city commission controlled the municipal government with the aid of black voters. To boost turnout in elections, Armstrong employed black ward heelers who canvassed and distributed literature in the three African American neighborhoods. His principal contact in the black community was businessman Joe Harris. Nicknamed "Daytona's black Mayor," Harris was the most powerful of several black politicos assisting Armstrong in African American districts. Armstrong rewarded his black supporters by building playgrounds and swimming pools in their neighborhoods, paying the funeral expenses of indigent families, and most significantly, by providing patronage in the form of city jobs.[10]

Armstrong had left a lasting legacy of empowerment and high self-esteem among black Daytonans that few African American communities in the Old South experienced prior to World War II. Yvonne Scarlett-Golden, a two-term mayor of Daytona Beach (and the city's first black mayor) whose father chauffeured for Armstrong, recalled that "very few blacks feared whites in Daytona Beach. There used to be a saying among [white] people: 'We don't want to deal with those blacks in Daytona. They have too much power.'"[11]

The strength of Daytona Beach's political machine and the benefits blacks derived from it diminished with Armstrong's death in 1938. The late mayor's fearsome political juggernaut became fragmented after his passing, and the city commissioners who had allied with him soon faced formidable challenges from reform candidates. As Daytona's political machine weakened, the benefits that blacks had derived from it, which included jobs and improved community services, also diminished. Furthermore, as reformers began to challenge the machine for control of city hall, it became apparent that black Daytonans would now pay a heavy price for their long-term loyalty to the machine. Most reformers viewed Daytona's black community as the machine's most loyal block and therefore sought to marginalize its influence.

It was not only city reformers who thwarted black aspirations. The machine bosses upheld Old South traditions of racial segregation and the exclusion of blacks from public office. Before the war, given the unquestioned pervasiveness of segregation and white political dominance, blacks Daytonans tolerated its subordinate status within the political machine. However, this arrangement no longer proved satisfactory after the war as blacks voiced new demands for equal status. Once black Daytonans began seeking public office and racial integration, they met with unbending resistance from reactionary political bosses steeped in the racial notions so characteristic of Dixie. Thus, as Daytona Beach entered the modern civil rights era, its black citizens could rely on neither white reformers nor machine bosses for assistance in their struggle for equality.

Discontent among African Americans with the racial status quo quickened during and after World War II. Wartime jobs provided blacks with greater economic security, and service to their country gave them an undeniable claim to equal citizenship. Returning to a South determined to uphold white supremacy, blacks resolved to assert their newfound pride and establish a New South free of racial barriers.[12] While black Daytonans joined African Americans elsewhere in realizing economic gains during the World War II and postwar years, the economic disparity between blacks and whites remained enormous. In Daytona Beach the percentage of blacks holding skilled or professional jobs increased from 11 to 15 percent between 1940 and 1950. However, by 1950 white Daytonans were more than three times as likely to hold such jobs as blacks. In 1949 the median income of black families and unrelated individuals stood below $900, compared to over $2,000 for whites. Low wages for black males meant that black women often had to work to support their families. From 1940 through the 1950s, approximately half of the black women in Daytona Beach worked for wages. In contrast, only about one-quarter of white women earned incomes during those years. Similar to Florida at large, fully three-fourths of the African American women working in Daytona Beach at mid-century toiled in low-end service jobs, mostly as domestics.[13]

Pride among black Daytonans soared on March 17, 1946, when Jackie Robinson took the field at City Island Ball Park for the Montreal Royals, a minor-league team affiliated with the Brooklyn Dodgers. This marked the first integrated professional baseball game in the United States in more than fifty years. Dodger owner Branch Rickey had chosen

Daytona Beach as the spring training site for the Royals because of the city's reputation for racial moderation, and because he had received assurances from the mayor and city manager that Robinson would be welcomed at City Island Ball Park as long as the municipal segregation ordinances and customs were obeyed. Thus, black baseball fans had to cheer Robinson from the Jim Crow stands, and while his white teammates roomed in a whites-only hotel, the Robinsons stayed at the home of Duffrin and Joe Harris, an influential couple in Daytona's African American community (as noted earlier in this study, Joe Harris, dubbed Daytona's "black Mayor," had been the leading black politico in the Armstrong machine). The following spring Robinson integrated major-league baseball after being called up by the Brooklyn Dodgers.[14]

Jackie Robinson's appearance proved inspirational to blacks in Florida's most famous beach town. As thousands filled the "Negro section" of City Island Ball Park and other black spectators crowded behind the right field foul line to cheer their hero, many in the crowd must have wondered whether integration could be moved from the playing field to everyday life.[15] Daytona Beach now seemed poised for meaningful racial uplift, but would it occur? Would the city embrace a bona fide New South posture or adopt Down South delaying tactics meant to preserve white privilege?

Imbued with a new sense of pride and a determination to challenge generations of white supremacy, black Daytonans stepped up their political activities after the war. As noted, African Americans had comprised as much as one-third of Daytona Beach's registered voters in the halcyon days of the Armstrong machine, but their numbers dwindled following the mayor's death in 1938. In 1944 only about 18 percent of Daytona's registered voters were black, but then the percentage rose, so that by the end of 1946 blacks comprised 20 percent of the city's electorate, and one-third by 1948.[16]

Much of the surge in postwar voter registration stemmed from the Supreme Court's groundbreaking decision in *Smith v. Allwright* (1944), which mandated that the Democratic parties in the southern states admit blacks. In Florida the Court's ruling stimulated black voter registration, primarily on the peninsula where the influx of white northerners had tempered traditional Deep South opposition to enfranchising African Americans—a complex story in itself and one not yet fully contextualized in the literature.[17] Also, the ruling precipitated a massive realignment in political party registration among blacks—a realignment that accelerated when President Truman ran for election in 1948. Truman had introduced anti-lynching and anti-poll tax legislation in Congress, and had issued executive orders desegregating the armed forces and banning discrimination in federal employment. Now able to register as Democrats, black Floridians switched party allegiance in droves. All of the estimated 20,000 black Floridians registered in the two major political parties in 1944 were Republicans. By November 1948, approximately 90 percent of the more than 85,000 registered black Floridians were Democrats, up from 67 percent just 30 months earlier. An even more dramatic realignment occurred in Daytona Beach, where over 98 percent of the more than 3,700 registered blacks were Democrats by November 1948, up from 77 percent the previous year.[18]

The *Allwright* decision and Truman's election bid gave impetus to the massive voter-registration drive organized by the Florida Progressive Voters League (FPVL), a state-wide black political association. Organized after World War II, the FPVL was the brainchild of Harry T. Moore, president of the Florida Conference of the NAACP from 1941 to 1946, and NAACP coordinator for Florida after 1946, until his assassination by Klansmen on Christmas night, 1951. Major partners of the FPVL voter registration drive included the Florida conference of NAACP branches and the Florida Negro Elks Association. The latter was headed by Albert Bethune Sr., son of Mary McLeod Bethune and coordinator of Bethune-Cookman College's vocational school in Daytona. About 10,000 African American men belonged to the Elks, and almost as many African American women joined the Elks auxiliary in Florida. The organization's bylaws required members to register to vote, and the club urged them to register as Democrats in 1948 because "only in this way can we [blacks] have any voice in electing public officials." Albert Bethune's involvement in the Democratic voter registration drive, together with Moore's close attachment to Daytona Beach (he and his two daughters had graduated from Bethune-Cookman College, and the Moores frequently visited the city) help to explain the nearly total conversion of Daytona's black electorate to the Democrats by 1948.[19]

The voter registration drive also revitalized African American political activity in the city. About 1,000 city blacks registered as Democrats in the months preceding the May 4, 1948, primary election, and over 70 percent of them voted in the primary. In early October several of Daytona Beach's African American leaders organized the Daytona Beach Citizens League (DBCL), which sought to enhance the influence of blacks in local politics and upgrade community services. Most DBCL organizers were progressive, middle-class blacks, such as church officials, school administrators and teachers, and assorted professionals, including a doctor and an insurance company manager. They chose as their leader Dr. Richard V. Moore, president of Bethune-Cookman College. At one of DBCL's early meetings the organizers addressed approximately one hundred concerned citizens and lamented about the inadequate sewage system, unpaved and unlighted streets, and suspected vote-buying attempts of city officials. The speakers implored their audience to work together and use the ballot to improve community conditions, and to "show them [elected officials] that you can't be bought."[20]

Following the 1948 presidential election, the DBCL turned its attention to electing George Engram as the city's first black commissioner. After graduating from Tuskegee Institute, Engram moved to Daytona Beach in 1933, planning to operate a black theater in town. Instead, he found himself barred from the all-white projectionist union. Undaunted, Engram became a certified electrician. After being excluded from the white-only electrical union, he established his own electrical contracting company. The union tried to restrict Engram to black neighborhoods west of the railroad tracks; when he crossed the tracks, union members threw bricks and scrawled "KKK" on his truck.[21]

Like the DBCL, Engram rejected machine rule. As discussed earlier, though the machine had provided considerable patronage and other favors in exchange for black votes, it strictly enforced racial segregation and white political rule, and condoned vote-buying and other corrupt practices. Moreover, the machine's patronage system devolved into a form of debt peonage. Many blacks worked at the city yards, where most non-civil service positions fell to machine loyalists. At the start of each workday, men lined up and white officials selected them for work assignments. It was common practice in Daytona, though of questionable legality, to give paychecks directly to employee creditors rather than to the employees. Former city manager LeRoy Harlow explained the system as it had existed at mid-century: "When payday arrived, the storekeeper came in, got the check, cashed it, took his share, and gave the rest to the employee. In some instances the pay-roll office made out the check directly to the creditor. . . . In most instances, the creditor got the check without the employee's formal consent by merely presenting evidence that the employee was indebted to him."[22] Engram and the DBCL represented a new generation of black Floridians unwilling to tolerate Old South-style corruption and Jim Crow belittlement.

Candidate Engram condemned corruption and promised several improvements for his district if elected, including paved streets, new sidewalks, lights for the Negro base-ball field, improved garbage collection, and sewer lines for all residences. Despite these modest objectives, his candidacy generated considerable racist opposition. Pre-election forums traditionally open to all candidates excluded Engram; he also suffered contin-ued harassment. Engram's truck remained a target of abuse and on election eve five high school students tried to burn a cross near his home. Bethune-Cookman president Rich-ard V. Moore received anonymous letters that threatened violence if the college's students actively supported Engram's candidacy. Unfazed, Moore led thirty students to the polls on election day.[23]

Engram forced a runoff by finishing a close second in a five-candidate primary elec-tion, but lost to the machine favorite in the runoff. In black precincts, white election officials slowed voting by meticulously checking voters' qualifications. Lines were so long that many blacks gave up in disgust and went home. Engram later claimed that many voted illegally for the machine candidate. Forty years later he remained bitter about the election: "I won the election [but] . . . the political machine controlled things in Daytona Beach. In the runoff they really took me for a ride." After Engram's crushing defeat, no African American would seek public office in Daytona Beach until 1960, and none would be elected until 1965, a full decade after *Brown*.[24]

Although the city's more progressive black leaders rejected machine rule, they received little support from the white political reformers who viewed the city's black electorate as corrupt supporters and dupes of the political machine. Reform leader Ollie Lancaster Jr., who briefly served as mayor after his election to the city commission in 1950, voiced the concerns of many reformers when he publicly opposed the city-wide election of commissioners "as long as Negro votes could be bought." When a reform majority swept the city commission in 1950, blacks found little cause to rejoice. The new office-holders maintained the city's color line and gerrymandered commission zones to ensure that no precinct contained a black majority. The reformers also instituted new voter registration procedures that required illiterates to be fingerprinted before being allowed to register. Touted as a mechanism to reduce fraud, the fingerprint requirement, in reality, diminished Daytona Beach's black electorate since illiteracy was more prevalent among blacks than whites. Not surprisingly, most African Americans rejected reform candidates. In 1954 machine candidates regained control of the city commission with the aid of 70 percent of the black vote.[25] Despite its tradition of racial moderation, Daytona Beach offered little in the way of meaningful uplift for its African American citizens.

Thus, at a time when the 1954 *Brown* decision held out hope that Jim Crow's demise was at hand, black Daytonans were marginalized by a die-hard racial caste system, with neither the machine politicians nor the self-styled reformers supporting their aspirations. While the machine thwarted efforts to elect blacks to political office and loosen the city's rigid color line, white reformers—those who presumably could have transformed Daytona Beach into an enlightened, New South burg—viewed most black Daytonans as vice-ridden and corrupt allies of the city's old-line political bosses. Consequently, attempts by Daytona Beach's African American community to improve its status met with stiff resistance from white machine politicians and reformers alike. Only after considerable grassroots organization, protests, and perseverance would black Daytonans be able to make headway against the city's exclusionary beliefs and practices.

One of the first victories over blatantly racist city policies was achieved by the West Side Business and Professional Men's Association (BPMA). Organized in 1948 by several of Daytona's progressive-oriented black business leaders, the BPMA promoted the interests of African American businessmen and professionals. The next year, however, it became embroiled with the city over the newly constructed Peabody Auditorium. This impressive facility, built for whites only, stood in stark contrast to the Spartan auditorium the city constructed for blacks, which contained half the number of seats and cost less than one-tenth as much to build as the Peabody. Shortly after the Peabody opened, the BPMA brought suit against Daytona Beach in federal court, claiming that since the auditorium was built with public funds, blacks had the same right to be admitted as other citizens under the Fourteenth Amendment's equal protection clause. Contesting the suit, the city argued that because African Americans had their own auditorium, Daytona Beach had no legal obligation to admit them into the Peabody. Ultimately, the BPMA stunned the city by winning the suit. In June of 1952, the Federal District Court in Jacksonville ordered that blacks be allowed to attend public performances, with separate but equal accommodations provided for both races.[26]

Grudgingly, city and auditorium officials admitted blacks to the Peabody, but the facility remained strictly segregated. Even more galling to African Americans than the Jim Crow arrangement was their admission being limited to city-sponsored events. Most programs at the auditorium were private, and with its manager openly discouraging the contracting parties from admitting blacks, they were allowed into only one performance during the Peabody's first nine months of operation following the court's ruling. Mary McLeod Bethune then interceded, informing the commissioners that "Negroes have gone a long way when they accept a segregated section, but it is unfair for the auditorium to be rented to people when Negroes cannot attend." The protests of the nationally acclaimed leader, now close to eighty years old, produced the desired result. City manager LeRoy Harlow instructed the Peabody's manager not to discourage contracting parties from allowing blacks to attend events at the auditorium.[27]

Despite this small step forward, other challenges to racial bias proved more problematic. In 1950, the BPMA and a newly formed organization, the South Side Voters League, petitioned the county commission to set aside a section of the beach for black bathers. The commission refused the request. The year prior to *Brown*, Daytona's Negro PTA delivered a petition to the school board, signed by 600 residents, protesting inferior facilities as well as double and triple sessions at the city's black schools. Although the school board indicated it would correct the matters, it adopted a classic Down South delay attitude, and by 1960 African American organizations still were protesting the "deplorable" conditions at several black schools, with one having "only one toilet, no electricity, and no drinking water."[28] Thus, as Daytona entered the 1960s, the city's heritage of racial moderation had done little to enhance its prospects for a smooth and rapid transition to New South racial behavior.

Grassroots efforts against entrenched racial exclusion and segregation in Daytona gained momentum following the *Brown* decision, as everyday citizens of the city's long-suffering black community rose up anew to protest Florida's traditional caste system. As John Dittmer has documented in *Local People: The Struggle for Civil Rights in Mississippi*, many important civil rights battles were primarily fought at the grassroots level, and this certainly proved to be the case in Daytona Beach. During the summer of 1955, 125 blacks petitioned the city commission to clarify the municipality's policy on the use of the beach by people of color. After the commission failed to respond, several African Americans approached the beach, only to be ordered away by police proclaiming that "the city would lose revenue by letting them swim." In June 1956, as the Montgomery, Alabama, and Tallahassee, Florida, bus boycotts energized African American communities nationwide, seventeen black Daytonans petitioned the city commission to integrate the municipal golf course. And in December the Citizens Welfare League (CWL), one of more than twenty civil rights-oriented organizations to form in Daytona Beach between 1945 and 1970, met to discuss the case of Louise Wade, a black laundry worker who was verbally abused, kicked, beaten, and fired by her white employer. This incident induced twenty-one laundry workers to quit their jobs in protest against "inhumane treatment and low wages." A month later, several black community leaders objected to the creation of segregated junior colleges in the city, an outgrowth of Governor LeRoy Collins's vision of an expansive statewide network of two-year colleges, albeit on a segregated basis.[29] Clearly, in these initial post-*Brown* years, the old order of segregation in Daytona came under increasing attack. The combination of federal actions, a tourist-conscious civic leadership eager to avoid racial discord, and most importantly, an aroused black community, now ensured that interaction between the city's blacks and whites was destined to enter a new phase.

As similar desegregation efforts in the South intensified, white efforts to preserve the old order increased as well. In the wake of *Brown*, most southern officials adopted a "massive resistance" approach to integration. Subsequently, White Citizens Councils, dedicated to maintaining racial segregation, formed throughout the South, and in 1956 seventy-seven of 105 southern congressmen and nineteen of twenty-two southern senators signed the "Southern Manifesto," which vowed allegiance to upholding Jim Crow. Both Florida senators and six of Florida's eight congressmen signed the declaration, including Albert S. Herlong Jr., who represented Daytona Beach. In June 1956, militant segregationists in Florida formed a statewide Citizens Council based in Tallahassee, and issued a Florida version of the Southern Manifesto. The following month a Daytona Beach chapter of the Citizens Council formed, drawing about 200 people to its initial meetings. Three years later massive resistance still engendered strong support, as demonstrated when twenty-four state legislators signed the "Florida Manifesto" while attending the first Daytona 500 car race in February 1959.[30]

Despite their efforts, integrationists had barely dented Daytona's color bar by 1960—the beaches, golf courses, schools, and every public facility, with the exception of the buses, remained segregated. The buses had integrated in 1956, probably in response to the successful Montgomery and Tallahassee bus boycotts of that year.[31] In 1960 Daytona Beach, blacks and whites were born in separate wings of Halifax hospital, grew up in separate residential areas, attended separate schools and churches, played in separate parks and playgrounds, dined in separate restaurants, and were even interred in separate cemeteries. Blacks could neither set foot unmolested on "The World's Most Famous Beach," nor check into the hotels that catered to the throngs of northern tourists visiting the famed resort. No blacks lived on the peninsula, or "beachside," where they were only welcomed as laborers and maids. Whites were two and a half times more likely than blacks to have skilled or professional jobs, and almost three-quarters of all black women employed were "service workers," mostly maids. Twice as many whites as blacks owned their own home or automobile, and fewer than half of black households possessed a telephone compared to more than 85 percent of whites. An extensive academic survey conducted during the early 1960s concluded that although the city's blacks were "better off" than those in many other communities, "their position relative to white people was the same. They were socially and culturally inferior. Their problems were those that faced Negroes all over the nation—undereducation, low income, occupational inferiority, inadequate housing, and pervasive segregation."[32] Almost a decade after *Brown*, the day when Daytona Beach could be deemed a New South metropolis still appeared distant.

Although socioeconomic disparities between blacks and whites would persist during the 1960s, there were momentous federal and local efforts—against enormous obstacles—to dismantle Florida's Jim Crow edifice. By the end of the decade much of that edifice had, indeed, crumbled. The rising tide of protest against segregated public facilities that began with the Greensboro, North Carolina, lunch counter sit-ins in February 1960 quickly spread to other southern cities, including those in central Florida. Within days of the Greensboro sit-ins, nearly identical demonstrations broke out in DeLand, Volusia's county seat, located only twenty miles west of Daytona Beach. Calls abounded for similar protests in Daytona Beach, and on March 2, twelve Bethune-Cookman College students staged a lunch counter sit-in at the downtown Woolworth's.[33]

However, Daytona Beach's black elite, consisting of educators, businessmen, church leaders, and political operatives, preferred less confrontational tactics to achieve integration. The local NAACP chapter opted to organize an economic boycott of downtown department store lunch counters rather than support sit-ins as advocated by aroused Bethune-Cookman students. Meanwhile, the college's president, Richard V. Moore, negotiated behind-the-scenes with the mayor, chief of police, and other city officials to integrate the lunch counters quietly. President Moore convinced these officials that the spectacle of police dragging students out of department stores would damage Daytona's tourist image. Moore and the city leaders reached an agreement in early August of 1960 to conduct peaceful demonstrations whereby small groups of black students would enter four major downtown department stores, sit at the lunch counters and order, be served, and then leave. After five consecutive days of such demonstrations, the *Daytona Beach Morning Journal* reported that the nonviolent "experiment" had been "successful" and that the lunch counters in these stores now catered "to persons of all races."[34]

Also in 1960, there were renewed attempts to integrate the municipal golf course, where blacks were forbidden from playing until evening. In June 1956, after three blacks had unsuccessfully attempted to play during the daytime, seventeen African Americans petitioned the city commission to clarify its policy. A city spokesman claimed that "there was no set policy regarding the course's use by Negroes, but it's customary on most courses to let caddies play free of charge after 5 p.m." The 1956 protest had failed to alter this practice, but in August of 1960 a local civil rights group, the Social Engineers, sent letters to municipal leaders requesting meetings on the issue. When no response was received, three black leaders attempted to play the course, but were rebuffed by the starter. After appeals by the three at a city commission meeting, the commissioners voted unanimously in early January 1961 to integrate the Municipal Golf and Country Club. The decision irked many white golfers, but it demonstrated nevertheless how city officials would yield to protests that might draw unfavorable state and national attention to their vacation mecca.[35]

Despite the integration of the golf course and the four lunch counters, the vast majority of Daytona's public establishments remained segregated. By the late spring of 1963, while the Birmingham, Alabama, confrontation dominated the television news, many black Daytonans lost patience with their community leaders' often-unsuccessful efforts to desegregate facilities through behind-the-scenes maneuvering. After several Bethune-Cookman and Daytona Beach Junior College students were arrested for staging demonstrations at a segregated downtown theater and diner, about one hundred representatives of several religious and community organizations met in May to urge nonviolent protests.

They also passed a resolution denouncing the city's failure to immediately desegregate public facilities and end job discrimination.[36]

Following the meeting a rash of protests broke out in early June, with demonstrators picketing the segregated lunch counter of a downtown drug store, an all-white movie theater, and a cafeteria. Several black youths were arrested in the demonstrations, which was sensational enough to reach the pages of the *New York Times*. After one week of protests, black leaders agreed to suspend them after Mayor J. Owen Eubank reactivated the city's long-dormant biracial committee, and the president of the Volusia County chapter of the NAACP, Horace Reed, received an invitation to meet with a city commissioner. Little was accomplished during this hiatus, and sporadic demonstrations soon resumed and continued through the fall. At the end of September 1963, the Social Engineer's president and Bethune-Cookman College chaplain, Rogers P. Fair, lamented that only seventeen restaurants and two hotels and motels out of 400 had desegregated, and that "in the area of desegregation Daytona Beach falls far below . . . Cocoa, Orlando, Gainesville, Miami, and falls in the category of Tallahassee, St. Augustine, and similar cities" so indicative of the Deep South. A native of Greenwood, South Carolina, Fair came to Daytona Beach in 1946 at the behest of Mary McLeod Bethune. In 1956 he helped found, and served as president of, the Daytona-based Halifax Area Ministerial Association, the first interracial ministerial association in the South. During the early 1960s Rev. Fair led demonstrations that integrated movie theaters and the municipal golf course in Daytona Beach, and his two children were among the plaintiffs in a 1960 federal law suit seeking to integrate Volusia County's public schools.[37]

Desegregation languished partly because the state laws and directives emanating from Tallahassee assisted local jurisdictions in their efforts to delay or thwart federal integration measures. Rabid segregationists from the panhandle, known as the "Pork Chop Gang," dominated the Florida legislature during the 1950s and early 1960s. Florida's governors during this era proved virtually powerless to challenge segregation with the Pork Chop Gang in control, even if they had been inclined to do so. And only one governor, LeRoy Collins, even hinted that some limited and gradual desegregation should be pursued as a strategy to remake Florida into a New South state. Collins, governor from 1955–1961, and often characterized as a racial moderate, quashed efforts by the legislature to enact extreme anti-integration laws in the wake of the *Brown* decision, but he refused to move aggressively to dismantle Florida's Jim Crow institutions. In contrast, the next three governors, Farris Bryant, Haydon Burns, and Claude Kirk, vehemently opposed integration.[38]

Fear by Daytona's elected officials and business leaders that integrating the beach and beachside hotels would drive away white tourist dollars also prolonged segregation. One beach hotel in the early 1960s lost customers after admitting blacks, and subsequently closed. As was the case with so many other Florida cities, it took decisive federal action to foil the efforts of die-hard segregationists to preserve the color line. Not until after the enactment of the landmark Civil Rights Act of 1964 could blacks enjoy the beach, eat in most restaurants, and stay at most hotels and motels.[39]

Meaningful school integration took even longer to achieve. For years after the *Brown* decision, Volusia County schools remained totally segregated. The Court itself muddied the waters in its 1955 *Brown II* ruling which, instead of setting deadlines, declared that desegregation should proceed at "all deliberate speed." Tired of a half-decade of Down South delay, forty-five black and white parents, many from Daytona Beach, petitioned the Volusia County School Board in 1960 to obey the Court's rulings and come up with a desegregation plan immediately; that same year the parents of several black children sued the school board for failing to develop one. The suit forced the board to institute a program over the next few years that allowed blacks to transfer to white schools under Florida's Pupil Assignment law. But the law required the child's parents to appear in person at the school and file a written request for transfer. If admission was denied, the parents could appeal by petitioning the school board for a hearing. Only if they attended and prevailed at the hearing would black parents be assured that their children could attend white schools.[40]

Implementation of the pupil assignment program resulted in only token desegregation of Volusia's schools. As of September 1964, just seventy-four black students were enrolled in predominantly white schools in the county. That number rose to 157 in the fall of 1965, but as late as 1969, ten of Daytona Beach's twenty-four schools remained completely segregated or consisted of more than 90 percent of one race. Widespread school integration did not occur until 1970, and only then after the federal courts had ordered immediate integration in late 1969.[41]

In contrast to the gradual and limited integration that occurred in Daytona's public schools during the 1960s, Daytona Beach Junior College (DBJC) integrated suddenly. Consistent with the dual junior college system established by Governor Collins and the state in 1957, Daytona Beach built all-white DBJC and all-black Volusia County Community College (VCCC). The Civil Rights Act of 1964, as well as growing agitation for racial integration throughout the South that year, prompted the State Division of Community-Junior Colleges to request that counties end the dual two-year college system. The Volusia County School Board responded in May 1965 by ordering VCCC to close, and for all its students to transfer to DBJC. VCCC remained open during the 1965–66 school year so that matriculating students could finish; by the fall of 1966 the black community college had ceased operating.[42]

Most VCCC administrators and faculty and many black community leaders objected to the terms of consolidation. The college's president, J. Griffin Greene, warned that the hasty merger would prove detrimental to many black students who had received inferior instruction "under an unequal dual public school system."[43] Another complaint involved the loss of jobs and the demotion of black professionals that resulted from the merger. Despite the school superintendent's assertion that 95 percent of VCCC's personnel would work at DBJC, the Junior College hired only ten of the sixteen black full-time faculty. The remaining instructors were offered positions in Volusia County's K-12 schools. President Greene, a highly respected educator and leader, was unceremoniously demoted. Given a minor administrative position at DBJC following the black college's closure, Greene soon retired. Interviewed in 1974, one year after leaving Daytona Beach Community College (formerly DBJC), Greene lamented, "I would have stayed if I had been offered a meaningful vice presidency. However, I could not in good conscience continue to be treated like a 'Field Hand.'"[44]

The slow pace of integration and its often one-sided implementation were among several disappointments black Daytonans experienced during the 1960s. In 1965, the same year that the federal Voting Rights Act became law, the city commissioners schemed to keep the commission lily white. Obliged by a federal circuit court ruling to dismantle gerrymandered city zones, the commissioners had little choice but to accept a plan that would leave two zones with black majorities. Then, in a blatant move to block the election of black commissioners, the commission voted to switch from single member district to citywide elections. Economic inequality remained a barrier for black Daytonans as well. In 1970 almost 44 percent of Daytona's African Americans were classified as poverty stricken compared to just 15 percent of whites, and while 64 percent of the city's white adults possessed a high school degree, only 34 percent of black adults held one.[45] The racial inequalities that existed reflected both nationwide disparities and the persistence of a Down South delay mentality in Daytona. The unfulfilled promises of the civil rights movement fomented increasing militancy by the late 1960s. National advocates of Black Power issued strident calls for a prompt end to all vestiges of racial injustice.

Black militancy in Daytona Beach found expression with the formation of the Citizens Coordinating Committee (CCC) in 1969. Ostensibly an umbrella organization for Daytona's disparate civil rights groups, in reality militants dominated the CCC. Local black activist Charles Cherry set the agenda of the CCC. Cherry, who worked as Bethune-Cookman College's chief accountant and as Volusia County Community College's business manager during the 1950s and early 1960s, ran for a city commission seat in 1960 (after several attempts he was finally elected to the city commission in 1995). Dissatisfied with the conservative leadership and tactics of the NAACP's adult branch, Cherry sponsored a Youth Council branch in Daytona in 1963. Organizing students at B-CC and VCCC, he led several demonstrations against segregated facilities in the city during the early and mid-1960s.[46]

In 1969 and 1970, Cherry utilized the resources of the CCC to his new cause, organizing Daytona's large contingent of poor black workers. When ten black bus drivers, tired of operating old and unsafe vehicles, walked off the job in 1969, Cherry took the lead in forming the Committee for Better Buses, and raised enough money from the community in one day to pay the salaries of the striking drivers for two weeks. Following a citywide bus boycott, the strikers returned to work in January 1970 after improvements to the busses were made. Next, the CCC took up the cause of striking black garbage workers in early 1970. As a consequence of Cherry's appeals, Local 385 of the Teamsters Union intervened in the strike, resulting in Daytona's garbage contractor recognizing the union and signing a contract that provided the garbage men with job security, substantially higher wages, and improved working conditions.[47]

Also in 1970 Cherry and the CCC addressed the plight of Daytona's black maids, arguably the most oppressed of the city's working poor. After conducting a series of interviews, the CCC's *West Side Rapper* (initially called *West Side of the Track*), concluded that the average maid earned $1.30 per hour and took home $35 per week. As one maid bluntly retorted, "That's not enough money to pay for bare necessities." One mother of seven children lamented that, "I was laid off last week without any way to feed my kids. . . . Sometimes [my oldest children] have to stay out of school to work. . . . I don't want my kids to stay out of school, but we have to live some way. We have to eat." Cherry's efforts to unionize the maids ultimately failed, and almost twenty years later he reflected on the lack of progress in narrowing the income gap between the races. Speaking on behalf of the large black underclass, he noted that by 1969, "we could go and eat anywhere, go to any hotels. . . . Now we wanted better jobs, improvement in the quality of life. . . .but we don't have any money, so we can't take advantage of these things."[48]

Mimicking the pronouncements of such national Black Power advocates as Stokely Carmichael and Charles V. Hamilton, Daytona's militants, including Cherry and his mostly young followers, were particularly disparaging of the traditional black leaders who urged gradual legal change and cooperation with the city's white elites. These conservative leaders were soon dubbed "Uncle Toms" by young, more militant blacks who favored confronting racism head-on. As one African American observed, Daytona's black community had divided between "Toms and bombs"—"Uncle Toms" and Black Power militants.[49]

The proliferation of local civil rights organizations during the 1950s and 1960s reflected the intensifying activity of the movement in Daytona Beach, but it also demonstrated that the movement spoke with many voices. Conflicting personalities and egos among the African American leadership proved divisive, as did opposing stances on key community issues. While city officials and some black leaders praised urban renewal for dramatically improving housing in the black community, critics, including Charles Cherry and the staff of the *West Side Rapper*, charged that thousands of African Americans had been uprooted, with their property falling into the hands of white developers. James "Jimmy" Huger, Daytona's lone black commissioner and a leading proponent of urban renewal, came under particularly harsh attack from grassroots militants who viewed urban renewal as "Negro removal." Ironically, Huger was elected in 1965, the same year that citywide elections were instituted in a bid to keep the city commission lily white. But citywide elections meant that Huger needed approval from Daytona's predominantly white constituency, and his reaching out to them prompted black militants to label him an "Uncle Tom." School integration also polarized the black community. Although many African Americans viewed segregation's demise as a momentous victory following a long-fought struggle, many others equated the closure of black schools with the loss of jobs and traditions. School desegregation plans called for African Americans to shoulder most of the burden—black students rather than white students would have to adjust to new, often-inhospitable schools.[50]

The racial violence that had mostly eluded Daytona Beach throughout the 1960s finally erupted in the fall of 1970 with such intensity that it received national media attention. A dispute between black and white students at the newly integrated Mainland High School sparked the unrest. Racial tensions rose at the school after several rock- and bottle-throwing incidents occurred following football games. At the end of October, fights between black and white students broke out on campus, and in early November approximately two hundred blacks walked out of classes. For a few days the situation seemed to improve as students, parents, school officials, and community leaders from CCC, the interracial Advisory Board, and the Halifax Area Council on Human Relations met and discussed grievances. However, violence resumed on November 5 when black youths threw rocks at a gas station and the attendant shot one of them. Crowds then gathered in the neighborhood and began attacking passing cars and police. Over the next few days, racial violence spread to various locations throughout the city, with the police reporting 150 incidents of fire bombings and sniper fire. Believing that the CCC incited much of the violence, heavily armed police surrounded its office and ordered the surrender of its twenty-five to thirty occupants. The police later broke up a protest march on one of Daytona's main thoroughfares; as reported in the *New York Times*, they arrested nineteen of the approximately 150 marchers, including several CCC activists.[51]

A study conducted by the Southern Regional Council (SRC) blamed Daytona's Old South-style power structure for much of the racial violence, accusing it of being largely insensitive to the city's racial and economic divisions. The SRC was especially critical of those officials who believed that the city's racial strife could be solved with greater law enforcement, and warned that Daytona's difficulties "are social and political. Solving them by adding more policemen and riot equipment . . . could be disastrous." The council articulated the grievances of many black Daytonans: student dissatisfaction over the closure of black schools and the racism displayed at "integrated" schools, high unemployment, incidents of police brutality, the paucity of blacks in city departments, and the preponderance of blacks in menial jobs. In the wake of the riots, the council urged city leaders to "drop its cocksure attitude and reach out in a genuine effort to improve the lot of Daytona Beach blacks."[52] But city officials paid little attention to the council's recommendations. As the 1970s progressed, *Brown* retreated from memory, civil rights agitation waned, and Daytona Beach failed to remake itself into an enlightened New South metropolis.

In sum, Daytona's civil rights struggle proved to be unexpectedly arduous and fostered a mixed legacy. In the afterglow of the *Brown* decision, enlightened Daytonans believed their city would forsake Jim Crow and rapidly transform itself into a New South municipality. Daytona's long tradition of relatively harmonious race relations and black political activity, the positive influence of Bethune-Cookman College, a progressive newspaper that supported desegregation, a steady influx of new residents and tourists from the North, and a city leadership determined to preserve the lucrative tourist trade all suggested swift progress. But for several reasons many of Daytona's racially divisive tendencies stubbornly persisted. Reactionary state leadership conspired to delay desegregation, and many local officials, steeped in the Old South mores and folkways, often hindered meaningful change through overt and covert Down South delays. Northern liberal influence was often negated by the concerns of the city's business community that integration would drive away white tourist dollars. Furthermore, traditional black allegiance to the corrupt political machine and long-held beliefs that the black vote was "for sale" hampered the formation of a meaningful alliance between blacks and progressive whites. The actions of civil rights militants during the late 1960s also alienated many whites, including those city officials who "tuned out" legitimate black grievances and relied on the police force to crush perceived violent militants.[53]

Bethune-Cookman College's role in promoting the goals of the civil rights movement engendered mixed results as well. The college's students, professors, and administrators certainly played important roles in fostering change, ranging from the constructive, often behind-the-scenes desegregation efforts of President Moore and other top officials, to the street protests led by students and faculty. However, as some students and faculty embraced militancy during the late 1960s, the campus came to be seen by many in the white community as a hotbed of subversive ideas and violent demonstrations. Ironically, black militants viewed Bethune-Cookman as a "bastion of Tomism" because of its moderate leadership and largely conservative, middle-class faculty and student body. Thus, the college came under criticism from white conservatives and black radicals alike by late 1969.[54]

In the final analysis, the struggle for racial justice in Daytona Beach proved to be long and, at times, violent, and by the 1970s had achieved only limited success. By the time my wife and I arrived in 1980, the rigid segregation of the Old South had vanished from Daytona Beach, only to be replaced with a less visible but still discernable color line of the Down South variety that has stubbornly persisted into the twenty-first century.

## NOTES

1. See James W. Button, *Blacks and Social Change: Impact of the Civil Rights Movement in Southern Communities* (Princeton, N.J.: Princeton University Press, 1989), 95, 220.

2. James "Jimmy" Huger, former Daytona Beach city commissioner and Director of Community Development, claimed that Fairway Estates was the first housing development in Daytona Beach to allow any racial integration. James Huger, interview by author, Daytona Beach, June 2, 1988, in author's possession.

3. "Daytona Beach City Segregation: Dissimilarity Indices," CensusScope, www.censusscope. org (accessed January 3, 2006); "Florida Cities Ranked by White/Black Dissimilarity Index," CensusScope, www.censusscope.org (accessed January 3, 2006); U.S. Bureau of the Census, *August 2004 Supplement to the Current Population Survey (CPS), Poverty in the United States*, www.census.gov (accessed September 23, 2004).

4. Manuscript Census Returns, *Tenth Census of the United States, 1880, Volusia County, Florida, Population Schedules*, National Archives Microfilm Series T-9, roll 102, frames 406–09; "Census Recalls 1880 Daytona," *Daytona Beach Sunday News Journal*, October 7, 1990; "GOP Bucked History to Emerge in Volusia," *Daytona Beach Sunday News Journal*, November 13, 1988; John Milton Hawks, *The East Coast of Florida: A Descriptive Narrative* (Lynn, MA: Lewis and Winship Publishers, 1887), 72.

5. Ianthe Bond Hebel, "Daytona Beach, Florida's Racial History," photocopy, 1966, P. K. Yonge Library of Florida History, University of Florida, Gainesville, 1; Howard Thurman, *With Head and Heart* (New York: Harcourt, Brace Jovanovich, 1979), 10; Anthony Mark Stevens, interview by Joseph E. Taylor, Daytona Beach, August 28, 1976, typewritten transcript of interview in author's possession.

6. Leonard Lempel, "African American Settlements in the Daytona Beach Area, 1866–1910,"

*Annual Proceedings of the Florida Conference of Historians, March 11–13, 1993*, vol.1 (Jacksonville: Florida Conference of Historians, 1993): 112, 117, 119; Hebel, "Daytona Beach, Florida's Racial History," 2; L. D. Huston to Maria Huston, Daytona, August 1, 1884, in *All We Have to Fear is the Lonesome: The Letters of L. D. Huston From Pre-Civil War Days Through His Relocation to the Florida Frontier in 1874*, ed. Maria M. Clifton (Daytona Beach: by the author, 1993), 211; quotation from Thurman, *With Head and Heart*, 9.

7. Minutes, Daytona City Commission, April 10, May 8, August 8, August 14, August 28, September 11, 1905, February 12, 1906, January 27, 1908 (microfilm, Daytona Beach City Hall), hereafter cited as City Commission Minutes; "The Booker T. Washington Idea of Education Demonstrated," *Daytona Morning Journal*, February 2, 1919, 8; quotation from "Industrial School Meeting A Success," *Daytona Morning Journal*, January 15, 1916, 10; Record of Daytona Ordinances July 26, 1876–January 1912, 254–55, Records Department, City Hall Annex, Daytona Beach; Leonard Lempel, "'The Mayor's Henchmen and Henchwomen, Both White and Colored': Edward H. Armstrong and the Politics of Race in Daytona Beach, 1900–1940," *Florida Historical Quarterly* 79 (Winter 2001): 276–77.

8. Jesse Walter Dees, Jr., "Bethune-Cookman College (1904–1954)," in *Centennial History of Volusia County, Florida, 1854–1954*, ed. Ianthe Bond Hebel (DeLand, Fla.: College Publishing Co., 1955), 56–61; Horace E. Hill, interview by author, Daytona Beach, August 12, 1989, in author's possession; first quotation from Huger interview; second quotation from Thurman, *With Head and Heart*, 23.

9. Lempel, "The Mayor's Henchmen and Henchwomen," 292–93, 274, 278–79; Leon Litwack, *Trouble in Mind: Black Southerners in the Age of Jim Crow* (New York: Alfred A. Knopf, 1998), 13.

10. Yvonne Scarlett-Golden, interview by author, Daytona Beach, July 8, 1997, in author's possession; former "meat inspector" of Daytona Beach, interview by Wilhelmina Jackson in Ralph J. Bunche, *The Political Status of the Negro in the Age of FDR*, ed. Dewey W. Grantham (Chicago: University of Chicago Press, 1973), 482; Scarlett-Golden interview; City Commission Minutes, November 22, 1928, June 19, 1929; Lempel, "The Mayor's Henchmen and Henchwomen," 293–94.

11. Lempel, "The Mayor's Henchmen and Henchwomen," 292–93; quotation from Scarlett-Golden interview.

12. See A. Russell Buchanan, *Black Americans in World War II* (Santa Barbara, Calif.: CLIO Books, 1977), especially 113–34; Richard M. Dalfiume, "The 'Forgotten Years' of the Negro Revolution," *Journal of American History* 55, no. 2 (1968): 90–106; and the collection of essays in Glenn Feldman, ed., *Before Brown: Civil Rights and White Backlash in the Modern South* (Tuscaloosa: University of Alabama Press, 2004).

13. Bureau of the Census, *Population*, vol. 2 part 10: *Seventeenth Census of the United States, Report by States Showing the Composition and Characteristics of the Population, 1950* (Washington, D.C.: Government Printing Office, 1952), 66, 68, 70; Bureau of the Census, *U.S. Census, Population Characteristics, 1940* (Washington, D.C.: Government Printing Office, 1942), 129, 131; see Maxine D. Jones, "No Longer Denied: Black Women in Florida, 1920–1950," in *The African American*

*Heritage of Florida*, ed. David R. Colburn and Jane L. Landers (Gainesville: University Press of Florida, 1995), 241–74.

14. Jules Tygiel, *Baseball's Great Experiment: Jackie Robinson and His Legacy* (New York: Oxford University Press, 1997), 102, 104–5, 110–11; Chris Lamb, *Blackout: The Untold Story of Jackie Robinson's First Spring Training* (Lincoln: University of Nebraska Press, 2004), 91–93; Chris Lamb, Glen Bleske, and Marc Bona, "As Different as Black and White: Media Coverage of Jackie Robinson's First Spring Training," (presented at the Jackie Robinson 50th Anniversary Conference, Daytona Beach, FL, March 15–17, 1996), 6, 14, 16, paper in author's possession.

15. Lamb, *Blackout,* 105.

16. Ordinances of the City Commission, September 8, 1953 (microfilm, Daytona Beach City Hall); Voter Registration and Election Returns Records, Volusia County Board of Elections Office, DeLand, FL, hereafter cited as Volusia County Election Records.

17. H.D. Price, *The Negro and Southern Politics: A Chapter of Florida History* (New York: New York University Press, 1957), 32–33, 40–45.

18. Price, *The Negro and Southern Politics,* 33, 58; *Congressional Quarterly Background: Revolution in Civil Rights* (Washington, D.C.: Congressional Quarterly Service, 1968), 3; Volusia County Election Records.

19. Caroline Emmons, "'Somebody Has Got to Do That Work': Harry T. Moore and the Struggle for African-American Voting Rights in Florida," *The Journal of Negro History* 82 (Spring 1997): 232–43; Jake C. Miller, "Harry T. Moore's Campaign For Racial Equality," *Journal of Black Studies* 31 (November 2000). 214–31; quotation from *Daytona Beach Morning Journal*, February 8, 1948; see Ben Green, *Before His Time: The Untold Story of Harry T. Moore, America's First Civil Rights Martyr* (New York: The Free Press, 1999).

20. "State Election," *Daytona Beach Morning Journal*, May 5, 1948, 1, 2; quotation from "Call On Negro Voters To Gain Voice," *Daytona Beach Morning Journal*, October 15, 1948, 1.

21. George Engram, interview by author, Daytona Beach, June 7, 1988, in author's possession.

22. LeRoy F. Harlow, *Without Fear or Favor: Odyssey of a City Manager* (Provo, Ut.: Brigham Young University Press, 1977), 233–34, 263, quotation from 234.

23. "Engram Gets Endorsement of League," *Daytona Beach Morning Journal*, November 9, 1948, 2; "Business Men Won't Endorse Candidates," *Daytona Beach Morning Journal*, November 12, 1948, 9; "200 Persons At Engram Rally," *Daytona Beach Morning Journal*, December 4, 1948, 1; "Hotelmen Talk Politics Tonight," *Daytona Beach Evening News*, November 16, 1948, 7; "B-C President Sees Letter On City Hall Stationery As Intimidation Effort," *Daytona Beach Evening News*, November 19, 1948, 1; "Election Tense; Voting Heavier Than Primary," *Daytona Beach Evening News*, December 7, 1948, 1; Leonard Lempel, "George W. Engram: Daytona Beach's Black Political Pioneer," *Halifax Herald* 16 (December 1998): 11–14.

24. "ICL Checkers Barred At One Poll," *Daytona Beach Evening News*, November 22, 1948, 1, 5; "Election Tense; Voting Heavier Than Primary," *Daytona Beach Evening News*, December 7, 1948,

1; "Brown-Sage Engram-Hall Races on Dec. 7 Ballot," *Daytona Beach Morning Journal*, November 23, 1948, 1; quotation from Engram interview; Lempel, "George W. Engram," 11–14.

25. Quotation from "Few Citizens Hear Candidates Speak," *Daytona Beach Evening News*, November 12, 1950, 1; "Daytonans To Ballot On 7 Issues Today," *Daytona Beach Morning Journal*, May 20, 1952, 1; "Four Charter Changes Lose In Close Vote," *Daytona Beach Morning Journal*, May 21, 1952, 1; "City Registration Totals 11,439; Most Of 674 Loss Is In 8D," *Daytona Beach Morning Journal*, November 7, 1952, 7; "Runoffs Are Necessary In Zones 1, 2, And Five," *Daytona Beach Morning Journal*, December 1, 1954, 1.

26. "To Protest Cut In Funds for Negro Center," *Daytona Beach Morning Journal*, August 19, 1949, 2; "City Seeks Ouster Of Negro Suit," January 4, 1950, 1; "City Has 4 More Days To File Answers In Auditorium Suit," *Daytona Beach Morning Journal*, May 2, 1950, 3; "Court Lowers Peabody Ban," *Daytona Beach Morning Journal*, June 6, 1952, 1, 6; *Harris v. City of Daytona Beach*, 105 F. Supp. 572 (1952); Leonard Lempel, "The Black Struggle for Admittance to Peabody Auditorium," *Halifax Herald* 17 (December 1999): 3–5.

27. "Final Decree Handed Down On Peabody," *Daytona Beach Morning Journal*, June 24, 1952, 1; "Peabody Board Sets Plans For Admitting Negroes To 'Carmen'," *Daytona Beach Morning Journal*, September 17, 1952, 2; "Negroes Win Common Entrance To Peabody," *Daytona Beach Morning Journal*, September 24, 1952, 1, 3; quotation from "Admittance Asked For Negroes," *Daytona Beach Morning Journal*, March 4, 1953, 1, 5; "City Takes Stand On Negro Ban At Auditorium Shows," *Daytona Beach Morning Journal*, March 6, 1953, 1; Lempel, "The Black Struggle for Admittance to Peabody Auditorium," 3–5.

28. "Negroes Ask For Use Of A Section Of The Beach," *Daytona Beach Evening News*, March 16, 1950, 1; "Vol. Board Has No Power To Reserve Negro Beach," *Daytona Beach Evening News*, April 6, 1950, 1; "Negro Group Files School Protest," *Daytona Beach Morning Journal*, January 26, 1953, 1; Minutes, Volusia County Board of Public Instruction, January 27, 1953, hereafter cited as, Volusia County School Board Minutes; quotation from "School Conditions Scored By Negro Civic Leaders," *Daytona Beach Morning Journal*, October 31, 1960, 9.

29. John Dittmer, *Local People: The Struggle for Civil Rights in Mississippi* (Urbana: University of Illinois Press, 1994), 1–430; "Negroes Petition For Statement About Beach," *Daytona Beach Morning Journal*, June 30, 1955, 3; first quotation from "Beach Use Statement Delayed," *Daytona Beach Morning Journal*, July 6, 1955, 1; "Negroes Ask What Golf Rights Are," *Daytona Beach Evening News*, June 26, 1956, 1; second quotation from "Negro 'Problem' Group Formed," *Daytona Beach Morning Journal*, December 13, 1956, 1; "Negroes Form 'Voice,' Oppose College Plan," *Daytona Beach Morning Journal*, January 25, 1957, 1, 3; Martin A. Dyckman, *Floridian of His Century: The Courage of Governor LeRoy Collins* (Gainesville: University Press of Florida, 2006), 87, 89, 158, 161.

30. James T. Patterson, *Brown v. Board of Education: A Civil Rights Milestone and Its Troubled Legacy* (New York: Oxford University Press, 2001), 98; *The Southern Manifesto*, 84th Cong., 2nd sess., *Congressional Record* vol. 102, 4 (Washington, D.C.: Government Printing Office, 1956), 4459–60; "Pro- Segregation Group Meets," *Daytona Beach Morning Journal*, July 17, 1956, 3; "That

Manifesto Hit By Pastors," *Daytona Beach Evening News*, April 7, 1959, 1.

31. "Not Segregated Here," *Daytona Beach Morning Journal*, November 14, 1956, 3.

32. Lewis Killian and Charles Grigg, *Racial Crisis in America: Leadership in Crisis* (Englewood Cliffs, N.J.: Prentice Hall, 1964), 30, 36–37, quotation from 42–43; Bureau of the Census, *Characteristics of the Population, Vol. I, Part 11, Tables 74 and 78: Eighteenth Census of the United States* (Washington, DC: Government Printing Office, 1963), 11–207.

33. "No Disorder At Lunch Counters," *Daytona Beach Evening News*, February 11, 1960, 30; "Counters Closed," *Daytona Beach Evening News*, February 12, 1960, 11.

34. "Economic Boycott Of Four Beach St. Stores Proposed At NAACP," *Daytona Beach Morning Journal*, March 1, 1960, 3; "Proposed Negro Boycott Of Some Beach St. Stores To Start Friday," *Daytona Beach Morning Journal*, March 2, 1960, 9; "12 Negro Students Refused Service At Counter," *Daytona Beach Morning Journal*, March 3, 1960, 9; "College Won't Back Any Demonstrations," *Daytona Beach Morning Journal*, March 4, 1960, 13; "Survey Shows Few Negro Shoppers," *Daytona Beach Morning Journal*, March 5, 1960, 9 ; Rogers P. Fair, interview by author, Daytona Beach, June 6, 1988, in author's possession; James Huger, interview by author, Daytona Beach, June 2, 1988, in author's possession; quotation from "Stores Adopting Changed Policy," *Daytona Beach Morning Journal*, August 16, 1960, 9.

35. Rogers P. Fair interview; James Huger interview; quotation from "Negroes Ask What Golf Rights Are," *Daytona Beach Evening News*, June 26, 1956, 1; "Desegregation Of City Facilities Asked," *Daytona Beach Morning Journal*, April 6, 1960, 9; "New Movement Begun To Dodge Integration Of Golf Course," *Daytona Beach Morning Journal*, August 2, 1960, 3; "Golf Board Declines to Rule," *Daytona Beach Morning Journal*, December 14, 1960, 11; "Ministers Back Course Integration," *Daytona Beach Evening News*, January 3, 1961, 9; Integration of Golf Course Approved," *Daytona Beach Evening News*, January 4, 1961, 1.

36. "City Judge Suspends Sentences," *Daytona Beach Evening News*, May 30, 1963, 1, 2; "Group To Press Race Relations," *Daytona Beach Morning Journal*, June 1, 1963, 2.

37. "Demonstrations, Negotiations" (editorial), *Daytona Beach Evening News*, June 4, 1963, 4; "White, Negro Leaders Call For Truce," *Daytona Beach Evening News*, June 7, 1963, 1, 2; "Negroes Push Drive in Daytona Beach," *New York Times*, June 7, 1963, 17; "Negroes in Fla. Suspend Protest," *New York Times*, June 8, 1963, 10; "Integration Negotiations Continue," *Daytona Beach Evening News*, June 10, 1963, 1; quotation from "Mayor Praised, Racism Hit By Negro Group," *Daytona Beach Evening News*, September 30, 1963, 13; "2 Cafeterias Picketed," *Daytona Beach Sunday News-Journal*, October 27, 1963, 2A; Leonard Lempel, "Reverend Rogers P. Fair: Champion of Black Equality and Interracial Harmony," *Halifax Herald* 24 (Summer 2006): 2–5.

38. See Dyckman, *Floridian of His Century*, 93–189; David R. Colburn and Richard K. Scher, *Florida's Gubernatorial Politics in the 20th Century* (Tallahassee: University Presses of Florida, 1980), 175–79, 224–28.

39. Button, *Blacks and Social Change*, 158; Rogers P. Fair interview.

40. "To Petition For School Integration," *Daytona Beach Morning Journal*, March 10, 1960,

19; Volusia County School Board Minutes, April 26, 1960; "Volusia Schools Sued," *Daytona Beach Evening News*, June 3, 1960, 1; *Eugene C. Tillman, Jr., et al. v. The Board of Public Instruction of Volusia County, Florida*, Civil Action File no. 4501, U.S. District Court for the Southern District of Florida, Jacksonville Division (June 3, 1960); Darryl Paulson, "Unfinished Journey," *Florida Humanities Council Forum* 28 (Spring 2004): 10–11; "Integration Plan Filed By County School Board," *Daytona Beach Evening News*, October 29, 1962, 1; "Integration Plan For Schools OK'd," *Daytona Beach Evening News*, September 8, 1964, 11.

41. "Integration Plan For Schools OK'd," *Daytona Beach Evening News*, September 8, 1964, 11; "157 Negro Pupils To Be Reassigned," *Daytona Beach Evening News*, June 15, 1965, 9; Button, *Blacks and Social Change*, 89.

42. Leonard Lempel, "Volusia County Community College," *Halifax Herald* 17 (June 1999): 8–11; Walter L. Smith, *The Magnificent Twelve: Florida's Black Junior Colleges* (Tallahassee: Four-G Publishers, 1994), 121–48.

43. Greene quoted in Smith, *Florida's Black Junior Colleges*, 44.

44. "Negro Group Hits Poverty Plan In Schools," *Daytona Beach Evening News*, April 26, 1966, 9; Arthur O. White, "The Desegregation of Florida's Public Junior Colleges, 1954–1977," *Integrated Education* 16 (May-June 1978): 35; Smith, *The Magnificent Twelve*, 146–47, Greene quoted on 147.

45. Leonard Lempel, "Single Member District vs. At-Large Voting in Daytona Beach," *Halifax Herald* 21 (Summer 2003): 7–9; Button, *Blacks and Social Change*, 87, 90.

46. Charles Cherry, interview by author, Daytona Beach, July 7, 1988, in author's possession.

47. Cherry interview; "Says NSB Bus Is Only Cancellation," *Daytona Beach Evening News*, June 17, 1969, 11; "Bus Boycott Called By NAACP Youth Organization," *Daytona Beach Morning Journal*, June 21, 1969, 12; "Buses Running Despite Efforts By NAACP," *Daytona Beach Evening News*, June 23, 1969, 7; "Some Bus Service Restored, But Boycott Will Continue," *Daytona Beach Morning Journal*, July 15, 1969, 12; "Guidelines For Truce Set Up In Boycott," *Daytona Beach Morning Journal*, August 7, 1969, 9; "Refuse Collections Under Way Here Despite Strike," *Daytona Beach Evening News*, January 5, 1970, 1 (City Edition); "B-CC Students In the Movement," *Daytona Beach Westside of the Track*, February 5, 1970, 5; "Hear Erskine Hepburn, Leading Labor Union Organizer In The South," *Daytona Beach Westside Rapper*, February 24, 1970, 2; "Garbage Workers' Victory Encourages A.L.A. To Continue Support," *Daytona Beach Westside Rapper*, October 10, 1970, 1.

48. First and second quotations from "The Big Struggle," *Daytona Beach West Side Rapper*, September 19, 1970, 1; third quotation from Cherry interview.

49. Stokely Carmichael and Charles V. Hamilton, *Black Power: The Politics of Black Liberation in America* (New York: Vintage Books, 1967), especially vii–xii; Quotation from Mike Bowler, "Southern Regional Council Report on Daytona Beach," *Daytona Beach Sunday News-Journal*, December 13, 1970, 2–3C.

50. James Huger interview; Bowler, "Southern Regional Council Report."

51. "Game At Memorial Stadium Followed By Rock Throwing," *Daytona Beach Evening News*, October 7, 1970, 11; "Rocks Thrown Again," *Daytona Beach Evening News*, October 16, 1970, 11;

"Police Probe 'Incident' At MHS," *Daytona Beach Evening News*, November 2, 1970, 9; "Mainland Classes Suspended For Day," *Daytona Beach Evening News*, November 3, 1970, 1; "MHS Pupils In Walkout For 3rd Day," *Daytona Beach Evening News*, November 4, 1970, 1, 12; "MHS Issue In Talk Phase," *Daytona Beach Evening News*, November 5, 1970, 9; "Police Ask Cooperation To Ease Race Tensions," *Daytona Beach Evening News*, November 6, 1970, 1, 2; "City Police Close CCC Office," *Daytona Beach Morning Journal*, November 9, 1970, 1, 2; "Police Praised For Keeping Racial Unrest 'Well In Hand,'" *Daytona Beach Evening News*, November 9, 1970, 11; "Calm Restored in Fla. City After Weekend Of Racial Strife," *New York Times*, November 10, 1970, 51; Button, *Blacks and Social Change*, 90.

52. Quotations from Bowler, "Southern Regional Council Report."

53. Rogers P. Fair Interview; Button, *Blacks and Social Change*, 91, 158; Bowler, "Southern Regional Council Report."

54. Bowler, "Southern Regional Council Report."

# CHAPTER FIVE

# PLANTING THE SEEDS OF RACIAL EQUALITY

## FLORIDA'S INDEPENDENT BLACK FARMERS AND THE MODERN CIVIL RIGHTS ERA

### CONNIE L. LESTER

In 1950 Charley Duncan bought a tractor. He paid cash for the machine that he planned to use on the 140-acre farm he owned in Columbia County, Florida, where he produced corn, watermelons, peanuts, and tobacco. The purchase of a tractor was, by itself, nothing unusual; both black and white farmers engaged in a variety of new cultivation practices, hoping to cash in on the mechanized commercial agriculture of the post-World War II era. But Duncan's investment received special attention when an article about his Florida farm was printed in the *Pittsburgh Courier*, an African American newspaper with a national circulation. Submitted by the local Negro Farm Extension Agent, the accompanying article highlighted this southern black farmer's rise from sharecropper to landowner, his diversified farm management practices, his frugal use of credit, and his homegrown search for dignity.[1]

The focus on Duncan's success in his climb from tenancy to landownership suggested a model for participation in the economic promises of the postwar New South in a state still marked by racial constructs and restraints long associated with the Old South. Looking backward after more than fifty years, historians can discern the presence of more subtle barriers to advancement for blacks in rural areas than those faced by urban blacks—a white power structure that avoided overt confrontation and violence but delayed equality through the foot-dragging tactics that this work has defined as "Down South" obstructionism. As Mark Schultz noted in his work on black farmers in Georgia, the face-to-face quality of rural power relationships complicated social interaction. On the one hand, the nature of rural life allowed greater flexibility and tolerance of some black assertiveness. On the other hand, the intimacy of the countryside and the transformation of agriculture after World War II created social and economic vulnerability that mitigated against public confrontations over civil rights.[2]

The absence of independent landowning farmers like Charley Duncan from the modern civil rights narrative ignores an important segment of African American and Florida history. For black farmers, the road to equality did not begin in 1954 with the landmark *Brown v. Board* decision, and it did not end in 1964 with the passage of the Civil Rights Bill. For black farmers, the Old South, New South, and Down South merged in ways that illuminate the ongoing struggle for civil rights and complicate the historian's understanding of the fight against racism and for racial equality.

The Old South was characteristically agricultural and white supremacy emerged from an agrarian paternalism that enforced strict racial inequality. The land tenure and labor arrangements characterized by sharecropping imposed a system historians describe as debt peonage. Sharecropping provided planters with the labor they needed, while croppers' contracts dictated social and economic constraints that kept blacks impoverished and limited their ability to climb the agricultural ladder to land ownership and economic independence. The power of the state and the courts stood behind the legalistic façade of contractual language and sanctioned the violent history of white supremacy.

Beginning with the Great Depression of the 1930s and the New Deal programs created to address the nation's economic woes, the South experienced an economic transformation with unparalleled social and political consequences. World War II brought additional upheaval as federal money and "Yankee" conscripts flowed into the South. The promise of a "New South" had taken root by the mid-1940s as rural blacks and whites joined northern transplants in the booming southern cities.

However, the New South was not necessarily one of racial equality. As courts increasingly undercut the legal supports of white supremacy—finally culminating in *Brown v. Board* in 1954—white Floridians adopted a presumed position of "moderation" toward integration. However, in what came to be recognized as a typical "Down South" stance, moderates hoped to either delay or stall integration indefinitely.

The historiography of the modern civil rights movement is largely that of the concentrated, urban black communities; the actions of rural blacks have been routinely ignored. Southern cities provided the landscape of confrontation with easily identifiable icons of Jim Crow segregation and sufficiently large concentrations of blacks to sustain a social revolution. Cities were the centers of black intellectual and professional life and the sources of leadership for the movement. The cumulative African American wealth in the urban centers overrode the poverty of individual black families and made economic boycotts a viable tactic in the "New South" battle to strike down the color line. Finally, the concentration of African Americans in urban ghettos provided a sense of community and solidarity that sustained the movement in its most trying time. The story of the urban civil rights movement is well known and has been essential to understanding the ideology and mechanisms of effective nonviolent dissent.[3]

The isolated geography of agriculture and the dependency of black farmers on white-controlled institutions for credit and marketing defined a landscape for reform that differed significantly from that of urban blacks. In the cities, under the intense scrutiny of newspapers, radio, and television, the coercive and oppressive face of white supremacy became apparent, and the push for civil rights made important gains through public activism. In the less-transparent countryside, rural African Americans tended to eschew the W. E. B. Du Bois and Martin Luther King Jr. ideological underpinnings of sustained black activism for the slower, racial "uplift" promoted in Booker T. Washington's prescriptions for worldly success. Even so, despite their absence from the civil rights narrative, rural blacks were not merely observers of the efforts to transform the South and give life to the nation's democratic ideals.

While choosing a different path did not provide rural blacks with sanctuary from the consequences of challenging white supremacy, it did alter the dynamics of the confrontation and it offered a starker and more troubling insight into the dimensions of "moderation." Florida's black farmers experienced the violence of the Old South as vigorously as African Americans in the state's cities did. Pursuing the path of landownership and rural progress, black farmers anticipated a New South and struggled to gain the economic, social, and political benefits post-World War II America promised. Yet, unlike their urban counterparts, their struggles characteristically took place out of sight of the national consciousness. For rural blacks, social, educational, and political equality came more slowly and "moderation" was not simply a stalling tactic of southern segregationists. The foot-dragging and sometimes obstructionist actions of rural white power brokers and the United States Department of Agriculture (USDA) limited the progress of black farmers long past the era of modern civil rights actions and gains largely identified with the urban scene.

At first glance, Charley Duncan's life as an independent agricultural producer seemed no different from that of white farmers of the day. Close ties to the local community, dependence on the county agricultural extension service for farming advice, careful balancing of savings and credit, and increasing mechanization characterized American agriculture everywhere. Nevertheless, for black farmers Florida's heritage of racism at every level of economic and social interaction imposed hurdles that white farmers did not face. Locally, black farmers negotiated credit for production and sold their crops or livestock against the backdrop of customary and legal white supremacy. Within the state and federal agricultural bureaucracies, the needs of black farmers took a backseat to those of whites, and the Negro Agricultural Extension Service operated with a reduced budget and under the watchful eye of white supervisors. Local white supremacists, banking and credit interests, buyers and processors, the Florida Department of Agriculture, and the USDA separately and together defined and threatened the existence of independent black farmers like Duncan. His rise from sharecropping to landownership, his allocation of limited economic resources, and his diverse production attest to his careful planning and his willingness to "make haste slowly" in a milieu that could reclaim blacks' hard-won gains at any moment.

The geography of Florida's black landownership provides a mechanism for understanding the racial climate in which farmers like Charley Duncan operated. Black farmers worked the land as landowners, tenants, sharecroppers, and field workers in all parts of the state, but whereas tenancy and sharecropping characterized black agriculture in most southern states, they played a smaller role for all farmers in Florida. In 1938, the state Commissioner of Agriculture, Nathan Mayo, commented on the differences in tenancy rates, claiming that, "although Florida inherited the plantation type of farm operation . . . it [had] consistently remained (as a whole) free of the sharecrop system . . . and particularly the more objectionable features of that system."[4]

Mayo attributed the difference to the fact that the Sunshine State's greatest agricultural development had occurred within the first three decades of the twentieth century and that the nature of the state's production in citrus, cattle, and truck crops did not lend itself to tenancy and sharecropping, which had produced the debt peonage system so characteristic of other Deep South states. He proudly noted that from 1900 through 1935, tenancy accounted for only 25 percent of Florida's farmers, at a time when tenancy rates in other Southern states ranged from 46 percent in North Carolina to 70 percent in Mississippi. Mayo ignored the fact that most blacks in agriculture worked as farm laborers, pickers, packers, and field hands, who toiled for miniscule wages and lived in unsafe and unhealthy conditions. Often imported labor, Florida's unheralded agricultural workers constituted the state's "dirty secret" for much of the twentieth century. As late as 1990, 21,676 men and 3,747 women continued to earn their living as poorly paid farm laborers.[5]

Nevertheless, census data confirm Mayo's assessment of Florida's landowning and tenancy patterns. In 1900, 41 percent of those classified as black farmers owned their own land.

By 1910, that percentage had climbed to 49 percent. On the eve of the modern civil rights era, the 1950 census recorded 5,779 black farm owners, who represented 73 percent of Florida's black farmers. By 1950, almost 77 percent of Florida's black farmers owned land in one of eleven counties (Alachua, Columbia, Gadsden, Hamilton, Jackson, Jefferson, Leon, Madison, Marion, Sumter, and Suwannee) concentrated in the reactionary Old South panhandle and in a line that originated on the Georgia border and ended in Central Florida.[6]

**Black Landowning Farmers in Florida, 1900–1964**

|  | 1900 | 1910 | 1920 | 1930 | 1940 | 1950 | 1964 |
|---|---|---|---|---|---|---|---|
| Total black farmers | 13,526 | 14,822 | 12,954 | 11,043 | 9,732 | 7,506 | 2,832 |
| Number of land owners | 5,607 | 7,267 | 6,347 | 5,522 | 5,549 | 5,779 | 2,379 |
| Percent black owners | 41% | 49% | 49% | 50% | 56% | 73% | 84% |

Source: Barbara R. Cotton, *The Lamplighters*, 101; *U.S. Census, 1900–1950*

Landowning patterns for Florida's African American farmers both confirmed their "Southern-ness" and challenged accepted norms of black behavior. Florida's "pioneer" status, which lasted through the 1930s, opened opportunities for immigrants and migrants that had been closed in other, more settled states with well-established and seemingly unassailable hierarchies of wealth and power. Florida's history of slaveholding and Confederate alliance, however, marked the state as a bulwark of segregation and black disfranchisement. If opportunities for blacks to acquire land remained somewhat higher in Florida than in other states of the Old South, the problems of retaining the land and advancing economically remained relatively the same as the surrounding states. Moreover, the landholding patterns of black farmers placed them largely within the areas most closely allied to the Old South in history and custom.

Black farmers in Florida struggled with the racial status quo that threatened the sustainability of the "family farm," while also battling public and private barriers to educational, fiscal, and institutional aid designed to protect small, independent producers. As Charley Duncan's example shows, many black farmers in the post-World War II years closely followed the "practical" advice of Booker T. Washington, putting down their "buckets" where they were and building on incremental economic gains to establish themselves as essential members of the larger, county farming community. It was a goal that faced enormous sociological and institutional barriers, but one that Florida's black farmers, in particular, believed held the promise of a better future.[7]

The role of Booker T. Washington in the fight for African American civil rights has been contested ground for black activists and African American historians. Hard work and economic success, not agitation and protest, were the keys to political and economic equality according to Washington. Southern whites initially viewed Washington's agricultural program and his Tuskegee Institute with skepticism, fearful that his practical admonition to "cast down your buckets where you are" and his promise of uplift threatened the established racial and economic hierarchy. Thus, in 1903, Gainesville's white citizens refused to allow Washington access to the community auditorium—an action that even drew negative headlines in the *New York Times*. Over time, however, whites developed a grudging respect for his efforts and for Tuskegee. By mid-century, black farm extension agents and professors at Florida A&M College proudly displayed their association with Tuskegee as evidence of their agricultural professionalism, and whites offered the institute a grudging degree of respect.

More troubling than white resistance to Washington's tactics were the criticisms of black leaders. W. E. B. Du Bois famously attacked Washington for his accommodationist advocacy of agricultural and "mechanical" vocations for blacks. In *The Souls of Black Folk* (1903), Du Bois spared no words in condemning Washington, accusing him of selling black citizenship for a pittance. Rigorous classical education of the "talented tenth" assured racial equality, according to Du Bois. Practical education in agriculture and the mechanical arts guaranteed second-class citizenship. In the first half of the twentieth century, black farmers and many professionals adopted the accomodationist "Tuskegee model" rather than Du Bois's more strident demand for immediate political, educational, and social equality. A close examination of the history of Florida's black farmers suggests that Booker T. Washington's practical approach could be used to accomplish W. E. B. Du Bois's revolutionary ends.[8]

In the 1960s, when civil rights leaders recognized the need to organize the southern countryside, they discovered that rural blacks needed agricultural and economic assistance as well as voting rights. Moreover, Booker T. Washington still had many things to teach. CORE and SNCC sent student workers into the southern countryside where they established Freedom Schools, registered voters, and, although less well known, organized farmer cooperatives. In his analysis of the Black Power movement of the 1960s, Harold Cruse asserted that "Black Power was nothing but the economic and political philosophy of Booker T. Washington given a 1960s militant shot in the arm and brought up to date."[9]

Old South Florida farmers were by no means adherents of the Black Power movement, but they were examples of Cruse's point that Washington's promotion of "economic self-help, black unity, bourgeois hard work, law-abiding, vocational training, stay-out-of-the-civil-rights-struggle agitation" provided a viable mechanism for political and social advancement.[10] An examination of individual farmers and Florida's rural communities sheds light on the complexities of the protest praxis of confrontation and economic self-help and reveals the contributions of the countryside to the advancement of the civil rights movement.

Black farmers acquired land through a variety of avenues, ranging from inheritance to advancement up the agricultural ladder. Simon Watson, a farmer in the Prop community was the second son of Robert Watson Sr., "one of the old settlers of Columbia County."[11] Simon began farming on forty acres of land in 1932, and, through careful additions to his original farm, owned 500 acres by 1952 on which he raised corn, hay, peanuts, cotton, and tobacco.[12]

Sim Jordan, another North Florida farmer, inherited forty acres in the Bethlehem community from his father, Henry Jordan. Jordan acquired an additional twenty acres and by the time of *Brown* was raising tobacco, corn, peanuts, and hogs on his sixty acres.[13] Like Charley Duncan, James Carter and Tom Banks sharecropped and rented land before purchasing small farms of forty acres each on which they raised corn, tobacco, cotton, peanuts, and hogs.[14]

Finally, some farmers, such as Marion County's Jack Daymon Santos and Alphonso Stewart, negotiated the labyrinth of government paperwork to obtain assistance through the World War II G.I. Bill in order to improve and modernize family farms. Santos entered the veteran farm-training program in 1947 and used his benefits to purchase a tractor for cultivating his 130-acre tomato farm. After serving in the South Pacific, Stewart took over his father's sixty-acre farm, where he raised peanuts and a variety of vegetables, in addition to maintaining small herds of hogs and cattle.[15] No matter how they acquired the land, black farmers recognized that holding onto their acreage and providing for their families demanded close attention to land use, farm practices, and labor needs as well as careful negotiation of the social space of race relations in color-conscious Florida.

While most attention has been focused on political advances, Florida's rural blacks knew all too well that white supremacy rested on an economic foundation that demanded a subservient position for African Americans. For that reason, economic success represented a revolutionary outcome, and also one with potentially violent consequences for rural blacks. Racially charged confrontations occurred in the fields and marketplaces of the rural South as planters, farm managers, ginners, packers, and shippers imposed wages and prices that black farmers, tenants, and field workers often disputed, sometimes at great risk. Whites entered market negotiations with all the advantages of wealth, education, power, and class privilege; increasingly, gender also worked to their advantage.

In 1955, Albert N. D. Brooks toured the South Atlantic states in an effort to understand the "practical considerations of daily life" for African Americans living in Virginia, North Carolina, Georgia, and Florida. His resulting report focused on an unnamed Florida community and the conditions that trapped tenant farmers in a situation that Brooks described as "modern day slave[ry]."[16]

Brooks argued that white supremacy and economic servitude rested on the dual pillars of white bookkeeping and black illiteracy. He also understood that segregationists had incorporated the highly charged landscape of white southern womanhood into the marketplace in an effort to keep blacks economically dependent. Black tenants often lived at the mercy of "the white lady's figures," the ledger entries made by the landlord's wife. She calculated the costs incurred by tenants for seed, fertilizer, and "furnishing" and deducted those costs from crop profits to arrive at the final "pay-out" for a year's work in the fields. By the time of *Brown*, the growth of business schools and high school accounting classes provided training for young white women eager to enter the business world as clerks, bookkeepers, and secretaries. In contrast, Brooks recognized that education in basic arithmetic learned in the poorly funded, one-room, segregated schools of rural Florida offered no protection against a bookkeeping system that disadvantaged black tenants. Because of this, countless confrontations between clerks and bookkeepers and black farmers and tenants occurred. The fact that many such confrontations had resulted in varying levels of retaliatory white violence convinced Brooks that "a Negro dare not dispute a white woman."[17]

Although generally pessimistic, Brooks found some reasons to hope for a better future for Florida farmers. He found "Negroes [who] were progressive and courageous in spite of the odds against them." He was particularly impressed with black teachers in rural towns and in small country schools. Often conducting classes in sub-standard buildings and with few resources, they "paint[ed] a picture of higher standards of living" their students could acquire through "education and the courage to change the conditions."[18] Brooks believed that rural teachers inspired hope and by 1954 had inspired a new generation of blacks who would demand change.

Albert Brooks's assessment of the value of black teachers was not overstated. Although he focused on classroom education, an expanded view of rural education provides evidence to support his confidence. The community of farm families, northern philanthropists, and federal agricultural agents contributed to knowledge that improved farm incomes and inspired youth to achieve higher goals, including advancements in civil rights.

Farm families and northern philanthropists worked together to construct school buildings and staff classrooms. Julius Rosenwald, president of Sears, Roebuck and Company and patron of Tuskegee Institute, established the Rosenwald Fund to build schools for black children in the rural South. The fund, which required local recipients to raise one-third of the cost of construction, built five thousand schools in sixteen states, 120 of them in Florida, including one in Lee County in the deep southwest region of the state. The Jeanes Foundation, endowed by Philadelphia philanthropist Anna T. Jeanes, provided funding to train black teachers. According to Altermese Smith Bentley, a Jeanes teacher at a school in Live Oak, parents and teachers used their own money to buy books and school supplies, "selling fish, chicken, ice cream, and roasted peanuts" to raise the needed funds.[19]

Landowning farmers also raised money for schools and assisted in the construction and maintenance of the buildings. Their wives and daughters taught the children of other farmers and tenants. In addition, farmers worked with black merchants and professionals in towns to assist farm youths in attending agricultural conferences and institutes and obtaining scholarships for college. Inez Watson, the wife of Simon Watson, taught at Kings Welcome School in Columbia County. Reverend George Clark, another Columbia County farmer, drove the school bus for the St. James School in the Mt. Tabor community, where his wife taught. In 1952, the Clarks' oldest son was a student at Bethune-Cookman College and their daughter was preparing to enter the nursing program at Grady Memorial Hospital in Atlanta. In Marion County, farmers, town merchants, and professionals worked together to aid promising students. A 1950 photograph in the Florida Cooperative Extension Service records shows Hansel Washington receiving a check from local businessmen to assist in his attendance at the regional 4-H meeting in Virginia. Samuel Wilson, the winner of a Sears, Roebuck agricultural scholarship to Florida A&M is also featured in the image.[20] Collectively, these anecdotal and pictorial snapshots inform our understanding of the commitment black farm families made to rural education and the promise of a more equitable future and racial dignity for them and their children in white-dominated, Old South Florida.

Outside the classroom, the farm extension service educated farmers in new cropping methods, taught planning and organizational skills, and encouraged black youth to practice management and leadership through 4-H programs. In the process, Negro Extension agents increased the financial security of black agrarians and gave farmers and their children the tools and confidence they needed to advance in a state palpably transitioning to an urban-focused New South status.

Beginning in 1909, the Agricultural Cooperative Extension Program established a working relationship between the USDA, land grant universities, and local government. It served white farmers for several years before creating a separate Negro Extension Service, which operated in some, but not all counties served by white agents. As subsequent federal legislation provided for crop allotments and imposed consumer standards that favored highly capitalized farms, black agents quickly realized that their best opportunity for improving the farm output, home life, and future advancement of black farmers, tenants, and their offspring rested with their advocacy of the Tuskegee model.[21]

Florida's black extension agents oversaw every phase of the rural transformation from subsistence to commercial production, and documented it in carefully crafted reports they knew would be read and critiqued by white supervisors in Gainesville and Washington. The bureaucratic language of their yearly narrative reports could not obliterate the racial minefield black farmers negotiated to secure credit, obtain cotton or tobacco allotments, and market agricultural products. Banks and rural credit agencies required proof of credit worthiness, county allotment committees favored white farmers, and marketing facilities imposed consumer-driven standards that cash-poor black farmers found difficult to meet. Too much success invited white scrutiny and could lead to charges of "uppity-ness" that brought retribution and violence against rural blacks perceived by whites as overstepping Jim Crow boundaries. Conversely, failure to meet the standards imposed by state and federal agencies limited access to credit and markets. Negotiating the boundaries of the "New (rural) South" drew black farmers into a closer relationship with the segregated extension service.

Black extension agents routinely reported their role as facilitators in a variety of interactions between farm families and public and private agencies. Working out of segregated offices with few amenities, the agents provided technical expertise in all areas of agriculture, vouched for credit worthiness, promoted health and sanitation initiatives, encouraged conservation practices, organized and supervised 4-H clubs for rural youths, arranged social services for families in desperate need of relief, and generally advanced ways to ease the possible tensions between black farmers and whites who were neighbors, political elites, and businessmen. As the few college-educated blacks in the county, both male Negro Farm Agents and female Negro Home Agents provided role models for aspiring black youth, albeit within a government agency that placed little value on the contributions of black farmers.

Agents' annual reports proudly pointed to success stories and simultaneously recorded Old South barriers to advancement. McKinley Jeffers's reports brimmed with newspaper clippings, photographs, and statistical evidence of black agricultural successes in the region near Lake City. Simon Watson, a Columbia County farmer whose successes appeared in many reports, secured a nine-acre tobacco allotment in 1952. Using techniques recommended by his county agent, Watson produced 12,500 pounds of tobacco that sold for 51 cents per pound.[22] The Jackson County agent, Virgil Elkins, recognized the difficulties black farmers faced in obtaining allotments and helped farmers develop other strategies for advancement. Writing in 1949, Elkins tersely observed, "The swine enterprise is growing as a result of the allotment on many of the cash crops."[23] Shifts in production represented considerable investment and planning, and were often undertaken through cooperative efforts. The Negro Farmers Club of Bushnell in Sumter County purchased purebred sows and distributed them to 4-H club boys and individual farmers to raise on shares. Their efforts yielded two benefits: improvement of local herds in order to raise profits, and use of the proceeds to purchase a tractor that would be used by the members of the cooperative.[24] Although some black farmers obtained crop allotments, others found themselves shut out of traditional cash crop production and turned to a variety of cooperative strategies to maintain their status as proud landowning farmers in an increasingly commercialized agricultural market.

Cooperativism was not new to post-World War II Florida. Historically, survival in rural Florida had depended on a variety of communal networks where friends and kin exchanged labor and tools, supported one another in good times and bad, relieved the isolation inherent in farms separated by poor roads and few institutions, and discussed the prospects for a better life for their children in a society promoting white hegemony. The transformation to modern agricultural practices did not obliterate earlier practices, and African American farm communities sustained strong communal networks throughout the 1950s and 1960s—a reflection of the importance of traditional rural cooperativism in a period of unprecedented social upheaval.

Along with the country schools, rural churches provided the most recognizable example of community. Religion had sustained African American communities since the time of slavery, and extension agents tapped into the existing networks developed by rural congregations to disseminate information and organize farmers for implementing new agricultural practices. McKinley Jeffers, working in the panhandle, assured his superiors that he worked "with all churches . . . in the development of greater spiritual and social values of all citizens, young and old."[25] J. A. Gresham, the black district supervisor, reinforced the importance of working with churches and civic groups in his 1952 annual report. "We have worked closely with State and district officials, county agents, business, fraternal, and civic groups, also church and school groups in assisting county agents," he wrote. The development of strong community bonds assisted extension "efforts to promote useful and serviceable progress which would improve the lot of Negro farm people of Florida."[26] Here, in the small rural congregations, black leadership emerged to help congregants cope with Jim Crow oppressions in the countryside and improve the life of the community and the next generation.

Simon Watson, the son of a Baptist minister, served as superintendent of the Sunday school and senior deacon at the Jerusalem Baptist Church in Columbia County. Tom Banks and his wife Viola were also members of the Jerusalem congregation. Both husband and wife were Sunday school teachers, and Viola was president of the Missionary Society. James Carter was a member of the Mt. Pleasant Baptist Church, where he held multiple positions, including Sunday school superintendent, assistant ward leader, treasurer of the building fund, president of the Sunday Morning Band, and trustee of the cemetery. Several black farmers served as pastors of local congregations. The Reverend George A. Clark, farmer and pastor of the Mt. Zion Baptist Church, had served that congregation for ten years. Extension reports routinely included information about community projects to build, repair, or make improvements to local churches.[27]

A careful reading of the extension agents' reports suggests the organized efforts to improve rural homes, schools, and churches masked an underlying social revolution. Independent black farmers increasingly had capital to invest in home improvements such as indoor plumbing and electrical appliances. Moreover, their economic progress extended to the larger community, fostering building and landscaping projects that beautified properties and added amenities. In order to accomplish their tasks, county agents established leadership committees made up of representatives from each of the black farm communities under their supervision. In addition to completing agricultural and community projects, the farmers learned parliamentary and organizational skills, traveled to Florida A&M College (University after 1953) for agricultural conferences, and established important contacts outside their segregated communities. For an advancing generation of rural youth, particularly those determined to move out from under the shadow of Jim Crow Florida, the contacts would prove valuable in numerous ways.

Through their associations with Florida A&M in Tallahassee, farmers gained an appreciation for higher education that had a long-term impact. Personal savings bought land and tractors, but farmers also used their accumulated capital to educate their sons and daughters in local schools, regional high schools, and black colleges. The pursuit of higher education by the children of successful black farmers in the civil rights era represented a social revolution that is not yet fully appreciated. In a state that persistently lagged behind other southern states in the percentage of college-educated blacks, the commitment by African American farmers to educate their children added substance to the promise of a New South.[28]

Both farmers and extension agents saw 4-H as a key component of the emerging, new black farm identity and the avenue for educational advancement for their sons and daughters. First organized in the early twentieth century, 4-H clubs taught modern farming methods and rural social development through their emphasis on "Head, Heart, Hands, and Health." Until 1928, the name 4-H applied only to white youth clubs; Jim Crow organizations for African Americans in Old South Florida were designated simply as boys' or girls' clubs or as farm and homemakers clubs.[29] No matter what they called the organizations, the already overworked black extension agents depended on local leadership to assist in the arduous task of organizing and supervising 4-H clubs in the isolated crossroads communities scattered across their counties. In addition to their exposure to better farming techniques and university-based agricultural programs, 4-H members learned civic communal lessons that instilled a sense of social responsibility. The sons and daughters of black farmers participated in research projects, developed work plans, competed in public debates, traveled to state and national 4-H meetings, and earned scholarships to land grant universities. As one Duval County girl said of her 4-H experience, "4-H Club work has helped me and my family not only improve our home, but also improve us and our surroundings." She anticipated a continuing association with 4-H and predicted, "when I finish school, I plan to enter college and take home economics." Using local black farmers as their mentors, 4-H prepared boys and girls not only for modern farming but also for leadership and mobility in the emerging New South.[30]

In 1953, on the eve of the *Brown* decision, the annual report of the Florida (Negro) extension service contained a note of reassurance for whites worried by the advances blacks were making into a New South. After detailing the measures used by county agents to secure and train community leaders among black farmers, the state supervisor inserted a word of caution, ostensibly intended for the agents, but in fact directed to white concerns. "It is a must that all county agents maintain a high standard of conduct," he wrote, "and not be identified with anything that is shady in the sight of local people."[31] As challenges to Jim Crow segregation and disfranchisement increased, the organization of rural black leaders and their education in planning and parliamentary procedure excited concern among Old South segregationists. The simultaneous activities of the NAACP in rural communities only confirmed what whites feared—and in Florida, white fear often translated into violence.

Although the state had cultivated a reputation as the nation's tourist playground, Florida was, in fact, "a haven for lynching." From 1900 to 1930, the state recorded 4.5 lynchings per ten thousand African Americans, the highest rate in the South. Between 1900 and 1917, Florida recorded ninety episodes of lynching, and an additional fifty lynchings occurred between 1918 and 1930.[32]

A gruesome recital of the most notorious outbursts of violence (all occurring in rural communities) demonstrates the level of brutality that supported white supremacy in Old

South Florida in the decades prior to the modern civil rights movement: the Ocoee Riot (1920), Taylor County (1922), the Rosewood Massacre (1923), the lynching of Claude Neal (1934). Although the educational efforts of Florida's NAACP resulted in a decline in the number of lynchings during the 1940s and 1950s, the state remained in the forefront of Old South violence and captured national attention with the Groveland rape trial and the bombing deaths of black civil rights workers Harry and Harriette Moore. For rural black Floridians, the death of Moore must have held special meaning. His commitment to the construction of small-town NAACP chapters earned him the respect of rural blacks and the opposition of the organization's national leadership. Nevertheless, his murder on Christmas Eve in 1951 shocked black farmers, not only for its brutality, but also as the latest episode of a violent Old South heritage that often found its bloodiest expression in rural Florida.[33]

Even though one historian concluded that violent acts in the Sunshine State ensured that "Black Floridians knew their place in society, and few dared to step outside it," the evidence suggests a more complex reading of black accommodation to white supremacy. After the U.S. Supreme Court outlawed the white primary in *Smith v. Allwright* (1944), Florida blacks exercised their rights and began registering as Democrats and casting their ballots in the party's primary elections, a tactic that gave them new influence in the state's contemporary political decisions. From an estimated twenty thousand Republican voters in 1944, black voting rolls grew to 106,420 registered Democrats in 1950, while black Republican numbers shrank to 9,725.[34] Although not fully contextualized in the studies of this era, many of the local black actions following *Smith v. Allwright* occurred in rural rather than the more studied urban areas of the period.

In Liberty County, an area the state NAACP secretary called the "Panhandle's most rural region," the Rev. Dee Hawkins found twelve black citizens willing to challenge white supremacy by registering to vote. The consequences were immediate and terrifying. Hawkins reported nightly visits by men who hid "in the brush behind trees" around his isolated farm house and "talked about burning me out of the house." Intimidated by the Ku Klux Klan, ten of the twelve would-be voters "voluntarily" withdrew their names from the voting rolls. Appeals for protection to Governor LeRoy Collins were denied, with the state's executive officer disingenuously citing the right of citizens to withdraw their names of their own accord as the reason for his failure to act. In the end, Hawkins paid a stiff price for his courage: segregationists burned the timber he cultivated on the land he owned in Liberty County and forced his removal to Tallahassee.[35]

Intimidation was not the only means for limiting rural voter registration in an Old South system that was now transitioning into a Down South mode of stonewalling. The lack of uniform statewide voter registration laws supported the Down South put-off tactics of local registrars and their accomplices who intimidated rural, black would-be voters. As late as 1954, Madison, Gadsden, and Jefferson counties, with large black populations and a sizeable number of independent farmers, had no registered black voters.[36] In "moderate" Florida, physical and economic intimidation, and the lack of media pressure against entrenched white power, made black farmers cautious in their efforts to attain voting and civil rights and thus delayed the promises of *Brown*.

Caution did not mean that rural blacks failed to act. Students in Marion, Columbia, and Volusia counties organized Youth Councils. Boycotts of county seat theaters and stores ended Jim Crow practices in entertainment and shopping venues. Increasingly, rural and small town blacks successfully registered to vote, and local politicians courted the ballots of African Americans. Although change occurred more slowly than in urban areas, rural counties were electing black officeholders by the 1970s, hiring black sheriff's deputies to patrol African American communities, and consolidating and integrating schools.[37] For rural blacks, the integration of public spaces and the acquisition of voting rights were accompanied transitions that undermined country life—the closing of rural schools and the decline in the membership in country churches as sons and daughters increasingly moved to New South cities in Florida and other southern states. Moreover, old customs died hard in tradition-bound rural communities, and the reluctance of rural white power brokers to accept the social and political reality of a state now in racial transition after the passage of the Civil Rights Act of 1964 and the Voting Rights Act of 1965 only complicated matters. Perhaps the most unexpected persistence of the Old South's color line occurred within the very agencies that were supposed to improve farm and rural life.

The 1960s proved to be a time of transition for Florida's farm families in ways that reflected the collapse of Jim Crow and changes in farming. Independent, landowning farmers, always a minority within the larger black community, had maintained their numbers throughout the first half of the twentieth century. But in 1959, Eugene P. Smith, the Marion County agent, recognized a trend that would be pervasive within another decade. "From all directions one can see the . . . farm families drifting to town and . . . to city work and industry occupations," he wrote. "Some of these families sell their land, others rent it, some are part-time farmers and will return to the farm at farming season."[38]

The message was clear. Black agrarians in Florida were now rejecting the legendary Booker T. Washington's words that, "we will serve ourselves best, we will serve our race best, when we keep away from the large cities," for the economic promise and egalitarian hope of the Sunshine State's exploding urban areas. In the process, black farmers and their sons and daughters left behind the rural support networks of churches, extension agencies, and 4-H Clubs, and joined a new city environment of segregated schools and neighborhoods which, in many cases, would propel them into new thoughts about civil rights and how they should be acquired. That notion did not rest on the Washingtonian concept of hard work and racial reward but rather on the belief that urban-centered activism and legal corollaries would force a recalcitrant "Down South" system of denial or delay to ultimately deliver on the promises of the U.S. Constitution. As "country folk" turned into "city folk," the modern civil rights movement in Florida took on new and often profound personal and public dimensions.[39]

By 1964, when African Americans celebrated the passage of the landmark Civil Rights Bill, and agricultural bureaucracies finally made plans to abolish separate agencies for blacks and whites, the statistics showed a steep drop in the number of black farmers. More than half of Florida's black farmers operating in 1950 were gone by 1964. The mechanization dream that had so intrigued the Charley Duncan generation of farmers, now worked in powerful economic and philosophical ways to drive their sons and daughters off the land and into the cities.[40]

For some landowning farm families, the migration to urban jobs did not end their connection to the countryside. As Smith predicted, some farm families transitioned back and forth between urban and country life, working in factories and businesses in town and intermittently cultivating the family land. Like many of their white neighbors, some black siblings retained ownership of farms their forebears had struggled to make productive, even if they no longer cultivated the land. Others put the land to new uses that required less effort, but still provided an economic return. Located near Marianna, the Gainer brothers continued to utilize the family land as a working farm. The 270 acres on which Andrew Bowers raised dairy cattle were now planted in peanuts and pine trees, and the farm operated as a family business for his children. Most of those children lived urban lives as college-educated professionals and businessmen and women. Richard Hartsfield's 440 acres, acquired after years of sharecropping, also continued as a land-legacy for his family.[41]

Ironically, the education that farmers provided for their children accelerated migration from these types of farms and produced a rural New South unlike anything men and women of the mid-twentieth century expected. Blacks who remained on the farm grappled with the slow pace of the civil rights crusade in Florida, the rapid transformation of agriculture, and the unexpected lingering racism in the agricultural agencies after the implementation of the Civil Rights Act. In one example of foot-dragging, Florida provided county commissioners with greater power in determining the employment of local agricultural extension agents, a veiled effort to prohibit or delay the assignment of black agents.

In 1979, long after civil rights agitation had waned and intransigent Florida had finally come to grips with the inevitability of new federal mandates, Madison County erupted in a protracted controversy over the hiring of an extension agent. The best qualified candidate was a black man with the necessary credentials and impressive experience. When the county objected, the district supervisor visited with one commissioner, who wanted the message relayed to the Extension Service and the University of Florida that "we have heard about enough in Madison County about Affirmative Action."[42]

In more subtle ways, the needs of rural blacks succumbed to overt and veiled racism. At mid-century, black farmers and farm workers depended on the Negro Extension agent to advise and assist them in negotiating the multitude of agencies and services designed to meet their needs. With the USDA directed toward agribusiness, poorer farmers found fewer resources to meet their needs. As farm regions lagged further behind in the economic boom that swept the state, the two land grant colleges, the University of Florida and Florida A&M, struggled to preserve small farms and address the needs of poor blacks, whites, and Hispanics. In a four-pronged program that focused on agriculture, community resource development, home economics, and 4-H Clubs, Florida largely delegated responsibility for implementation of educational and developmental programs for "limited resource residents" in the black, white, and Hispanic communities to "paraprofessionals."[43]

The USDA's failure to address the needs of independent black farmers had long-term consequences. At the century's end, class action suits challenged USDA failure to administer allotments and loans fairly. In 2001, nearly a half-century after *Brown*, the USDA finally agreed to restitution for black farmers in the settlement of *Pigford v. Glickman*, a class action suit charging discrimination by the USDA between the years 1981 and 1996.[44] Today, black agrarians continue the struggle as both farmers and African Americans fighting for racial justice and economic fairness.

The story of the civil rights movement in Florida, as elsewhere, is a complex blending of confrontation and compromise as African Americans battled the Old South of white supremacy in order to bring forth a New South of racial equality. Another South, the Down South, often delayed the benefits of the federal court cases and congressional acts that were meant to restore constitutional equality to both rural and urban black societies. In their own "practical" way, independent black farmers played an important role in challenging the old white order and in shaping the civil rights future of black Floridians. In isolated rural communities, they served as role models to families struggling to survive and as advocates for education, civic responsibility, and brighter futures. Supported by the peculiar rural phenomenon of extension agents, they took leading roles in their churches, in local schools, and in agricultural and civic societies, and negotiated on their terms the contested ground of segregation. They also mentored black youths and found funding to introduce them to a broader world of hope and opportunity.

Perhaps, they succeeded too well. Sons and daughters left the land for Florida's booming cities to teach school, practice law and medicine, pastor churches, establish businesses, and build a new world as engineers, bankers, and politicians. In doing so, they harvested both the rural seeds of dignity and self-worth planted by their parents and grandparents and the urban seeds of impatient and informed protest that, after a long and delayed struggle, forced Florida beyond the Jim Crow shadow of the Old South into the sunlight of opportunity of the New South.

## NOTES

1. Newspaper clipping from the *Pittsburgh Courier*, April 22, 1950, in Annual Narrative Report of Negro Farm Demonstration Work in Columbia County, Florida, 1950, Public Records Collection, Series 91B, box 7, Florida Cooperative Extension Service Annual Reports, George A. Smathers Libraries, University of Florida Archives, Gainesville, Florida (hereafter reports from this collection will be cited by agent, county name, year, and box number only).

2. Mark Schultz, *The Rural Face of White Supremacy: Beyond Jim Crow* (Urbana: University of Illinois Press, 2005).

3. See, for example, Glenn T. Eskew, *But for Birmingham: The Local and National Movements in the Civil Rights Struggle* (Chapel Hill: University of North Carolina Press, 1997); Raymond A. Mohl, "The Pattern of Race Relations in Miami since the 1920s," in *The African American Heritage of Florida*, ed. David R. Colburn and Jane E. Landers (Gainesville: University Press of Florida, 1995), 327–65; Abel A. Bartley, *Keeping the Faith: Race, Politics, and Social Development in Jacksonville, Florida, 1940–1970* (Westport, Conn.: Greenwood, 2000); David R. Colburn, *Racial Change and Community Crisis: St. Augustine, Florida, 1877–1986* (New York: Columbia University Press, 1985); Randall M. Miller and George E. Pozzetta, eds., *Shadows of the Sunbelt: Essays on Ethnicity, Race, and the Urban South* (Westport, Conn.: Greenwood, 1988). While fewer in number, literature on rural civil rights activities includes Stephen J. Whitfield, *A Death in the Delta: The Story of Emmett Till* (Baltimore: Johns Hopkins University Press, 1992); Kay Mills, *This Little Light of Mine: The Life of Fannie Lou Hamer* (New York: Dutton, 1993); Richard A. Couto, *Lifting the Veil: A Political History of Struggle for Emancipation* (Knoxville: University of Tennessee Press, 1993); John Dittmer, *Local People: The Struggle for Civil Rights in Mississippi* (Urbana: University of Illinois Press, 1995); Neill McMillan, *Dark Journey: Black Mississippians in the Age of Jim Crow* (Urbana: University of Illinois Press, 1990); Schultz, *The Rural Face of White Supremacy*.

4. Quoted in Florida Department of Agriculture, *A Graphic View of Florida Agriculture* (St. Augustine, Fla.: The Record Company, 1938), 59.

5. Florida Department of Agriculture, *A Graphic View of Florida Agriculture*, 59. Figures for 1990 farm labor found in Maxine D. Jones, "The African-American Experience in Twentieth-

Century Florida," in *The New History Florida*, ed. Michael Gannon (Gainesville: University Press of Florida, 1996), 380.

6. Barbara R. Cotton, *The Lamplighters: Black Farm and Home Demonstration Agents in Florida, 1915–1965* (Tallahassee, Fla.: The United States Department of Agriculture in Cooperation with Florida Agricultural and Mechanical University, 1982), 101; *Census of the United States, 1900, 1910, 1920, 1930, 1940, 1950* http://fisher.lib.virginia.edu/collections/stats/histcensus (accessed July 15, 2006).

7. For discussions of southern rural communities and race, see Melissa Walker, *All We Knew Was to Farm: Rural Women in the Upcountry South, 1919–1941* (Baltimore: Johns Hopkins University Press, 2002); Rebecca Sharpless, *Fertile Ground, Narrow Choices: Women on Texas Cotton Farms, 1900–1940* (Chapel Hill: University of North Carolina Press, 1999); Glenda Elizabeth Gilmore, *Gender and Jim Crow: Women and the Politics of White Supremacy in North Carolina, 1896–1920* (Chapel Hill: University of North Carolina Press, 1996); Robin D. G. Kelley, *Hammer and Hoe: Alabama Communists during the Great Depression* (Chapel Hill: University of North Carolina Press, 1990); James C. Cobb, *The Most Southern Place on Earth: The Mississippi Delta and the Roots of Regional Identity* (New York: Oxford University Press, 1992); and J. William Harris, *Deep Souths: Delta, Piedmont, and Sea Island Society in the Age of Segregation* (Baltimore: Johns Hopkins University Press, 2001).

8. *New York Times*, January 30, 1903; see David H. Jackson Jr., "Booker T. Washington's Tour of the Sunshine State, March 1912," in *Go Sound the Trumpet!: Selections in Florida's African-American History*, ed. David H. Jackson Jr. and Canter Brown Jr. (Tampa: University of Tampa Press, 2005), 173–99; W. E. B. Du Bois, "Of Mr. Booker T. Washington and Others," in *The Souls of Black Folk* (New York: Penguin Classics, 1996 [1903]), 36–50; Rebecca Caroll, *Uncle Tom a New Negro?: African-Americans Reflect on Booker T. Washington and "Up From Slavery"* (New York: Harlem Moon/Broadway Books, 2006), and Michael Rudolph West, *The Education of Booker T. Washington: American Democracy and the Idea of Race Relations* (New York: Columbia University Press, 2006).

9. Quoted in Karen J. Ferguson, "Caught in 'No Man's Land': The Negro Cooperative Demonstration Service and the Ideology of Booker T. Washington, 1900–1918," *Agricultural History* 72 (Winter 1998): 33.

10. Ferguson, "Caught in 'No Man's Land,'" 33.

11. McKinley Jeffers, Columbia County Annual Report, 1952, box 15, Negro Extension Service.

12. Jeffers, Columbia County Annual Report.

13. Jeffers, Columbia County Annual Report.

14. Jeffers, Columbia County Annual Report.

15. Eugene P. Smith, Marion County Annual Report, 1950, box 7, Negro Extension Service.

16. Albert N. D. Brooks, "Behind the Segregation Curtain," *The Negro History Bulletin*, 18 (May 1955).

17. Brooks, "Behind the Segregation Curtain."

18. Brooks, "Behind the Segregation Curtain."

19. National Trust for Historic Preservation, "The Rosenwald Rural School Building Program," www.rosenwaldschools.com/history (accessed October 30, 2006); quoted in Jim Robinson, "On the Road to Better Education," *Black Family Today* (January/February 2001): 19–20. On Rosenwald and the Rosenwald schools, see Peter M. Acoli, *Julius Rosenwald: The Man Who Built Sears, Roe-buck and Advanced the Cause of Black Education in the American South* (Bloomington: Indiana University Press, 2006), and Mary S. Hoffschwelle, *The Rosenwald Schools of the American South* (Gainesville: University Press of Florida, 2006).

20. Newspaper clipping in "Annual Report, Columbia County, 1952," folder Columbia, box 15 (1952), Florida Cooperative Extension Service; newspaper clipping in Annual Report, Marion County, 1950, folder Marion, box 7 (1950).

21. Historians have amassed a considerable historiography on the role of the USDA and the Cooperative Extension Service in the twentieth-century transformation of agriculture. See Debra Reid, "African Americans and Land Loss in Texas: Government Duplicity and Discrimination Based on Race and Class," *Agricultural History* 77 (2003): 258–93; Valerie Grim, "African American Landlords in the Rural South, 1870–1950, A Profile," *Agricultural History* 72 (Spring 1998): 399–416; Valerie Grim, "Black Participation in the Farmers Home Administration and Agricultural Stabilization and Conservation Service, 1964–1990," *Agricultural History* 70 (Spring 1996): 321–36; Jeannie M. Whayne, "Black Farmers and the Agricultural Cooperative Extension Service: The Alabama Experience, 1945–1965," *Agricultural History* 72 (Summer 1998): 523–51; Gary Zellar, "H.C. Ray and Racial Politics in the African American Extension Service Program in Arkansas, 1915–1929," *Agricultural History* 72 (Spring 1998): 429–45; Karen J. Ferguson, "Caught in 'No Man's Land': The Negro Cooperative Demonstration Service and the Ideology of Booker T. Washington, 1900–1918," *Agricultural History* 72 (Winter 1998): 33–54.

22. McKinley Jeffers, Columbia County Negro Extension Service Report, 1952, box 15.

23. Virgil Elkins, Jackson County Negro Extension Service Report, 1949, box 4.

24. Richard L. Bradley, Sumter County Negro Extension Report, 1950, box 8.

25. McKinley Jeffers, Columbia County report, 1953, box 20.

26. J.A. Gresham, 1952 Annual Report, box 15.

27. Jeffers McKinley, Columbia County Report, 1952, box 15.

28. See Stephanie Y. Evans, "'I Was One of the First to See Daylight': Black Women at Predominantly White Colleges and Universities in Florida Since 1959," *Florida Historical Quarterly* 85.1 (2006), 46–7.

29. Barbara Cotton, *Black Farmers and Home Demonstration Agents in Florida*, 74.

30. Annual Report, 1959, box 59; Virgil Elkins, Jackson County Report, 1950, box 7; Eugene P. Smith, Marion County Report, 1950, box 7; Cotton, 84–86, quote on page 86.

31. "Extension (Negro) Annual Report 1953," box 20 (1953).

32. Quoted in Ben Green, *Before His Time: The Untold Story of Harry T. Moore, America's First*

*Civil Rights Martyr* (Gainesville: University Press of Florida, 2005 [1999], 45; see Margaret Vandiver, *Lethal Punishment: Lynchings and Legal Executions in the South* (New Brunswick: Rutgers University Press, 2006), 70–88, 201–2.

33. Jones, "The African-American Experience in Twentieth-Century Florida," 379; see James R. McGovern, *Anatomy of a Lynching: The Killing of Claude Neal* (Baton Rouge, Louisiana State University Press, 1982), 138–9; Robert L. Zangrando, *The NAACP Crusade Against Lynching, 1909–1950* (Philadelphia: Temple University Press, 1980), 213–15, and data on 6–7; Steven F. Lawson, David R. Colburn, and Darryl Paulson, "Groveland: Florida's Little Scottsboro," in *The African American Heritage of Florida,* 398–325.

34. Figures found in Jones, "The African-American Experience in Twentieth-Century Florida," 376; see Green, *Harry T. Moore,* 117–18.

35. Robert W. Saunders Jr., *Bridging the Gap: Continuing the Florida NAACP Legacy of Harry T. Moore* (Tampa: University of Tampa Press, 2000), 149–50.

36. Maxine D. Jones, "The African-American Experience in Twentieth-Century Florida," 376: Green, *Harry T. Moore,* 54.

37. See Canter Brown Jr., *None Can Have Richer Memories: Polk County, Florida, 1949–2000* (Tampa: University of Tampa Press, 2005), 88–89; Edward F. Keuchel, *A History of Columbia County, Florida* (Tallahassee: Sentry Press, 1981), 207–209; Gilmore Academy-Jackson County Training School Alumni Association, Inc., *Jackson County, Florida* (Charleston, S.C.: Arcadia Publishing, 2000), 65.

38. Smith, 1959, box 56.

39. Quoted in West, *The Education of Booker T. Washington,* 108.

40. See Raymond A. Mohle, "The Pattern of Race Relations in Miami since the 1920s," in *The African American Heritage of Florida,* 326–65.

41. *Jackson County, Florida,* 35, 37, 61, 62.

42. Maurice F. Cole to Dr. John Woeste, memo, April 27, 1979, University of Florida Archives, Public Records Collection Series 93b, Institute of Food and Agricultural Science, Office of the Dean for Extension Administrative Policy Records, 1969–1979, box 5, folder "District Agents, 1979," George Smathers Library, University of Florida, Gainesville, Florida (hereafter the collection cited as IFAS Policy Records).

43. B.B. Archer, Administrator, Florida A&M Programs to Dr. W. Neill Schaller, Deputy Director for Extension USDA, Washington, D.C., March 22, 1979, IFAS Policy Records, box 3, folder "Community and Rural Development, 1978–79."

44. Debra A. Reid, "African Americans and Land Loss in Texas: Government Duplicity and Discrimination Based on Race and Class," *Agricultural History* 77 (2003): 258–92; Federation of Southern Cooperative Land Assistance Fund, "Class Action Suit Index," http://www.federationsoutherncoop.com/classaction.htm (accessed October 30, 2006); *Pigford v. Glickman* 182 F.R.D. at 352, www.pigfordmonitor.org/orders/19990414op.pdf (accessed October 30, 2006).

# CHAPTER SIX

# JUSTICE DELAYED IS JUSTICE DENIED

## FLORIDA'S "PUBLIC MISCHIEF" DEFENSE AND VIRGIL HAWKINS'S PROTRACTED LEGAL STRUGGLE FOR RACIAL EQUALITY

### AMY SASSER

Scholars have long presumed that *Brown v. Board of Education* of 1954 and its spin-off, the *Brown II* decision of 1955, provided the impetus for the modern civil rights struggle in Florida, even though that struggle remained rather muted in comparison to the other states of the Deep South. Yet the historical record reflects a challenge to this premise, especially regarding *Brown* as the lynchpin of black protest in Florida and the notion that the state itself adopted a more enlightened and progressive posture toward racial advancement than many of its neighbors in Dixie. An examination of the origins, developments, and long-delayed results of the *Hawkins v. Board of Control* case, beginning in 1949, illustrates just how entrenched Florida was in its Old South ways in the pre- and post-*Brown* years and how equally determined the state's power brokers were to ignore, prolong, or actually stymie Virgil D. Hawkins's fight for racial equality in the 1940s and 1950s. Like many events occurring in the dramatically changing local environs of Florida in the era of modern civil rights, the complexities of the *Hawkins* case defy ready-made typecasting. As historians and other scholars deliberate the factors suggesting that Florida was or perhaps was not "moderate" in its approach to racial legacies and racial issues, it would be instructive for them to ponder the personal and institutional experiences of Virgil Hawkins and his search for equal access to higher education in post-World War II Florida.

In 1949, civil rights pioneer Virgil Hawkins applied to the all-white law school at the University of Florida (UF) but was denied admission on the basis of his race. As a result, he fought for the next nine years in the courts for his right to attend law school. *Hawkins v. Board of Control* resulted in four Florida Supreme Court cases, three U.S. Supreme Court cases, and three final federal court reviews. Through its decisions, the Florida Supreme Court ignored judicial precedent and even defied the U.S. Supreme Court in its Old South-style opposition to admitting Hawkins, claiming immediate integration would cause irreparable "public mischief."[1]

Although white claims of racially motivated "public mischief" was nothing new to the Sunshine State in the 1950s, the evidence that the state used to support its Down South delay of integration in actuality showed a population perhaps more ready to integrate than the state leadership maintained. It is notable that when Florida did begin to integrate in 1959, few incidents of violence occurred that year (although that would not be the case in the following years). This "mild" initial reaction to integration corresponded with the beginnings of New South priorities in Florida, especially its leaders' focus on economics in rapidly growing and diversifying urban areas. Even so, the Old South commitment to segregation by much of Florida's leadership caused protracted delay in implementing New South practices of social and racial uplift. This Down South delay and stonewalling ultimately denied justice to Virgil Hawkins, who never obtained a law degree in his home state. In this regard, Hawkins's legal struggle offers a useful case study by which to evaluate the accuracy of many assumptions now held by historians of Florida's past.

Virgil Hawkins (1906–1988) was one of eight children of a black family that lived in Okahumpka in Lake County, Florida, a region known widely for its entrenched racism. The sheriff during the civil rights era, Willis McCall, was particularly notorious for his open racism. According to Robert Saunders, former field secretary for the National Association for the Advancement of Colored People (NAACP) in Florida, few counties had such "bigotry and brutality" as Lake County. Hawkins was the only child in his family who desired to obtain an education. He started college at Lincoln University in Pennsylvania, but returned to Florida and enrolled at Bethune-Cookman College, where he obtained his bachelor's degree in 1952. He worked as a teacher, a principal, an insurance salesman, and as the public relations director of Bethune-Cookman College before attempting to attend the law school at the University of Florida at forty-two years of age.[2]

Writing in the *Florida Coastal Law Journal*, Harley Herman, an associate of Hawkins during his brief law career in Leesburg, relayed the story of why Hawkins wanted so much to be a lawyer. When Hawkins was about six years old, he saw several black men in a court, without the aid of counsel, who had no ability to understand what the judge was saying. According to Herman, this left Hawkins with a "burning desire to be the voice to deliver his people from similar scenes of injustice." His dream of a law career seemed unobtainable in his youth when the public universities were segregated and the black college in Tallahassee, Florida Agricultural and Mechanical College (FAMC), did not offer a degree in law.[3]

Despite such obstacles, Virgil Hawkins held onto his dream to attend law school. On May 13, 1949, Hawkins and five other African Americans applicants were denied admission to the University of Florida by the Florida State Board of Control, the governing body of the public universities of Florida. The chairman of the board, Thomas Gurney, instead offered the applicants scholarships to out-of-state schools. Rather than admitting students to an all-white state school, the board was so dedicated to maintaining Old South segregation that they were willing to spend public funds to send the applicants to another state and pay a high price to do so.[4]

In 1949, the Florida Constitution still prohibited integrated schooling. However, this part of the constitution referred specifically to children, "White and colored children shall not be taught in the same school, but impartial provision shall be made for both." Even though it had been the practice and assumption, the constitution did not specifically say that this provision applied to students of adult age, such as Hawkins. It was only the Florida Supreme Court's ruling on the *Hawkins* case that gave the Florida Constitution formal and legal application to segregated higher education.[5]

The applicants rejected the out-of-state scholarships. Twelve days after they were offered the scholarships, five of them and their attorney, former Florida House member Alex Akerman Jr., filed suit against members of the Florida Board of Control and petitioned the Florida Supreme Court to order their admission to the University of Florida. Akerman then decided to argue the benefits of studying in the applicants' home state, since FAMC did not offer the applicants' desired curriculum. The NAACP later joined this case, with Hawkins acting as the lone plaintiff.[6]

In the years preceding Hawkins's court challenge, there were several U.S. Supreme Court cases that specifically addressed segregation in higher education. The cases cited by the U.S. Supreme Court in the 1956 *Hawkins v. Board* opinion as precedents were *Sipuel v. Board of Regents of the University of Oklahoma* (1948), *Sweatt v. Painter* (1950), and *McLaurin v. Oklahoma State Regents for Higher Education* (1950). All these cases occurred before or at the time Virgil Hawkins was applying to law school and signaled to the Old South that the Court was no longer turning a blind eye towards color lines in higher education. In all three cases, the Supreme Court "ordered the admission of Negro applicants to graduate schools without discrimination because of color."[7]

It would seem on the face of these decisions that Florida's white officials would have recognized the folly in persisting in race-based discrimination in admission to law schools, but the Old South habits of the Sunshine State's white leadership still underscored public policy, even in defiance of the U.S. Supreme Court. Indeed, as Martin A. Dyckman has highlighted in a recent study, the state legislature even sent the governor an appropriations bill requiring that state colleges remain segregated in the face of such legal challenges. In their review of Hawkins's challenge to the color bar of UF's law school, Darryl Paulson and Paul Hawkes argued that the established court rulings and the newly-filed *Hawkins* brief were the very actions that led the legislature to resurrect the issue of institutional segregation, in this case thinly veiled in a general appropriations bill.[8]

*Sweatt v. Painter* was decided on June 5, 1950, two months before the first decision in *Hawkins*. In *Sweatt*, a black applicant was denied admission to a Texas law school because of race; the applicant rejected the offer to attend a newly created, separate law school for African Americans. It was decided that a legal education at this new law school would not be "substantially equal" to the education the applicant could receive at the all-white law school. The Court found that the two law schools in Texas were unequal, not only in funding issues like books and teachers, but also in intangible aspects such as prestige and acquiring professional contacts. *Sweatt* established that a state's duty is to provide the petitioner with an equal legal education under the Fourteenth Amendment, and that this could not be done through the separate law school. *McLaurin* was decided on the same day. This decision also upheld that separate did not mean equal in higher education.[9]

These legal precedents and Florida's Jim Crow now seemed to be on a collision course. Hawkins and the other applicants petitioned the Florida Supreme Court for admission to their respective graduate school programs. The Florida Board of Control responded by devising a plan that would maintain segregation according to Jim Crow customs. Although the board members preferred out-of-state scholarships, they seem to have anticipated that the U.S. Supreme Court case of *Gaines v. Canada* (1938) had rendered out-of-state scholarships unequal. Board members devised an alternative plan to create comparable graduate studies, such as a law school, at Florida Agricultural and Mechanical College. This plan also allowed African American students to attend classes at white public colleges until the new courses were offered at FAMC. The board subsequently petitioned the Florida court not to force admission of Hawkins to the University of Florida.[10] In reality, the board's plan ushered in a Down South tactic of continued delay to prevent integration.

The Florida Supreme Court ruled on the *Hawkins* suit on August 1, 1950. It denied the applicants admission to white colleges, but did approve the Board of Control's plan to temporarily allow African Americans to attend classes at the white colleges. The chief justice, Harold L. Sebring, of the Florida Supreme Court in 1950 said that the out-of-state scholarships did not provide equal opportunity. The court cited U.S. Supreme Court ruling *Gaines v. Canada* in support of not allowing out-of-state scholarships, but completely ignored the recent rulings of *Sweatt* and *McLaurin*. The 1950 *Hawkins* decision declared that the court would later examine whether equal facilities existed at the separate school for African Americans. As reported in the national press, Justices Terrell, Chapman, Adams, Hobson, and Roberts concurred with Chief Justice Sebring to deny admission and approve this plan.[11]

Justice Sebring commented on the Fourteenth Amendment, "The object of the amendment was undoubtedly to enforce the absolute equality of the two races before the law, but, in the nature of things, it could not have been intended to abolish distinctions based upon color, or to enforce . . . a commingling of the two races upon terms unsatisfactory to either."[12] As mentioned, however, the Florida court's opinion did allow African Americans to attend the white universities until the requisite facilities were built at FAMC (FAMU after 1953). Although this was not the permanent desegregation that civil rights advocates wanted, it was a significant enough change in the practices of segregationist Florida to warrant a story in the *New York Times*.[13] Integration in Florida's graduate and professional schools, though, would not occur for almost another decade. In retrospect, it appears that the Sunshine State, bowing to the new legal realities of civil rights in the 1950s, simply replaced Old South blatant forms of discrimination with a new ruse to delay or even ultimately prevent desegregation in public higher education.

Hawkins would not accept the compromise of the new law school. He and his lawyers argued, "the belated attempt of the respondents to now set up Schools . . . at the Florida A&M School for Negroes would still be a denial of rights guaranteed . . . under the Constitution of the United States."[14] Hawkins recalled in a 1983 interview that he did not accept attending the school at FAMC because he did not feel that a law school in existence for only one year would be as good as the one at the University of Florida.[15] *The Nation* magazine noted that the board had also decided to suspend out-of-state scholarships for future students. The magazine believed that this was retaliation for the petitioners' refusal to accept "makeshift and unaccredited" programs at FAMC.[16]

On June 15, 1951, the Florida Supreme Court again denied the African American applicants, including Virgil Hawkins, admission to the University of Florida. In the midst of these early Florida cases, Hawkins's case made it to the Supreme Court of the United States on November 13, 1951.

The U.S. Court delayed making a decision on the case "for want of a final judgment" from the Florida court.[17] The year 1952 also brought another disappointment for Hawkins;

the Florida Supreme Court denied a new motion, stating that Hawkins had not provided any evidence about the inequality of the programs at Florida Agricultural and Mechanical College and the University of Florida. According to *Sweatt*, however, the practical equality or inequality of the schools should not have mattered; segregated law schooling had been declared unequal by the U.S. Court. The Florida Supreme Court instead emphasized that equality did not have to mean exactly identical progress.[18] This Old South loyalty of the Florida court indicated that New South practices still lay in the distant future.

Hawkins was able to advance his case to the U.S. Supreme Court again in 1954, because on May 17 of that year, the nation changed irrevocably with the ruling of *Brown v. Board of Education*. *Brown* found that "Segregation of white and Negro children in the public schools of a State solely on the basis of race . . . denies to Negro children the equal protection of the laws guaranteed by the Fourteenth Amendment. . ." The Court added, "The 'separate but equal' doctrine adopted in *Plessy v. Ferguson* in 1898 has no place in the field of public education." *Brown* was, however, specifically concerned with lower education and discussed children, rather than adults, in the opinion. It was unclear, therefore, whether *Hawkins*, a case for higher education involving an adult, would have fallen under *Brown*. Even so, the Supreme Court ruled on May 24, 1954, that the Florida court must reconsider Hawkins's case in light of *Brown*. Many authors argue that the *Brown* decision galvanized the black protest community of Florida, and this may be in part accurate; yet, as Theodore Hemmingway and Algia R. Cooper, among other researchers, have argued, *Brown* did not awaken black agency in Florida but simply served to re-energize local black activism—it was actually the Hawkins's case of 1949 that instituted a new era of black demands for equality.[19]

The Florida Supreme Court "reconsidered" Hawkins's case on October 19, 1955, over a year after ordered to do so by the U.S. Supreme Court. By this time, Hawkins was the only one of the five original African American applicants still pursuing the case.[20] One of Hawkins's lawyers from the NAACP, Constance Baker Motley—later to become the first black female federal judge—faced the difficulty that civil rights lawyers had in breaking through the southern legal system. As black Floridians closely monitored the situation, she argued the 1955 case before the Florida Supreme Court, what she called "a group of stone-faced white male judges."[21]

The decision of the Florida Supreme Court in 1955 nominally matched the sentiment of the U.S. Court. It acknowledged that the Supreme Court ended segregation in public schools. However, in practice, Florida's decision was a new disappointing and delaying step for civil rights advocates in a state now acquiring a reputation for moderation on the civil rights front. The court decided that the applicant's admission would be withheld until officials could determine when necessary "adjustments" in Florida's university system could be made. Florida used the *Brown II* (1955) "implementation decision," a second decision by the U.S. Supreme Court that left implementation of *Brown* up to local authorities due to the local nature of education, to justify this continued delay. In essence, *Brown II* left much room for the local courts to delay in their own creative ways. Historians would be wise to note that Florida did just that. Florida's Justice Sebring maintained that the implementation decision "does not impose upon respondents a clear legal duty to admit . . . immediately."[22]

In their answer to Hawkins's petition, the Board of Control had argued that integration would cause "grave and serious problems" in the school system, requiring "numerous adjustments." In summary, the board ignored the higher education decisions of the U.S. Supreme Court and argued that *Brown* did not even apply to an adult student such as Hawkins. The board argued that there were still decisions to be made about "the means and manner and practical effective date" of desegregation.[23]  In this 1955 case, the Board of Control and the majority of the Florida Supreme Court switched their old argument—that they had created an "equal" law school at FAMU—to one of indeterminate delay of integration due to the threat of "serious problems."  However, at least one Florida Supreme Court justice showed that his loyalty to segregation was not purely from a concern for public safety. Justice William Glenn Terrell said in his 1955 concurring opinion, "Segregation is not a new philosophy generated by the states that practice it. It is and has always been the unvarying law of the animal kingdom . . . and when God created man, he allotted each race to his own continent according to color . . ."[24]  In a blatant departure from accepted jurisprudence, Terrell's statements were reminiscent of the antebellum South's justification for slavery itself.

Not all justices agreed with Terrell's Old South position. In the 1955 decision, Justice Sebring, in a differing statement from his past opinions in 1950 and 1952, both agreed and dissented with the decision of the court. He agreed with the need for some adjustments to provide for integrated education in Florida. He disagreed, however, on legal grounds with acting against the federal government. Instead of avoiding *Sweatt v. Painter*, as in past decisions, he now cited it as a guiding precedent. Sebring said that it was clear that the *Brown* decision was meant to apply to public schools at every level and not just for children. Although *Brown II* might not require immediate admission, Sebring did not agree with other justices that the adjustments needed were major ones and instead felt that delaying would deprive Hawkins of his constitutional rights. In addition to Justice Sebring, Justice Elwyn Thomas also dissented.[25]

Was the Florida Supreme Court trying to integrate "as soon as possible," as *Brown II* demanded of local authorities, or was it trying to evade integration for as long as possible?

As Florida civil rights historian Glenda Alice Rabby notes, the Florida Supreme Court was "apparently desperate to find a way to avoid admitting Hawkins while appearing to be in compliance with recent judicial mandates. . ." Desegregation scholar Jean L. Preer also found that the *Hawkins* case "demonstrates how the unresolved conflict in higher education . . . was compounded by applying public school precedent to delay rather than advance the end of segregation." The loophole in *Brown II* for delay complicated the resolution of Hawkins and opened the door for anti-integration stonewalling, as Florida leaders took advantage of its provisions.[26]

As noted, it was not clear at the time of *Hawkins* whether *Brown* applied to higher education. Arguments either way could be used against Hawkins. For instance, the Florida Supreme Court in *Board of Public Instruction v. State* (1954) said that "the Brown case comprehends all levels" of schooling. Florida Attorney General Richard Ervin also argued that the "least dangerous method of making the change would be as a part of one over-all desegregation program affecting all levels of education." Even when applying *Brown* to higher education, though, the Attorney General still used the *Brown II* loophole as a way to delay desegregation for all schools.[27]

The 1955 *Hawkins* case gained prominent coverage in Florida media. Comments in these articles implied that the state would eventually comply with the federal government's order to desegregate. For instance, the *Orlando Sentinel* stated that this was the second ruling, after Texas, in the "Deep South that fully supports segregation orders of the U.S. Supreme Court." The newspaper also noted that the decision determined that Florida could not lawfully refuse Hawkins's admission to UF.[28]

In reality, however, *Hawkins v. Board of Control* in 1955 was a continued victory for denying integration. As part of the delay, the court gave a circuit judge the responsibility of determining when it would be possible for Virgil Hawkins to attend the University of Florida without creating "public mischief." The judge was to report in four months, but the survey took much longer.[29] The University of Florida Faculty Senate voiced its opposition to the survey and declared that it "foresaw no serious conflicts, incidents or disturbances resulting from integration." The University of Florida Student Government Cabinet also stated that its members thought that "the majority of students do not advocate violence or demonstrations" in regard to desegregating the campus.[30]

During the inevitable postponements, Hawkins again went to the U.S. Supreme Court for an order admitting him to the University of Florida. Hawkins and his lawyers argued that the Florida 1955 decision was not in his interest, and after losing six years to delays, "could well deprive him completely of his constitutional rights." According to Hawkins's position, in the past Court cases on higher education, the removal of racial barriers in these institutions occurred immediately. It appeared to Hawkins, his legal team, and other supporters at that time that applicants had less protection after *Brown* because of reprehensible state tactics.[31]

It was in this context that, for the third time in seven years, the U.S. Supreme Court rendered a decision in the *Hawkins* case. On March 12, 1956, the Court issued a unanimous decision, finding that *Brown II* did not imply that desegregating graduate school represented new problems and necessitated delays that were allowed for elementary and secondary education. The Supreme Court made it clear with this decision that the differences in public schools and graduate schools led to different legal obligations.[32] As reported in national newspapers such as the *New York Times*, Florida could not legally bar or delay Hawkins's admission to UF any longer, since the legal obligation for graduate schools had been decided in 1950 in *Sweatt*.[33]

The wording of the U.S. Supreme Court's 1956 ruling seemed a victory for Hawkins, who said that he planned to enter the law school in the fall of 1956. The *New York Times* reported that the Supreme Court's ruling was "ending a 7-year fight." However, the fight did not end, and the case was not that simple for Old South Florida leadership. By December of 1956, Hawkins still had not been admitted, and the Florida Supreme Court still planned to decide by itself when Hawkins would be permitted to enroll.[34]

The Florida Board of Control also maintained its argument that Hawkins's admission would "cause trouble" and this type of "mixing" should be delayed until a "safer" time. The board said that admitting Hawkins would "create 'an atmosphere of hate and fear in university communities likely to result in violence and other actions endangering the public interest, welfare and safety'" or "the potential of causing serious public discord and disturbances in the state." Attorney General Ervin stated that anti-integration demonstrations in places such as Tennessee and Texas showed the type of trouble that might occur in Florida.[35]

The board also cited "administrative problems," such as black students leaving colleges like FAMU and increasing the overcrowding problems at the white universities, as factors necessitating delay. Although overcrowding and other problems may have been real, those concerns were not the same as the problem of "public mischief" that the Florida Supreme Court cited as the reason for delay.[36] It is arguable the usual cry of "public mischief" was really motivated by Old South commitments to segregation rather than the reality of potential violence.

The Florida Supreme Court finally made its decision in response to the U.S. order in March of 1957. This new ruling denied Hawkins immediate entrance but would allow him to renew his petition by showing that his admission "could be accomplished without doing great public mischief." In addition to transferring the burden of proof off the state and onto the petitioner, the court again technically maintained that Florida had to admit Hawkins as the U.S. Supreme Court's ruling ordered, but that the right time for admission had not yet been established, and that the Supreme Court would not deny a sovereign state the right to decide "the effective date of its own discretionary process." According to the *Orlando Sentinel*, with this decision, "the Florida Supreme Court . . . threw up a states' rights barrier to block immediate entrance" of Hawkins to the University of Florida.[37]

Indeed, Florida Supreme Court Justice B. K. Roberts argued in the 1957 opinion that states' rights were of utmost importance to civil liberties. Roberts maintained that Florida had a duty to admit Hawkins but also had a duty to protect the public peace.[38] However, not all of the justices agreed. Justice Thomas dissented, saying that Florida's right of discretion has "been abused, has been exhausted and the time has arrived to obey the mandate of the higher court." Justice E. Harris Drew also dissented, stating in what are now time-honored words, "It is a fundamental truth that justice delayed is justice denied." Justice Drew not only disagreed with the defiance of the U.S. Supreme Court, but he also felt that the duty of his court was to not delay but rather expedite justice.[39] Although the dissent advocated New South practices, on the whole the Florida Supreme Court was still so dedicated to its Old South ways that it was willing to openly defy the U.S. Supreme Court.

Some may argue that the Florida Supreme Court cases were a step forward for civil rights, because the cases did say that, after *Brown*, Florida could not deny admission to public education on the basis of race. This argument was seen, for example, in one of the many letters that the president of the University of Florida received about the integration question. This letter came from a white supremacist who linked integration to a communist conspiracy. The author felt that even a meeting called to determine whether admission of Hawkins would cause "public mischief" was "just another attempt to integrate us."[40] Nevertheless, it was not until the 1958 decision by a U.S. District Court that integration was actually ordered in Florida. The state courts did not do this, but instead further delayed implementation as a way to once again defer integration.

The governors of Florida in the 1950s were an integral component of the debate over segregation. *Brown* inflamed the segregation issue and created a difference in tone in the governors' races. Segregation had not been a key issue in the 1954 election, but the segregation debate greatly intensified by the time of the 1956 gubernatorial election. As Martin Dyckman has noted in his recently published study of LeRoy Collins, by 1956 Governor Collins, after becoming intensely aware of and concerned about the implications of the *Hawkins* lawsuit, came to oppose desegregation because he felt it had not been accepted in Floridians' minds and attitudes. While professing that "separate but equal" was a reasonable dictum in the Sunshine State, Collins opposed a proposal to vest all power over university entrances in the office of the governor. Nevertheless, Collins did react to *Hawkins* by saying that he would personally try all legal possibilities to oppose integration. As a result, during the 1956 gubernatorial elections Collins campaigned with a solid segregation platform.[41]

It seems as if political factors pushed Florida leaders, including Collins, into a strict segregationist stance. Tom Wagy's biography of LeRoy Collins states that as the segregation issue in Florida became important, Collins was not able to focus on his own priorities, such as creating the economic base for a New South state. Wagy writes that political factors in Florida, such as the Florida legislature taking a reactionary, segregationist stance, made it difficult for Collins to publicly display his feelings about desegregation. In the 1993 Hawkins documentary, produced by Lawrence Dubin, author Harley Herman said that the candidates in 1956 "chose to all run against Hawkins rather than each other."[42]

Professor Helen Jacobstein notes, "The temptation to make political capital out of the issue was too great for the opportunists. Southern office-holders who formerly had been moderate on the racial question now found themselves pushed into a more extreme position."[43] H. D. Price in *The Negro and Southern Politics* finds a dilemma for a white candidate: "If the candidate's constituency contains both a sizable Negro vote and a large number of race-conscious whites, any overt appeal to either group is likely to turn the other group against him." Price argues that after the 1954 desegregation decision, an anti-Negro campaign became more politically advantageous. A pro-Negro campaign or even a pro-Negro label, then, became politically dangerous. Whether or not this sort of political intrigue moved a "moderate" Collins to a strong segregationist position in 1956 is a matter of historical speculation. Nevertheless, in 1956, his and others' strong segregationist actions delayed justice for Hawkins.[44]

The results of the study ordered by the Florida Supreme Court in 1955 concerning the appropriate time for integration and protection of the public interest were part of the argument in 1957 for continuing delay and as evidence of "public mischief." Justice Roberts, in his opinion, found that the study showed that a "substantial" number of students and parents would take positive action to persuade "Negro students to leave the University or make it . . . unpleasant for them." Roberts also said that the study "leads inevitably to the conclusion that violence in university communities and a critical disruption of the university system would occur if Negro students are permitted to enter the state white universities at this time . . ."[45] Attorney General Ervin used the results in his petition to the U.S. Supreme Court, arguing that the case confirmed that integrating would represent "public mischief" and would result in a "serious disruption."[46]

However, the potential for "serious disruptions" were not, in actuality, suggested by the survey. It was mailed to 62,000 alumni, students, and parents of the three state colleges and to high school seniors. The survey asked whether the respondents "favor immediate integration, whether there should be a reasonable period of adjustment, whether integration should be delayed as long as legally possible, or whether it should never occur in Florida."[47] Faculty members were the most tolerant in the survey, more than "92 percent were willing to start teaching black students in the classroom immediately."[48]

Approximately half of students surveyed felt that African Americans should be admitted "after a reasonable period of preparation for integration." Only 5.96 percent of students surveyed said they would try to discourage African American students from attending the white school, and only 1.66 percent said they would drop out of college if African Americans enrolled. A mere 2.52 percent would try to make it so unpleasant for African Americans in the dormitories that they would move out. Parents, however, showed more resistance to integration, with about 40 percent saying that African Americans should never be admitted. Alumni were also resistant, with 52 percent saying they would cease to financially support their school if integration occurred.[49]

Although the survey found resistance to integration, there were no indications of impending violence or rioting, contrary to the argument from the Florida Supreme Court that a "critical disruption of the university system would occur" and a "substantial" number of students would try to make integrated life unpleasant.[50] Even if alumni would have followed through with their intent to stop financial support, thus creating financial difficulties for integrated universities, the Board of Control and the Florida Supreme Court were arguing against integration because of the potential for "public mischief," not financial changes. Evidence of loss of financial support did not sustain opponents' argument about the potential threat to public safety and order. The use of the survey by Hawkins's opponents shows the distortion in these opponents' arguments.

There were other indications of Floridian sentiment in the Hawkins years. A survey done for the *Independent Alligator* at the University of Florida found that 75 percent of law students at the school did not see any harm in integrating their school.[51] There is no way to assure the accuracy of this survey, but it was widely reported in the media. More than two hundred University of Florida students also signed a petition saying that they would welcome any new student. This provoked segregationists, who burned a cross on campus and threatened to have faculty fired.[52] Despite such disruptions, President Reitz praised the students and faculty for their "calm and orderly manner" in responding to the 1956 Supreme Court's decision.[53]

According to Glenda Rabby, the justices believed that the desegregation decision had "engendered . . . strife, tension, hatred, and disorder." She argues that this belief was "contrary to any evidence in Florida. . ."[54] However, the state did have its fair share of racially motivated violence. For example, Hawkins said in an interview in 1983 that when he approached the law school entrance test facility at UF, he felt intimidated by armed white bystanders.[55] The justices would have been wrong, though, if they were implying that the desegregation cases began such disorder in Florida. For instance, "The Florida Terror," multiple bombings targeting minority communities and religious centers in Miami and Orlando, actually had occurred three years prior to *Brown*.[56] It is unfortunate for Hawkins that "public mischief" concerns were not fully addressed by Florida leadership then or even decades earlier, but instead were being "addressed" by an indeterminate delay of integration after 1955.

Scholar Earl Black adds, "Florida campaigns for governor have contained more segregationist rhetoric than the political demography of the state might suggest."[57] In March 1956, the *New York Times* reported on the condition of integration in each Southern state. Although the *Times* reported that segregation still "reigns in Florida," the piece also said, "human and climatic temperatures remain mild."[58] There were factors in the state that contributed to a general mildness by 1956. For instance, business-moderates in states on the periphery of the South, such as Florida, opposed massive resistance to integration. Wagy also finds that factors such as economic dependence on tourism influenced Florida's "mild climate."[59] Jacobstein quotes noted political scientist V. O. Key on the nature of Florida politics, summarizing the differences between urban and rural areas: "In urbanization may be found a major explanation of Florida's relative unconcern about the Negro. While the state's politics is by no means free of Negro-baiting, the dominant attitude on the race question is comparatively mild."[60]

The moderation hypothesis can be further examined by breaking the state into demographic areas. North Florida was mostly rural and contained the majority of the highly concentrated African American counties. These were also the core segregationist counties.[61] The difference between rural Florida and urban Florida was also demonstrated in the state legislature's opposition to the more pragmatic actions of Governor Collins. The legislature overwhelmingly represented the rural minority of Florida.[62]

The results of the 1956 election highlighted these divisions between northern and peninsular Florida and urban and rural areas. For instance, although Collins won the 1956 election, his radical segregationist opponent, Sumter Lowry, won almost all of North

Florida and actually placed second in the Democratic primary. The remarkable results of politically inexperienced Lowry in Florida showed how fiery racism still had widespread support in Florida. Interestingly, though, Collins showed strength in Hawkins's home county, Lake County.[63] Although this county was notorious for its racism, its voting may have been moderated by its proximity to the urban area of Orlando and its changing economic priorities.

Jacobstein underscores these types of demographic factors. North Florida was composed of "native 'Crackers'" and "most meaningful of all, huge numbers of immigrants from other states . . . settled in peninsular Florida." Old South sentiment was notably weaker in Florida cities like Miami and St. Petersburg that were "populated by new Floridians and concerned with tourism." Areas with largely new transplants from the northern U.S. showed a certain willingness to integrate public facilities.[64] Price agrees with Jacobstein's argument that those in South Florida were "not willing to make every sacrifice to avoid" integration like other parts of the state might have been, although it would be incorrect to conclude that wave of the new "Yankees" to the state were as progressive on the racial issue as they were on political issues.[65] Thus, transplants and New South economics and attendant  characteristics were beginning to arise and shape Florida into a new national image by 1957, but the *Hawkins* fallout suggests that historians today must carefully evaluate the roots and accuracy of that image.

In 1957 the question was, then, what the U.S. Supreme Court should do when a state court defied its decision and continued the state's history of Jim Crow, especially based on Florida's specious assumption of "public mischief." After 1957, the U.S. Court chose to "bypass" the state court by sending the *Hawkins* case to a federal court in Florida.[66] The U.S. Supreme Court did this because federal courts were not as sensitive to arguments of "public mischief" as state courts and did not have the problems of federalism versus states' rights that were demonstrated by Florida's refusal to comply with the Supreme Court decision. To some, however, this was interpreted as a lack of action by the U.S. Supreme Court. Authors Stephen L. Wasby, Anthony A. D'Amato, and Rosemary Metrailer found that this move showed "some deference to the state courts even after their delays."[67] This was an acceptable compromise for Florida. It was based on a theory that because Federal District court judges live in the states over which they preside, they were more sympathetic towards their state even though they were under federal jurisdiction.[68]

Hawkins continued to fight and appealed his case to the Federal District court. This case was different from past *Hawkins* cases because Hawkins combined his petition to be admitted to the University of Florida for himself with a class action request that sought to prevent the defendants from refusing to admit any qualified African Americans to the law school. Down South delay was once again successful, this time assisted by the Federal District court. Hawkins wanted to be admitted to the spring 1958 class while the court determined his eligibility for permanent tenure at the school. Nevertheless, Federal District Judge Dozier DeVane refused. In 1958 the U.S. Court of Appeals for the Fifth Circuit reversed DeVane and ordered a new "speedy" trial, and said that the judge had not given Hawkins a chance to introduce evidence.[69]

When this "speedy trial" occurred, the defendants sought to dismiss the case by discrediting Hawkins's eligibility.[70] Complications had developed with Hawkins's eligibility by 1958. Hawkins had taken a law school admission test in August 1956 and scored 200. Previously, applicants took the exam, which was established in November of 1948, but there was no requisite score for admission. However, in 1958 the Board of Control resolved to set a minimum score of 250.[71] Test scores are a legitimate way of regulating admission to law school, but this change in admissions standards for all applicants seemed like an additional tactic by the board to delay Hawkins's admission. As *Hawkins* historians Darryl Paulson and Paul Hawkes state in their *Florida State University Law Review* study of the case, Virgil Hawkins was deemed in 1950 to have "all the scholastic, moral and other qualifications, except as to race and color."[72]

Judge DeVane defined the issue for Hawkins. If Hawkins remained in the lawsuit, he would be allowing the state to litigate his qualifications, which would mean many more years of legal battles.[73] Hawkins decided to drop his part of the suit and instead just focus on admission for any qualified African American. The court ruled favorably for Hawkins on this part of the suit and restrained the Board of Control "from enforcing any policy, custom or usage of limiting admission to the *graduate* schools . . . of the University of Florida to white persons only."[74] This ruling was unusual because normally when the plaintiff fails in a class action suit, the rest of the suit is also dismissed. The attorneys for Hawkins and the state "conscientiously overlooked" this "serious legal difficulty."[75]

Even so, the decision was a step towards integration of Florida's graduate schools. It seemed to be a compromise for everyone, except for Hawkins. The deferred judgment on his case for so long left him without his desired justice. Judge DeVane had actually delayed his retirement when he took the *Hawkins* case, and Lawrence Dubin in a *Florida Law Review* article argues that perhaps DeVane wanted to "exercise a hidden agenda to ensure that Hawkins never would become a law student in a white Florida law school."[76]

Hawkins later explained to journalist and Florida chronicler Al Burt his ultimate decision not to go to UF. "I knew they were settin' for me, ready for me. I would have been the whipping boy. I didn't want to do that anymore."[77] His capitulation, though, allowed for the desegregation of the University of Florida College of Law. In September of 1958, George H. Starke, a black man from Orlando, registered as a law student at the University of Florida. Although the event made the news across Florida and the nation, no major disturbances occurred when UF actually undertook this integration process.[78] As Helen Jacobstein notes about the relative lack of violence in Florida, "Perhaps what did not happen in Florida was most significant of all."[79] Although Jacobstein has a valid point, this line of reasoning seems to ignore that something else did not happen in Florida: that after almost a decade of pursuing his federal and personal rights, Down South delays in the Sunshine State still prevented Virgil D. Hawkins from enrolling in the law school at the University of Florida.

Instead of attending law school, in 1961 at the age of fifty-four, Hawkins went to Boston and earned a degree in public relations. He later attended the New England School of Law to finally attain his dream. The disappointment in Hawkins's story continued when he returned to the Sunshine State and the Florida Bar rejected his application because the New England institution was not a nationally accredited law school. In 1977, the Florida Supreme Court, through special order, finally allowed Hawkins to be admitted to the Florida Bar.[80]

Hawkins was seventy years old in 1977 when he began his legal practice in Lake County.[81] According to the Associated Press, "Hawkins resigned from the Bar in 1985 after a complaint was filed against him alleging incompetence and misuse of client monies." After his resignation, Hawkins said, "When I get to heaven, I want to be a member of the Florida Bar." Hawkins was reinstated to the Bar posthumously, only eight months after his death on February 11, 1988. In 1999, the Florida Supreme Court apologized for the "hatred and discrimination" coming from the bench during the Hawkins cases.[82] The forty years it took for Florida to officially recognize Virgil Hawkins's sacrifice for the cause of civil rights reveal how distanced the legal system of Florida in the 1950s was from true New South ideals. Whatever the motivating factors, it is now obvious that Down South delay played a crucial role in denying integration of higher education in the "moderate" Sunshine State. Even though Florida did not manifest the high-profile violence and disruptions of other former Confederate states, the Hawkins case demonstrates a victory for Down South delay and the perseverance of an Old South mentality.

## NOTES

1. *Florida ex rel. Virgil D. Hawkins v. Board of Control*, 93 So. 2d 354 (March 8, 1957).

2. *A Lawyer Made in Heaven: The Virgil Hawkins Story*, VHS, dir. Forest Godsey, (1993; Birmingham, MI, Weil Productions); Robert W. Saunders Sr., *Bridging the Gap: Continuing the Florida Legacy of Harry T. Moore* (Tampa: The University of Tampa Press, 2000), 212; Al Burt, *The Tropic of Cracker* (Gainesville: University Press of Florida, 1999), 89; Algia R. Cooper, *"Brown v. Board of*

*Education* and Virgil Darnell Hawkins Twenty-Eight Years and Six Petitions to Justice," *Journal of Negro History* 64 (Winter 1979): 1–20; Samuel Selkow, "Hawkins, the United States Supreme Court and Justice," *Journal of Negro Education* 31 (Winter 1962): 97; see Tom R. Wagy, *Governor LeRoy Collins of Florida: Spokesman of the New South* (Tuscaloosa, Ala.: The University of Alabama Press, 1985), 66.

3. Harley Herman, "Anatomy of a Bar Resignation: The Virgil Hawkins Story: An Idealist Faces the Pragmatic Challenges of the Practice of Law," *Florida Coastal Law Journal* 2 (2000): 81.

4. "Out of State Scholarships Are Declined," *Daytona Beach Morning Journal*, May 14, 1949.

5. Robert B. Mautz (Assistant Dean, University of Florida) to David F. Cavers (Law School, Harvard University), July 15, 1955, Office of the President J. Wayne Reitz, Subject files 1953–1967, University of Florida Archives, Gainesville, Fla.; J.B. Culpepper to Fred Kent (Chairman of the Board of Control), September 12, 1955; Florida Constitution of 1885, Article XII, Section 12.

6. "5 Negroes Ask for Order Admitting them to U of F," *Daytona Beach Morning Journal*, May 26, 1949; "Out of State Scholarships are Declined," *Daytona Beach Morning Journal*, May 14, 1949; Constance Baker Motley, *Equal Justice Under Law: An Autobiography* (New York: Farrar, Straus, and Giroux, 1998), 112.

7. *Sipuel v. Board of Regents of University of Oklahoma*, 332 U.S. 631, No. 369 (January 12, 1948); *Sweatt v. Painter*, 339 U.S. 629, No. 44 (June 5, 1950); *McLaurin v. Oklahoma State Regents*, 339 U.S. 637 (June 5, 1950).

8. Martin A. Dyckman, *Floridian of His Century: The Courage of Governor LeRoy Collins* (Gainesville: University Press of Florida, 2006), 50; Darryl Paulson and Paul Hawkes, "Desegregating the University of Florida Law School: Virgil Hawkins v. The Florida Board of Control," *Florida State University Law Review* 12 (1984): 59–70.

9. *Sweatt v. Painter*, 339 U.S. 629, No. 44 (June 5, 1950); John R. Howard, *The Shifting Wind: The Supreme Court and Civil Rights from Reconstruction to Brown* (Albany: State University of New York Press, 1999), 293–96; *McLaurin v. Oklahoma State Regents*, 339 U.S. 637 (June 5, 1950).

10. "Florida Plan for Co-Racial Education Set," *Orlando Sentinel*, January 21, 1950; A Certified Copy of Excerpts Taken From the Official Minutes of a Meeting of the Board of Control, December 21, 1949, series 776, box 117, file folder 5, LeRoy Collins Papers, Florida State Archives, Tallahassee (hereafter Collins Papers); *Gaines v. Canada*, 305 U.S. 337, No. 57 (December 12, 1938).

11. "Court Rules on Negroes," *New York Times*, August 1, 1950; "Negroes Lose Suit to Enter Universities," *Orlando Sentinel*, August 2, 1950; *State ex rel. Hawkins v. Board of Control of Florida*, 47 So. 2d 608 (1950).

12. *State ex rel. Hawkins v. Board of Control of Florida*, 47 So. 2d 608 (1950).

13. "Florida White Colleges Plan to Admit Negroes," *New York Times*, January 21, 1950.

14. "Motion for Leave to File Supplemental Brief," in the Supreme Court of the State of Florida, Filed June 29, 1950.

15. "A Lunchtime Conversation with a Man Who Took 25 Years to Become a Lawyer," *Florida Flambeau*, February 17, 1983.

16. "The Shape of Things," *The Nation*, October 1951, 269.

17. "High Court Rejects Students' Petition," *Orlando Sentinel*, June 16, 1951; *State of Florida, ex rel. Hawkins v. Board of Control of Florida*, 342 U.S. 877 (1951); Darryl Paulson and Paul Hawkes, "State Obstruction to Desegregation in Higher Education: *Virgil Hawkins v. the Florida Board of Control*," *Florida State University Law Review* 12 (Spring 1984): 59.

18. *State ex rel. Hawkins v. Board of Control of Florida*, 60 So. 2d 162 (1952); Jean L. Preer, *Lawyers v. Educators: Black Colleges and Desegregation in Public Higher Education* (Westport, Conn.: Greenwood Press, 1982), 139.

19. *Brown v. Board of Education*, 347 U.S. 483 (1954); *State of Florida ex rel. Hawkins v. Board of Control of Florida*, 347 U.S. 971 (1954); Theodore Hemmingway, "The Rise of Black Student Consciousness in Tallahassee and the State of Florida," in David H. Jackson Jr. and Canter Brown Jr., *Go Sound the Trumpet!: Selections in Florida's African American History* (Tampa, Fla.: University of Tampa Press, 2005), 261; Cooper, "*Brown v. Board of Education*," 1–20.

20. "Segregation Case Handed to Court," *Ft. Myers News-Press*, January 19, 1955; Brief of Respondents, in the Supreme Court of Florida, Filed June 18, 1956, S 776 box 117, FF5, Collins Papers.

21. Motley, *Equal Justice Under Law*, 113.

22. *State ex rel. Virgil D. Hawkins v. Board of Control*, 83 So. 2d 20 (1955); *Brown v. Board of Education*, 349 U.S. 294 (1955).

23. "Amended Answer of Respondents," in the Supreme Court of the State of Florida, Filed 1954, Florida State Archives (hereafter FSA), Tallahassee, Florida.

24. *State ex rel. Virgil D. Hawkins v. Board of Control*, 83 So. 2d 20 (1955); "Terrell Says Mix Mandate Reverses God," *Orlando Sentinel*, October 20, 1955.

25. *State ex rel. Virgil D. Hawkins v. Board of Control*, 83 So. 2d 20 (1955).

26. Glenda Alice Rabby, *The Pain and the Promise* (Athens, Ga.: University of Georgia Press, 1999), 210; Preer, *Lawyers v. Educators*, 128.

27. "Brief of Respondents on Amend Petition for Alternative Writ," in the Supreme Court of the State of Florida, FSA, from the Harley Herman collection, 9; *Board of Public Instruction v. State*, 75 So. 2d 832, 837 (1954).

28. "Segregation Held Against Constitution," *Orlando Sentinel*, October 20, 1955.

29. Rabby, *The Pain and the Promise*, 210–11.

30. "Faculty Group Delays Action on Integration," *Florida Star Jacksonville*, December 17, 1955; "Collins Discourages Segregation Proposal," *Daytona Beach Morning Journal*, March 15, 1956.

31. "Petition for Writ of Certiorari and, in the Alternative, Motion for Leave to File and Petition for Writ of Common Law Certiorari and/or Writ of Mandamus to the Supreme Court of the State of Florida," in the Supreme Court of the United States, October term 1955, FSA, from the Harley Herman collection, 10–11; "Along the N.A.A.C.P. Battlefront," *The Crisis* (March 1956): 167.

32. *Hawkins v. Board of Control*, 350 U.S. 413 (1956); Preer, *Lawyers v. Educators*, 139–40; "Along the N.A.A.C.P. Battlefront," 165.

33. "Court Bars Delay in Granting Negro Law School Seat," *New York Times*, March 13, 1956;

"1956 Events Put State in National Spotlight," *Palm Beach Post*, December 30, 1956.

34. "Hawkins Plans Entry in Fall, Doesn't Anticipate 'Trouble,'" *Orlando Sentinel*, March 13, 1956; *A Lawyer Made in Heaven*, VHS; "Court Bars Delay in Granting Negro Law School Seat," *New York Times*, March 13, 1956; "1956 Events Put State in National Spotlight," *Palm Beach Post*, December 30, 1956.

35. "Florida to Argue 'Fear' in Mix Case," *Ocala Star Banner*, September 4, 1956; "Court Told it Can Delay U of F Mixing," *Orlando Sentinel*, September 5, 1956; "Brief of the Respondents," in the Supreme Court of Florida, Filed 1956, series 776, box 117, file folder 5, Collins Papers, 9–14, 14–17, 23–24.

36. "Brief of the Respondents," in the Supreme Court of Florida, Filed 1956, series 776, box 117, file folder 5, Collins Papers, 9–14, 14–17, 23–24.

37. *Florida ex rel. Virgil D. Hawkins v. Board of Control*, 93 So. 2d 354 (March 8, 1957); "Court Rules Negro Can't Enter U of F," *Orlando Sentinel*, March 9, 1957.

38. *Florida ex rel. Virgil D. Hawkins v. Board of Control*, 93 So. 2d 354 (1957); "Integration and Public Mischief," *Orlando Sentinel*, March 12, 1957.

39. *Florida ex rel. Virgil D. Hawkins v. Board of Control*, 93 So. 2d 354 (1957).

40. Sterling R. Booth to Honorable President of the University of Florida, December 30, 1955, Office of the President J. Wayne Reitz, Subject files 1953–1967, University of Florida Archives.

41. "Race Relations 1954–1960: Excerpts from Report of Saul A. Silverman, Staff Assistant to the Fowler Commission on Race Relations," in *Florida Across the Threshold: The Administration of Governor LeRoy Collins* (Tallahassee: no publisher, 1961), 54; Wagy, *Governor LeRoy Collins*, 61; "Collins Discourages Segregation Proposal," *Daytona Beach Morning Journal*, March 15, 1956; "Collins Won't Hesitate to Call Special Session," *Daytona Beach Morning Journal*, March 13, 1956; "Full text of Collins' Speech: Firm, Calm Position Urged for Segregation," *Orlando Sentinel*, March 13, 1956; Dyckman, *Floridian of His Century*, 101–26, quoted on 103.

42. Wagy, *Governor LeRoy Collins*, 59–61; *A Lawyer Made in Heaven*, VHS; Dyckman, *Floridian of His Century*, 167–81.

43. Helen L. Jacobstein, *The Segregation Factor in the Florida Gubernatorial Primary of 1956* (Gainesville: University of Florida Press, 1972), 5–6.

44. H.D. Price, *The Negro and Southern Politics* (New York: New York University Press, 1957), 59–60, 63; Wagy, *Governor LeRoy Collins*, 69–70.

45. *Florida ex rel. Virgil D. Hawkins v. Board of Control*, 93 So. 2d 354 (1957).

46. "Integration and Public Mischief," *Orlando Sentinel*, March 12, 1957.

47. Quoted in Jacobstein, *The Segregation Factor in Florida*, 8–9.

48. Rabby, *The Pain and the Promise*, 211.

49. State of Florida, Board of Control for State Institutions of Higher Learning, "Study on Desegregation, Part I" (Tallahassee, 1956), 4–5, 13; "Integration and Public Mischief," *Orlando Sentinel*, March 12, 1957.

50. *Florida ex rel. Virgil D. Hawkins v. Board of Control*, 93 So. 2d 354 (March 8, 1957).

51. *Jacksonville Chronicle*, October 28, 1955.

52. "Students Burn Cross Before Law Library," *Orlando Sentinel*, March 13, 1956; Jacobstein, *The Segregation Factor in Florida*, 8–9.

53. "Students Burn Cross Before Law Library," *Orlando Sentinel*, March 13, 1956; "Court Bars Delay in Granting Negro Law School Seat," *New York Times*, March 13, 1956; President Reitz, letter, Office of the President J. Wayne Reitz, Subject files 1953–1967, University of Florida Archives.

54. Rabby, *The Pain and the Promise*, 212.

55. Vogt, "A Lunchtime Conversation"; Jacobstein, *The Segregation Factor in Florida*, 77.

56. "FBI Joins in Hunt for Killers," *Orlando Morning Sentinel*, December 27, 1951; Jeff Truesdell, "Race Against Time," *Orlando Weekly*, April 7, 1999.

57. Earl Black, *Southern Governors and Civil Rights* (Cambridge, Mass.: Harvard University Press, 1976), 90.

58. "Report on the South: The Integration Issue: Florida," *New York Times*, March 13, 1956.

59. Numan V. Bartley, *The New South, 1945–1980: The Story of the South's Modernization* (Baton Rouge: Louisiana State University Press and the Littlefield Fund for Southern History of the University of Texas, 1995), 213; Wagy, *Governor LeRoy Collins*, 59–60.

60. Jacobstein, *The Segregation Factor in Florida*, 8.

61. Black, *Southern Governors and Civil Rights*, 90–91, 92, figure 8.

62. Jacobstein, *The Segregation Factor in the Florida*, 74.

63. Rabby, *The Pain and the Promise*, 214, 217; Wagy, *Governor LeRoy Collins*, 72–73; Jacobstein, *The Segregation Factor in Florida*, illustration 3.

64. Jacobstein, *The Segregation Factor in Florida*, 11–13.

65. Price, *The Negro and Southern Politics*, 96; Jacobstein, *The Segregation Factor in Florida*, 8, 71, 77.

66. Motley, *Equal Justice Under Law*, 116; Rabby, *The Pain and the Promise*, 213.

67. Stephen L. Wasby, Anthony A. D'Amato, and Rosemary Metrailer, *Desegregation from Brown to Alexander: An Exploration of Supreme Court Strategies* (Carbondale, Ill.: Southern Illinois University Press, 1977), 162.

68. Raymond Tatalovich and Byron Daynes, ed., *Moral Controversies in American Politics: Cases in Social Regulatory Policy* (Armonk, New York: M.E. Sharpe, 1998), 45.

69. *Florida ex rel. Hawkins v. Board of Control*, 253 F. 2d 752 (April 9, 1958); *Florida ex rel. Hawkins v. Board of Control*, 162 F. Supp 851 (June 18, 1958).

70. *Florida ex rel. Hawkins v. Board of Control*, 162 F. Supp 851 (June 18, 1958).

71. Rabby, *The Pain and the Promise*, 213; Board of Control Resolution, June 2, 1958, Office of the President J. Wayne Reitz, Subject files 1953–1967, University of Florida Archives; President Reitz to James Love, May 29, 1958, Office of the President J. Wayne Reitz, Subject files 1953–1967, University of Florida Archives.

72. Paulson and Hawkes, "State Obstruction to Desegregation in Higher Education," 59.

73. *A Lawyer Made in Heaven, VHS*.

74. *Florida ex rel. Hawkins v. Board of Control*, 162 F. Supp 851 (June 18, 1958).

75. Motley, *Equal Justice Under Law*, 117.

76. Lawrence A. Dubin, "Essay: Virgil Hawkins: A One-Man Civil Rights Movement," *Florida Law Review* 51 (December 1999): 913, 946; see Harley S. Herman, "A Tribute to an Invincible Civil Rights Pioneer (Part II)," *The Crisis*, August/September 1994, 22.

77. Quoted in Burt, *The Tropic of Cracker*, 89.

78. "First Negro is Admitted to University of Florida," *New York Times*, September 16, 1958; Dubin, "Virgil Hawkins: A One-Man Civil Rights Movement," 913, 942; Samuel Selkow, "Hawkins, the United States Supreme Court and Justice," *Journal of Negro Education* 31 (Winter 1962): 101.

79. Jacobstein, *The Segregation Factor in the Florida*, 77.

80. *A Lawyer Made in Heaven, VHS*; Associated Press State and Local Wire, "High Court Honors Man Who Led Battle for Integrated Law School," May 26, 1999, www.lexisnexis.com (accessed October 31, 2006); see Burt, *The Tropic of Cracker*, 88–90.

81. Lawrence A. Dubin, "Virgil Hawkins: A One-Man Civil Rights Movement"; Harley S. Herman, "A Tribute to an Invincible Civil Rights Pioneer (Part II)," 23.

82. Associated Press State and Local Wire, "High Court Honors Man Who Led Battle for Integrated Law School," May 26, 1999; Herman, "Anatomy of a Bar Resignation: The Virgil Hawkins Story," 79; "An Apology for an Old Wrong," *Lakeland Ledger*, May 27, 1999.

# CHAPTER SEVEN

# "WAIT" HAS ALMOST ALWAYS MEANT "NEVER"

## THE LONG ROAD TO SCHOOL DESEGREGATION IN PALM BEACH COUNTY

### LISE M. STEINHAUER

"'Wait' has almost always meant 'Never,'" Dr. Martin Luther King Jr. lamented in 1963 while exhorting both black civil rights workers and white elected officials to reject repeated demands by southern segregationists to delay the enactment of federally mandated desegregation measures. To those who waited almost two decades for Palm Beach County, Florida, to comply with the U.S. Supreme Court's 1954 school desegregation order in *Brown v. Board of Education*, King's words had proved all too prophetic.[1]

Located in South Florida far from the influence of other former Confederate states with deep-seated Jim Crow traditions, Palm Beach County had never been rabidly "Old South" like much of the Panhandle, which bordered such extremist entities as Georgia and Alabama. The Palm Beach area's development, in fact, had been minimal until generations after the demise of the Confederacy. Although it had grown to 114,688 residents by 1950, Palm Beach County was not technically becoming "New South" as has been argued about the larger urban areas of Tampa and Miami, where economic growth was presumably taking precedence over white supremacist practices. Yet, like much of Florida, Palm Beach County was still "Down South," where it could take time to effect real change, and strong motivation would be needed for white school officials to comply with *Brown* any sooner than they deemed necessary.[2]

The message for many years spoke, after all, not of urgency but of defiance and delay—the conventional Down South strategy to place a brick wall in front of Court-mandated desegregation. *Brown* itself stated no timetable for implementation of public school desegregation. Florida officials, from the panhandle capital of Tallahassee, urged districts to resist while they searched for ways to avoid the Supreme Court's decree. Palm Beach County leaders would not find sufficient motivation to desegregate until much later, when local groups unified, and even more so, when the messages from *outside* the county and state foretold change. Evolution of an effective motivation for racial change took *time*, the very thing Florida asked for following the federal dictate of *Brown*. This state-sanctioned policy of delay must have, however, seemed like "never" to the black citizens of Palm Beach County.

Although Florida is geographically a southern state, as early as 1949, political scientist V. O. Key Jr. recognized that Florida was unusual, calling it "scarcely a part of the South" and "a world of its own." And just as Florida was not typical of the Deep South, South Florida was not typical of the rest of the Sunshine State. Much of the Florida population that grew from 269,493 in 1880 to 1,897,414 by 1940 had made its way increasingly further south on the peninsula, at first following Henry Flagler's railroad that, in 1893, reached the future Palm Beach. At that time, Palm Beach was essentially a clean slate, with little history of social behavior either to continue or to overcome. Despite segregation in Florida by custom or law, early pioneers often worked together to create a sense of community in this subtropical wilderness. Black or white, they depended on one another for survival. Until Palm Beach County was created in 1909, the settlements around Lake Worth were part of Dade County, as was most of the South Florida wilderness. In 1890, in all of Dade County, census-takers located 640 whites and 87 "Negroes"; by 1900, the count rose to 3,548 whites and 1,298 blacks.[3]

As more wealthy guests of Flagler's luxurious Palm Beach hotels became seasonal residents, the ratio as well as the socio-economic gulf widened between the races. Black workers first formed a rustic community in Palm Beach called the "Styx." When the land's owners decided to develop it, they moved the tenants across Lake Worth to establish a self-sufficient neighborhood in West Palm Beach. According to retired black judge Edward Rodgers, by the time he arrived in the 1950s, the affluence and mild climate contributed to a feeling that there was room for everybody—if color lines were honored. The abundance of undeveloped space likely helped as well. In 2006, Rodgers described the West Palm Beach he had moved to: "They really had a separate-but-equal doctrine. All the service stations, stores and things were all owned by black people [in certain areas], and they did not allow that philosophy to be abridged. . . . It was unique to that extent."[4]

The black slums characteristic of many other Florida cities never developed in West Palm Beach. Those blacks who were employed by wealthy Palm Beach whites often enjoyed hand-me-down clothes, extra food, and exposure to culture and travel, said Rodgers. In western Palm Beach County, black farm workers had a harder life but generally were better off than blacks in many other Florida communities. In the north end of the county, the Limestone Creek community was formed by blacks who had labored for and with the town of Jupiter's white pioneers. The City of Lake Worth, on the other hand, posted warning signs for blacks not to remain past sunset. Edward Rodgers recalled, "We studiously avoided being in Lake Worth after dark."[5]

At the county's south end, many early pioneers of Delray Beach were black. Although the town became known for what black educator C. Spencer Pompey called "a fine, accommodating relation between the races," segregation remained the norm. William McLaughlin, a white man who moved to Delray Beach in 1955, later made it clear that this situation had been neither his choice nor a difficulty: "My children had all types of friends up in Rhode Island. I mean, it was 'the school,' everybody went there . . . . Schools [in Delray Beach] were segregated, of course. . . . [T]he whole situation of segregation was foreign to us [but] it caused no problems in my family at all." McLaughlin's experience seems to support Key's 1949 observation that in Florida, "the whites of the newly settled areas do not seem to be governed by a Negrophobia to the same extent as the long settled agricultural areas of the Old South."[6]

Rodgers and McLaughlin joined Florida's rapid growth during the 1950s and 1960s, after which more than 64 percent of the state's residents had been born elsewhere. In the Palm Beach area, early white settlers came less often from other southern states than from the North and the Midwest, and more so from the Northeast as the decades passed. Without many southerners, the Old South mentality became less prevalent than in North Florida, where, influenced by nearby Alabama, Georgia, and South Carolina, hardliners remained wedded to states' rights to maintain their way of life.[7]

Although northerners may have been shocked by the openness of Florida's racism as they populated South Florida in greater numbers, they apparently adapted to the Jim Crow system rather than challenged it. Social historians Raymond A. Mohl and Gary R. Mormino concluded, "Jim Crow practices found easy acceptance even in Florida cities without Southern-born populations, such as . . . Palm Beach." Florida historian David R. Colburn described what U.S. Senator Bob Graham called the "Cincinnati Factor," whereby migrants to Florida remained so connected to their home states that they seldom engaged with Florida issues. At the most, said Colburn, they were focused on local issues rather than on the state's racial divide and civil rights struggles. This attitude contributed to a complex racial environment in areas like Palm Beach County that was somewhat difficult to define.[8]

Even though poor and working-class blacks were not generally outspoken about unequal treatment until the civil rights era, a determination to effect change formed much earlier in two African American youths who would have an impact in Palm Beach County: William Holland of Orange County and Isaiah Courtney Smith of Volusia County. Smith later recalled of his 1930s youth: "The County furnished a little raggedy school bus to pick [the white kids] up and we had to walk. . . . [A]ll of the books came from white schools. . . . You learn to live with it. But you keep it in the back of your head, so when the time comes and I have the opportunity to do something about it—things should be changed." Smith found that "opportunity" in Palm Beach County, where he and William Holland became allies.[9]

In 1941, Smith and Holland met on a train, both bound for all-black Florida A&M College in Tallahassee. Smith later said, "We talked about things, and we felt something should be done . . . So we decided that we'd go to law school." Holland went to Boston University Law School and, after World War II, opened the first black law practice in West Palm Beach in 1951. Another black attorney, F. Malcolm Cunningham, opened an office across the street. After graduating from Brooklyn Law College, Smith joined Holland in August of 1954; he recalled a half-century later, "Holland and I . . . still talked about what should be done about the schools."[10]

Just three months before Smith arrived in West Palm Beach, the U.S. Supreme Court had reversed the 58-year-old *Plessy v. Ferguson* ruling on public education with *Brown v. Board of Education*. The new chief justice, Earl Warren, crafted the twelve-page decision, arguing in part: "Any language in *Plessy v. Ferguson* contrary to this finding is rejected and we conclude that in the field of education, the doctrine of 'separate but equal' has no place. Separate educational facilities are inherently unequal."[11]

A ruling with such far-reaching consequences, on what for many was a deeply emotional issue, was certain to affect Florida's Old South ways. Historian Joseph Tomberlin concluded, "Nearly every journal in Florida commented on the [*Brown*] matter, and generally, editorial remarks reflected restraint and reason." The *Palm Beach Post*, however, carried no editorial comment or story of local reaction—only stories from Atlanta, Tallahassee, and Washington, D.C.—even though Acting Governor Charley E. Johns was in West Palm Beach when *Brown* was announced. Johns suggested a special session of the legislature was in order and asked Attorney General Richard Ervin to execute an "exhaustive study" of the ruling.[12]

Ervin predicted a considerable delay before Florida would actually need to desegregate. He assured the public that, "It may be . . . years," and that the state would play a part in setting the conditions and timing: "This our state will do." Florida's U.S. senators echoed

Ervin's lack of concern about imminent change. Spessard Holland spoke of "patience and moderation," while George Smathers expressed "hope in that the effective date was left open." Increasing their optimism for continuation of Jim Crow in the state was the Court's request for input as to how the ruling might be implemented.[13]

Palm Beach County residents saw no sign that local officials had anticipated or even heard the decision. Maintaining their traditional ways, school officials proceeded with planned segregation. Only a month before the Supreme Court announcement, the Board of Public Instruction (later renamed the Palm Beach County School Board) had appropriated funds for a new all-white school in Riviera Beach, which they proceeded to build. According to black educator Carleton Bryant, blacks quickly concluded that the county did not intend to abide by *Brown*. The racial climate had not sufficiently changed in 1954 for blacks to do anything but "wait."[14]

Just prior to the *Brown* case, from 1945 to 1953, Florida had funded all-black schools as a way to avoid desegregation. Just after the *Brown* announcement, State Superintendent of Public Instruction Thomas D. Bailey told the *St. Augustine Record*, "My presumption is that Negroes attending a good school are going to prefer to remain there." Palm Beach County's all-black schools did have high standards, and the black community had equally high pride in those segregated schools. Yvonne Lee Odom, the first black student to attend Seacrest High in Delray Beach in 1961, recalled her earlier days at all-black Carver High: "Black teachers knew the obstacles that we had to face, that we could not just be equal to a candidate, we had to be much better. . . . And what I learned when I went over [to Seacrest] was dang, I know a lot more than these kids. 'Cause we were told that all white kids were smarter than we were, that white kids did everything right."[15]

The memories of H. Ruth Pompey, a retired black teacher, showed that the message had not changed since she attended Delray's schools thirty years earlier: "They used to say to us a lot, you've got to be better prepared to get a job than the white child has, because their parents own the jobs. . . . [W]e had to be better than that in order to be as good." Mary Reddick Fleming, Shirley Rivers Farr, and Norman Walker recalled a similar situation at Roosevelt High School, from which they graduated in 1960. Walker said that academics were always a priority at Roosevelt, but attitude—respect, discipline, and self-esteem—was important, too. "We had teachers who believed in us and taught us to believe in ourselves."[16]

Black parents also preached to their children that education was the path out of oppression, as Pompey noted: "You just get yourself a good education and you won't have to do this, that or the other, or you won't have to be segregated." In the 1930s and 1940s in Delray Beach, Alfred Straghn's siblings worked in the rural fields, but Straghn said his grandfather told him, "'You'll fill the church house, the schoolhouse, or the jailhouse. Now you choose.' So that was his way of tellin' me, 'You're goin' to school.'"[17]

School, church, home, and the struggle for dignity were closely related in local black communities like those of Palm Beach County, partly because segregation forced blacks to look inward for sustenance and support in a white-controlled world. School plays, concerts, sporting events, and similar activities were often the center of the community's social life and brought teachers and families together. Pompey explained, "Your parent either belonged to one of those churches that the teachers attended or they would see them at the grocery store.... [As a teacher] kids in my class, I knew them, all of their parents."[18]

Ruth Pompey's husband, the late teacher C. Spencer Pompey, once called all-black Roosevelt High School in West Palm Beach one of the best high schools in Florida. The late U. B. Kinsey, who had been a student, teacher, and principal in Palm Beach County's black schools, agreed: "The black schools were absolutely better." The difference was not that the teachers were more qualified academically, but that they cared enough to help their students, whose families they knew, move up in society. Ruth Pompey added, "They, too, had come through poorly equipped schools, and most of them had an A.A. [degree], and they were going to summer school for most of their B.A.s."[19]

Black schools may have delivered a high-quality education, but they did it with a handicap. Inferior facilities, equipment, and materials were standard in black schools, as Alfred Straghn recalled: "The books that was in the white schools was handed down, and some of them was raggedy, but they enforced us to please take care of the books." The situation had not changed when attorney William Holland came to West Palm Beach in 1952: "Even the textbooks for white and 'Negro' students were kept in different warehouses . . . 'Separate but equal' was unconstitutional, but the ruling had been mostly ignored in Palm Beach County. All of our supplies were handed down from white schools. Our books were out of date with pages missing. The blackboards were so old, they had holes in them."[20]

Most black residents believed that mixed-race schools were their only chance for the same quality of education and supplies (e.g., current books and lab equipment) as white children, although the relief or enthusiasm instilled by *Brown* was often coupled with anxiety. Optimism increased in 1955 when the Supreme Court addressed the inequalities between black and white schools in what became known as *Brown II*: "The Courts may consider problems related to administration, arising from the physical condition of the school plan, the school transportation system, personnel." According to C. Spencer Pompey, Palm Beach County instituted a ten-year building program "that all but equalized the facilities in black schools" and caused many blacks to become less interested in integrated schools. The goal, after all, was not access to white classrooms, but to their level of funding and quality support materials.[21]

*Brown II* resulted in part from the Supreme Court's request for input regarding a time frame for implementation of school desegregation. Florida Attorney General Ervin was the first to file an *amicus curiae* (friend of the court) brief, on October 1, 1954. Richard Kluger, a scholar of *Brown*, called Florida's brief "the most extensive and spirited," while C. Spencer Pompey of Palm Beach County said it was "by far the most chilling at the out-start but perhaps the best for its long-run effect." In the brief, Ervin asked the Court to consider that the psychological and sociological damage that had been recognized in blacks due to segregation would affect the white population as well, unless a slow (i.e., Down South) transition was allowed. Most significantly, as reported in the *New York Times*, Ervin asked for flexibility: "If [desegregation] must come eventually, it should come only after a reasonable period of time, and then only on a county to county or local basis, pursuant to administrative determinations made by local school authorities."[22]

A month later, the Florida Supreme Court echoed Ervin, insisting that segregation could end only with a "gradual adjustment," and called *Brown* "a great mistake." When the U.S. Supreme Court met on April 11, 1955, the central question was: Should the Court permit "an effective gradual adjustment"? The decision, announced on May 30, 1955, stated, in part, that: "The Courts will require the defendants to make a reasonable and prompt start toward full compliance with the 1954 ruling. [Then] the Courts may find that additional time is necessary."[23]

By omitting a timetable, the Federal Court appeared to accept Florida's argument that time and flexibility were essential to an unprecedented transition to integration. The timetable omission sent a message to school districts across the United States, including Palm Beach County: there was no need to rush into dismantling the system they had lived under since 1885. Traditionalists in the Florida Senate had also heard the decision, and promptly passed Resolution 1432, praising Ervin and Superintendent Bailey for helping the Supreme Court to reach "a more realistic decree of desegregation in the public schools of the nation." According to the *New York Times,* Florida representatives Prentice Pruitt and Farris Bryant said *Brown II* "appeared to mean segregated schools could be maintained for . . . years." The *Times* article continued, "Gov. LeRoy Collins said the decision, by taking into account local conditions, would give Florida extra time to work out the problem."[24]

Although Collins was committed to segregation, he was more committed to a growing economy. With strong support from South Florida, he and his political allies held off the militant segment of the state government that could ruin the state's image. According to David Colburn and Lance deHaven-Smith in *Florida's Megatrends: Critical Issues in Florida*, "Few among recent arrivals had a personal or economic commitment to segregated schools and a segregated society." The election of Collins, said C. Spencer Pompey, had been an encouragement to some in Palm Beach County that "Florida had, indeed, left the 'old Confederacy.'" Collins advised whites not to fight the Supreme Court, encouraged voluntary integration, and said "racial progress, under the law, was necessary." But such talk created only an illusion of progress for blacks. Collins left office in 1961 with only one Florida school "desegregated"—by a mere four black students in Dade County.[25]

Looking beyond Florida during the mid-1950s, Palm Beach County residents would have seen other southerners putting off desegregation successfully enough to expect an interminable delay in enforcement of *Brown*. The Supreme Court turned over implementation to the South's district judges, whom Court scholar Richard Kluger called "a blend of Old South aristocrats and New South urbanites . . . about the best of the white South." Kluger theorized that Washington's judges believed all they could do was to decree that segregation was unconstitutional and let the white South free its black citizens at its own pace.[26]

The nation watched and reported on steps taken—and not taken—toward integration of southern schools. The *New York Times* commented in February 1956: "So far in Florida there has been no move. . . . And surprisingly, there has been little public talk about the matter and no agitation on the part of Negro parents to force the issue." Such articles both captured and reinforced the inaction by school officials in Palm Beach County. But in May 1956, two black attorneys decided the time was right to force the issue into the public arena. Holland and Smith had not forgotten why they became lawyers.[27]

By 1960, 33 percent of school-age children would be non-white in the metropolitan West Palm Beach area. Several local black organizations worked toward desegregation—some were even formed with that express mission. William Holland was education director of the Vanguard Club, started by a group of West Palm Beach black businessmen to challenge discriminatory practices. Although Holland wanted to test *Brown*, the club maintained a cautious attitude. This hesitancy and the lack of a family to volunteer as a test case held Holland off until 1956. He said later, "I could not get one single black parent at that time to use their children." Many leaders in the black community were also educators, and they were unsure where they would fit in integrated schools and wary of angering their white superiors. I. C. Smith later said he and Holland had understood that: "I'm quite certain . . . all of them had our sense, but what do you do? You have to keep your mouth closed and go along and do what you have to do . . . Holland said, 'Billy is ready to go to school now, we will use him.'" Both blacks and whites questioned Holland's motives in giving this role to his son, but as no one else came forward, the fact that William Holland Jr. reached school age in 1956 allowed Holland and Smith to begin pushing the school district to comply with *Brown*.[28]

Holland and Smith knew that the school board was not prepared for black resistance to segregation; thus, they pushed officials into a test case. In 1957, when the County denied William Jr. ("Billy") entrance to Northboro Elementary a second time, Holland and Smith filed a class-action suit. The Court's 1958 ruling stated, in part: "The primary responsibility rests on the County Board of Public Instruction to make 'a prompt and reasonable start,' and then proceed to 'a good faith compliance at the earliest practicable date' with the Constitution."[29]

Like other southern states, Florida had adopted a "pupil placement law" to allow assignment of students to schools using non-racial criteria, such as available facilities, ability of a student to grasp a school's curriculum, and psychological profiles. Generally, parents could request a transfer if an assignment did not suit them. By 1961, such laws had been retracted in Tennessee and Virginia, and blacks in West Palm Beach and Riviera Beach challenged Palm Beach County's version. Billy Holland remained in all-black schools until 1963, when a court ruling allowed the eighth grader to transfer to Central Junior High School, where he was one of six black students. Holland and Smith continued to pursue equal education in the Courts for all citizens until 1973, when Palm Beach County schools were officially, and finally, considered integrated by the U.S. Fifth Circuit Court.[30]

After Holland's death in 2002, Dr. Joseph Orr, the first president of the biracial Palm Beach County Classroom Teachers Association, recalled that "Bill was the most dedicated of all of us and he took the most flak because he got the most exposure. He's one of my heroes." Over many years, Holland's "flak" included death threats and attacks on his home with bottles and explosives. In later years, as he told the *Palm Beach Post*, "There were times I felt very lonely . . . We put a lot of pain and bloodshed into those early battles." Smith said he encountered no such problems because he had referred reporters to Holland as the client and kept his own name out of the press: "I knew Holland would lay it on them . . . how he felt about it."[31]

A probable beneficiary of the ongoing *Holland* case was Yvonne Lee, who became one of the first black students to integrate a Palm Beach County school. She was born in 1946 in Daytona Beach, Florida, where she enjoyed theaters, beauty salons, and other facilities for blacks, into a family that she described as focused on education instead of race: "My father . . . graduated from Bethune-Cookman College in 1948. My grandfather graduated from Florida Memorial College. . . . My only experience with whites was if you went downtown to Daytona. I think my father shielded us from a lot of it." When Lee's family came to Palm Beach County in 1959, five years after *Brown*, no progress had been made toward integrated schools. Lacking incentive to do otherwise, members of Palm Beach County's all-white school board had maintained the status quo in their customary way.[32]

Palm Beach County officials found their first incentive to change in 1961, when they were forced to take a tentative step forward in testing the tolerance of the community. A Federal Court order, resulting from William Holland's lawsuit, required that second-ary students be permitted to attend the schools nearest their homes if they so requested. To comply, Palm Beach County offered the Freedom-of-Choice Plan, which allowed high school students to apply to any school with available space within their geographic attendance area. In 1961, eighty-seven black students applied for transfer to white high schools. Four were approved.[33]

This token effort became unforgettable to those involved. Until this time, black high school students who lived between the southern county line and Lake Worth were bussed to all-black Carver High School in Boynton Beach in preparation for industry or vocations but not for college. Lee was one of the teens targeted for an all-white school: "I learned later, there was a movement to try to integrate the school system here. And they wanted to draft kids they thought would be successful." The committee that was seeking such students included Lee's father, the Rev. Randolph Lee. Both races wanted to minimize problems by choosing students carefully, but Rev. Lee later admitted to another motive: "We were trying to get the top kids so they could not say we were dumb." Although only four black students attended white schools in 1961, School District administrators rejected many other applications, and still others withdrew on their own.[34]

When those first four students were asked on the fiftieth anniversary of *Brown* in 2004 to recall their first days in white schools, Iris Hunter Etheredge was the only one to mention the threat of violence. She recounted how an elderly white woman threatened her with a shotgun near Jupiter High School before police removed the woman: "She said, 'If that little nigger bitch goes into the school, I'm going to shoot her' . . . [A teacher] said she wasn't accustomed to having 'nigras' any place but [working in] her home, and I'd do well to remember my place . . . I cried. . . . The girl I was sitting behind passed me a tis-sue. . . . The name-calling died down, but it never stopped."[35]

Theresa Jakes Kanu and Johnnie Green were chosen to attend Lake Worth High. Kanu remembered in 2004 her mother's reasons to apply to the white school: "I'd be closer to home and it would be a chance for me to impact what happened with other students." Even in retrospect, Kanu felt it had been challenging: "Every word that came from my mouth, I thought about it. The magnitude of it all hit me as I became older. When I think about it, I probably should have been afraid." Instead of fear, the teen felt isolation, both from most of her white classmates and from some of the black students still at Carver High School, who felt she had deserted them.[36]

Lee, perhaps the most outgoing of the four, remembered her determination: "I was going to get an education. . . . Yes, I had incidents of name-calling, but the adults were able to minimize it . . . I was not going to avoid any situation. . . . They asked me to use the faculty restrooms and I told them, 'No, I'll use the restrooms everybody else uses.'" In 2004, Kerry Koen recalled the preparation for Lee's arrival at Seacrest High, where he was a senior: "Principal Fulton came into the student council homeroom and . . . made it clear we were to act as leaders in that time of transition." Most white students did not seem to have a problem with the presence of black classmates in 1961; there were few of them and they had been carefully chosen for success. Lee was impressed by Principal Fulton: "Children know when you're fair and sincere." In May 1964, he was elected superintendent of schools, a change that would prove to be important to Palm Beach County's civil rights future.[37]

The climate beyond Palm Beach County also changed in the mid-1960s, starting with President Lyndon Johnson's signing of the Civil Rights Act of 1964. Title VI of the Act prohibited racial discrimination in federally assisted programs and would prove to be a powerful weapon of educational and racial progress in the Sunshine State. Meanwhile, the Fifth Circuit Court in New Orleans, assigned by the U.S. Supreme Court to enforce *Brown* in Florida, responded to the lack of compliance with an order that desegregation begin by 1964 and be complete by 1967. Although it seemed they would have no choice but to integrate at last, the board had not exhausted its stonewalling tactics.[38]

The two governors who led Florida through the period of heightened federal oversight tried, as Collins had, to avoid racial eruptions in favor of economic growth. Farris Bryant (1961–65) and Haydon Burns (1965–67) preferred to maintain segregation but they, like LeRoy Collins, also preferred to bring new business and profits into Florida. At the same time, two factors caused north Florida politicos to lose their influence over race relations in the Sunshine State, according to Colburn and deHaven-Smith. First, with the Civil Rights Act of 1964 and the Voting Rights Act of 1965, the state lost most of the local control to keep blacks "in their place"; despite pockets of white resistance, Jim Crow was now legally dead, in many cases a direct casualty of Federal Court mandates and actions. Second, fast-growing Central and South Florida, where racism had always been the least intense due to "Yankee" influences, grew more powerful.[39]

The national progress and these statewide changes prepared a path in Palm Beach County for now-Superintendent Fulton to effect change. He began the process in 1965 by recommending that the two organizations representing black and white teachers merge.

Although it took two years to create the new Palm Beach County Classroom Teachers Association, the interim period's unified leadership was a catalyst for calm. The teachers jointly supported Fulton's Three-Year Plan for desegregation, which provided for a gradual transition, while the county established standards to protect black educators during the process. Fulton brought desegregation into the public arena by announcing his plan at a press conference: "We are not all made alike," Fulton said. "However . . . our way of life does seek to offer all Americans equal opportunities under the law." Fulton's commitment was welcomed by black parents who sought the best preparation for their children under the new federal mandates.[40]

As required by the Civil Rights Act, Palm Beach County filed reports with the U.S. Office of Civil Rights in Atlanta. In 1965, although they reported only 137 of the county's 15,000–plus minority students attending predominantly white schools, they earned an "integrated" status for eleven of the county's 102 schools. According to the federal government's *Survey of School Desegregation in the Southern and Border States, 1965–1966*, Palm Beach County was not alone in its failure to enact total school integration: "While many previously segregated school districts adopted a policy of desegregation for the first time during the school year 1965–66, the number of Negro children in the deep South who are actually attending school with whites, is still very low." Even so, Palm Beach County's compliance plan was one of the first twelve approved in the South.[41]

By March 1966, U.S. Commissioner of Education Harold Howe II became impatient with the slow progress of southern and border states in achieving desegregation. Howe found an effective weapon to accelerate the process in Title VI of the Civil Rights Act, as noncompliance would cost schools their federal funding. Although most districts had filed plans as required, many, including Florida's, had not been enacted. Commissioner Howe made three issues clear: (1) that he required schools to pledge to begin desegregation in 1965 and complete it by fall of 1967, and to make progress toward faculty desegregation; (2) that he would only accept the Freedom-of-Choice plan—which was being used in Palm Beach County and elsewhere to sidestep the intent of *Brown*—if it resulted in significant progress; and (3) that he would order the closing of "inadequate schools maintained for Negroes." Howe expressed his frustration: "Somehow we seem to have been lulled into a blind faith in gradualism, a mindless confidence that some morning, some year, a suddenly transformed electorate will spontaneously and joyously decide that this is the day to integrate America. Well, it's not going to happen."[42]

Although the Palm Beach County School District had pledged compliance to the federal government, by 1967 only Jupiter High School had achieved full desegregation; about one third, or 1,884 of 6,322 black secondary students in the county, were attending predominantly white schools under Freedom-of-Choice options while all of its black schools remained open. Since the first four students integrated its high schools in 1961, Palm Beach County had progressed little. In December 1968, the district was called before the U.S. Department of Health, Education, and Welfare (HEW) in Atlanta.[43]

The hearing was attended by Robbie T. Littles of the United Front, an education watchdog group of representatives from Palm Beach County's black social, charitable, and religious organizations, and one of several active black organizations in Palm Beach County during the late 1960s. According to Littles, HEW's lead investigator stated, "There is nothing wrong with maintaining black high schools in Palm Beach County. I am only interested in having the board meet Title VI provisions and comply." Although the county had planned to close all black schools during the 1966–67 school year as required, it had not followed through. Now, it seemed, the federal government was sending mixed messages.[44]

Based on the HEW hearing, the United Front saw the closures as unnecessary and presented the school board with alternatives. When they were denied, the group organized two boycotts. For eight days in March and April of 1969, about 2,500 black students stayed home from school, until fear of being denied promotion or graduation ended their resistance. Another black group, the Imperial Men's Club of Riviera Beach, presented questions to the school board in June 1969 concerning school boundaries. Although the club was dissatisfied with the response, it had produced a new dialogue. In the face of this new action, the school board continued its "wait" strategy by announcing a Five-Year Plan for vocational preparation and individual attention in schools; yet the black community still complained of its marginal status in the field of educational reform and updating.[45]

The United Guidance Council (UGC), a biracial group composed of lay citizens, educators, ministers, and business people, then formed. They met in September 1969 with School Superintendent Lloyd Early, Deputy Superintendent Russell Below, and School Board Attorney Michael Jackson. The UGC maintained that the black community was doing most of the bending and that racism was rampant among faculty and administrators. Attorney Jackson explained that officials had tried to adopt boundary lines that would satisfy the Civil Rights Act of 1964's mandate to "maximize desegregation": "It's easier ordinarily to assimilate the minority group into the majority, and that presents a problem because of the loss of identity of the black people . . . We have identified some of the reasons why we are unsuccessful . . . [like] too many damn reasons for [white] reassignments."[46]

United Guidance Council's black co-chair, John Cartwright, asserted that black students chose white schools to get a quality education: "He can get a quality education right there in his school if the man downtown would . . . stop . . . taking out our top blacks and putting them in white schools and giving us first-year teachers. Stop draining the blood out of our community." Below admitted, "We have taken the very best negro [sic] teachers . . . and transferred them to white schools, because the majority of the power structure demanded [it]. We are attempting now to change this."[47] As UGC's white co-chair Leo Schwack observed, this frank discussion of issues and attitudes was yet another step forward: "This is probably a new era in this community's lifetime. Could you look back at any time in the past when a group such as this could sit down with a so-called 'power structure,' air your thoughts . . . get responses . . . ? Everything we have gone through has not been in vain."[48]

This dialogue encouraged mutual understanding between the races, and progress toward desegregation soon materialized, including the appointment of two blacks to new positions. The School District ended its delay in phasing out all-black schools, and by the end of the 1969–70 school year, out of thirteen former all-black schools in Palm Beach County, only one remained above 90 percent black. In compliance with HEW's continuing directives, the School District converted its four all-black high schools to junior highs. Although principals remained employed, teachers were reassigned, many of them losing leadership and other senior positions.[49]

Positive changes made under Superintendent Fulton, however, left Palm Beach County educators better off than elsewhere in Florida. A 1970 study showed one thousand black teachers and fifty-seven black administrators had lost their jobs in Florida schools in the prior three years, while the student population had increased by one hundred thousand— none of these losses occurred in Palm Beach County.[50] Black student leaders also lost their positions in changing schools. Although the UGC's Cartwright had said, "We want a school where our black students can go in and take some leadership," it would take time for black leaders to rise in predominantly white schools.[51]

At the 1969 UGC meeting, Deputy Superintendent Below described the inaction that had delayed desegregation: "Most plans have been developed to circumvent integration nationwide, and . . . I am one of the educators who hasn't had guts enough to stand up to the man on the street and say it has got to go this way for good education programs, but instead we stood aside and let HEW become God." As Below had suggested, instead of adopting voluntary measures to satisfy Court mandates, Palm Beach County took little initiative until forced to do so by the federal threat of lost funding. Palm Beach County's leaders were not alone in their exclusionary tactics, but their actions were possibly not as racially motivated as blacks may have believed, nor were they as defiant as many other school districts in the Sunshine State.[52] The county's history of relatively harmonious race relations, its historical cohesive and dignified black community, and its evolving "Yankee factor" in the 1960s may have accounted partly for this moderation, although the issue is a complex one and, therefore, defies facile characterization.

Finally, in 1969, the U.S. Supreme Court decisively rectified the three words in *Brown* that had permitted so many years of delay of school integration in locales like Palm Beach County: "all deliberate speed." It was not the Court's first attempt. When *Green v. New Kent County* (1968) had ordered states to dismantle their segregated systems "root and branch," Justice William Brennan wrote in a private note to Justice Earl Warren: "When this opinion is handed down, the traffic light will have changed from Brown to Green. Amen!"[53]

But *Green* was neither the first nor the final word to achieve implementation of *Brown*. In *Alexander v. Holmes County Board of Education* (1969), Justice Hugo Black traced earlier efforts: "In Brown II the Court declared that this unconstitutional denial of equal protection should be remedied, not immediately, but only 'with all deliberate speed.' Federal courts have ever since struggled with the phrase 'all deliberate speed'... and I am of the opinion that so long as that phrase is a relevant factor they will never be eliminated. 'All deliberate speed' has turned out to be only a soft euphemism for delay." Justice Black cited *Griffin v. County School Board* (1964), which had acknowledged the same deficiency in *Brown*: "The time for mere 'deliberate speed' has run out, and that phrase can no longer justify denying... children their constitutional rights." In 1968, the *Green* decision, citing *Griffin*, added: "The burden on a school today is to come forward with a plan that promises realistically to work, and promises realistically to work now." But *Alexander* also had a problem with *Green*'s verbiage: "There is language in that opinion which might be interpreted as approving a 'transition period.'" *Alexander* sought to stop the ongoing delays, demanding desegregated schools, "not only promptly but at once—now." The opinion stated, in part: "There is no longer the slightest excuse, reason, or justification for further postponement of the time when every public school system in the United States will be a unitary one, receiving and teaching students without discrimination."[54]

When the Court declared in 1969, "Enough," Palm Beach County was one of a number of school districts in the Sunshine State that could no longer employ Down South delay, regardless of its motivation or reaction of its citizenry. By this time, Palm Beach County—if not Florida, the South, and the nation—was realizing that the federal government would no longer tolerate non-compliance with school desegregation at the grassroots level. The message, though fifteen years after *Brown I*, resonated through Palm Beach County and the South at large that Down South-style delays were now moribund.

Although Palm Beach County did end its "wait" strategy and followed through with desegregation, few were celebrating in either the black or white communities. While many blacks had protested the years of delays, others were frustrated or angry over their loss of identity in predominantly white schools. White parents were also angry when their children were bussed to schools located in black neighborhoods. The relative calm that had prevailed in Palm Beach County since 1954 ended for a time as both races resisted the changes. There were sporadic incidents at the start of both the 1970 and 1971 school years, the latter including a boycott against bussing. Some white parents held rallies, chanting, "Hell no, mine won't go," or moved their children to private schools. While William Holland was in New Orleans attacking Palm Beach County's desegregation plan before the Appeals Court, a group of white parents incorporated and asked the U.S. District Court for permission to intervene in Holland's class-action suit as a plaintiff, claiming Holland did not "represent the class of people the intervenor [sic] represents." Not surprisingly, Judge Joseph Eaton denied the request.[55]

During the 1971–72 school year, Palm Beach Gardens High School, the largest school in Palm Beach County, received the most transfers of blacks (549 out of 2,063 students). In a spirit of cooperation, its principal, Edward M. Eissey, met with ministers, police, new students and their parents, and formed a biracial student committee. Eissey told reporters, "I had to learn what they thought the problems of both groups of young people would be, and learn I did. It takes time." Years later, Eissey shared his interpretation of those events:

> Neither the white nor the African-American community was ready to integrate. [The blacks] felt as though . . . [t]hey were losing their own identity. . . . I am sure that the [School Board] cared, but a lot of the people who were in politics knew that if they pushed integration . . . Afro-American people . . . [and] white people who didn't want to integrate would be opposed to them. . . . It was delayed and delayed and delayed by excuses and reasons that were not real.[56]

Despite Eissey's efforts, conflict in February 1972 earned heavy press coverage. One faculty member reportedly said, "You just cannot put us together if we've been apart for 100 years and expect racial harmony overnight." Black activist Carleton Bryant later wrote that local blacks called 1972, "The Year of Turmoil." Their black high schools were gone, their teachers and principals were relocated, and black students were bussed to formerly all-white schools. Community-based activities that had been part of their schools, such as sports, musical, and dramatic performances, were over.[57]

Many people felt the price demanded of blacks had been too great. Maxine D. Jones, a scholar of Florida's black heritage, wrote that while school desegregation erased "many of the apparent educational disparities," it also destroyed many of the black community's strengths. Black former principal U. B. Kinsey believed this to be true in Palm Beach

County. A year before his death, Kinsey told the *Palm Beach Post* that a sense of community had been destroyed in the name of racial equality, and that integration did as much harm as it did good: "Minority kids in Florida, or in Palm Beach County, or the United States, got the short end of the stick." An article in *American Educational Research Journal* in 2004 referenced the "frustration and despondency by black parents, who felt that the burden of desegregation was being placed disproportionately on black students," as the United Guidance Council had complained in 1969.[58]

The black community was still forced to deal with the specter of "never" in terms of equity in splitting that burden. Thus, while the Down South scenario of school integration in Palm Beach County evolved out of an aggressive and sustained struggle by the black community, that very community was forced to adapt to the enviro-sociological changes demanded of school integration. The beloved black community perhaps never came to full terms with the long, unfolding delays after *Brown*, but it did adapt realistically to the pain of losing its black schools and authority figures, although that process took time.

On July 9, 1973, U.S. District Court Judge Joseph Eaton issued the final ruling in the *Holland* case. He declared Palm Beach County School District to be officially integrated, although the Office for Civil Rights continued to monitor the county's schools until 1999, when it judged "appropriate steps" had been taken. "Wait" had not meant "never," but it had meant nineteen years of unsettling delays from *Brown*'s 1954 ruling to the final decree. Some of the blacks who had waited saw the all-white school board as hostile and unfairly wanting to deny black rights. Attorney I. C. Smith later said, "The School Board [was] bucking us on every move, after being told they must integrate. They did everything to get around it." The record, however, is more complex than that. As long as the messages from all levels were inconsistent and contradictory, the white power structure found no compelling reason to desegregate immediately, or even a decade, after the momentous findings in *Brown*.[59]

## NOTES

1. Dr. Martin Luther King Jr., "Letter from Birmingham Jail to the Fellow Clergymen," April 16, 1963, in *Letters of a Nation: A Collection of Extraordinary American Letters*, ed. Andrew Carroll (New York: Broadway Books, 1999), 212. Many people who lived through segregation and the long transition to desegregated schools in Palm Beach County recounted their memories of those times, experiences, and expectations decades later through local oral history and related interview projects. The words of many such individuals are interspersed in this essay with other sources of historical memory in an effort to add a significant personal and intra-community dimension to the long school desegregation process in Palm Beach County.

2. U.S. Bureau of the Census, *1950 Census of Population*, vol. 2, 10–6.

3. V. O. Key Jr., *Southern Politics in State and Nation* (New York: Alfred A. Knopf, 1949), 83; U.S. Bureau of the Census, *Sixteenth Census of the United States: 1940*, vol. 1, 220; U.S. Bureau of the Census, *Twelfth Census of the United States: 1900*, vol. 1, Pt. 1, 532.

4. Edward Rodgers, interview by author, January 6, 2006, Oral History Collection, Historical Society of Palm Beach County, West Palm Beach, Fla.

5. Edward Rodgers, phone conversation with author, February 2006; Lynn Lasseter Drake, "Limestone Creek History" (paper presented to the Loxahatchee Historical Society, December 2004); Edward Rodgers interview.

6. C. Spencer Pompey, *More Rivers to Cross: A Forty-Year Look at the Quest for Fair and Equitable Fulfillment of the "American Dream," 1940–1980* (West Palm Beach: Star Group, 2003), 346; William McLaughlin, oral interview, 2003, Kitty Oliver Oral Histories Collections on Race and Change, African-American Research Library and Cultural Center, Ft. Lauderdale, Fla. (hereafter Oliver Oral Histories Collection); Key, *Southern Politics*, 669.

7. Charlton Tebeau and William Marina, *A History of Florida* (Coral Gables, Fla.: University of Miami Press, 1999), 420; David R. Colburn and Lance deHaven-Smith, *Florida Megatrends: Critical Issues in Florida* (Gainesville: University Press of Florida, 2002), 39.

8. Raymond A. Mohl and Gary R. Mormino, "The Big Change in the Sunshine State: A Social History of Modern Florida," in *The New History of Florida*, ed. Michael Gannon (Gainesville: University Press of Florida, 1996), 441; David R. Colburn and Lance deHaven-Smith, *Government in the Sunshine State: Florida Since Statehood* (Gainesville: University Press of Florida, 1999), 33; David R. Colburn, "Florida Politics in the Twentieth Century," in *The New History of Florida*, ed. Michael Gannon (Gainesville: University Press of Florida, 1996), 361.

9. I. C. Smith, interview by author, October 13, 2005.

10. I. C. Smith interview.

11. *Brown v. Board of Education*, 347 U.S. 483, 74 Sup. Ct. 686 (1954), 495.

12. Joseph Tomberlin, "Florida Whites and the Brown Decision of 1954," *Florida Historical Quarterly* 51 (July 1972): 25; quoted in "Johns Hints Special Meet of Legislature," *Palm Beach Post*, May 18, 1954.

13. Holland and Smathers quoted in "Defiance, Caution Greet Court Ruling," *Palm Beach Post*, May 18, 1954; "New Hearings Set on How to Effect Ruling," *Palm Beach Post*, May 18, 1954.

14. B. Carleton Bryant, "With More Than Deliberate Speed: A Historical Study of Six Major Issues in Secondary Education in Palm Beach County, Florida, 1954–1971 From A Black Perspective" (PhD diss., Florida Atlantic University, 1975), 35.

15. *St. Augustine Record*, May 19, 1954, quoted in David R. Colburn, *Racial Change and Community Crisis: St. Augustine, Florida, 1877–1980* (Gainesville: University of Florida Press, 1991), 25–6; Yvonne Lee Odom, oral interview, February 28, 2004, Oliver Oral Histories Collections.

16. H. Ruth Pompey, interview by Nancy Stein, February 19, 2004, Oral History Collection, Department of History, Florida Atlantic University, Boca Raton, Fla.; "Reunion Renews Black

School Ties," *Palm Beach Post*, August 7, 2005.

17. H. Ruth Pompey interview; Alfred Straghn, oral interview, February 14, 2004, Oliver Oral Histories Collections.

18. H. Ruth Pompey interview.

19. Pompey, *More Rivers*, 601; "Brown vs. Board of Education," *Palm Beach Post*, May 14, 2004; H. Ruth Pompey interview.

20. Alfred Straghn interview; Holland quoted in "William Holland, Civil Rights Champion, Dies," *Palm Beach Post*, July 25, 2002.

21. *Brown v. Board of Education*, 349 U.S. 294, 75 Sup. Ct. 753, 99 L. Ed. 1083 (1955): 300–301; Pompey, *More Rivers*, 597.

22. Richard Kluger, *Simple Justice: The History of Brown v. Board of Education and Black America's Struggle for Equality*, (New York: Vintage Books, 2004), 727; Pompey, *More Rivers*, 318; Ervin, quoted in Luther A. Huston, "Florida Opposes Fast Integration in High Court Bid," *New York Times*, October 2, 1954.

23. "Top Florida Court Hits Bias Decision," *New York Times*, November 17, 1954; "Argument is Set on Integration," *New York Times*, April 11, 1955; *Brown v. Board* 349 U.S. 294 (1955).

24. *Summary of 1955 Legislative Action Pertaining to Education* 1955–06–14, Box 12, Folder 9, Item 58, Papers of Governor C. Farris Bryant, University of Florida Libraries, Department of Special and Area Studies Collections, Manuscript Collections: 4, 8, 9; "Florida," *New York Times*, June 1, 1955.

25. Colburn and deHaven-Smith, *Florida's Megatrends*, 46–47.

26. Kluger, *Simple Justice*, 749.

27. "School Integration Report: The Situation in 17 States," *New York Times*, February 19, 1956.

28. Holland quoted in Flannery, "William Holland," *Palm Beach Post*; I. C. Smith interview.

29. *Holland v. The Board of Public Instruction of Palm Beach County*, 258 F. 2nd 730, (1957), No. 16897, U.S. Court of Appeals Fifth Circuit, August 25, 1958.

30. Jeffrey A. Raffel, *Historical Dictionary of School Segregation and Desegregation: The American Experience* (Westport, Conn.: Praeger, 1998), 204; U.S. Commission on Civil Rights, *Survey of School Desegregation in the Southern and Border States, 1965–1966*, February 1966, 12.

31. Orr and Holland quoted in Flannery, "William Holland," *Palm Beach Post*; I. C. Smith interview.

32. Yvonne Lee Odom interview.

33. "Junior College Integrated by Negro Girl's Enrolling," *Palm Beach Post*, September 12, 1961; "The Segregation Debate Re-Emerges: Some Black Parents Want Their Children Back in the Neighborhood. Educators Warn It Could Be A Big Mistake," *Sun-Sentinel* (Ft. Lauderdale, Florida), February 16, 2002; U.S. Commission on Civil Rights, *Survey of School Desegregation*, 12.

34. Yvonne Lee Odom interview; quoted in "In 1961, Two Teen-Agers Broke Down a Barrier," *Sun-Sentinel*, February 26, 1994.

35. "Brown vs. Board of Education: 50 Years Later," *Sun-Sentinel*, May 9, 2004; Etheridge quoted in "Integration Pioneers," *Palm Beach Post*, May 16, 2004.

36. Etheridge and Kanu quoted in "Brown vs. Board of Education"; "Integration Pioneers," *Palm Beach Post*, May 16, 2004.

37. Koen quoted in "Integration Pioneers"; Yvonne Lee Odom interview.

38. See Pompey, *More Rivers*, 580, 583.

39. Colburn and deHaven Smith, *Florida Megatrends*, 48.

40. Pompey, *More Rivers*, 587, 614, 627.

41. Palm Beach County School Board Report to U.S. Office of Civil Rights, 1965, cited in Pompey, *More Rivers*, 583–84; U.S. Commission on Civil Rights, *Survey of School Desegregation*.

42. Howe quoted in "Schools in South Ordered To Desegregate Faculties," *New York Times*, March 8, 1966; Howe quoted in "Educators Told Integration Fails," *New York Times*, June 9, 1966.

43. Bryant, "Deliberate Speed," 51, 47, 181.

44. Robbie T. Littles, Report to the United Front, December 12, 1968, in Bryant, "Deliberate Speed," Appendix G, 181–84.

45. Bryant, "Deliberate Speed," 74, 77, and 55–57; Minutes, Imperial Men's Club, June 19, 1969; Bryant, "Deliberate Speed," Appendix F; Palm Beach County Education Plan, Department of Secondary Education, July 1969, cited in Bryant, "Deliberate Speed," Appendix F, 55.

46. Jackson quoted in "Meeting of United Guidance Council, September 23, 1969," in Bryant, "Deliberate Speed," 153.

47. Cartwright and Below quoted in "United Guidance Council," in Bryant, "Deliberate Speed," 156.

48. Schwack quoted in "United Guidance Council," 156.

49. IPET-ISUT Historical Preservation Foundation, "Commemorating the 50th Anniversary Brown v. Board of Education," 2004, http://www.palmbeach.k12.fl.us/African American/documents /BrownvBoardPBCTimeline.pdf (accessed September 15, 2005).

50. IPET-ISUT Historical Preservation Foundation, "Commemorating the 50th Anniversary"; "Vanishing Florida Educators," *Journal of the Florida Education Association* (November 1970), cited in Pompey, *More Rivers*, 625.

51. Cartwright quoted in "United Guidance Council," in Bryant, "Deliberate Speed," 156.

52. Below quoted in "United Guidance Council," in Bryant, "Deliberate Speed," 159–60.

53. *Green v. School Board* 391 U.S. 430 (1968); IPET-ISUT "50th Anniversary."

54. *Green v. School Board*; IPET-ISUT "50th Anniversary"; *Alexander v. Holmes County* 396 U.S. 19 (1969).

55. William E. McGoun, *Southeast Florida Pioneers: The Palm and Treasure Coasts* (Sarasota: Pineapple Press, 1998), 158; Jan Tuckwood and Eliot Kleinberg, *Pioneers in Paradise: The First 100 Years* (Marietta, Ga.: Longstreet Press, 1994), 88; "Official: More 'Misplaced' Students Than Boycotters," *Palm Beach Post*, September 11, 1971; quoted in "Judge Denies Desegregation Plan Challenge," *Palm Beach Post*, September 11, 1971.

56. Edward M. Eissey, interview with author, January 17, 2006, Oral History Collection, Historical Society of Palm Beach County, West Palm Beach, Fla.; Eissey quoted in "Palm Beach Gardens

Has Its Own Desegregation Plan—A 'Human Plan,'" *Palm Beach Post*, September 12, 1971.

57. Nelson quoted in "Gardens' Problems: No Answer," *Palm Beach Post*, February 28, 1972; quoted in Bryant, "Deliberate Speed," 64.

58. Maxine D. Jones, "The African-American Experience in Twentieth Century Florida," in *The New History of Florida*, 384, 389; Michael Browning, "Brown vs. Board of Education: 50 Years Later: Mr. U. B. Kinsey," *Palm Beach Post*, May 14, 2004; Kathryn M. Borman, et al, "Accountability in a Postdesegregation Era: The Continuing Significance of Racial Segregation in Florida's Schools," *American Educational Research Journal* 41 (Fall 2004): 605–32.

59. Flannery, "William Holland," *Palm Beach Post*; Bryant, "Deliberate Speed," 113; I. C. Smith interview.

# CHAPTER EIGHT

# THE TRIUMPH OF TRADITION

## HAYDON BURNS'S 1964 GUBERNATORIAL RACE AND THE MYTH OF FLORIDA'S MODERATION

### ABEL A. BARTLEY

Throughout the twentieth century, Florida's population steadily increased as northern migrants, retirees, and businesses relocated to the state in pursuit of its mild climate and low taxes. It is often theorized that these new residents, transplanting their northern progressive or moderate views on race relations, helped transform the state socially and create a new civil rights mindset. Yet the question of how a pluralistic society like Florida's stood in terms of civil rights moderation during the modern struggle for civil rights is a complex one that requires an equally complex analysis process to answer. Indeed, the evaluation of historical processes as complex as those characterizing Florida during the post-*Brown* decade may, of necessity, lead to conflicting interpretations. As a case in point, an examination of the Florida gubernatorial election of 1964 and the racial positions of its leading candidates, particularly segregationist William Haydon Burns, sheds useful light on the enduring interpretation of Florida as an exceptional state of moderation in the region, especially given the troubling nature of race relations there after the nation and much of the South had come to terms with the inevitable.[1]

Since Reconstruction, African Americans in Florida had been caught in a caldron of racial prejudice and legalized discrimination. The white supremacist system in the state had denied African Americans most benefits of citizenship, reducing them to a second-class, caste status. Even so, African Americans constituted a large percentage of the state's population, making them a potentially critical political force. But up to 1964, segregation, discrimination, and intimidation had kept blacks from gaining a real measure of political power or effectively altering the caste system in Florida.

After the Supreme Court's ruling in the 1944 *Smith v. Allwright* case, African Americans gained access to the formerly all-white Democratic primary, now giving them an unprecedented opportunity to influence the system. As a result, in several corners of the state, black voters and white politicians formed uneasy coalitions in attempts to protect their interests and gain access to political channels. Prominent politicians like self-proclaimed "moderate" William Haydon Burns built a political career by forming such expedient coalitions with voters. Burns's fifteen-year tenure as mayor of Jacksonville was largely the result of a political coalition composed principally of small businessmen, middle-class whites, and, occasionally, African Americans. In this sense, Burns's political career provides a useful model of an Old South machine politician, someone willing to make or break alliances to serve his needs. He often used this process to project a progressive public face while adhering to a rigidly private conservatism. In 1964 he put together a coalition that would provide Florida's Old South adherents a final gasp and opportunity to use the Down South delaying tactics that had become so common to the Sunshine State.[2]

Indeed, 1964 was a watershed year for African Americans. In 1963 President John F. Kennedy proposed a sweeping civil rights bill that would end the nation's long affair with segregation and legalized discrimination. Speaking to a national audience on June 11, 1963, Kennedy said, "It ought to be possible . . . for every American to enjoy the privileges of being American without regard to his race or his color . . . this nation will not be fully free until all its citizens are free."[3] Kennedy's statements were fired by the heavy resistance he encountered in Dixie while trying to protect civil rights leaders and workers from reactionary violence. He was especially incensed by the actions of Alabama Governor George Wallace, who stood defiantly in the doorway of the University of Alabama, symbolically blocking black students from registering in 1963. Although Florida had no George Wallace to annoy Washington, it did have an equally staunch segregationist in the person of Haydon Burns.

After Kennedy's assassination, President Lyndon B. Johnson proclaimed civil rights legislation as part of his larger Great Society initiative. He pressured Congress to pass the martyred president's civil rights bill as a memorial to JFK's legacy. On the face of it, the sweeping Civil Right Act of 1964 would finally emasculate such segregationist politicians as Florida's Haydon Burns. But it didn't.[4]

Throughout the South, including Florida, there was entrenched opposition to the proposed legislation. In Congress, southerners, including the two U.S. senators from Florida, had supported a prolonged filibuster to block the bill from even reaching a vote. In the heat of the fight on Capitol Hill, politicians in Florida used the debate over the legislation to shore up their conservative credentials, as most remained anchored in the reactionary policies so characteristic of the Deep South. With few exceptions, whites overwhelming supported political race-baiting. As a result, federal civil rights measures became a major factor in Florida's 1964 governor's race.[5]

For Florida, the drama of 1964 actually had begun in early 1963, when local officials in St. Augustine began planning for their quadricentennial. St. Augustine, which was founded by Spanish explorer Pedro Aviles de Menendez in 1565, was the oldest permanent European settlement in North America. As 1963 approached, the city prepared to celebrate its 400th birthday. This celebration was meant to bring national and international publicity and dollars to Florida.[6]

However, there was serious racial baggage to overcome. St. Augustine was one of the most rigidly segregated cities in the South. Its mayor and police chief ran a sort of urban plantation system designed to keep African Americans in a second-class status with little or no access to civil services and citizenship rights. In 1963, the same year as Kennedy's proposed civil rights bill (and his assassination), African Americans in St. Augustine declared a new civil rights era locally and began a renewed campaign to challenge the system. Dr. Robert Hayling, a local African American dentist and NAACP Youth Council advisor, energized St. Augustine's black community by organizing new protests against city leaders. In reaction, the local Klan held a mass rally at which a speaker stated that the "burr-headed bastard of a dentist [Hayling] ought not to live." After several demonstrations, shots were fired and the black and white communities hunkered down for a long and painful confrontation.[7] St. Augustine, quadricentennial celebration notwithstanding, was not ready to yield ground on its Old South lifestyle.

The Ku Klux Klan, which had a historical presence in the city, took the lead in attacking African Americans participating in civil rights activities. Blacks responded to the violence by killing a Klansman. To pressure local officials to change and take advantage of his newfound success in Birmingham, Dr. Martin Luther King Jr., by now an internationally renowned civil rights figure, supported a direct-action campaign in St. Augustine to correspond with the city's planning for its 400-year celebration. At the very same time, Haydon Burns was planning for election advancement to Tallahassee with one eye on his opponents and one eye on the racial dilemmas of his state. As with most state-level politicians and candidates, no campaign was possible without addressing the intrusive issue of segregation and racial subjugation in Florida. Thus, the unfolding protests and white, conservative backlash in St. Augustine took on more than a local significance in what was widely touted as racially "moderate" Florida.[8]

St. Augustine's association with the KKK in 1963 began when a shady minister named Charles Conley Lynch brought his Church of Christ white supremacy message to the city. Lynch preached a message of black inferiority often tinged with specious biblical quotations. Nevertheless, his message had a strong appeal to the poor whites that gathered at his rallies. He gave them a convenient scapegoat for their troubles and prejudices. As Lynch told a white crowd, "Martin Lucifer Coon. That nigger says it's gonna be a hot summer. If he thinks the niggers can make it a hot summer, I will tell him that one hundred forty million white people know how to make it a lot hotter . . . When the smoke clears, there aint gonna be nothing left except white faces."[9]

As the situation deteriorated, Governor Farris Bryant, himself a proclaimed segregationist, called for an end to night demonstrations and sent highway patrolmen into the city to monitor the protests and deteriorating situation. The NAACP thereafter dismissed Dr. Hayling and some of the other leaders of the disturbances. Hayling then called Rev. C. T. Vivian and asked if the Southern Christian Leadership Conference (SCLC) would be interested in creating a presence in St. Augustine. Vivian accepted the challenge. The SCLC organized its first large-scale protest on March 26, bringing dubious national attention to the country's oldest city while simultaneously underscoring Florida's racism as an issue in the pending gubernatorial election.[10]

In May 1964, King himself had joined the rising conflict in St. Augustine, calling it a "small Birmingham," in comparison to the Alabama city known to civil right workers as "Bombingham." If city leaders did not negotiate an end to the ancient city's race divide, King promised to launch a direct-action campaign on May 26, a few days after the Florida primary. Fresh off his successes in Birmingham, King hoped to use the momentum and national recognition he gained there to pressure St. Augustine and the "moderate" State of Florida into accepting integration. However, he quickly found that the Sunshine State's racists could be just as vicious and unyielding as those in any other entity of Dixie. He also encountered a political process in Florida that still revolved around the segregationist mentality of outright resistance to civil rights, or more covertly, *sustained delays* in response to any federal measures meant to counteract racial inequality.[11]

This affair once again pitted the reality of Old South Florida against the image of New South Florida. St. Augustine's mayor, Joseph Shelley, in the mold of Jacksonville's Haydon Burns, was a Dixie-first holdover who rejected compromise, and usually even dialogue, with African Americans. And just like Burns and other white supremacists in the state, he accused those involved in civil rights activities of being communists and refused to negotiate or to establish a biracial committee to study the situation. Throughout these actions, Shelley became an ideal foe for the media-savvy King, as did Police Chief Virgil

Stuart, also a Gestapo-style segregationist. Both officials refused to provide civil rights activists with protection and served to highlight St. Augustine's and Florida's romance with the Old South while much of the nation had moved on to racial healing. Indeed, a State Legislative Investigation Committee's findings on the disorders of St. Augustine highlighted their effects on the state's New South image but conveniently ignored the issue of racial accord and justice in Florida. As stated in the very first words of the report: "Racial strife and civil commotion last summer cost the economy of St. Augustine, Florida an estimated five million dollars loss of business. Lost business also means lost state taxes. . . . In addition there is the most intangible factor of adverse publicity."[12] Apparently, Tallahassee's image-makers did not even attempt a moderate commitment to honestly address Florida's racial fault line. Rather, those image-makers sought only to highlight the state's economic priorities.

Since the 1950s, Florida's "New South" politicians like Governor LeRoy Collins had publicly touted the Sunshine State as a "moderate" force for racial progress and as an economic and demographic magnet for new economic ventures. In September 1957, Jacksonville's mayor Haydon Burns had gained national attention when he called for "a day of prayer" for southern governors who met with President Dwight Eisenhower about segregation. Burns prayed "for a truly American and Godlike solution to the problem." Yet as the gubernatorial elections of 1964 approached, there was nothing moderate about the nation's oldest colonial city and, as the gubernatorial campaign would yield, there was little moderation in the electoral mode either. One might presume that had the state actually been moderate, segregation would not have been a pressing issue in its campaigns a full decade after *Brown*—but it was![13]

Meanwhile, in Mayor Haydon Burns's Jacksonville, one of the state's largest cities situated just to the north of St. Augustine, the NAACP had begun another sustained attack on segregation. In 1964, Mayor Burns was also the leading Democratic candidate for governor. Burns, like Shelley, refused to negotiate with civil rights protesters, making himself by design the sworn enemy of the NAACP. He took advantage of every opportunity to denounce the organization and the civil rights movement, including traveling to St. Augustine in a show of support for white city officials. Rutledge Pearson, the state NAACP president, had failed to get Mayor Burns to negotiate with civil rights protesters on minor issues such as organizing a biracial commission to study the racial problems of Jacksonville. Burns took advantage of Pearson's failed overture and the local protest to bolster his conservative credentials. The tactic seemed to be working well until March, when a riot erupted.[14]

In the midst of these civil disturbances, in two of Florida's most famous and economically significant "Sun Cities," six men competed for the Democratic nomination for governor: State Representative Fred B. Karl of Daytona; State Senators John E. Matthews of Jacksonville, Fred O. Dickinson of West Palm Beach, and Scott Kelly of Lakeland; Miami Mayor Robert King High; and Jacksonville Mayor Haydon Burns. Scott Kelly immediately staked his claim to the reactionary label by proclaiming himself as the "symbol of opposition to civil rights in Florida." He also promised to ignore the civil rights measures now before Congress and to halt any school integration in the Sunshine State. Robert High immediately embraced the more controversial position of encouraging his fellow candidates to support civil rights and any federal enforcement measures. He argued that this would be good publicity for the state and would foster better economic initiatives. Of the six gubernatorial candidates, High was the only candidate to publicly support civil rights progress and enforcement measures. Hailing from the heavily northern- and Jewish-influenced Miami area, High's progressivism in the election of 1964 possibly reflected as much political savvy as moral conscience.[15]

Against this backdrop, and even in the midst of protest and violence in his own city and its backyard (St. Augustine), Burns sought to project the image of a "realist" on the race issue, even though he simultaneously stated his opposition to almost all civil rights gains and demands. Unable to straddle the issue with image building, Burns eventually centered his campaign on his opposition to civil rights measures and protesters, labeling the more temperate Robert King High as the NAACP candidate. Burns openly used racial issues like this to solidify his own segregationist constituency. In so doing, he became the target of the other candidates. They all attacked him for his duplicity and for his inept handling of protest in Jacksonville, often accusing him of using the city's racial disturbances in the early 1960s to further his political career.[16]

Who was Haydon Burns and why was he Florida's leading candidate for governor in 1964? William Haydon Burns, whose family had roots in Kentucky, was born on St. Patrick's Day, March 17, 1912, in Chicago, Illinois. The Burns family moved to Jacksonville in 1922. Young Haydon attended the public schools of Jacksonville before graduating from all-white Jackson High School in 1930. During the depression years of the late 1930s, he found employment in Tallahassee working for the state auditor's office. After a few years absence, he returned to Jacksonville to pursue work as a salesman. He soon resigned that post and opened a small appliance store in the downtown area. Later he started an aviation company. When World War II erupted, Burns was offered a naval commission as an aeronautics salvage specialist. When the war ended, he was appointed manager of the federal War Housing Center in Jacksonville. Burns then operated a business-consulting firm, until friends convinced him to run for the $6,600 a year mayor's office.[17]

In 1949 several prominent members of the Jacksonville Chamber of Commerce encouraged Haydon Burns to challenge incumbent Mayor Frank Whitehead. Most people only knew of Burns's reputation as chairman of the local war bonds drive. Except for helping his father, Harry, win a County Commissioner seat, Burns had almost no political experience. In the 1949 election in Jacksonville, one of Mayor Whitehead's most prominent supporters was C. Daughtry Towers, a powerful local attorney, businessman, and major investor in the city's bus and taxicab company. Just prior to the election, the municipal bus company raised fares and changed routes. Many in the community accused the City Council, which regulated the bus company, of being manipulated by powerful forces associated with the bus cartel.[18]

Burns saw a potential issue in the bus controversy and sought to exploit it. Casting himself as a protector of tradition, who would bring stability and the voice of the people to the mayor's office, Burns undertook a populist campaign to woo the masses. He stated "Jacksonville being potentially the finest city in the South, cannot afford to let the position of Mayor reduce itself to that of greed alone." By accusing Whitehead of cronyism, Burns was able to win a stunning victory over the sitting mayor.[19] In Old South Florida, the Democratic nomination meant he had won the office. Despite his opposition to civil rights measures, most African Americans hoped Burns's populist victory would also usher in a new era in race relations in Jacksonville. Indeed, he actually captured the election with both black and white support. Even so, Mayor Haydon Burns's victory actually meant progress for downtown merchants and building programs, but those types of urban renewal priorities, as James Crooks has noted in his study of Jacksonville, did not encompass the city's African American community.[20]

This first campaign demonstrated a trait that would define Haydon Burns throughout his political career. To win the election, Burns had quietly formed a political alliance of convenience with African Americans, and they had given him the margin of victory. Secondly, people either admired him or despised him, but few were indifferent to his stand on preserving traditional life in the Sunshine State. This had the effect of motivating large numbers of voters to express their opinion one way or the other on Burns. It also set the pattern for Burns of promises made and promises betrayed to the black community. In this regard, Burns was not unlike many old-guard Florida politicians who recognized the significance of the black vote, from those who could actually exercise the franchise, while simultaneously arguing for the significance of the "old way of life" in order to solidify the prevailing white vote. Burns was an old-line promoter who sold Jacksonville as a model for racial and economic development.[21] But those who purchased his goods came away with image rather than reality.

Burns began what would be a fourteen-year stint as mayor as a self-professed New South politician, championing a massive public works and office building program and attempting to attract out-of-state investment for his city of over two hundred thousand residents. He promised African American leaders improved access to city services though he was intent on maintaining Jim Crowism in all aspects of his administration.[22]

While carefully avoiding media attention, Burns made cautious, low-level overtures to black leaders. Blacks responded to him because of his willingness to acknowledge the black community as a factor in city politics. In the process, Burns developed a political, yet uneasy, dialogue with important black leaders. Burns's victory opened a long reign as Jacksonville's mayor, followed by two years as Florida's governor. For most of that period, Burns maintained the white community's support without losing a part of the African American vote, an incredible feat considering the complex social, political, and racial climate of booming Jacksonville.

During his first campaign in the Sunshine State, Burns made two important vows to black voters. First, he promised to hire black police officers, and secondly he promised to build a swimming pool for African Americans. Two years after his election, city officials approved financing for the Blodgettville swimming pool on the corner of Fourth and Jefferson Street, an upscale black neighborhood that just happened to be home to potential black voters for the mayor. The swimming pool opened on Sunday, April 9, 1951, with pomp and circumstance as Burns sponsored a huge political rally attended by prominent citizens.[23]

Initially, Burns vacillated on the second promise. The need for black officers had been evident since World War II. Mistrust and apprehension characterized relationships between white officers and blacks for obvious reasons. Other southern cities had already experimented with the idea. For example, in September 1944, Miami had hired five African American police officers, the first full-time black officers hired in the South since Reconstruction.[24]

The hiring of African American police officers proved to be a divisive political issue. The report conducted by the Council of Social Agencies in 1946 had recommended that Jacksonville's leaders hire African American officers to patrol black neighborhoods. The report cited African American attitudes toward white police officers as the reason for their recommendations, the "average Negro believes that he will be exploited rather than helped by the police under almost all circumstances. Therefore, he refuses to seek assistance from the police and contacts these representatives . . . only when it is unavoidable." It recalled the success the city had with the African American shore patrol and military police operating in black districts during World War II. By 1948 many local organizations publicly endorsed the report and the hiring of African American police officers, somewhat easing the path to Burns's decision.[25]

In early February 1950, the *Jacksonville Journal* ran the headline "JAX COMMISSION SET TO OK NEGRO POLICE." Burns, ever the opportunistic politician, reminded blacks that he had initiated the idea.[26] On July 19, 1950, Mayor Burns swore in six African American officers. They were paid $180 a month during their probationary period and $200 a month after that, $20 less than white officers. They were also restricted to black neighborhoods by the mayor.[27]

When Haydon Burns relinquished office in 1964 to run for governor, African Americans had little else to show for their fifteen years of support. Ultimately, all that Burns had actually done was seek the black vote by hiring twenty-seven black police officers (restricted to black communities), suggesting minor modifications to Jim Crow divisions, and building a swimming pool in a black, tax-paying and voting neighborhood.

Often the mayor would stroll through black neighborhoods talking with residents; but in the tradition of reactionary Florida, Burns made few tangible improvements to black communities. The streets in the African American sectors remained unpaved, the sewage system primitive, and the problems of crime and social decay bothersome. Most blacks remained locked in an oppressive web of poverty and disappointment as the Burns administration refused to alter the Florida-style Jim Crowism that defined life for black Jacksonville residents, even after a decade of heightened civil rights activity on the national scene. For the sizable African American population during these actions, the only changes in race relations in Jacksonville had been Burns's effort to move the city from Old South intransigence to Down South delays. As a leading city of Florida, Jacksonville was characteristic of much of the state; as a leading politician in 1964, Burns too was characteristic of a large portion of the voting public in what scholars have termed "moderate" Florida.[28]

Yet everyday African Americans in Jacksonville, like those in other locales in the state, had not willingly acquiesced to Burns's "put-off-to-later" politics. The first cracks in the alliance between Burns and black Jacksonville had come in 1955, when Frank Hampton, a police officer and political activist, sued to get a local golf course integrated. Burns delayed responding until 1959 when the courts forced the issue. To stave off integration, Jacksonville's leaders attempted to sell the public golf courses. Hampton responded by filing an omnibus suit that asked the federal court to outlaw segregation at the Gator Bowl football stadium and municipally owned swimming pools, parks, and golf courses. Federal Judge Bryan Simpson ruled that the city had to desegregate the courses and open them to all patrons.[29]

On April 6, the City Commission met to discuss plans to delay implementing the court order. In Jacksonville the mayor served as chair of commission meetings, but had no more authority than the other commissioners. However, the mayor's support or opposition to an issue often determined its fate. The commissioners voted to defer action on most of the facilities and to close the two golf courses indefinitely.[30]

On September 22, the City Commission held a stormy meeting, during which African Americans introduced a petition seeking an end to segregation at municipally owned entities. The commissioners ignored the petitions, and instead opened bids to sell the golf courses. Several African Americans attended the meeting to protest the commission's actions. They presented a petition, signed by Frank Hampton and other black golfers, asking the commission to integrate the golf courses on a trial basis. The petition's language offended Burns, triggering heated exchanges between him and some of the petitioners. Burns, who was preparing for his 1960 gubernatorial bid, did not want to be associated statewide with any type of integration measures. Like most politicians, Burns knew that the vast majority of white voters, with the exception of some progressive northern transplants in places like the Miami-Dade region, were not ready to support a candidate who seemed willing to compromise on the Sunshine State's Old South folkways, even in the presumed New South milieu of the 1960s.[31]

In response to the criticism, Burns made an impassioned speech defending his actions during his eleven-year tenure. He concluded with this statement: "As long as I'm in the office of mayor, I'll continue to act in the best interests of all the residents of this city. All these petitions won't change my course. I do it, I feel, in the interests of the majority of the colored citizens as well as the white." Black spokespersons found Burns's words hollow and his actions illegal.[32] Nevertheless, as the nation moved forward with the election of John F. Kennedy and new federal civil rights measures and protections in 1960, Mayor Haydon "Traditionalist" Burns kept Florida's number two city in the reactionary grips of segregationists.

Many African-Americans lost confidence in Burns after the golf course fiasco. "We expected Burns to step forward and make the decision to fight the commission and open the courses on an integrated basis," said one African American. "I believe that had he fought for the open courses the other commissioners would have fallen in line."[33] In the midst of the nation's heightened civil rights activities of the late 1950s and early 1960s, Haydon Burns, one of Florida's leading political figures and a future governor, had the opportunity and national climate to finally repay black leaders for their political support over the years. In typical Sunshine State fashion, Burns rejected moderation and endorsed segregation. In the end, the mayor of Florida's economic/urban giant had defiantly clung to the divisive politics of the past. The mayor fashioned himself a New South moderate, but many who used that label in Florida were minimalists like Haydon Burns who actually did the least amount of work required to maintain what they viewed as positive race relations. The stratagem did not impress black Floridians.[34]

The 1960 gubernatorial race highlighted the second crack in Burns's alliance with blacks, who were then intensifying their challenge to segregation in Jacksonville and in many other cities across the state. The local NAACP branch organized massive sit-in campaigns—aimed at desegregating lunch counters, hotels, and theaters—that coincided with Burns's campaign in the gubernatorial primaries. The local NAACP used the situation to force the mayor to deal with Jacksonville's race problems. Even though this was the NAACP's goal, a byproduct of it was to shift the attention of the entire state onto Burns's home turf of Jacksonville. Moreover, the way Burns handled the demonstrations in Jacksonville would, in large part, define the nature of his candidacy in the rest of the Sunshine State: a population in support of a New South candidate would spurn Burns; a population in favor of Old South barriers would support Burns. Although Haydon Burns lost the Democratic primary for governor in 1960, he captured 166,352 votes and used that support as his base to win the gubernatorial nomination in 1964, with 56.1 percent of the popular vote.[35]

In retrospect, Burns missed an opportunity to repay African American voters for their years of loyal support and to make his mark as a progressive on racial issues. If he were going to take advantage of this challenge, Burns would have to lead Jacksonville into a racially as well as an economically new era. That would also mean his abandoning his segregationist stance. If Burns took such a position in 1960, his chances of being elected governor of Florida might end. The Sunshine State had a notorious segregationist history, and Burns's choice of intransigence over moderation comported with that experience.[36]

Relations between Burns and the black community continued to deteriorate as the civil rights movement intensified. In 1960, Jacksonville experienced a weekend of violent rioting as Klansmen armed with axe handles and baseball bats attacked peaceful black demonstrators in downtown Jacksonville while police refused to act. The frightened demonstrators retreated to their own communities, but finally fought back against the pursuing attackers. They used bottles, sticks, baseball bats, and other weapons to successfully counterattack the Klansmen and drive them from their neighborhood.[37]

Florida Governor LeRoy Collins blamed the disturbances on the reluctance of local leaders to deal effectively with the civil rights protesters. He all but ignored the real cause as Burns's stonewalling and Florida's love affair with its color-coded way of life. Collins openly chastised local government for refusing to establish a biracial committee to deal with racial issues and to improve communications with Jacksonville's 110,000 black residents. The governor advocated interracial committees as the best way to prevent conflict in racial tinderboxes in places like Jacksonville. Collins contended that prejudice and intolerance caused racial conflict, "It [racism] is un-American, un-Christian and morally wrong but at the same time it exists and should be challenged so that we can move forward." Unfortunately for Jacksonville's and the state's black and progressive communities of the early 1960s, Collins uttered these words while still supporting separate-but-equal as a mainstay of life in the Sunshine State.[38]

Burns attacked Collins's statements as unwarranted, but agreed that local government in the state was responsible for keeping the peace. In a backhanded criticism of the governor, Burns stated that the best way to maintain law and order was when, "state officials withhold their actions and their comments until their assistance is requested by local responsible officials." Burns denied that the city had experienced rioting, and predicted that there would be none in the future if state officials stayed away.[39]

African Americans hoped that "separate-but-unequal" Burns would change after 1960, but he did not. Burns remained the same resourceful politician and segregationist mayor he had always been. By 1960 black expectations were changing as a result of the growing civil rights movement; it awakened a new spirit of freedom and protest in black communities across the state. In Jacksonville, African Americans were now determined anew to not accept the crumbs tossed to them from a politician whose reelection was his sole concern. Although this was reality, Burns, ever the traditionalist, refused to accept it.[40]

Race and civil rights activism thereafter became the central issues in the 1960 gubernatorial campaign. After the first primaries, ultra-conservative North Florida's Farris Bryant faced Doyle E. Carlton Jr. in the runoff. Well-known segregationist Bryant embraced a backward-looking platform and advocated states' rights and open resistance to forced integration. He challenged Carlton to clarify his position on segregation, accusing him of duplicity on racial issues. Maintaining segregation still appealed to most white Florida voters; Farris Bryant won the run-off election. Although Haydon Burns lost his bid for statewide office in 1960, his regressive stand on race relations still carried the day in "moderate" Florida, only in the form of another candidate, Farris Bryant.[41]

In 1963 Haydon Burns made his fifth bid for mayor, using the slogan, "Continue progress with Burns." The gulf between the African American community and him had so widened that Burns realized he could not count on certain black precincts to support him as they had in the past. Burns's opponent, John F. Lanahan, charged the mayor with corruption and unethical conduct. As a result of Lanahan's accusations, the federal government investigated Burns's relationship with a Caribbean company. There arose damaging charges of illegal payoffs and of siphoning public funds.[42]

Despite the negative campaigning and black voter disdain, Burns easily won reelection. In previous elections, like the 1960 mayoral election, Burns had run well in every black district; this heavy African American vote had proven decisive. Only a few months later, in the first Democratic primary for the governorship, those fifteen precincts had all voted against Burns. By ignoring the civil rights activism of the nation, state, and local scene, Burns was alienating his black voter base in order to maintain, and perhaps even expand, his impact as a racial divisionist. In this regard, Burns's experience and success with the local reactionary electorate would in some ways mimic his success with the statewide electorate in 1964.[43]

Although Burns lost considerable ground in the African American community, he more than recouped that loss in the white community. White precincts, which had voted against Burns in previous elections, backed him in the 1960 and 1963 mayoral elections. While Haydon Burns promised to be "the mayor for all people," the chasm between the black community and the mayor continued to widen. In the process, he was losing patience with the civil rights movement and the constant locally organized protests and demonstrations that he felt destabilized his vision of "progressive" race relations. In essence, Haydon Burns and the black community simply had two diametrically opposed visions of life and justice in the Sunshine State. The final break between the black community and Haydon Burns came in 1964, when Burns made his second bid for Florida's top office. On December 6, 1963, Burns announced his candidacy at a huge rally at the Jacksonville Coliseum. Few blacks expressed interest in the meeting.[44]

It was now 1964—ten years after the monumental *Brown v. Board* decision and the very year of implementing the nation's most far-reaching Civil Rights Act—and Haydon Burns was still underscoring his campaign for statewide office with his "traditionalist," "separate-but-equal" rhetoric. The fact that Burns did not remain a lone voice in the 1964 election speaks volumes about the state's commitment, or lack thereof, to New South politics and prevailing racial attitudes. The fact that Haydon Burns actually won the gubernatorial election speaks even more demonstrably about the false notion that Florida was a "moderate" state during the contemporary civil rights movement.

Burns's campaign was principally supported by a group of close friends, who formed what became known as the "Burns Blitzers." This organization was founded in 1960 to help Burns drum up support for his first run at governor. What had started as a small-scale organization centered in Jacksonville had expanded into a statewide entity. The Blitzers served as an army of supporters, which at its peak numbered 150,000 supporters. Burns and his Blitzers promoted a "progressive" platform, which included increased aid to education, tax reform, constitutional revisions, reapportionment of the legislature, expanding road projects, and protecting Florida's beaches, but neither he nor they said anything about desegregating schools or enacting civil rights measures in the state.

Though the frontrunner, Burns remained vulnerable. Jacksonville's schools had recently been disaccredited, there were race riots going on in the city, and several policemen had been indicted for accepting bribes to protect gambling interests. Burns's opponents had a number of weak points to attack, especially his duplicity on race issues. Perhaps the *Miami News* best summed up the reasons for Burns's particular vulnerability on the issue of race progress: "We lament, too, the reply of Negroes to express their feelings in Jacksonville or anywhere else [in the state]."[45]

Burns then adopted a politically expedient strategy. He basically ignored his opponents and centered his campaign on opposition to the public accommodations section of the pending 1964 Civil Rights Act. He also touted "The Jacksonville Story," a slide show of building projects and economic programs completed during his term as mayor as the blueprint for delaying federal mandates and for his vision of a New South Florida.

African Americans in the state found little uplifting news in "The Jacksonville Story" and showed their disdain by subsequently opposing Burns's candidacy. They instead supported Robert King High, because High, representing the more politically progressive region of Southeast Florida, supported civil rights progress, even though racially progressive and Jewish voters of Miami seemed somewhat disinterested in the statewide civil rights movement itself. In Jacksonville, Burns's home area in Northeast Florida, blacks abandoned him for High and lamented their former alliance with him. For reasons of political impact in the state, Burns had hardened his position against integration and increased the police presence in black neighborhoods. He calculated that this show of force against civil rights demonstrators would play well in conservative areas of Florida. He was correct.[46]

As Burns and his fellow candidates debated the issues of the governor's race, Jacksonville again exploded into racial violence. In March 1964, the unrest began when police officers attacked students who were trying to organize a boycott of Jacksonville's downtown businesses. For nearly a week, the city experienced racial upheaval. Burns reacted by deputizing 469 firefighters, thus strengthening his image as a "law and order" politician. Many in the black community interpreted "law and order" as a "put blacks in their place" gambit rather than an anti-crime policy, as the issue would at first appear. Ironically, the rioting and subsequent law and order approach helped Burns in the gubernatorial election. His hard-line stand against the protests and staunch support of the racist conventions of the Sunshine State bolstered his support, particularly in the conservative panhandle and central regions.[47]

Between the time that Burns was elected mayor in 1949 and his 1964 run for governor, Florida had undergone dramatic economic and demographic changes, but most of that change occurred outside the panhandle. Florida's population was increasing even more significantly than in previous years. Between 1830 and 1945, the state's population had increased from 34,730 to 2,250,061. Following World War II, Florida began a new period of rapid population increase, which created a political divide between the slower-growing rural areas of the Panhandle (western, northern parts) with the more progressive, fast-growing southern parts of the peninsula. Between 1945 and 1970, Florida's population ballooned from 2,250,061 to 6,789,443. By 1960, Florida had 4,951,560 residents. Between 1960 and 1970, Florida's African American population had also increased by 161,465. The Miami and Dade County region became the largest demographic area of Florida, overtaking Jacksonville, which held to its Jim Crow roots even though the city was growing increasingly African American.[48] Mayor Haydon Burns's Jacksonville of the early 1960s seemed to epitomize a common saying in the Sunshine State: "the farther north one goes in Florida, the more southern it gets."

As the 1964 gubernatorial election took shape, Burns immediately became a frontrunner in this state of profound change, diversity, and tradition. Burns had run a respectable third in the 1960 campaign. Since then he had worked on building support for his 1964 run: he sought and won re-election as mayor of Jacksonville while he continued to establish his statewide credentials as a traditionalist politician. Burns won in the May 5 primary election with 312,453 votes, though he lost a large segment of the African American vote. Those ballots went almost exclusively to Miami mayor Robert King High, the candidate endorsed by the Florida NAACP. High, who received 207,280 votes, had a reputation as a racially moderate mayor of a city that had moved far ahead of most Florida urban areas on civil rights issues. Tellingly, nearly every major newspaper of Florida endorsed Mayor Burns as its candidate. The editorials pointed to his years of experience and his success in governing Jacksonville, and his well-known Florida traditionalism. Few of the newspapers, however, pointed out Burns's backward racial tendencies, civil rights stalling tactics, or the divisiveness caused by the recent race riots in his city. Apparently, Burns's segregationist stand in the "moderate" state of Florida in 1964 was not an issue important enough for either the newspaper or voters to address.[49]

Burns implored voters to use the May 23 runoff election as a referendum of rejection for the federal civil rights bill. According to Burns, Robert Saunders, the field secretary of Florida's NAACP, had issued a call for all African Americans to raise their voice in support of the Civil Rights Bill now before Congress and against Burns. Haydon Burns then called for all "thinking people" of both races to back him and oppose the bill. He described High as the "NAACP candidate," implying that a vote for Miami's mayor was a vote for integration. He also charged that African Americans from across Florida had told him that they were afraid to vote against the NAACP. Burns said blacks "live in an atmosphere of fear and dread if they oppose the NAACP. Those who do are marked and branded as traitors to their race. This is the sinister force I have alluded to in the press." The mayor claimed a vote for him would underscore the state's actual feelings regarding the civil rights proposal and strengthen the hand of Florida's two senators who, he said, were fighting for true democracy by actively opposing the measure.[50]

Burns preached his segregationist message in the conservative counties of central and northern Florida, but not in the modernizing southern part of the state. During his campaign swing through the central counties, he blasted the public accommodations section of the Civil Rights Bill, calling it "the most dastardly thing that can happen to any individual."[51] He claimed that the articles in that section destroyed individual rights and deprived people of their economic opportunities. He went on to accuse High of catering to African American voters and ignoring the wishes of other voters. Then, in another significant political coup, he announced that he would not debate High. This kept him from having to answer uncomfortable questions on civil rights disturbances in Jacksonville and his regressive stand on the impending Civil Rights Act of 1964. Instead of debating High, Burns spent his time accusing the Miami mayor of being an NAACP stooge. He constantly argued that High's actions were undermining the efforts of Florida's U.S. Senators George Smathers and Spessard Holland to derail the Civil Rights Bill.[52]

Burns went on the offensive against the NAACP itself in May. In a half-page advertisement in the *Florida Times-Union*, Burns urged the citizens to "PROTECT FLORIDA'S FUTURE: BLOCK [sic] VOTING THREATENS." He warned that the NAACP had used bloc voting against him in the May 19 primary and in favor of his opponent, Mayor High. Burns's advertisement listed the May 19 returns from certain black precincts in Florida in an attempt to tie High to the NAACP.[53]

High continued to attack Burns's integrity and regressive stand on separation of the races. He accused Burns of being dishonest. He challenged Burns to list his income. He questioned the use of Jacksonville police officers and other city officials as Burns's Blitzers. And most significantly, he highlighted Burns's segregationist actions in Jacksonville and accused the mayor of being a racial extremist. He said that Burns's election could turn Florida into a publicity disaster for those touting its New South achievements and potential. He said that Burns was using racial issues as a smokescreen to cover the real issues of the campaign. He maintained (correctly) that the Civil Rights Bill was not an issue for the governor's race, because Congress was debating the issue and the governor's role was to enforce federal law.[54]

Unfortunately for High, the major issue for the white electorate was the Civil Rights Bill and not constitutional guarantees and roles. In 1964, most Florida voters saw a rare opportunity to delay positive actions on civil rights by employing stonewalling tactics for at least one more election. As a result, they took advantage of the opportunity and chose to do exactly what Burns had accused the NAACP of doing. They bloc voted, using race as the coalescing issue. The election coverage and results were clear; race was, indeed, a unifying issue that transported white voters to the polls in 1964.[55]

The actual vote proved anticlimactic. Burns won the day with a 56.1 percent victory, winning sixty-four of Florida's sixty-seven counties. In some reactionary counties, Burns won by a stunning margin of 10 to 1. Even in his home region where High hoped to gain strong support from "Yankee" voters, race trumped the opportunity to elect the first moderate to statewide office in Florida. High won unimpressive margins only in Dade and Broward counties in South Florida and in "rapidly aging" Pinellas County in the Tampa Bay region. The margin of victory seemed to lend credence to the theory that northern and Jewish transplants to Florida were not energized by such statewide issues as a social change and Burns's "keep 'em where they are" campaign.[56]

Haydon Burns's gubernatorial victory says much about Florida in the early to mid-1960s. Despite claims of being the most "northern of southern states," Florida's voters demonstrated a palpable affinity in their voting patterns for the Old South/Down South mentality in their overwhelming support for Haydon Burns. They had an opportunity to chart a different path and support a candidate who did not espouse the old order. Instead, they chose to follow the business-as-usual model of other, "more radical" southern states. Though Florida continued to evolve politically and socially following Burns's election, it still maintained its association with the region's "now-is-not-the-time-for-racial-progress" mindset. In retrospect, the 1964 election showed that Florida's progressive public face was perhaps only an illusion. While Florida fought to delay the inevitable, it continued to have more in common with Alabama, Georgia, and Mississippi than it had with Massachusetts, New York, California, or even many of the states of the upper South.

Traditionalist, "Jim Crow" Burns spent two tumultuous years as governor. In 1966, he lost his bid for a second term. After facing charges of corruption and incompetence (but not facing charges of forcing integration), he lost a controversial primary race to a more politically savvy Robert King High, his 1964 nemesis. Burns's conservative supporters across the state found it difficult to support High during the general election. They instead switched sides and voted for his conservative, racially regressive Republican opponent, Claude R. Kirk Jr. Once again Florida's less-than-moderate tendency surfaced in the heat of an election, this time fully a dozen years after *Brown*.

For the first time since Reconstruction, Florida voters elected a conservative Republican candidate. Kirk, who switched to the Republican party during the time of the student sit-in movement of 1960, represented the Richard Nixon, "law and order," conservative wing of the party. Kirk was an archetypical Down South, "put off civil rights" candidate and governor, who slowed Florida's progress in race relations, reduced governmental spending, and once again actively sought to delay Florida's drive towards public school integration. One of the highlights of the Kirk administration was his help in attracting the Republican Party's convention to Florida in 1968, at which time the attendees nominated ultra-conservative Richard Nixon as its standard bearer. In the general election, Florida gave 40.5 percent of its vote to reactionary Richard Nixon, 30.9 percent to the racially progressive Democrat Hubert H. Humphrey, and in another challenge to the conventional wisdom on the temperance of the state, gave another 28.5 percent to racial demagogue George Wallace of Alabama.[57] One can only speculate on what "moderate" Florida might have given to Haydon "Jim Crow" Burns had he been a candidate that year.

Some could argue that the 1964 election simply continued the Sunshine State's Old South folkways and electoral patterns. However, it is clear that Florida did embrace some New South changes, which occurred in later years. After the chaotic four-year term of Claude Kirk, Florida voters continuously elected moderate Democrats to office until the mid-1980s, and African Americans increasingly became part of that new political landscape, rising to positions of prominence across the Sunshine State. Though it would take a long, painful process, the last of Florida's holdout schools were successfully integrating by the early 1970s, as well. In a real sense, Florida's renowned segregationist and gubernatorial victor in 1964, Haydon Burns, served as both a vision of past racial injustices and harbinger of future racial progress in the state. No matter how doggedly Burns and his ilk attempted to hold onto the old ways, the Sunshine State was destined for change. Unfortunately, that change did not sweep "moderate" Florida until years after Governor Burns had left state office in early 1967.

## NOTES

1. See Gary Mormino, *Land of Sunshine, State of Dreams: A Social History of Modern Florida* (Gainesville: University of Florida Press, 2005), 1–43; Abel Bartley, *Keeping the Faith: Race, Politics, and Social Development in Jacksonville, Florida, 1940–1970* (Westport, Conn.: Greenwood Press, 2000), 59–72; David R. Colburn and Richard K. Scher, *Florida's Gubernatorial Politics in the Twentieth*

*Century* (Tallahassee: Florida State University/University Presses of Florida, 1980), 220–36.

2. *Smith v. Allwright*, 321 U.S. 649 (1944); Francis Adams and Barry Sanders, *Alienable Rights: The Exclusion of African-Americans in a White Man's Land, 1619–2000* (New York: Perennial Books, 2004), 262–63; Albert Blaustein and Robert L. Zangrando, *Civil Rights and African-Americans: A Documentary History.* (Evanston, Ill.: Northwestern University Press, 1991), 396–97. For the early and evolving civil rights movement in Florida, see Ben Green, *Before His Time: The Untold Story of Harry T. Moore, America's First Civil Rights Martyr* (Gainesville: University of Florida Press, 1999); Glenda Alice Rabby, *The Pain and the Promise: The Struggle for Civil Rights in Tallahassee, Florida* (Athens: University of Georgia Press, 1999); Marvin Dunn, *Black Miami in the Twentieth Century* (Gainesville, University Press of Florida, 1997); David H. Jackson and Canter Brown Jr., eds., *Go Sound the Trumpet!: Selections in Florida's African American History* (Tampa: University of Tampa Press, 2005), Section 6, 255–331; Maxine D. Jones, "The African-American Experience in Twentieth-Century Florida," in *The New History of Florida*, ed. Michael Gannon (Gainesville: University Press of Florida, 1996), 373–90; Maxine D. Jones, "No Longer Denied: Black Women in Florida, 1920–1950," in *The African American Heritage of Florida*, ed. David R. Colburn and Jane L. Landers (Gainesville: University Press of Florida, 1995), 240–74; J. Irving E. Scott, *The Education of Black people in Florida* (Philadelphia: Dorrance and Company, 1974).

3. Blaustein and Zangrando, *Civil Rights and African-Americans*, 486.

4. See Robert Dallek, *Flawed Giant: Lyndon Johnson and His Times, 1961–1973* (New York: Oxford University Press, 1998), 37–38, 111–21; Eric Goldman, *The Tragedy of Lyndon Johnson* (New York: Dell Publishing, 1974), 374–76.

5. See David R. Colburn and Lance deHaven-Smith, *Government in the Sunshine State: Florida Since Statehood* (Gainesville: University Press of Florida, 1999), 40–41.

6. David Garrow, *Bearing the Cross: Martin Luther King, Jr. and the Southern Christian Leadership Conference* (New York: Vintage Books, 1988), 316–18; David R. Colburn, *Racial Change and Community Crisis: St. Augustine, Florida, 1877–1980* (Gainesville: University Press of Florida, 1991), 13–17; *New York Times*, April 14, 1963; Robert Cook, *Sweet Land of Liberty: The African-American Struggle for Civil Rights in the Twentieth Century* (New York: Longman, 1998), 138–44; David Garrow and David Colburn, eds., *St. Augustine Florida, 1963–1964: Mass Protest and Racial Violence* (Brooklyn: Carlson Publishers, 1989), 232;

7. Colburn, *St. Augustine*, 36–44; *New York Times*, July 7, July 26, July 27, and July 29, 1963; quoted in Patsy Sims, *The Klan* (New York: Stein and Day, 1978), 154.

8. Garrow, *Bearing the Cross*, 316–17; Colburn, *St. Augustine*, 13–17, 32, 33; *New York Times*, June 27, and July 5, 1964.

9. Quoted in Robert Hartley, "A Long Hot Summer: St. Augustine Racial Disorders of 1964," in *St. Augustine, Florida*, 63.

10. Adam Fairclough, *To Redeem the Soul of America: The Southern Christian Leadership Conference and Martin Luther King, Jr.* (Athens: University of Georgia Press, 1987), 181–91; Colburn,

St. Augustine, 63; Garrow, Bearing the Cross, 317–25; Cook, Sweet Land of Liberty, 138–44; New York Times, June 26, 1964.

11. New York Times, June 26, 1964; quoted in Fairclough, To Redeem the Soul, 141.

12. New York Times, June 14, 1964; State of Florida, Racial and Civil Disorders in St. Augustine: Report of the Legislative Investigation Committee (Tallahassee: Florida State Legislature, 1965), iii.

13. Washington Post and Times, October 1, 1957; see Colburn, St. Augustine, 36–60; Martin A. Dyckman, Floridian of His Century: The Courage of Governor LeRoy Collins (Gainesville: University Press of Florida, 2006), 72–205.

14. "Where Violence Has Started: Jacksonville Riots," U.S. News and World Report, April 6, 1964, 35–36; Florida Times-Union, March 23, 1964.

15. Colburn, St. Augustine, 73; Florida Times-Union, April 15, 1964, June 8, 1964.

16. Florida Times-Union, March 23, April 2, April 5, April 6, April 15, and May 3, 1964; New York Times, May 24, 1964.

17. Florida Times-Union, November, 23, 1981; Allen Morris, comp., The Florida Handbook, 1973-1994 (Tallahassee, Peninsular Publishing, 1993), 343–44.

18. Florida Times-Union, November, 23, 1981; New York Times, March 29, 1964.

19. Florida Times-Union, April 3, 1949, November 23, 1981.

20. Florida Times-Union, May 18, and May 1, 1949; Brian Hennessey, "The Racial Integration of Urban Police Departments in the South: Case Studies of Three North Florida Cities" (M.A. thesis, Florida State University, 1974), 17; Jacksonville Chronicle, July 21, 1950; Frank Hampton (Jacksonville civil rights activist), interview by author, January 2, 1993, Jacksonville; James B. Crooks, Jacksonville: The Consolidation Story, from Civil Rights to the Jaguars (Gainesville: University Press of Florida, 2004), 4.

21. New York Times, March 29, 1964; Florida Times-Union, November 23, 1981, February 21, 1999.

22. Florida Times-Union, November 23, 1981; Florida Times-Union, February 21, 1999; see James Robertson Ward with Dena Elizabeth Snodgrass, Old Hickory's Town: An Illustrated History of Jacksonville (Jacksonville: Old Hickory's Town, Incorporated, 1985), 221–22; Crooks, Jacksonville: The Consolidation Story, 2–36, for background on Brown and the black community of Jacksonville; Bartley, Keeping the Faith, 43–74.

23. Florida Times-Union, April 5, 1951; Bartley, Keeping the Faith, 43–74.

24. Miami Herald, February 9, 1992; see Dunn, Black Miami, 143–70.

25. Quoted in "The Council of Social Agencies, Jacksonville Looks At its Negro Community: A Survey of Conditions Effecting the Negro Community in Jacksonville and Duval County, Florida" (Jacksonville, 1946), 74–78; Hennessey, "The Racial Integration of Urban Police Departments," 11.

26. Jacksonville Journal, February 3, 1950; see Florida Times-Union, February 3, 1950.

27. Florida Times-Union, July 20, 1950, November 23, 1981; Hennessey, "The Racial Integration of Police Departments in Urban Areas," 19.

28. Interview, Frank Hampton; Florida Times-Union, April 7, 1959; Bartley, Keeping the Faith, 43–74.

29. Florida Times-Union, April 7, and September 23, 1959.

30. *Florida Times-Union*, April 7, 1959, September 24, and September 24, 1959; Roger Thurow, "Blues to Greens: A Golf Course Rising From Bigotry's Ruins Is a Game's New Hope—Racism Closed Brentwood Decades Ago; Tigermania Helps to Revitalize It—Mr. Hampton's Sacrifices," *Wall Street Journal*, April 9, 1998.

31. *Florida Times-Union*, September 23, 1959; see Bartley, *Keeping the Faith*, 43–74.

32. Quoted in *Florida Times-Union*, September 23, 1959; see Bartley, *Keeping the Faith*, 65–66.

33. Frank Hampton interview; *Florida Times-Union*, April 7, 1959.

34. Eric Simpson (former editor of the *Florida Star*), interview by author, January 3, 1993, Jacksonville,; Frank Hampton interview; *Florida Times-Union*, August 21, 1983; Bartley, *Keeping the Faith*, 43–74.

35. *Florida Times-Union*, September 2, 1960; Morris, *Florida Handbook*, 344, 622.

36. Bartley, *Keeping the Faith*, 43–74.

37. *Florida Times-Union*, September 2, 1960; Crooks, *Jacksonville*, 18–24.

38. Quoted in *Florida Times-Union*, September 2, 1960; see Tom Wagy, *Governor LeRoy Collins of Florida: Spokesman of the New South* (Tuscaloosa, University of Alabama Press, 1985), 170–72; Dyckman, *Floridian of His Century*, 190–205.

39. Quoted in *Florida Times-Union*, September 2, 1960.

40. Frank Hampton interview; *Florida Times-Union*, May 14, 1960; Bartley, *Keeping the Faith*, 43–74.

41. See Morris, *Florida Handbook*, 342–43.

42. *Florida Times-Union*, April 17, 1963; see Charlton W. Tebeau and William Marina, *A History of Florida* (Coral Gables: University of Miami Press, 1999), 435.

43. *Florida Times-Union*, April 17, 1963; see Charlton W. Tebeau and William Marina, *A History of Florida* (Coral Gables: University of Miami Press, 1999), 435.

44. *Florida Times-Union*, May 23, 1964; *Miami News*, March 24, 1964; Crooks, *Jacksonville*, 3–36.

45. *Florida Times-Union*, November 30, 1981; *Miami News*, March 24, 1964; Crooks, *Jacksonville, the Consolidation Story*, 3–36.

46. *Florida Times-Union*, May 24, 1964, November 30, 1981.

47. *New York Times*, March 29, 1964; *Florida Times-Union*, March 26, May 23, and May 24, 1964; Bartley, *Keeping the Faith*, 104–14.

48. William Frey, "Census 2000 Shows Large Black Return to the South, Reinforcing the Regions 'White-Black' Demographic Profile Before 1960–1970," 17; see "Florida's Rank by Population, 1900–1990," Morris, *Florida Handbook*, 559.

49. See *Florida Times-Union*, May 15, May 17, May 23, and May 24, 1964; *New York Times*, May 6, May 7, and May 24, 1964; *Sheboygan Press*, May 27, 1964.

50. Quoted in *Florida Times-Union*, May 18, 1964, see May 24, 1964.

51. Quoted in *Florida Times-Union*, May 18, 1964.

52. *New York Times*, May 10, and May 24, 1964; *Florida Times-Union*, May 23, and May 24, 1964.

53. Quoted in *Florida Times-Union*, May 27, 1964; *New York Times*, May 20, and May 24, 1964.

54. *Florida Times-Union*, May 10, May 21, and May 24, 1964.

55. See *Florida Times-Union*, May 3, May 17, May 23, and May 27, 1964; *New York Times*, May 24, 1964; Colburn and Scher, *Florida's Gubernatorial Politics*, 80.

56. *Florida Times-Union*, May 27, 1964; *New York Times*, May 27, 1964; Edmund F. Kallina Jr., *Claude Kirk and the Politics of Confrontation* (Gainesville: University Press of Florida, 1993), 19–45.

57. *Miami Herald*, August 31, 1967; Morris, *The Florida Handbook*, 617.

# CHAPTER NINE

# FROM OLD SOUTH EXPERIENCES TO NEW SOUTH MEMORIES

## VIRGINIA KEY BEACH AND THE EVOLUTION OF CIVIL RIGHTS TO PUBLIC SPACE IN MIAMI

### GREGORY W. BUSH

Virginia Key Beach is an eighty-two-acre waterfront park on a one thousand-acre barrier island about a mile from the city of Miami. In 1945, a bathing beach for people of African descent was established there by the Dade County Commission in accordance with the Old South Jim Crow segregation laws and practices of the state. The park became an unprecedented gathering spot in South Florida, a place of pride and fellowship and an important link to nature for the black community. It also arose as one of the first sites in mid-century Florida where a dramatic episode of civil disobedience was successful in expanding public accommodation and creating a new, although segregated, leisure space within the state's fast-growing urban centers.

Virginia Key Beach is not only an unusual and revealing symbol of the complex history of civil rights in Florida's largest city, but it also illustrates the recurring challenges for the black community to redefine and preserve its "special" public spaces made so in association with protest actions.[1] Thus, this study will address the evolution of the civil rights struggle for Virginia Key Beach in relation to changing struggles for access to a recreational space impacting all local residents. The ironic role played by the memories of locals focused around the fight for a segregated place to bathe in the sea in 1945 are set against the more recent use of memory to retain the site as a historically unique public space in the face of intense commercial pressures.²

The establishment of the beach was in response to a protest that demanded a bathing beach in accordance with the segregation laws and practices of the time. In a real sense, the lessons of Virginia Key Beach, and the civil rights struggle in Miami to preserve it, transcended the Miami-Dade region of the state. Miami's race problem and long-standing habit of denying equitable treatment of public spaces to its African American community—whether by intention or oversight—demonstrates that Florida's civil rights movement originated before, lived through, and reappeared after the traditional demarcation of 1954–1965. Moreover, an examination of the beach protest sheds useful light on the much-debated notion that the migration of northerners to South Florida in the period under review did little to temper the racial codes and practices of a dramatically transforming and increasingly complex demographic landscape in the Sunshine State, especially that of the most "northern" region of Florida, South Florida. Therefore, two critical lessons of the Virginia Key Beach experience are that the periodization of civil rights in Florida itself is debatable and that the "Yankee" influence on the racial temperament of the state remains an issue in need of further historical analysis.

Virginia Key remains a unique island of modern, mobile people—black and white—searching for their roots. The island separated from what became Miami Beach as a result of tidal changes and hurricanes in the early nineteenth century. Although evidence is scant, it likely once harbored small, marooned colonies of people of African heritage, including black Seminoles. It may also have served as part of the Underground Railroad escape route to the Bahamas and the Caribbean. The key became an informal recreational gathering place for blacks in the early twentieth century when it remained largely uninhabited and unconnected to the mainland. Today, Virginia Key is also emblematic of the confused values, oversight, and fragile sense of public involvement involving the planning and disposition of public space as well as the preservation of racial memory in the Sunshine State. Its poorly planned land uses should act as a fire bell in our contemporary air-conditioned nights.³

Ever since the founding of Miami, blacks had no place to swim in the Atlantic Ocean or Biscayne Bay, one of the most scenic bodies of water in the southern states. Such oppression was common throughout much of the South as well as the North and West. After an early attempt to create a black beach on what is now Fisher Island by a black real estate leader failed in the early 1920s, the need to create a "colored beach" in the Miami area became conceptualized by white leaders as part of their efforts to remove blacks from downtown Miami in the 1930s. The aim was, in part, to prevent blacks from interacting with white tourists while also responding to blacks' discontent over their lack of any legalized oceanfront access. Conversely, the beach issue had a starkly different set of meanings to the African American community. Although the beach was initiated after a May 1945 wade-in, many African Americans saw it as a triumph of personal relationships with white leaders that Miami's black elite had built over the years. Others, in a later era, saw the facilities of Virginia Key Beach as a second-rate place compared to nearby white beaches, an embarrassing memory and offensive use of public space. At yet another level, through its role in local religious ceremonies, seasonal celebrations and entertainment, family lore, and romance, the beach became a major center of community life for several critical decades after World War II in the state's critical demographic change and its transition from Old South segregation to what passed as New South integration.[4]

Virginia Key Beach also fits within a much larger and emerging national context of the civil rights movement. Around the nation, public spaces of human interaction—voting booths, schools, recreational and sports parks, plazas, streets, cemeteries, and libraries—often became the actual theaters where the human dramas of direct discrimination, personal humiliations, and sustained confrontations occurred. Urban historian Raymond Mohl notes that much recent scholarship has tended to focus on the local dimension and social significance of race and public space protests. "As a result of this work," Mohl notes, "it is now clear that the civil rights movement was in reality many civil rights movements, innumerable local groups confronting segregation and discrimination, energized by local leadership and moved to action by local conditions or events. . . outside the national spotlight and with little or no connection to national leaders or organizations." Within this context, Miami provides an important illustration of the local dimension of the civil rights movement in Florida. Thus, the struggle for Virginia Key Beach, prior to and again following the modern civil rights movement, illustrates important local initiatives involving race relations, territoriality, public access, and broader notions of urban memory that are now re-emerging within multicultural places like Miami.[5]

Memories of Miami's waterfront access have been important forces in the distribution of power when defining and facilitating recreation and the value of living in harmony with nature. "Lived inequalities yield unequal historical power," Michel-Rolph Touillot wrote in his study of the Haitian Revolution, and that can equally be said of Miami.[6] Remembering the meaning of places of humiliation, resistance, joy, and terror has helped to retrieve some of the pervasive silences in African American history, the hidden history of the decades-long forms of oppression experienced in daily life under the racial caste system that dominated the Old South life of rural and urban Florida. Remembering has also become a part of a broader process of re-appropriating urban-space access as Americans of all backgrounds have redefined the value of place and forms of leisure, and have reassessed the function of power over land use and race relations in contemporary "special" locales like the beach in New South Miami. Collectively, these changes have raised fundamental questions about marginal groups' civil rights to public space and the proper role of collective memory.

Boyd Shearer Jr., who created a path-breaking web site on the history of segregated parks in Lexington, Kentucky, notes that "black parks, like schools and churches for African American communities, were crucial daily geographies that empowered black identities despite the dehumanizing eclipse of racism, which initially created this segregated landscape." Sites for leisure thus became places for an African American sense of community and intra-group nurturing. Historian Robin Kelley adds that, "They were places that enabled African-Americans to take back their bodies, to recuperate, to be together. . . . Knowing what happens in these spaces of pleasure can help us understand the solidarity black people have shown at political mass meetings, [and] illuminate the bonds of fellowship one finds in churches and voluntary associations."[7]

Reviving Virginia Key Beach, one of Miami's special "spaces of pleasure," was initiated in 1999 by whites—in some cases by locals and northern transplants, myself included—but in recent times has been predominantly led by elder African Americans. They are predominantly professional women, who lived a significant portion of their lives under Jim Crowism and wanted to pass on an understanding of their times and that of their forbears to a younger, New South generation. Their determination to pass on a legacy in relation to a place of public interaction has been pivotal to the evolving concept of civil rights in Miami and, perhaps, in the Sunshine State itself. This approach to a civil rights agenda makes it an important turning point in Florida's race movements. It illustrates how subtle strategies of dialogue and protest over issues focused on memory of public spaces existed in Miami, but, so far, have eluded many scholars of civil rights in the state.[8]

From its inception in 1896, Miami remained mired within the social and racial context of its segregated land use patterns. Most blacks lived in strictly demarcated neighborhoods; generally either Coconut Grove or what was then called Colored Town near Miami's present-day urban core. For years, the KKK dominated the Miami police force and bullied blacks to stay within the strict boundaries of race-based segregation. Even within that context, there were powerful successes in forging black community life in Jim Crow Miami—as in many other Florida cities. In a recent study of black activism in Florida, Paul Ortiz has demonstrated how African Americans in the state "called on their mutual aid institutions to maintain the one thing that legal segregation always threatened to destroy: their dignity."[9] Colored Town, later known as Overtown, was not merely a place of widespread poverty, but a vibrant community where signs of dignity and some prosperity were clearly evident. Still, up to 1945, in typical Dixie fashion, African Americans had no recreational waterfront space in Miami and, subsequently, no significant public space in which they could nurture special values like group solidarity and dignity. Only with the impact of Supreme Court decisions and federal legislation following the *Brown* decision (1954)—notably cases involving public parks such as *Baltimore* (1956), *Watson v. Memphis* (1963), and finally the sweeping Civil Rights Act of 1964—did white control over beach access become seriously threatened in the South.[10]

Yet the story also involves numerous local commitments and actions by professional *and* everyday blacks in bringing the issue into sharp focus. In part, the issue of beachfront access illustrates diverse experiences and geographies, but several patterns can be identified from the past. First, informal recreational use existed for blacks throughout the east coast, often at isolated places or small towns, where blacks could only swim at dangerous inland rock pits or use the water along their industrial waterfront. Examples of this occurred in rock pits in Miami and in the Fort Lauderdale area.

A second pattern involved black ownership of beachfront land and the evolution of specific traditional spaces associated with particular black communities. As noted earlier, black developer Dana Dorsey bought Fisher Island off the south coast of Miami Beach at the end of World War I to be used as a black beach, but limited boat access and economic factors forced him to quickly sell it. In the 1930s, at the same time that Zora Neale Hurston was writing about the significance of black community life in her moving novels (often associated with Eatonville in the Orlando area), blacks often sought to own or use waterfront land for their own enjoyment. Several of the best examples in Florida are Frank Butler's purchase of land on Anastasia Island near St. Augustine in 1926 and A. L. Lewis's American Beach on Amelia Island near Jacksonville in 1935. Cookman-Volusia Beach in Deerfield Beach involved an assemblage of land including beachfront property brought together by national race leader and President of Bethune-Cookman College, Mary McLeod Bethune. These places sometimes possessed summer cottages for leading blacks in the state, and hosted various public picnics, religious gatherings, and occasionally commercial establishments.[11]

Third, in a few instances, protracted negotiations with local officials brought about a limited number of segregated beaches sanctioned by local white leaders, often in undesirable market locations for white buyers. Pablo Beach near Jacksonville is one such example. It was opened for blacks in 1884 but only on Mondays; even so, there were numerous excursions by black civic and religious groups to Pablo Beach. After Henry Flagler extended his railroad to nearby Mayport in 1899, blacks began buying property on Manhattan Beach. This soon became an important haven for blacks in North Florida until the Great Depression.[12]

World War II changed the context for those models. Historian Steven Lawson notes that the "World War II era furnished the staging ground for the black revolution. It revitalized black solidarity, tested innovative protest tactics, and moved the federal government closer to the side of racial equality. . ." Lizabeth Cohen adds, "the infuriation that worked its way into so many memories of World War II service was the preferential treatment given to white, German prisoners of war in commercial establishments where blacks were excluded." A few miles south of Miami, at the present-day site of the massive Dadeland Shopping Mall, once stood a World War II prisoner of war camp. Prisoners were allowed in many establishments where southern practices and laws excluded blacks. Many black servicemen in the states of Dixie—and most pointedly in Miami—were bitter to come back to a segregated city after they had served under combat to free the world of intolerance and fascism.[13]

Having been denied access to Miami's waterfront for years, black leaders focused on this issue after the war as a civil rights test case. While the Supreme Court in *Smith v. Allwright* (1944) had outlawed the white primary, and the NAACP used various other legal strategies in attacking segregation, Miami leaders became increasingly focused on gaining their own legal access to beaches.[14] As the Miami experience demonstrated, local people tended to localize their grievances. Thus, as the nation, and even parts of Florida, witnessed more conventional attacks on Jim Crow practices, the black community of Miami imbued its particular brand of civil rights into new demands for waterfront access, based largely on its own local needs for gratification and modification, if not destruction, of Florida's racial barriers.

As a result, a fourth model evolved over time from many places in the South but can be seen, perhaps in its first postwar iteration, in Miami. This demonstration model reflected not only impatience and anger but also an emerging recognition of the need for a localized focus on civil rights, if necessary, born out of nonviolent confrontation. Although usually associated with the protest tactics developed so effectively by Martin Luther King Jr. and the Southern Christian Leadership Conference (SCLC), this tactic may have actually been first demonstrated in postwar Miami, eventuating in the creation of Virginia Key Beach. Yet the seeds for this discontent were sown in an earlier time.[15]

George Merrick, founder of Coral Gables and head of the local county planning commission, reflected the white awareness of a need to create beach access for blacks far from the gaze of the white tourists; he identified Virginia Key in the late 1930s as a possible site. The tone of his plan sounded conciliatory rather than biased. "Today one-third of our present population is Negro. . . . Today this third of our present citizenry are effectively denied water access and 'water use.' Now collectively, as well as individually, we cannot receive fairness, unless we give fairness to this deserving one-third of our citizenry." The intent of his message, however, seemed clear, especially given his simultaneous plan for "slum clearance . . . effectively removing every Negro family from the present city limits." He saw the best model to be in Nassau's Grants Town with half-acre plots, presumably created further west in the Everglades, linked by a "county wide, county controlled transportation system, whereby these Negroes and other workers can be brought back and forth at a very cheap rate." This was arguably an early manifestation of Down South delay, simply perpetuating the color line and denying meaningful changes by pushing blacks out of the downtown area while creating beach access for them away from white tourists.[16] In retrospect, the plan was simply a stratagem to placate blacks and to delay meaningful negotiations with them until some distant future date.

In the following war years, the National Park Service cooperated with the County Park Department to study Dade County's recreational parks. An anonymous author concluded that it would be "wiser . . . to confine the Negro park problem to simple lines of development in order to more adequately satisfy the needs of the colored population as it exists here." The average "Negro is in a very low income bracket, and relatively few possess cars . . . their travel radius is largely restricted to close-to-home movement and activity." The author then rationalized continued exclusion of blacks from beaches due to the influx of northern tourists and the potentially high cost of surrounding land values, concluding that "since any Negro development would be ruinous to a large neighborhood area, it would be unwise and impractical to set off a Negro reservation on the beach." In practical terms, the plan simply validated delaying black access to evolving public space in the Miami area. The extant color line in this case seemed to be updated once again, but also applied in a newly conceived Down South constraining pattern.[17]

The work of several interracial committees as well as federal funding had kept the issues of black access to beaches alive during the war. The Interracial Committee of the YWCA offered to work with the city's recreational department in planning playground programs for black children. "The needs for a swimming beach available to Negroes, mentioned in the recent committee survey, was urged for consideration by city and county commissioners," the *Miami Herald* noted in 1943. The informal tradition of black use of the area east of Bear's Cut on Virginia Key was also reinforced by the action of the navy, which set aside the area for blacks near the end of the war.[18]

As late as January 1945, though, Virginia Key remained a contentious hodgepodge of land uses and visionary plans. An array of jurisdictional fights, financial interests, and personalities subsequently competed to define the shape of the key. An airport and seaport were proposed, but Miami Beach, lying directly north of Virginia Key, objected strongly. Then an announcement was made by Commissioner Crandon in late January that a "half-mile Negro bathing beach, large enough for 100,000 bathers, will be established by the County on Virginia Key." As if to underscore what would become a common Down South refrain for Florida segregationists following *Brown I* in 1954, and *Brown II* in 1955, Crandon added that this was the "best that the City could do," for its citizens of color. The actual and psychological distance between Virginia Key Beach for blacks and the newly projected Crandon Park for whites, as a newspaper article pointed out, was that "Virginia Key Beach is separated from Crandon Park by an expanse of water known as Bear Cut, which is approximately a half-mile wide."[19] It was also notoriously dangerous place to swim, with currents that were to drown a number of African Americans in the years to come.

Yet no further county action to create the beach had taken place by May 1945 and returning black servicemen after the war and Miami's post-war black leaders were in no mood to continue waiting for beach access as the months dragged on. The "best that the City could do" translated into the all-too-common game of waiting and prolonged racial inequity. Black journalist and war veteran Garth Reeves recalled that, even as South Florida swelled with new populations, there was "a hard racial climate in Miami. . . . and maybe if I'd been some place else it would be better than what I was experiencing in Miami. I was pretty bitter." Another interviewee noted that, "soldiers came back determined that they simply were not going to take [racial oppression] after having risked their lives." Miami's black leaders echoed this post-war restlessness. Old South Miami, and its progeny, Down South Miami, were no longer acceptable options for them. [20]

In tandem with the NAACP, local leaders like attorney Lawson Thomas, Rev. John Culmer, and Dr. I. P. Davis made the tactical decision to combat segregation in general by focusing on securing what they had been promised: a waterfront park. Their concern was heightened after learning that Broward County officials had written a letter to African American clergy saying that Dade residents were no longer welcome—informal as it was—at Broward beaches. The message was clear: waterfront recreation in Southeast Florida was off-limits to black residents.[21]

In May 1945, Thomas, who had consulted with Thurgood Marshall of the NAACP in conceiving of test cases against segregation, organized a protest. As recounted by the son of one of the demonstrators, "There were two women, five men from the NAACP . . . And they were to wade in at the all white County beach at Baker's Haulover . . . they proceeded to do that." Later, Dr. Oscar Braynon, son of one of the participants in the subsequent demonstration, concluded that "what is significant [is that] this happened long before the other cities. It wasn't heard at that time. This was 1945 before the war ended . . . So this was very new. Those folks had no idea what was going to happen to them but they were willing to take that chance . . ."[22] No other local leaders joined Thomas in the protest, and his wife later expressed sadness at the timidity of the other black leaders in their lack of support of the action. Nonetheless, these few Miami blacks, absorbing the lessons of World War II and the new federal court cases, undertook one of the first documented civil rights actions in the South almost ten years prior to the Court's desegregation edict in 1954. Although *Brown* is often portrayed in national and state literature as the demarcation point for black civil rights action in the twentieth century, in reality local actions over the right to public spaces—like the beach in Dade County, Florida—actually helped lay the groundwork for the awakening of civil rights protests across the Sunshine State that occurred in the post-*Brown* era.

As Virginia Key Beach slowly gained amenities (i.e., food concessions, a miniature train, a carousel, dance pavilion, and overnight cabins) and attention as a segregated leisure location for African Americans, the political climate of the Miami area gradually reflected elements of the New South. From 1945 through the 1960s, although seemingly out of the media mainstream, the civil rights movement in the Miami area reflected some of the most progressive forces in the urban South, while the simultaneous impact of various federal policies also began to undermine the traditional color lines, poverty, and degraded living conditions for African Americans. Forces challenging the old racial order included: (1) the influx of some northern activists—white (notably Jews) and black, (2) the economic consensus that sought to avoid major racial incidents in order to attract northern tourists, (3) the burgeoning role of labor organizations, and (4) the assertive actions of the Civil Rights Congress, the NAACP's legal challenges, and the direct-action protests of CORE (Congress of Racial Equality). Yet the very power of all these factors also engendered a prolonged reactionary crusade that sought to link civil rights and the labor movement to communist conspiracies. The result retarded a local protest movement in one of the regions where it might have been most successful.[23]

Nonetheless, there were gains over segregation achieved through negotiation, protests, and legal strategies. For example, Miami hired its first black policemen in 1944, although, as had been the case in other large Florida cities such as Jacksonville, they were only allowed to arrest blacks. In 1949, fourteen local black leaders began their long challenge of racial exclusion at local golf courses. Lawson Thomas became the first black judge in the South in 1951, presiding over a court addressing a new black police precinct. The dominant news media, although often stereotyping black life as violent while ignoring its diversity and accomplishments, nonetheless sought to defuse racial conflict. This was seen most graphically in the 1956 WTVJ news broadcast, "Incident at Delray Beach," in which newsman Ralph Renick staged a round table discussion that forced black and white leaders to address problems of access to beaches and pools in nearby Delray Beach. (The program beamed throughout South Florida, suggested that issues of segregated access to the waterfront could be worked out through biracial dialogue.) Sit-ins to promote deseg-regation, led by Dr. John O. Brown and CORE, took place at Burdines Department store in 1959, a year prior to the Greensboro sit-ins that gained such widespread attention, and are often used as a demarcation point for such nonviolent actions of defiance in the mod-ern movement. De jure integration was initiated at Miami's Orchard Villa Elementary School in 1959, although it became a de facto all-black school as whites of all backgrounds refused to send their children to it (the problem of segregated schools continues to this day). Pools were at first integrated after black leaders merely pointed out to city officials that no ordinance mandated segregated swimming facilities, although the city commis-sion soon rescinded the order of the city manager.[24]

Black leadership of Miami's civil rights movement came from locals in the Negro Ministerial Alliance, the NAACP, and CORE. Due to the repressive climate, however, a large number of middle-class African Americans shunned involvement. The Civil Rights Congress, active in Miami and including some members of the Communist Party, was the target of newspaper and TV news attacks, grand juries, and police as well as FBI action in the early 1950s. In later years, the state legislature's infamous Johns Committee asso-ciated the civil rights movement with both communism and homosexuality and sought to access the membership records of the local NAACP chapters in order to harass them. The Supreme Court, in *Gibson v. Florida Legislative Investigative Committee* (1963), finally ruled the Johns Committee's action unconstitutional. By then, one Miamian, Albert D. Moore, had become a close associate of Martin Luther King Jr. Although it was seldom publicized, King frequently visited Miami and Virginia Key Beach to relax. With such post-World War II developments, Miami had been poised for civil rights gains even prior to the more prominent national actions in other locales.[25]

Therefore, even within the context of local repression, black community activists had made slow but measurable gains by the 1960s, somewhat in contradiction to other locals in Florida and in the South in general. A biracial committee, formed to combat hous-ing conditions in the western portion of Miami's Coconut Grove, was created in the late 1940s, led by Father Theodore Gibson and Elizabeth Virrick. Gibson was later elected to the City Commission. Funeral home director M. Athalie Range, who had cut her politi-cal teeth fighting for school desegregation in the late 1940s, became the first black City Commissioner in 1965 and was later appointed head of the state's Department of Com-munity Affairs by Governor Reubin Askew. Voter turnout increased, although by the early

1980s black effectiveness had been compromised by several political scandals involving charges of bribery.[26]

Central to understanding the social limits that continued to be imposed on African Americans were the structural changes brought about by such forces as technological "progress" and the impact of state and federal programs. Air conditioning and television, for example, promoted an increasing retreat into the privacy of home life as suburbanization (for whites and blacks) became the trend in the postwar period. Scholars have shown in recent years that the impact of "redlining" through the federal housing and highway policies reinforced poverty and isolation in Miami—a pattern practiced around the state as well. The federal highway system, notably through the construction of I-95, cut through downtown Miami and had a devastating impact on the black community of Overtown. Its population fell from 40,000 to 16,000, and those left often suffered joblessness and despair.[27]

Social and political tensions were also exacerbated by the rapid influx of Cubans into the Miami area, beginning in the late 1950s. Government and private assistance given to Cubans, combined with the jobs they were seen to have taken from blacks, and, in later years, the double standard in immigration status given to Cubans versus Haitians, all fed into economic and political resentment that found its most potent symbol in episodes of white police brutality. Culminating in the riots surrounding the Republican National Convention in 1968, and highlighted later in the 1980 riots, police violence, and the subsequent trial related to the death of Arthur McDuffie, Miami's racial setbacks often seized national headlines. The hard racial edge that Miami represented became even more pronounced in the late 1990s when the city was cited as having the highest poverty rate in the nation. Downtown Miami remained a devastated location, one largely uninhabited by whites, well into the new century before a new skyline building boom ensued. Black neighborhoods like Overtown and the West Coconut Grove area remained places of intense poverty and hopelessness. And within that context, Virginia Key Beach was lost as a place of community pride in the reactivated New South as modern commercial vitality continued many of the distinct racial and ethnic divides in Miami.[28]

Virginia Key Park operated for blacks from August 1945 until the desegregation of all county beaches produced its increasing isolation by the 1960s. Protests in the late 1950s and early 1960s opened nearby Crandon Park on Key Biscayne and other parks to blacks. In retrospect, the fate of Virginia Key Beach in the era of desegregation is revealing. It was a vital community location—a place of recreation, romance, and religious fellowship, an unusual environment for South Florida blacks that provided both intra-group bonding and unparalleled proximity to the natural world. Yet the very plasticity of its appeal proved its undoing after desegregation opened all beaches to blacks. Staff and amenities were cut back. Its popularity declined and the beach was finally transferred from Dade County to the City of Miami in 1982. The city was obliged to keep it open "for public park purposes only" and there was a clause in the deed stating the land would revert back to the county if the deed restrictions were not honored. Unfortunately, the county never provided the oversight of its own deeds to force the city to comply. As a result, the physical condition of the beach dramatically deteriorated. It was finally closed and remained off-limits to the public behind a locked fence.[29]

By the 1990s, as the City of Miami's fiscal condition deteriorated, its staff sought to privatize many of the underutilized public spaces on Virginia Key and the rest of the waterfront. By that time, the island contained a strange array of land uses and zoning classifications. Long before this, parcels of land had been leased out to the University of Miami for a Marine Science School, to a private tourist venture (the Seaquarium), several restaurants, and a major county sewage treatment plant that overshadowed much of the northwestern portion of the island. There was also a wildlife preserve on the western side and an anomaly called Shrimper's Lagoon on the north end that harbored Jimbo's, an unpretentious hangout and drinking location for whites and blacks.[30] Within this context, greater Miami continued to be challenged by its onetime promise to reserve Virginia Key Beach as a public place of special significance to blacks.

Even so—as oral history interviews have uncovered in the past dozen years—after 1945, Virginia Key Beach had provided a growing array of community experiences and recreational amenities for African Americans. Never equal to the funds spent on nearby Crandon Park for whites (opened after the causeway from Miami through Virginia Key to Key Biscayne was completed in 1947), Virginia Key Beach was, nevertheless, an important public space facilitating racial solidarity until the 1970s. Large numbers of people went there as documented in numerous photographs from the era. Recreational and cultural activities made it a kind of a local paradise for many blacks, a special black enclave in an ever-changing urban landscape. Local resident Fred Brown recalled:

> You had to get on the boat on Fifth Street . . . maybe 100 or 150 people on the boat. And they would make two or three trips to get everybody over there. . . . Certain days you could go over there and certain days you couldn't. Then they kept fighting until they got a black concession over there. More like hotdogs, hamburgers. They had a small, real railroad track with a small train that you could sit in . . . for the kids to ride around in. Then they had cabanas, small cabanas that people could rent and take their families alongside the beach.[31]

The founder of Miami's Black Archives, historian Dr. Dorothy Jenkins Fields, added that "the irony of it all was that there was no bridge [or] causeway . . . the currents were so swift that it was frightening. . . . We always thought, why would [whites] give us the water that had the bad spot, knowing that we were going to bring children."[32]

In its prime, many nationally known African American entertainers and leaders had visited the beach, helping to make it a major intra-group arena for fun and fellowship. On numerous occasions from the late 1950s until the end of his life in 1968, Martin Luther King Jr. visited what continued to be in many ways a color-coded South Florida. He often stayed at the Hampton House, the all-black resort in Brownsville, relaxed with friends, fished on segregated boats in Biscayne Bay, and swam at the area's only "colored beach," Virginia Key. From 1945 until King's era, it was the only place in Miami-Dade that blacks could officially frequent to bathe in Biscayne Bay. King is even reported to have delivered an early version of his legendary "I have a Dream" speech at the Hampton House. The champion of civil rights found Miami and the beach, albeit persistently segregated, an exciting and nurturing place to recharge his soul.[33]

Yet the desegregation of Dade County's public parks truncated this sort of recreational focus and memory for the black community, and, in the process, resulted in yet another round of struggles over public space. In the three decades following King's assassination in 1968, and in the midst of a continued northern influx into South Florida, tensions grew from the conflicting goals of expanding access to open space and pressures for commercialized forms of leisure. Following the revitalization of New York's Central Park in the 1970s, and the revival of waterfronts in Boston and Baltimore, urban waterfronts became exploding focal points for commercial development and public-private partnerships. The historical landscape of waterfronts changed from their earlier industrial focus into tourist attractions where restaurants, bars, shops, hotels, and parking facilities multiplied. Many also argued that, in a time of urban crisis and lean public revenues, it was smart to develop economic synergism with public spaces that both focused historical memory and expanded cultural tourism. However, Charles Birnbaum has recently warned that the national trend in which "the cluttering of reposeful park grounds with activity-oriented 'focal points' is lamentable and perplexing, not least because park users themselves aren't demanding change." In short, the character of parks was being undermined as nonprofit institutions seeking "free land" concessions or public agencies seeking new revenue increasingly privatized them. In this light, the recent development and preservation of Virginia Key Park fits into the national contemporary revival of civic participation in the design and revitalization of public parks and the rising interest in black heritage tourism, two goals often contested by corporate entities and public agencies. In a real sense, Virginia Key Park presents sort of a microcosm of the events and issues that have surrounded the revitalization and public memory preservation attempts of numerous other parks in the Sun Cities of Florida and across the nation.[34]

Almost predictably, Miami's waterfront became a major zone of conflict when funding for parks eroded in a city with a softening tax base and a divisive political arena increasingly moving away from old-line leadership to new Cuban-American political forces, all of which underscored South Florida's complex ethnic and cultural population base. City staff had orders to develop much of the largely abandoned and under-planned waterfront parkland by working with private entrepreneurs. In 1985, a large chunk of Miami's most famous waterfront park, Bayfront, was taken over and transferred to the Rouse Company to become a popular shopping mall and tourist destination in the stagnating downtown area (now called Bayside). Then in 1996, a county referendum was held to take nearby waterfront parkland for a new arena for the Miami Heat professional basketball team. The team won after an expensive advertising campaign. A full-scale assault on waterfront parks was in process by the late 1990s, seen most pointedly in the struggle to preserve the Miami Circle, an ancient Tequesta Indian site at the mouth of the Miami River, and the attempt by the Marlins to take over Bicentennial Park for a new baseball stadium—all contemporary events strikingly similar to those in so many other large cities of the New South. The attempts to privatize the largely forgotten Virginia Key Beach thus fit historically within a larger process of revenue generation and of selling off the public's assets through commercializing Miami's waterfront.[35]

By the late 1990s, Miami's waterfront parks, including the historically black Virginia Key Beach, were more threatened with extinction and neglect than those in any other major city in Florida. A complex array of political and economic developments had affected the site of Virginia Key Beach, undermining its value as public space and special memory for the black community. A city task force called for the creation of an eco-tourist resort on the land that would, presumably, bring revenue to the city. Decades after integration of public accommodations had been established in law, the former "black beach" had become largely forlorn, abandoned, forgotten, and seemingly set up to be leased out by the city as a high-end "eco-resort." That land thereafter became part of a broader contemporary struggle by a new multicultural coalition to reclaim and redefine public space along Miami's waterfront. Although many blacks had decried the loss of the park's status in the 1970s, predominantly white environmentalists, led by Mabel Miller and the Friends of Virginia Key, fought both to preserve the natural attributes of the island and to persuade public officials to accede to the deed restrictions up through 1998. In a manner eerily reminiscent of an earlier foot-dragging Florida, their appeals failed to achieve any concrete changes or future plan for the beach or the island itself. Time had eroded many positive associations by African Americans to the beach. It was closed to public use and few of Miami's new or old-line social activists seemed to be aware that actions on it had been delayed indefinitely, or, even worse, simply deferred.[36]

In 1999, however, the Virginia Key Park issue re-surfaced and signified in compelling ways the importance of remembering the meaning of segregation and the civil rights struggle by African Americans for recreational equality that had surfaced so strongly in South Florida at the end of World War II. The new struggle, led first by the Urban Environment League, gained attention in the *New York Times*, the *San Francisco Chronicle*, and other national newspapers. Ultimately, the identification with the land, forged through a sense of community traditions and the unique experience of African Americans in Miami, was to be revived in a broad-based civil rights crusade to end a new round of stalling after a long hiatus in the Sunshine State itself. According to Enid Pinkney, an African American and former president of the predominantly white Dade Heritage Trust:

> a lot of the history of the people who helped the civil rights movement can never be told because people don't know about it. You only know about the famous people, the people who became famous in the struggle. But other people . . . did things that called attention to the problems of segregation, [though] you will never read about them in the history books . . . they played an important part in bringing about changes in our society . . . It was our beach. Colored Only . . . [Later in 1999] we rallied when we heard that the City of Miami was going to turn it over to developers. . . . We took ownership again . . . I think it showed the strength and the depth of the ownership when we said, "Oh no, no, no. You can't do that to us because this belongs to us . . ." I see it as a steppingstone to means into fuller equality. [37]

The new grassroots crusade to which Pinkney referred galvanized many in the black and progressive white communities of Southeast Florida, including local heritage preservationists, environmentalists, and a few academics. In 1999, in my capacity as the newly installed president of the Urban Environment League and longtime director of the University of Miami's Institute for Public History, I spoke before the city's Ad Hoc Committee for Virginia Key and stated for the record that "what was being overlooked was the historical significance of the park to the black community. Why shouldn't the whole park be designated to honor the meaning of the civil rights struggle within the history of Miami? That would be a perfectly valid reason to deny the privatization of that land."[38]

Other civic-minded whites were moved by this line of reasoning and soon sought to collaborate with such African Americans as Gene Tinnie, Enid Pinkney, Dorothy Fields, and others in creating the idea of a Civil Rights Park for the site. But it was clear to everyone involved that the attempt to make the land into a civil rights memorial would once again succumb to an indeterminate destiny unless African Americans themselves forcefully defined and led the effort. It seemed in those early days of the local movement that many people thought any such effort was doomed to indefinite delay or failure if the actual users and heirs of the park's "special" memories did not spearhead a sort of Miami-based, neo-civil rights movement to preserve this unique place of public interaction.[39]

The decision was quickly made by the Urban Environment League to campaign aggressively for a civil rights park, and equally so to enlist the aid of South Florida's black leaders to orchestrate preservation of Miami-Dade's historical black beach. One of the first people contacted had once worked on the Miami Circle demonstration. Dinizulu Gene Tinnie, a tall, deep-voiced African American, was a calm man, an artist, a writer, and a profound thinker. He later captured the essence of what came to drive the black community of Miami in its aroused effort to preserve Virginia Key Beach, its public space of past and now present "special" significance: "one of the strategies that we have to have is looking at our sacred sites, places that have been consecrated by, labored by, the struggle. There are too many people with too many fond memories, too many people who have been baptized out there, had their honeymoons out there, had their first love affair out there . . . that was a place that brought together an entire black community."[40]

Support soon swelled within parts of the black community. While never a deafening roar, it was enough to end the city's delay in preserving the land as a park. Central to the overall success was the input from Gene Tinnie, who has kept at it to this day, writing columns for the *Miami Times*, published by Garth Reeves, previously noted as one of the demonstrators desegregating Crandon Park in the late 1950s.

Significantly, the *Miami Herald* (the leading media voice of greater Miami) had largely ignored coverage of the issue from 1997 through early 1999. Even so, the local history of blocking access to a waterfront beach and the habit of delaying (often endlessly) redress to grievances were surfacing to rescue Virginia Key Park through exposure by both local and national publications. For example, *Miami New Times* reporter Kirk Nielson wrote, "Today [1999] the long-closed beach on Virginia Key is a symbol of racial segregation, the black struggle against it, and the need to preserve history." Athalie Range told reporter Teresa Mears of the *San Francisco Chronicle*, "the struggle, the civil rights issues that have been part of Miami for now over 50 years, need to be remembered . . . I can think of no better way to remember it than by opening this park and doing what needs to be done to bring the citizens back." Rick Bragg of the *New York Times* wrote a pioneering article focused on the memories of African Americans rather than on the value of developing the park into an eco-campground. Drawing on the meaning of the memories of black residents toward the beach, he quoted Range's comment that "we forget about these things and when it comes to a point when someone wants to do something else, you remember."[41]

Among the many steps taken in the ensuing months was the use of oral history reminiscences of the site as a civil rights memorial in persuading the city administration to create another temporary task force to orchestrate the renewal of the park. The result was a charrette (or design workshop for the public) that began work in January 2000. The City Commission appropriated $25,000 for the project, a pittance in standard terms, yet nonetheless an encouraging sign of support. The charrette submitted an articulate and important message about a new climate for preserving memory and expanding public involvement. The plan called for both a civil rights memorial as well as natural areas. This had the effect of ending the long delaying action. The City Commission responded to the report with an ordinance creating the Virginia Key Beach Park Trust to oversee fundraising, events, and planning for revitalization of the eighty acres of the historical "colored beach." Another stride forward occurred in August 2002, when the site was placed on the National Register of Historic Places and honored with a State of Florida Historical Marker. The Virginia Key Beach Park Trust, headed by Range and Tinnie, now had its own substantial city budget and planning operation.[42]

The trust built on its earlier work by creating a documentary film and oral history collection that both revealed and institutionalized important overlooked aspects of Florida's hidden past. A Master Plan followed in 2003 and a study for the National Parks Service focusing on its historical significance for possible inclusion in the National Park System emerged by 2006. Until her death in November 2006, Athalie Range remained the dominating force behind the African American community's commitment to force the preservation of its "special" public space as well as shore up the Virginia Key Beach Park Trust, overseeing its role as a force to groups working to preserve a special place of civil rights and African American heritage for future generations of Floridians. But, the battle was not over. Public debate soon emerged about whether the rewards of National Park status, which would bring national stature and land use protections, outweighed the possible loss of local control and jobs related to the park. Tellingly, the fifty-year experience leading up to this juncture helped soften South Florida's color lines while highlighting the problem of preserving public places of "special memory" involved a web of racial, ethnic, cultural, and economic factors in a significant region of Florida undergoing dramatic changes since World War II.[43]

The proposal for an African American Memorial/Civil Rights Park was first brought forward in 1999 by the author and local activist Nancy Lee. The notion of ending delay in preserving this historic beach as public parkland by creating a major Civil Rights/ Memorial Park was at first ignored by a powerful and quasi-official city committee that seemed to be unrepresentative of the diversity of the City of Miami and, at least initially, unmotivated to preserve a place of "special" open-space significance to generations of Miami's black residents. This failure to act resulted in an important part of the African

American community's heritage, as well as the civil rights heritage of the Sunshine State, being given short shrift in regard to usage of public lands. When adequately publicized, this issue became politically powerful and subsequently interested many people of all backgrounds. Soon, representatives of these diverse groups came to argue that the struggle for civil rights and the related goal of preserving its public spaces were and are central to both the minority communities of urban areas and to all humanity interested in broadening the scope of urban planning to include such issues as the right to adequate public space for whom that space holds "special" memories.

The lessons involved in this historical debate provide useful insight into the complex, locally based civil rights movement, the conventionally cited dates for the advent of the modern movement in Sunshine State, and the much-debated "Yankee factor," as well as the basic question of how, when, and why cities like Miami must look both forward and backward when debating and deciding the issue of civil rights, "special" heritage, and public land usage.

Until recently, the silences of Virginia Key Beach have had powerful political and economic ramifications on the nature of Old South behaviors and New South African American priorities. The renewal of this waterfront area also illustrates the potential of New South forms of civic engagement in public planning processes that are designed to involve a broad, multi-cultural audience in honoring the experiences and memories of Florida's historical and still sizable African American population. Virginia Key Beach is, however, a compelling historical place of leisure and protest, fellowship and shared memories. This beach has become a common ground of hope for a better future than the experiences of color-coded Florida. It is also part of a broader effort to redesign the entire island through a new Master Plan process in which public participation by multi-racial residents can help ensure the redefinition of public space as true *public* space.

It remains a major challenge to redesign Virginia Key Beach Park as a usable place of leisure while remaining respectful of its powerful pioneering legacy in Florida's and the nation's civil rights movement. The beach's place in the order of civil rights experiences transcends not only generations of African American struggles to end delays and denial, but also reflects universal issues of equality and rights in the long journey towards social justice and environmental sensitivity. When and where, and even if, that historical struggle ended is yet a matter for intellectual inquiry. Arguably, that issue cannot be confronted comprehensively without understanding the unique role that Virginia Key Beach has played in Miami's and Florida's last half-century of civil rights goals, activism, failures, and successes.

## NOTES

1. This study draws from my National Park Service project, "Virginia Key Beach Park: Historic Context and National Significance," completed in May 2006. For further elaboration of several themes in the present study, see Gregory Bush, "Politicized Memories in the Struggle for Miami's Virginia Key Beach," in *"To Love the Wind and the Rain": African-Americans and Environmental History*, ed. Dianne D. Glave and Mark Stoll, (Pittsburgh: University of Pittsburgh Press, 2005), 164–88.

2. The best general work on Florida beaches is Gary Mormino, *Land of Sunshine, State of Dreams: A Social History of Florida* (Gainesville: University of Florida Press, 2005), ch. 9; see Martha Dean Phelts, *An American Beach for African-Americans* (Gainesville: University of Florida Press, 1997); and Russ Rymer, *American Beach, A Saga of Race, Wealth and Memory* (New York: Harper Collins, 1998).

3. For general background on the island, see Joan Gill Blank, *Key Biscayne* (Sarasota: Pineapple Press, 1996), 61–80, 157–61.

4. See Eileen Smith, "Black Churchgoers, Environmental Activism, and the Preservation of Nature in Miami, Florida," (PhD diss., Florida International University, 2003), especially ch. 6.

5. Raymond Mohl, "Civil Rights Movements," review of *Sunbelt Revolution: The Historical Progression of the Civil Rights Struggle in the Gulf South, 1866–2000*, ed. by Samuel C. Hyde Jr., H-Florida, December 2003, http://h-net.msu.edu/cgi-bin/logbrowse.pl?trx=vx&list=h-florida&month=0312&week=b&msg=cCt%2b3mBW5YAtEZFmJ3rOYA&user=&pw= 1, (accessed May 9, 2006).

6. Michael-Rolph Trouillot, *Silencing the Past: Power and the Production of History* (Boston: Beacon Press, 1995), 48; see the documentary on African Americans and urban parks by Austin Allen, "Claiming Open Spaces," VHS (ITVS, 1995), and http://www.pps.org/info/design/AustinAllen.

7. Quoted in "The Daily Aesthetic," website sponsored by the University of Kentucky and created by Boyd Shearer, http://www.uky.edu/Projects/TDA/welcome-tda.html (accessed March 13, 2007); Robin D. G. Kelly, "'We Are Not What We Seem': Rethinking Working-Class Opposition in the Jim Crow South," *Journal of American History* 80 (June 1993): 84–85.

8. This account makes extensive use of relevant oral history interviews.

9. See Helen Muir, *Miami, USA* (Miami: Hurricane House, 1953), ch. 6; Arva Moore Parks and Gregory Bush (with Laura Pincus), *Miami: The American Crossroad* (Englewood Cliffs, Prentice Hall, 1996), chs. 2–3; Alejandro Portes and Alex Steppick, *City on the Edge: The Transformation of Miami* (Berkeley: University of California Press, 1993), chs. 1, 8; Marvin Dunn, *Black Miami in the Twentieth Century* (Gainesville: University Press of Florida, 1997); Paul George, "Colored Town: Miami's Black Community, 1896–1930," *Florida Historical Quarterly* 56 (April 1979): 432–47; and a series of articles and books by Raymond Mohl, including "The Pattern of Race Relations in Miami Since the 1920s," in *The African American Heritage of Florida*, eds. David R. Colburn and Jane Landers (Gainesville: University Press of Florida, 1995): 326–65; Paul Ortiz, *Emancipation Betrayed: The Hidden History of Black Organizing and White Violence in Florida from Reconstruction to the Bloody Election of 1920* (Berkeley: University of California Press, 2005), 127.

10. On the legal history of public accommodation, see the National Park Service study "Civil Rights in America: Racial Desegregation in Public Accommodations" 2004, http://www.cr.nps.gov/nhl/themes/Pub%20Accom.pdf (accessed March 13, 2007).

11. Phelts, *An American Beach*, 1–13, 37–42, 62–77, 101–133; Rhymer, *American Beach*, ch. 3.

12. Phelts, *An American Beach*, 10; Donald Mabry, *The World's Finest Beach*: e-book located at http://historicaltextarchive.com/books.php?op=viewbook&bookid=70 (accessed March 13, 2007).

13. See Steven Lawson, *Running for Freedom: Civil Rights and Black Politics in America Since 1941* (New York, McGraw Hill, 1997), 28; Lizabeth Cohen, *A Consumer's Republic: The Politics of Mass Consumption in Postwar America* (New York: Alfred Knopf, 2003), 90, 93, 100; Harvard Sitkoff, "The Detroit Race Riots of 1943," *Michigan History* 53 (Fall 1969): 183–206; Howard Kleinberg, *Miami: The Way We Were* (Miami: Miami Daily News, 1985), 170–71.

14. *Smith v. Allwright*, 321 U.S. 649 (1944).

15. See Gary Mormino, *Land of Sunshine*, ch. 9; Michael D. Sproat, "A Beach Too Far: 50 Years Ago, Sarasota's Black Citizens Fought for the Simple Right to go to the Beach," *Sarasota Magazine* (June 2005), http://www.sarasotamagazine.com/Articles/Sarasota-Magazine/2005/06/A-Beach-Too-Far.asp?ht? (accessed March 13, 2007); Gilbert Mason, *Beaches, Blood and Ballots: A Black Doctor's Civil Rights Struggle* (Jackson: University of Mississippi Press, 2000), chs. 4–5.

16. George Merrick, "Planning the Greater Miami for Tomorrow," as given by Mr. Merrick before the Miami Realty Board on Monday May 17, 1937 and at the Miami Bayfront Park Friday May 28, 1937, 10–11, Special Collections, Otto Richter Library, University of Miami.

17. "Dade County's Recreation Parks: A Report to the People of Dade County Florida on the Present Extent and State of Development of the Several County Recreational Park Units Together with Recommendations for Future Development of the Park System," Dade County Park Department, 1941, 2–15; see Richard Dalfiume, *Desegregation of the United States Armed Forces: Fighting on Two Fronts, 1939–1953* (Columbia: University of Missouri Press, 1969).

18. "Playground Program Planned for Negro Children of Miami," *Miami News*, June 12, 1943, Agnew Welsh Scrapbooks, Vol. 23, Florida Room, Miami-Dade Public Library.

19. "Crandon Tells Virginia Key Beach Plans," *Miami Herald*, January 28, 1945; see Ernie Hill, "Virginia Key Airport: Plans Action Through Pepper," *Miami Herald*, February 9, 1945; Carl Ogle, "Round Table Demands Port Authority Push Virginia Key," *Miami Herald*, February 23, 1945; "Virginia Key Beach to Cover 46 Acres," *Miami Daily News*, January 28, 1945.

20. Garth Reeves, interview by Channelle Rose, 2005, Virginia Key Beach Park Trust; Rev. Austin Cooper, interview by author, 2002, Richter Library, University of Miami; see Channelle Rose, "The 'Jewel' of the South? Miami, Florida and the Black Struggle for Civil Rights in America's Vacation Paradise, 1896–1968" (PhD diss., University of Miami, 2007).

21. Eugenia Thomas, interview by Channelle Rose, 2005, Virginia Key Beach Park Trust.

22. Dr. Oscar Braynon, interview by Channelle Rose, 2005, Virginia Key Beach Park Trust.

23. See Raymond Mohl, *South of the South: Jewish Activists and the Civil Rights Movement in Miami, 1945–1960* (Gainesville: University of Florida Press, 2004), Part I.

24. Marvin Dunn, *Black Miami*, ch. 5; WTVJ broadcast, "Incident at Del Rey Beach," July 1956, Florida Moving Image Archive, Miami. On the integration of pools, see John Morton, "Pool Integration Revoked by Board," *Miami Herald*, October 28, 1959; Merrett Stierheim (former County Manager), interview by author, 2005, in author's possession.

25. Mohl, *South of the South*, 46–61; Gregory Bush, "'We Must Picture an Octopus': Anticommunism, Desegregation, and Local News in Miami, 1945–1960," *Tequesta*, 65 (2005): 48–63.

26. Dunn, *Black Miami*, 196–204.

27. Raymond Arsenault, "The End of the Long Hot Summer: The Air Conditioner and Southern Culture," *Journal of Southern History* 50 (November 1984): 597–628; Portes and Steppick, *City on the Edge*, ch 8.

28. See Dunn, *Black Miami*, chs. 7–8.

29. See Gregory Bush, "Politicized Memories in the Struggle for Miami's Virginia Key Beach," in *"To Love the Wind and the Rain,"* 164–88.

30. On the eclectic land uses in the period from 1982–1998, see "Virginia Key Beach Park Master Plan," 2003, http://www.virginiakeybeachpark.net/images/VKBPMasterPlanReport.pdf (accessed March 13, 2007).

31. Fred Brown, interview by Channelle Rose, 2005, Virginia Key Beach Park Trust.

32. Dr. Dorothy Jenkins Fields, interview by Channelle Rose, 2005, Virginia Key Beach Park Trust.

33. On Martin Luther King in Miami, see Albert D. Moore, interview by Kathy Hersh, 2001, in author's possession; Jody Benjamin, "Past Glory Fades Into History: The Hampton House Motel, Once A Bustling Hangout That Attracted Celebrities To The Black Community In Miami, Today Lies In Ruins," *Sun-Sentinel* (Fort Lauderdale), February 18, 2001.

34. Charles Birnbaum, "In Defense of Open Space," *Preservation* 57 (2005): 38–39. On the growing popularity of black tourism, see Sandhya Somashekhar, "Black History Becoming A Star Tourist Attraction," *Washington Post*, August 15, 2005.

35. "Parks and Profits: Believe It or Not, Miami's Planning Czar Jack Luft Says He Can Make Virginia Key both Lovely and Lucrative," *Miami New Times*, October 23, 1997; "Take Me Out to the Parking Lot," *Miami New Times*, January 27, 2000.

36. "A Noisy Fight Over Some Quiet Refuges," *Miami Herald*, March 3, 1995, "Blacks Say They Always Braved Beach," *Miami Herald*, February 19, 1975; "A Deserted 'Old World' Beach," *Miami Herald*, February 22, 1975; "A Historic Dip: Witnesses to the Segregated History of Virginia Beach Tell a Sorry but Inspiring Tale," *Miami New Times*, April 8, 1999; Julian Pleasants, *Orange Journalism: Voices from Florida Journalism* (Gainesville: University of Florida Press, 2003), 204–05.

37. Enid Pinkney, interview by Channelle Rose, 2005, Virginia Key Beach Park Archives.

38. Gregory Bush, notes at meeting of Ad Hoc Committee for Virginia Key, January 1999, in author's possession.

39. Jim Mullin, "Saviors of Virginia Key," *Miami New Times*, April 1, 1999, http://www.miaminewtimes.com/1999-04-01/news/saviors-of-virginia-key/1 (accessed January 4, 2008).

40. Resolution of the Urban Environment League Board of Directors, "Future Enhancement of Virginia Key Beach," February 22, 1999, in author's possession; Dinizulu Gene Tinnie, interview by Channelle Rose, 2005, Special Collections, Richter Library, University of Miami; Dinizulu Gene Tinnie, editorial, "Virginia Key in Jeopardy," *The Miami Times*, March 4, 1999; "Virginia Key Beach Trust," *The Miami Times*, December 20–26, 2000; and "3,000 Revive Easter Tradition on Virginia Key," *The Miami Times*, May 3–9, 2000.

41. "A Historic Dip," *Miami New Times*, April 8, 1999; "Alliance Fights a Plan to Develop a Florida Getaway Born of Racism," *New York Times*, March 28, 1999; "Black Pearl," *San Francisco Chronicle*, September 1999. For an illustration of how racial politics was inserted into the overall dialogue, see Gregory Bush, Letter to Dr. Virginia Newell, February 18, 1999, in author's possession.

42. See the National Park Service statement at http://www.nps.gov/legal/testimony/107th/virkeybe.htm (accessed March 13, 2007).

43. An online version of the Virginia Key Beach Park Trust Master Plan can be viewed at http://www.virginiakeybeachpark.net/images/VKBPMasterPlanReport.pdf (accessed March 13, 2007).

# Afterword

## Old South, New South, or Down South? Florida and the Modern Civil Rights Movement: Towards a New Civil Rights History in Florida

### Paul Ortiz

You born here?

Naw. Down south. Jacksonville, Florida. Bad country, boy. Bad, bad country. You know they ain't even got an orphanage where colored babies can go? They have to put 'em in jail. I tell people that talk about them sit-ins I was raised in jail, and it don't scare me none.

—Toni Morrison, *Song of Solomon*

This telling exchange between Milkman Dead and Freddie Guitar in *Song of Solomon* is rooted in a black perspective of Florida history. Australian Frank Sullivan, who settled in Jacksonville after World War I, learned about Florida from the other side of the color line. Sullivan served in the U.S. Army and married an American woman who convinced him to become a U.S. citizen after the Armistice. According to some local whites, however, Sullivan became too friendly with African Americans. Sullivan, in his own words, "born in a country where freedom of speech, and open discussion of community questions is an assured fact," began to publicly question Florida's Old South-style racism. When the army veteran attended an African American wedding as a guest of honor, Ku Klux Klansmen decided that a southern citizenship lesson was in order. They seized Sullivan and told him, "Sullivan, you get out of Jacksonville within three days. If you don't do so, we will kill you. No matter how many guns you may have in your home, we will get you.

We belong to a strong organization. . ." After the Klansmen tarred and feathered Sullivan, he fled from the state. Safely outside Florida, Sullivan rued his decision to become an American citizen, "I have sold my birth-right for a mess of pottage."[1]

Like Frank Sullivan, English Episcopal Church Reverend Philip S. Irwin would quickly learn about U.S. race relations in Florida. A federal agent who spied on the Miami churchman during the World War I era claimed that Irwin "has been instrumental in fomenting trouble between the negroes and whites. IRWIN has a great deal of influence among the colored population of Miami in view of the fact that the negroes [sic] are about 65 per cent BAHAMA NEGROES, aliens, and members of his church. His following is rather large." (Emphasis in original.)[2] The undercover federal operative understood that part of his job in securing domestic tranquility was to reinforce the racial status quo in Florida: "Agent is proceeding under the theory that it is not likely the feeling of the white population is apt to change regarding the segregation of the colored population, and that any disturbing element should be suppressed if possible." Shortly after Rev. Irwin was questioned by the Miami police "regarding his alleged preaching of race equality," members of the Klan abducted the pastor and flogged him. After tarring and feathering Rev. Irwin, the Klansmen ordered him out of town.[3] The bishop of the South Florida Episcopal Diocese believed that the KKK did not act alone. Bishop Cameron Mann publicly stated that the American Legion also participated in driving Irwin out of Miami.[4]

From North Florida to South Florida and from the Atlantic coast to the Gulf coast, the Sunshine State's restrictive system of race relations was skillfully guarded by local, state, and federal authorities, often in tandem with terrorist groups like the Klan. Open challenges to white supremacy were summarily dealt with in Jim Crow Florida, and candid public assessments of white supremacy were not tolerated. Individuals and organizations that fought against racism were routinely punished and even obliterated. Given this historical reality, recovering Florida's true racial past remains a daunting task.

In this light, the authors of the preceding essays have formidable obstacles to overcome. Foremost, they must sift through the beguiling edifice of image, illusion, and reality that governs Florida's portrayal of itself. I call this narrative "Florida exceptionalism," and it is informed by three significant assumptions. The first assumption is that race relations have been relatively benign in Florida, and that the Sunshine State stood apart from the racially oppressive Old South. Political scientist V. O. Key's declaration that Florida was "scarcely part of the South" has provided the foundation of this hypothesis for over half a century. "While the state's politics is by no means free of Negro baiting," Key maintained, "the dominant attitude on the race question is comparatively mild."[5] Key's claim is often coupled with the assertion that Florida's post-Reconstruction leaders were too busy encouraging outside investment, economic development, and seasonal tourism to maintain a rigorous system of white rule. There have been important challenges to this hypothesis; however, the idea that Florida was not quite a part of the hardcore segregationist South is still prevalent today.[6]

Advocates of Florida exceptionalism also argue that large numbers of white northerners brought more enlightened attitudes that softened the harder edges of white supremacy in their adopted state. This belief has been articulated by a number of prominent white Floridians, including former Governor LeRoy Collins. It is explicit in the dichotomy drawn between a conservative North Florida said to be dominated by Old South-style white leaders versus a "more progressive, urban south [Florida]" peopled by Yankee immigrants.[7] As a graduate student in history, I too embarked on my dissertation research on Jim Crow Florida with similar assumptions.

The third plank of the exceptionalist platform holds that black Floridians did not energetically organize and press for equal citizenship between the end of Reconstruction and the 1940s. For example, it is often stated that NAACP leader Harry T. Moore, assassinated by white supremacists in 1951, was the state's *first* civil rights activist and martyr. Prior to that, we are led to believe that African Americans retreated from politics and activism as Reconstruction faded into memory. The distinguished Florida historian Charlton W. Tebeau argued, "Most of the Carpetbag leadership had given up the unequal contest after 1876 and the Negroes, without that leadership and under the pressure of their white employers and on occasion fraud and intimidation, had largely surrendered the right to vote."[8] Governor Collins suggested to historian John Egerton that black Floridians had not been as active as African Americans in other parts of the South when it came to agitating for social change.[9] The notion that black Floridians did not challenge Jim Crow to any significant degree until the 1950s complements the first two components of the exceptionalist model. If Florida were already more progressive in race relations than Alabama, Georgia, or Mississippi, then there would have been less for black Floridians to protest.

Historians and scholars of southern politics have bolstered the exceptionalism paradigm by routinely excluding the state and black Floridians from major synthetic works on slavery, Reconstruction, and racial protests. Florida is sometimes missing altogether, even in the more recent works on segregation and civil rights. Several years ago, a leading scholar of U.S. history contacted me to inquire about primary sources on race relations in Florida. This historian was finishing a major monograph on the post-emancipation South, and stated that, "there just isn't that much on race in Florida for that time period." When this scholar's work was published a few years later, it was greeted with praise, and certainly deserved all of the accolades it received. Unfortunately, the book, like so many of its predecessors, placed Florida once again on the margins of the white supremacist Old South.

The broader scholarly literature frequently gives readers the impression that Florida managed to stave off the forces of racism that engulfed the rest of the nation after the defeat of Reconstruction. When Florida has been included in accounts of segregation and disfranchisement, the African American freedom struggle has commonly been overlooked or underemphasized. Michael Perman's impressive *Struggle For Mastery: Disfranchisement in the South, 1888–1908* asserts that there was little dissent to segregating Florida's railroads in 1887. In fact, black Floridians vigorously protested railway segregation that year, and ministerial leaders in Jacksonville called a boycott of railroad companies that enforced the ordinance.[10]

The essays in this collection have struck a decisive blow against such misrepresentations of Florida history and the state's long-presumed exceptionalism. Moreover, they have forever altered our understanding of Florida's history. The writers in this volume situate Florida squarely within a southern political order that ardently defended segregation, in many cases through Down South delay or stonewalling measures, long after its alleged demise. The authors also insist that scholars must listen more carefully to the voices of local people and movement activists in order to gauge *their* ideas of just how Old South in beliefs and practices white Florida really was. Abel Bartley aptly observes that black Floridians did not confuse Florida's beaches and images of tourism with the realities of everyday life in the Sunshine State. When the Rev. Thomas A. Wright arrived in St. Augustine in 1954, he observed that "the city was infested with hatred, divisiveness and cruelty toward minorities."[11] This cruelty endured well into the 1960s and was a critical factor in the defeat of Dr. King's SCLC campaign in the Ancient City. When Howard Thurman compared his youth in Daytona with his later experiences in Georgia, he saw no need to differentiate between race relations in the two states. "The fact that the first twenty-three years of my life were spent in Florida and in Georgia," Rev. Thurman recalled, "left its scars deep in my spirit and has rendered me terribly sensitive to the churning abyss separating white from black."[12]

A careful look at race relations in the decades leading up to World War II reveals the organizing challenges that civil rights activists faced in the Sunshine State. In 1907, Governor Napoleon Bonaparte Broward proposed to the legislature that Florida work with the U.S. Congress to expel African Americans to a "[foreign] territory purchased by the United States." In the same year, the legislature seriously considered a measure that would have abrogated the 14th and 15th Amendments to the U.S. Constitution, presumably to affirm the state's right to manage black citizenship without federal interference. Thirteen years later, Governor Sydney Catts proposed to the same body that Florida organize a special army of 5,000 white troops "to protect the homes of whites as a race war [in Florida] was pending within the next five years." In 1930, school boards in Orange, Osceola, Duval, and other Florida counties spent three times more funds on white students than on their black peers. Statewide, Florida school boards appropriated an average of $34.59 per white pupil compared with $10.56 per black student. Moderate race relations, indeed.[13]

Black Floridians viewed segregation at its inception as a system based on terror and economic extortion. In 1887, a black correspondent in Pensacola wrote, "Well, sir, I will tell you what they are doing with us down South. They are shooting us down as so many partridges; don't allow editors to speak the truth always through their papers to the people; kicking us off trains whenever they see fit to do so; distribute the school funds as their conscience directs, charging us very often as high as 24 per cent per annum for money when we are compelled to borrow it from them, and thousands of other things too numerous to mention."[14]

This tangled web of racial oppression and violence may have eluded distant observers. However, its actual legacy was dramatically exposed during the 1994 Rosewood hearings in Tallahassee. The African American survivors of Rosewood, Florida, reintroduced the world to the story of the 1923 massacre and destruction of their once-proud town.[15] Unfortunately, Rosewood was habitually dismissed thereafter as a terrible aberration, an isolated pogrom carried out by racist "crackers" in a backwoods part of the state.

In reality, the Rosewood Massacre was only one of many outbreaks of anti-black violence in the state. Florida had the highest per capita lynching rate in the nation between 1882 and 1930.[16] Mass white assaults of African Americans occurred in Hernando County in 1877 as well as in the statewide elections of 1880, 1884, and 1888, when hundreds of African American voters were assaulted, murdered, or driven out of their home counties for attempting to vote. The decade of the 1890s was scarcely less harrowing for black Floridians. White supremacists carried out multiple homicides of African Americans in Titusville (1892), Wildwood (1893), Manatee County (1896), and in Bradford County (1897). Two years later, white citizens murdered black miners near Dunnellon and drove African American turpentine workers out of Holmes County. My colleagues in Latin American history have suggested to me after reading my book, *Emancipation Betrayed*, that Jim Crow Florida looked much like Central America during its repressive periods. That is to say, stolen elections, paramilitaries, and acts of repression were part of the chaotic social fabric of segregating Florida much as they were in parts of Latin America and the Caribbean.

Anti-black violence in Florida was not driven by primordial hatred; it was the linchpin of the effort to exploit African Americans and rob them of their economic resources.

Drawing on the path-breaking work of Gary R. Mormino, Irvin D. S. Winsboro has suggested in these pages that Florida's political leaders sacrificed civil rights in favor of economic development. During the Jim Crow period, much of Florida's economic development was, in fact, *based on racial oppression*. Indeed, one of the primary goals of disfranchisement in Florida—and elsewhere in the region—was to create a pool of oppressed laborers without citizenship and redress rights. Such workers would be unable to mobilize in the political or economic arenas to defend their interests. Their loss of the ballot paved the way for the expansion of Florida's notorious and profitable convict labor system. One prison camp captain compared his state's network of convict camps to Czarist Russia's infamous prisons, dubbing Florida, "The American Siberia."[17] Florida's vagrancy statutes—initially designed to force African Americans to toil for cheap or non-existent wages—were also used by firms against Eastern European immigrants who found themselves reduced to debt peonage after being lured to Florida under false pretenses.[18] Winsboro's conception of Florida's history as one that subordinated civil rights to economic predation and designs may well merit closer attention by future scholars of the Florida experience.

Florida's history of vagrancy statutes and debt peonage remind us that racial and class oppression conveniently reinforced each other. Lillian Smith's stunning memoir, *Killers of the Dream*, was published in the same year that V. O. Key's *Southern Politics in State and Nation* appeared. Smith was a Florida native, born in 1897. She recalled that racial epitaphs, especially the word "nigger," were strictly banned in her Jasper, Florida, household. On the surface, civility between the races reigned. Yet, as Smith noted in *Killers of the Dream*, "I learned to believe in freedom, to glow when the word democracy was used, and to practice slavery from morning to night." Smith's father, a deeply religious man and a turpentine operator, "employed hundreds of colored[s] and . . . paid them the prevailing low wages, worked them the prevailing long hours . . . saw to it that a commissary supplied commodities at a high price, and in general managed his affairs much as ten thousand other southern businessmen managed theirs."[19] Lillian Smith believed that class domination bolstered racial apartheid.

White elites in Florida employed violence, one-party rule, and economic exploitation as strategies to control the state's resources. I refer to this form of economic development in *Emancipation Betrayed* as "white business supremacy." Historian J. Randall Stanley wrote that prior to the Civil War, white growers in Middle Florida had been "conservative" and peaceful. After the war, however, Stanley observed that the same people "became the disciples of violence because it had become a necessity—if not righteous—in combating white and black radical domination." "With the return of white supremacy," Stanley testified, "the able descendants of the Gadsden pioneers led their state to a revival of agriculture, industry and business which today far surpasses the grandeur of the 'Golden Age.'"[20]

Employers in Florida zealously guarded their prerogatives; however, black migration out of the state initially threatened white business supremacy. When African Americans began leaving the state in large numbers via Jacksonville in 1916 to seek higher wages in the North, the Jacksonville Chamber of Commerce denounced the exodus and demanded that Mayor J. E. T. Bowden take action. Jacksonville police were thereafter deployed and beat would-be escapees away from the train stations. The pro-business *Times-Union* attacked black efforts to leave while chamber leaders insisted that African Americans were sufficiently well paid. Political officials, employers, the police, and the media colluded to enforce white business supremacy. To paraphrase historian John W. Cell, this was Jim Crow at its highest stage.[21]

The idea that race relations in Florida were improved by waves of liberal white "Yankee" transplants presumes a uniformly liberal North and a monolithically reactionary South. In reality, the South did not invent segregation. In separate studies on the matter, John Hope Franklin's *From Slavery To Freedom* and Leon Litwack's *North of Slavery* have shown that Jim Crow actually originated in the antebellum North.[22] The New York and Pennsylvania state legislatures rewrote their respective constitutions in the 1830s and drove great numbers of African Americans off their voting rolls. Simultaneously, black workers were forced out of the better-paying manual occupations in the North by employers and European immigrants, who became "white" citizens in large part by adopting racist attitudes and practices. Political and economic disfranchisement was accompanied by waves of anti-black race riots in Northern cities.[23]

Ellen F. Wetherell's fascinating 1890s memoir of her time in Florida provides clues of the racial stereotypes that many northerners brought with them to the Sunshine State after the end of the Civil War. Wetherell interviewed an "Abolitionist's Daughter" who believed that African Americans "'have to be dealt with like children.'" She continued, "'My father was a Boston Abolitionist, and I'—throwing up her chin—'was born in Boston. But one must live a long time here at the South to know what is best for the colored race.... Sometimes I think the right of franchise is detrimental to them and the State; but there is one thing true: they must be treated as children, for they are nothing else.... The colored man is a child in politics; he has not the education for the right use of the ballot.... But the white race must be the rulers.'"[24] Wetherell's memoir is a reminder—if we actually need one at this late date—that the South had no monopoly on racism. The late nineteenth-century guidebooks published to promote northern investment, tourism, and white settlement in Florida generally mirror the racial sentiments that Wetherell found among Yankee transplants to the state. At the same time, elite Europeans who relocated to Florida brought with them ideologies of white superiority and racial hierarchies that mirrored their experiences in the colonial past and present.

John Hope Franklin asserts that the major thrust of northerners' involvement in the South after the end of Civil War hinged on economic development that was premised on racial disfranchisement. "They [southerners] were very firm on what they felt the position of the country should be in respect to race," Professor Franklin states. "And the North was interested primarily in the South's resources. It was the perfect trade-off, we'll let you take this race thing and run with it as long as you let us invest and exploit the South's resources. That was the gospel of the New South, and all the new legislation and Jim Crow stuff came when the Northerners were coming down in larger numbers investing in the South." Historian Darlene Clark Hine is equally explicit, "The white supremacists' major goal, after all, was to maintain a pliable, exploitable labor force that would remain permanently in a subordinate place." We will go a long way in understanding the origins of segregation in Florida, as well as its staying power, when we recognize that segregation, like slavery, is a labor system designed to extract resources from black communities and redistribute them (unequally) to the rest of the society.[25]

Commercial interests seized on the power that segregation gave to white employers. As demonstrated in business publications such as *The Florida Grower*, most transplanted white northerners came to Florida to take advantage of the state's non-union and low wage agricultural, service, and industrial sectors. Claude Pepper believed that George Smathers defeated him in the 1950 senatorial election due to an infusion of $700,000 into Smathers's campaign coffers from northern Republicans who sought to maintain the anti-labor status quo in Florida.[26] As new waves of white northerners poured into the state after World War II, they helped transform Florida's existing right-to-work statute into a constitutional amendment in 1968. To this day, Florida's rates of unionization remain quite low.[27]

What of the third plank of Florida exceptionalism, the belief in African American submission to Jim Crow? As I have found of earlier periods in *Emancipation Betrayed*, the authors in this volume have uncovered numerous examples of pioneering and sustained African American organizing against segregation. Marvin Dunn shows that the Congress on Racial Equality (CORE) held major sit-in protests against segregation in Miami six months *before* the well-publicized Greensboro, North Carolina, actions of 1960. Gregory Bush's essay on Virginia Key Beach demonstrates that African Americans in Miami conducted a "wade-in" and other protests almost a year before *Brown* to demand access to beachfront, leisure spaces that segregationist Florida routinely denied them. Leonard R. Lempel explains that black fraternal lodges served as vital links between the statewide

Florida Progressive Voters League and the local Daytona Beach Citizens League by requiring male and female members to register to vote. Thanks to *Old South, New South, or Down South?* we will be better able to place Harry and Harriette Moore's organizing work in the 1940s in a larger historical tradition of black protest that was statewide as well as deeply rooted in local communities and everyday people.

Moore's generation of courageous movement organizers had strong foundations on which to build. As historian Jane Landers and other scholars have argued, African American resistance to white supremacy, racial oppression, and political tyranny actually predates statehood in Florida. Enslaved African Americans seized on the imperial rivalry between Spain and England to carve out a measure of freedom in St. Augustine during the 1730s. By agreeing to bear arms for the Spanish Crown, scores of African Americans earned provisional freedom. A new cohort of black freedom fighters sided with the British in northern Florida during the War of 1812 in a bid to stave off American slavery. In 1816, Andrew Jackson ordered his soldiers to destroy the so-called Negro Fort on the Apalachicola River. Liberated slaves and their Indian allies used the citadel to wage guerilla warfare against slavery in Florida and Georgia. In the ensuing battle, more than two hundred men, women, and children perished. Escaped African Americans continued building interracial coalitions with Seminole Indians that challenged the growth of slavery and white oppression in the southeastern perimeter of the U.S.[28]

These types of black struggle in Florida provide excellent case studies in the ways oppressed people have struggled for liberty and justice in the Americas from the colonial era to the present. In fact, it may be that the most truly exceptional part of Florida history has been the depth, continuity, and creativity of black strivings for freedom in a hostile land of Old South values and practices.

African American resistance was also a defining theme of Florida history between the end of Reconstruction and the modern civil rights movement as uncovered in *Old South, New South, or Down South?* Irvin D. S. Winsboro introduces us to the Nelson Tillis family, who, along with other black homesteaders in Monroe (later Lee) County, demanded equal education for their children as early as 1867. Indeed, many of the institutions that birthed the modern civil rights movement in Florida in the 1950s traced their origins back to the post-Reconstruction era. This was especially true of secret societies and churches. The death of Rev. Albert Sidney James Allen in Alachua County in 1904 highlights the continuities of black movement organizing in Florida. Allen was a leading Methodist minister in north-central Florida as well as a highly respected educator. On April 2, Rev. Allen informed his neighbor (a white farmer by the name of J. L. Shaw) that his new fence encroached onto Allen's land. According to the Jacksonville *Times-Union*, the two men began arguing over the disputed boundary line whereupon Shaw pulled a weapon and shot the minister dead. Following the dictates of Jim Crow justice, the coroner's jury quickly exonerated the white man.[29]

Allen's murder exposed segregation's underbelly while also highlighting the ways that African Americans fought back in collective and personal ways against the system. The *Times-Union*'s correspondent sought to justify the murder by asserting that Rev. Allen was "regarded as a troublesome negro [*sic*] and had few friends even among his own race." African Americans in Alachua County would have none of this. Black lodges and churches mobilized to bring Shaw to justice. The Masons and Odd Fellows lodges raised funds for a legal team and hired a prominent lawyer from Jacksonville who was able to get the case heard before a grand jury. African Americans in Alachua were committed to proving the *Times-Union* and the rest of the white power structure wrong; in their minds, Rev. Allen was an integral member of their community and he, like any innocent man, did not deserve to be murdered. While this community mobilization did not change the outcome of the case (Shaw was exonerated by a grand jury), by so challenging the white systems of oppression, African Americans reminded white Floridians that they were human beings and should not be shot down in cold blood. In honoring Rev. Albert Sidney James Allen's memory, black Floridians were affirming their traditions and right to live and die with dignity, which, after all, are the foundations of all freedom struggles.

African American communities in Florida continued this tradition by organizing numerous social movements between the 1880s through the Great Depression. Local activists boycotted segregated streetcars and stores, took up arms to stop their neighbors from being lynched, and waged strikes for higher wages. Resistance to oppression was always costly, and black Floridians had to carefully weigh the consequences of protest. Whatever the era or locale, African Americans in the Sunshine State never accepted the legitimacy of Jim Crow and its brutal offspring. Black Floridians seized upon every space, no matter how small, to challenge white supremacy and to pass down a hatred of racial injustice to younger generations. Dr. Johnnetta B. Cole recalled that her great-grandfather, Abraham Lincoln Lewis, co-founder of the Jacksonville-based Afro-American Insurance Company, hated segregation. "There was always a streak of controlled emotion when my great-grandfather talked about the white folks," Cole observed. "He would be quite controlled, and yet his outrage at the injustice would be clear. This is not a man who could scream. This is not a man who would pound on the desk. . . . Outraged yes. Particularly if it had to do with black folks not being treated properly." Not surprisingly, agents of the Afro-American Insurance Company would play major roles in the dramatic civil rights movement that would emerge throughout the state during World War I.[30] Like so many other aspects of Florida's racial past, the history books generally remain silent or evasive on such subjects. Yet, and this is a major theme to note, there are countless additional episodes of meaningful and sustained black challenges to white oppression that have yet to be uncovered.

Black Floridians transformed the Great War into a full-scale assault on the political and economic dimensions of Jim Crow in Florida. African American workers organized unions and negotiated for improved working conditions. Fraternal lodges, churches, and black women's clubs purchased Liberty Bonds for the war effort, and expected and demanded full citizenship rights once the war concluded. African American men who served in France did not merely "return fighting," to paraphrase W. E. B. Du Bois. They demanded an equal stake in their society. L. A. Alexander, an artilleryman from West Palm Beach, proudly noted, "we played our part in the great struggle for Democracy," and also observed, "I voice the sentiment of every colored soldier in the United States when I say that we are hoping and expecting to reap the benefits of our toilsome struggles and that Democracy in its fullest meaning will be for the betterment of the [N]egro race as it will be for all other races."[31]

Black Floridians parleyed these sentiments into the first statewide civil rights movement in U.S. history. Beginning on Emancipation Day, 1919 (January 1st), African Americans began openly calling on each other to pay their poll taxes and register to vote. Leading activists of the movement included Mary McLeod Bethune, James Weldon Johnson, and Joseph E. Lee. The goal of the campaign was to regain the right to vote and to defeat white supremacy and Democratic one-party rule. Black Floridians envisioned a new society where they would be able to work towards economic justice, political rights, and educational equity for their children. African Americans across the state demanded the abolition of vagrancy laws, an end to corrupt law enforcement, and an end to lynching among other demands. In so doing, black Floridians underscored their long tradition of collectively protesting injustices.

There appears to be more continuity than discontinuity in the black freedom struggle between the 1880s and the 1950s. Many of the African American organizations that spurred activism in the earlier period—mutual aid lodges, churches, civic organizations, the NAACP—were also at the forefront of the local movements of the later period. Even newer organizations such as the Southern Christian Leadership Conference were built upon preexisting ministerial networks. Black organizers in the earlier era were just as sophisticated as their descendants were. In fact, in counties and cities across the state, including Gadsden, Pensacola, Jacksonville, and Miami, newer generations of organizers drew directly from the political wisdom of older activists who had survived and protested the repressive middle years of Jim Crow.[32]

Connie L. Lester's essay on black farming in this volume illuminates important intergenerational continuities in black protest traditions. Lester shows that African Americans who moved from rural to urban Florida in the 1950s brought with them lessons on cooperation and self-help that they had learned from their landowning elders and their community institutions (e.g., kin networks, churches, and secret societies). In turn, they translated many of these older rural values, which, after all, hinged on building and maintaining group solidarity, into new urban movement activism. Although more research is needed in this area, the evidence in this volume suggests the possibility of continuities in black protest traditions in rural communities. Because African American families sustained kin and network ties between the country and the city, these traditions may have developed symbiotically between rural and urban Florida.

Perhaps what changed more than anything else between 1920 and the post-World War II period was the complex interplay between local black protests and state, as well as federal, responses. The 1919–20 statewide voter movement in Florida confronted a national government and polity that blatantly reinforced black disfranchisement. When Walter White and James Weldon Johnson presented evidence of widespread violence and fraud against African Americans in the 1920 Florida election to the U.S. Congress, they were jeered by legislators who rejected the idea of free and fair elections. In other words, black Floridians had to confront both the local Klan *and* a hostile federal government.[33]

In contrast, Florida's civil rights organizers in the 1950s and 1960s operated in a new national environment. Now, millions of African Americans were members of active political and labor organizations in the North as well as South. As former Jacksonville resident and national black labor leader A. Philip Randolph pointed out, African American activism in the labor movement was a critical impetus for social change throughout the United States.[34] Black political organizers capitalized on the U.S. Supreme Court's 1944 *Smith v. Allwright* ruling outlawing the white primary.[35] By the presidential election of 1948, Harry Truman understood that he would have to court the African American vote in order to eke out a victory over Thomas E. Dewey. Both major parties were now at least temporarily forced to compete for black ballots in close national elections. Simultaneously, Third World liberation insurgencies as well as the Cold War rivalry with the Soviet Union forced national leaders to confront the hypocrisy of American apartheid. This shifting national landscape did not necessarily make civil rights activism in Florida any easier or less dangerous. However, it began to create new fissures in the Old South groundwork of separate and unequal.

One of the important contributions that the scholars in this volume have made is to encourage readers to reconsider the composition, depth, and subtlety of the segregationist forces in Florida. Traditionally, the history books have suggested that poorer whites were in the vanguard of resisting social change. According to this theory, the white middle classes were swept along by a popular tide of ground-level racism. *Old South, New South, or Down South?* disputes this thesis. In these new narratives it is often the middle and upper classes that are shown to be holding the line against racial progress. Judges, college presidents, government bureaucrats, newspaper editors, and other educated individuals appear to have been some of the most persistent defenders of white supremacy. Martin A. Dyckman notes that Governor Collins's successor, C. Farris Bryant, "an unconverted segregationist," was a graduate of Harvard Law School.[36] Florida governors Fuller Warren and Daniel Thomas McCarty had both been students at the University of Florida, and the notorious race-baiter Haydon Burns acquired his college education in New England.

The elite defense of segregation was highlighted in dramatic fashion during the Tallahassee Bus Boycott. According to Martin Dyckman, the presence of two state universities and the state capital in Tallahassee "made for a more sophisticated electorate than in any of the neighboring counties bordering Georgia."[37] This same electorate, however, opposed the campaign to end segregation on the city's buses and the local newspaper, the *Tallahassee Democrat*, served as its mouthpiece. "Tallahassee was just like any other Jim Crow city," recalled boycott organizer Cornelius Speed, who added that, "Leon County was just like any other Jim Crow county."[38]

In 1956, the *Democrat* savagely attacked the leader of the boycott, Rev. C. K. Steele. A half-century later, the newspaper's new leadership apologized to the family of Rev. Steele and tendered a public apology for the role it had played in opposing equal rights: "Leaders in that journey toward equality should have been able to expect support in ending segregation from the local daily newspaper, the *Tallahassee Democrat*. They could not. We not only did not lend a hand, we openly opposed integration, siding firmly with the segregationists."[39] The question is *why* did so many civic leaders, as well as the *Democrat* and most of Florida's media establishment, support and defend segregation so ardently?

The contributors to this volume have raised critical questions about the civil rights record of Governor LeRoy Collins, and their findings will stimulate new debates on Florida politics. In prior accounts, Collins has been judged to be a desirable alternative to many of his Dixie counterparts who took militant and vociferous stands in support of Jim Crow. When Collins is compared with fire-breathing segregationist governors such as Orville Faubus and George Wallace, he understandably appears moderate. However, as several essays in this volume attest, the bombastic Faubus could have learned a thing or two from the way Governor Collins quietly circumvented *Brown v. Board* in Florida's schools. Like his North Carolina ally, Governor Luther Hodges, LeRoy Collins avoided brash public statements supporting segregation, yet worked efficiently to maintain the status quo.[40] Marvin Dunn argues that Governor Collins was more concerned with upholding property rights and promoting economic growth than supporting civil rights or the physical safety of beleaguered movement activists during the Tallahassee sit-in protests. Amy Sasscer reminds readers that Collins rejected the racist vitriol of his more pugnacious gubernatorial opponents in 1956 only to weigh in publicly on the side of segregation in higher education.

Governor Collins' administration created an ingenious public school measure that allowed local school boards to dodge and stonewall desegregation. Like North Carolina's Pearsall Plan, Florida's Pupil Assignment Act of 1955 gave local school boards the autonomy and maneuvering room they needed to avoid implementing school integration.[41] Irvin D. S. Winsboro describes in his case study how effectively the Pupil Assignment Act worked to retard integration in Lee County. The NAACP and local activists in Lee County worked to prove that the school board was willfully avoiding the dictates of *Brown v. Board* by using the colorblind rhetoric of "Pupil Assignment Zones" and "Freedom of Choice" plans. Ultimately, African Americans challenged the ruse and pressed for federal legal intervention to break school segregation in Lee and many other Florida counties.

Historian C. Vann Woodward was chagrined that Governor Collins declared in 1956 that "'we are just as determined as any Southern state to maintain segregation.'"[42] With the benefit of a hindsight that Professor Woodward could not have enjoyed, we know that Collins would gradually shift in the direction of his party's leader, Lyndon Johnson, in matters regarding African American citizenship. Indeed, President Johnson appointed Collins to head the national Community Relations Service in 1964. This unit would play a role in Johnson's efforts to implement a pro-civil rights agenda nationally. It is important to understand, however, that Johnson and Collins were creatures of the political realities of their times. As journalist James Kilpatrick noted shortly after the 1964 presidential election, "There is substance in the Negroes' assertion that Lyndon Johnson carried such states as Virginia, North Carolina, and Florida only with their votes."[43] African Americans were becoming a political force to be reckoned with on a statewide as well as national level, and leaders such as Johnson and Collins ignored this reality at their own peril. Even so, there are still important questions to ask about just how much of a difference LeRoy Collins made to the actions and success of civil rights across the Sunshine State. Long after Collins's failed senatorial bid in 1968, African American parents in Florida were still struggling to enroll their children in nonsegregated schools in an effort to overcome the obstructionist legacy that Collins and others had left behind.

The essays in *Old South, New South, or Down South?* both confirm as well as challenge recent civil rights historiography. Abel Bartley's essay on the movement in Jacksonville dramatically highlights how African American parents, the NAACP, and younger black activists developed overlapping strategies of sit-ins, pickets, and lawsuits to confront school segregation and wider Jim Crow in the Gateway City. Bartley also suggests that civil rights organizing in Florida was most effective when it was grassroots and intergenerational in scope and scale. Bartley's argument is in line with the most innovative civil rights literature of late, and scholars would be wise to test his findings in other parts of the state.[44] Leonard R. Lempel's poignant story about the closure of the all-black Volusia County Community College and Lise M. Steinhaur's study of Palm Beach County's painful success in the name of "gradual" integration raise questions about the costs of desegregation on black institutions and African American communities.[45]

Through such lessons, the writers in this anthology demonstrate the complex interplay between grassroots activism, statehouse politics, and federal policy in the making of social change. These essays also put to rest the old maxim of Florida exceptionalism. Scholars will now be able to approach Florida without pre-conceived images and illusions. In reality, Florida was no more or less racist than the rest of the South or, indeed, the rest of the United States. Indeed, this is the very theme that the editor of this book seeks to establish in his introduction, as he concentrates on the often misleading role "image, illusion, and reality" have played in judging Florida's historical intersection with racial rights and justice. I believe that *Old South, New South, or Down South?* represents a major step forward in placing Florida's civil rights historiography on a level intellectually comparable with its peer works in other states of the region. Equally important, historians writing national treatments on the civil rights movement in the United States must now place Florida at or near the center rather than the conventional periphery of their narratives. Established historians, graduate students, and local history practitioners will, thus, be able to use this book as a reference point for future research projects in African American history, Florida politics, and civil rights studies.

The next generation of civil rights historiography in Florida should continue to draw liberally from the groundbreaking scholarship on other regions and time periods.[46] Historians working on Florida should pose such innovative questions as what made the civil rights struggle unusual or unique in a state that has been a major gateway between the United States, the Caribbean, and Latin America? For example, what kind of impact did the Cuban Revolution and its aftermath have on the movement in Florida? To what extent did interactions between African Americans, Jewish Americans, Haitians, Bahamians, and immigrants from Latin America shape new protest strategies after the Great Depression?

Florida scholars should also engage in the vibrant debate about the impact of the Cold War: did anti-Communism give civil rights organizers leverage to make demands on the state— as long as they framed these demands in the language of "100 percent Americanism"—or did the witch hunts engaged in by Charley Johns and his Tallahassee legislative committee all too effectively silence dissent?[47] Finally, are there connections between local theorists and movements in the Sunshine State with Third World liberation struggles immortalized by Frantz Fanon, C. L. R. James, and other anti-colonial intellectuals?

As the essays in this volume attest, we must work harder to understand the dynamic tensions between image and reality and the interactions between local movement activity, state politics, and federal agencies which played critical roles in aiding—or sometimes hindering—civil rights gains. We also need to further examine the social composition of local movements as well as tensions between organizers and activists across lines of class and gender especially. Charles Payne writes that by the early 1960s, the civil rights movement "was largely a movement of working-class people."[48] Payne's assertion challenges us to take a close look at the stories in this book that illuminate everyday, working-class activists in Florida. There is still a tendency in civil rights historiography to lionize middle-class organizers at the expense of everyday working people who formed the social backbone of the movement. What does the civil rights movement look like when we shift the lens from educational access to struggles for economic justice or affordable housing? Finally, scholars should ask whether black trade unionists in Florida (the home of noted labor leader A. Philip Randolph) played long-term roles in movement activities akin to those played by African American unionists in Tennessee, North Carolina, and other Southern states?[49]

Following the work of Barbara Ransby, civil rights scholars in Florida would do well to focus more closely on relationships and tensions between male and female activists as well as leadership styles and networks that may have privileged charismatic male leadership.[50] Yes, we should pay homage to the heroism of Harry T. Moore (while also honoring Harriette T. Moore!), but how does the narrative change when we include the countless female organizers active in women's clubs, religious groups, and other civic associations? What about African American women, such as those described by Connie L. Lester, who did not belong to formal institutions but nonetheless resisted Jim Crow on an everyday level? Gender, sexuality, and social class mattered enormously in the development of the broader civil rights, student, and anti-war movements of the 1960s, and we need to bring the insights developed in studying these movements to Florida.

The essayists in this volume understand that the civil rights movement in Florida was not a spontaneous outburst but rather—to borrow Vincent Harding's apt metaphor—part of a long, flowing river.[51] New studies on the movement in Florida should continue to probe both the undercurrents and branches of this historical phenomenon in state and region. To what extent, for example, did black Floridians nurture what Charles Payne has called an "organizing tradition," and what were its ideological and philosophical moorings? We know that African Americans in early twentieth-century Florida placed great emphasis on historical memories of slavery and the strides of Reconstruction in forging struggles against Old South habits of life. Did these historical memories become attenuated later in the century or did some African Americans continue to find ways to promote positive images of black history in a state that taught black inferiority as a matter of course? All these inquiries, I should add, are byproducts of this stimulating book that scholars and aficionados of Florida history will want to research, analyze, and, most importantly, address in future debates.

Of course, no single book on a state as complex as Florida can make claims of full coverage. Perceptive readers will note the absence of important cities and regions (i.e., Pensacola and the Tampa Bay area). Even though no work of this scope could appropriately address all the corners of a large state like Florida, the book does, nevertheless, establish patterns and lessons significant for the state at large, and in so doing challenges scholars to broaden their own geographical and demographic examinations of the Sunshine State. Certainly these types of examination can be most perplexing for a state in which Key West is about as far from Pensacola as Pensacola itself is from Chicago. As the true story of Florida's racial past grows over the years, the studies documenting and interpreting these events will, of necessity, encompass numerous large and more finitely focused works.

It is also important that the next generation of civil rights scholarship in Florida move beyond the intellectual boundaries of this book and the traditional North American-based black/white paradigm of race relations. Nancy Hewitt's *Southern Discomfort: Women's Activism in Tampa, Florida, 1880s–1920s* provides an excellent example of this type of avant-garde scholarship. Hewitt reminds us that generations of Cuban, Bahamian, and Central American female migrants created political and social institutions in Florida that did not easily fall into the U.S. racial binary. Likewise, the south Florida business billboard "We cater to white only: NIGGERS, MEXICANS & PUERTO RICANS not allowed," photographed by Stetson Kennedy in the early 1960s, reminds us that Florida has often been at the crossroads of European empire building and subsequent social stereotyping.[52] The Spanish, French, and English empires promoted distinctive ideologies on race mixing, or, in the Spanish context, *mestizaje*. However, all engaged in what poet Martín Espada calls "the orchestration of a racial caste system with its roots in slavery."[53] Studies placing Florida within a broader transatlantic colonial context—here one thinks of historian Rebecca

Scott's work on post-Emancipation Louisiana—may better allow scholars to understand how the modern civil rights struggle in Florida drew from and in turn influenced human rights and anti-colonial movements throughout the region and the world.

The next generation of civil rights researchers in Florida will also need to grapple with the continuing legacies of segregation and the unfinished agendas of civil rights activists. Central and south Florida contained some of the most highly segregated cities in the South decades after Brown.[54] Florida yet maintains its old reputation as a state buffeted by frequent incidents of debt peonage and forced labor. A Florida-based organization, the Coalition of Immokalee Workers, recently received an international anti-slavery award for exposing six major incidents in South Florida alone involving over 1,000 farm workers held in involuntary servitude.[55]

At the same time that African Americans were protesting de jure segregation, municipalities and private firms were dumping toxic chemicals near their neighborhoods and schoolyards. As a result, Florida has become increasingly associated with the phenomenon of environmental racism. African American and minority communities in Tampa, Jacksonville, and Orlando have been the victims of sustained toxic chemical dumping, and child rates of asthma among young African Americans, particularly in Superfund sites in and around Jacksonville, have reached epidemic levels.[56] This calls for new research into the interactions between environmental justice, civil rights, and sustainable development in Florida and throughout the South.

Nor has the question of universal enfranchisement in the Sunshine State been laid to rest. The U.S. Civil Rights Commission exposed modern-day voter disfranchisement of qualified African American voters in the 2000 Presidential Election.[57] Furthermore, human rights advocates have demonstrated that Florida's absolutist practice of taking the franchise away from convicted felons—a practice dating back to the nineteenth century—has substantially diluted African American and Latina/o political representation.[58] In terms of ethnic diversity, international trade, and urban development, Florida is undeniably a part of the *Nuevo*, New South. As this book suggests, however, many of Florida's seemingly new institutions are extensions of past racism in the state and thus imbued with historical segregationist practices. To paraphrase this volume's editor, much has been written about civil rights and Florida but much more needs to be done.

In light of these essays, how should we now characterize past and present Florida—as Old South, New South, or Down South? In terms of its race relations, Florida existed squarely within the segregationist South, and not on its margins or borders. Civil rights activists have always found racial inequality to be a persistent and perplexing organizing challenge in Florida. In fact, this volume demonstrates that Florida's guardians of

segregation were often far more sophisticated in both rhetoric and tactics than their counterparts in other parts of the region. Florida is genuinely part of the Old *and* New South.
But Florida is also unique. The same state that produced race baiters like Haydon Burns
was also the work site of extraordinary activists such as Mary McLeod Bethune, Luisa
Moreno, José Marti, and Stetson Kennedy. Yes, a part of Florida is rooted in a plantation
past. Nevertheless, that experience was dynamic and it includes the largest slave rebellion in the history of North America. Geographically, Florida stands at the crossroads of
a revolutionary transatlantic world with its polyphonic rhythms of oppression, rebellion,
and renewal. Natives, Spaniards, Afro-Cubans, African Americans, whites, British—all of
these and more have fought over the meanings of freedom, citizenship, and social justice
in this complicated entity known as Florida. And, the struggle lives on. Contemporary
scholars and students of social movements will find Florida to be a fruitful and revela-
tory site of study.

The field of civil rights studies in Florida is on the verge of a revolution. *Old South, New
South, or Down South?* gives us a solid foundation on which to build. We are now better
placed to understand how African Americans and their allies created social movements
for justice and dignity in the face of what seemed like impossible odds. At the same time,
however, there is much new work to be done. The questions posed here represent but a
fraction of potential research topics, historical and contemporary, relating to Florida. Let
us honor the known and still-to-be-discovered heroes and heroines of the Florida civil
rights movement by redoubling our efforts to dig deep for the answers to these issues. In
the process, the lessons we will learn about what it means to strive for equality and justice
in the face of adversity will, indeed, make the endeavor worthwhile.

## NOTES

1. "Tar and Feather Florida Farmer," *Chicago Defender*, February 5, 1921; "Attends Negro
Wedding, Gets Tars and Feathers," *Richmond Planet*, February 6, 1921. Mr. Sullivan told his story
to the NAACP; see "Statement by Frank Sullivan RE his treatment at the hands of Jacksonville,
Fla. Residents who claimed to be members of *The Ku-Klux-Klan*," n.d., Box C312, Folder "KKK
1921–Jan.," National Association for the Advancement of Colored People Papers, Library of Congress, Washington, D.C.

2. Agent Leon F. Howe, Field Report, "Dynamiting of Negro Houses," July 7, 1920, in *Federal
Surveillance of Afro-Americans 1917–1925: The First World War, the Red Scare, and the Garvey
Movement*, ed. Theodore Kornweibel (Frederick, Md.: University Publications of America, 1986),
Reel 13, Frame 155.

3. "The House Committee on Rules," *The Ku Klux Klan Hearings*, Sixty-Seventh Congress,
First Session (Washington, D.C.: Government Printing Office, 1921), 51; "White Caps Strike Terror

Over South," *New York Times*, July 19, 1921; "Tar and Feather Florida Rector: Episcopal Archdeacon Charged with Preaching Social Equality to Negroes," *Raleigh News and Observer*, July 19, 1921; "Investigates Floggings," *New York Times*, December 3, 1921; "We Do Not Have Forever," *Central Florida Episcopalian* 105 (August 2003), 12–13.

4. "Accuses Legion Official," *New York Times*, July 27, 1921.

5. V. O. Key Jr., *Southern Politics in State and Nation* (New York, A. A. Knopf, 1949), 85. A number of scholars have addressed the issue of Florida's moderation, including Danielle L. McGuire, "'It Was Like All of Us Had Been Raped': Sexual Violence, Community Mobilization, and the African American Freedom Struggle," *Journal of American History* 91 (December 2004): 906–31; Tom Wagy, *Governor LeRoy Collins of Florida: Spokesman of the New South* (Tuscaloosa, Ala.: University of Alabama Press, 1985); Steven F. Lawson, "From Sit-in to Race Riot: Businessmen, Blacks, and the Pursuit of Moderation in Tampa, 1960–1967," in *Southern Businessmen and Desegregation*, ed. Elizabeth Jacoway and David R. Colburn (Baton Rouge: Louisiana State University Press, 1982); Arthur O. White, *Crisis in Public Education: Changing Patterns of Leadership* (Gainesville: University Presses of Florida, 1975).

6. Important exceptions to this thesis include Stetson Kennedy, *Palmetto Country* (New York: Duell, Sloan & Pearce, 1942); Joe M. Richardson, *The Negro in the Reconstruction of Florida, 1865–1877* (Tallahassee: The Florida State University, 1965); Jerrell H. Shoffner, *Nor Is It Over Yet: Florida in the Era of Reconstruction, 1863–1877* (Gainesville: University Press of Florida, 1974); Larry Eugene Rivers, *Slavery in Florida: Territorial Days to Emancipation* (Gainesville: University Press of Florida, 2000); David R. Colburn and Jane L. Landers, eds., *The African American Heritage of Florida* (Gainesville: University Presses of Florida, 1995); Glenda Alice Rabby, *The Pain and the Promise: The Struggle for Civil Rights in Tallahassee, Florida* (Athens: The University of Georgia Press, 1999); Michael Newton, *The Invisible Empire: The Ku Klux Klan in Florida* (Gainesville: University Press of Florida, 2001).

7. LeRoy Collins, interview by David R. Colburn and Richard K. Scher, February 12, 1975, FP 38, The Samuel Proctor Oral History Program, The University of Florida (hereafter Proctor Oral History Program). The phrase "more progressive urban South," is taken from the web site of the Florida Legislative Research Center & Museum, *http://www.legislativeresearchcenter.org/book.html* (accessed December 3, 2006).

8. Charlton W. Tebeau, *A History of Florida* (Coral Gables: University of Miami Press, 1972), 289; exceptions to this thesis include Nancy A. Hewitt, *Southern Discomfort: Women's Activism in Tampa, Florida 1880s–1920s* (Urbana: University of Illinois Press, 2001); Canter Brown Jr., *Florida's Black Public Officials, 1867–1924* (Tuscaloosa: The University of Alabama Press, 1998); David R. Colburn, *Racial Change and Community Crisis: St. Augustine, Florida, 1877–1980* (Gainesville: University of Florida Press, 1991 [1985]); Robert Cassanello, "The Great Migration, Migrants and Identity in The Making of New South Jacksonville, Florida, 1865–1920" (PhD diss., Florida State University, 2000).

9. LeRoy Collins, interview by John Egerton, April 13, 1990, FP 39, Proctor Oral History Program.

10. Michael Perman, *Struggle For Mastery: Disfranchisement in the South, 1888–1908* (Chapel Hill: The University of North Carolina Press, 2001), 258.

11. Thomas A. Wright, *Courage in Persona: An Autobiography* (Ocala: Special Publications Inc., 1993), 102.

12. Howard Thurman, *The Luminous Darkness: A Personal Interpretation of the Anatomy of Segregation and the Ground of Hope* (Richmond, Ind.: Friends United Press, 1999 [1965]); Howard Thurman, *With Head and Heart: The Autobiography of Howard Thurman* (New York: Harcourt Brace & Company, 1979), 20–21.

13. Samuel Proctor, *Napoleon Bonaparte Broward: Florida's Fighting Democrat* (Gainesville: University of Florida Press, 1950), 252; Paul Ortiz, *Emancipation Betrayed: The Hidden History of Black Organizing and White Violence in Florida from Reconstruction to the Bloody Election of 1920* (Berkeley: University of California Press, 2005), 83; "Gov. Cats of Fla., Rebuked," *Birmingham Reporter*, June 14, 1919; Charles S. Johnson, *Statistical Atlas of Southern Counties; Listing and Analysis of Socio-Economic Indices of 1104 Southern Counties* (Chapel Hill: The University of North Carolina Press, 1941), 73–84.

14. "Pensacola Letter," *Christian Recorder*, October 27, 1887.

15. Michael D'Orso, *Like Judgment Day: The Ruin and Redemption of a Town Called Rosewood* (New York: Boulevard, 1996); Principal Director Maxine D. Jones, co-project director Larry E. Rivers, Investigators David R. Colburn, R. Tom Dye, and William R. Rogers, *A Documented History of the Incident Which Occurred at Rosewood, Florida, in January 1923: Submitted to the Florida Board of Regents 22 December 1993.* (Tallahassee, Fla: Board of Regents, 1993).

16. To review these acts of violence, see Ortiz, *Emancipation Betrayed*, 61–84.

17. J. C. Powell, *The American Siberia* (Chicago: Donohue, Henneberry, 1892).

18. Jerrell H. Shofner, "Mary Grace Quackenbos, A Visitor Florida Did Not Want," *Florida Historical Quarterly* 58 (January 1980): 273–90; Jerrell H. Shofner, "The Legacy of Racial Slavery: Free Enterprise and Forced Labor in Florida in the 1940s," *The Journal of Southern History* 47 (August 1981): 411–26.

19. Lillian Smith, *Killers of the Dream* (New York: W.W. Norton & Company 1961 [1949]), 29, 33.

20. J. Randall Stanley, *History of Jackson County* (Marianna: Jackson County Historical Society, 1950), 205.

21. Ortiz, *Emancipation Betrayed*, 128–41; John W. Cell, *The Highest Stage of White Supremacy: The Origins of Segregation in South Africa and the American South* (New York: Cambridge University Press, 1982).

22. John Hope Franklin, *From Slavery To Freedom: A History of Negro Americans* (New York: Alfred A. Knopf, 1974 [1947]), 164–87; Leon F. Litwack, *North of Slavery: The Negro in the Free States, 1790–1860* (Chicago: University of Chicago Press, 1961).

23. See David Roediger, *The Wages of Whiteness: Race and the Making of the American Working Class* (New York: Verso, 1991); Theodore W. Allen, *Racial Oppression and Social Control: The*

*Invention of the White Race* 2 vols. (London: Verso, 1994).

24. Ellen F. Wetherell, *Facts From Florida* (Lynn, Mass.: n.p., 1897), 27–30; see Harriette Beecher Stowe, *Palmetto Leaves* (Boston: J.R. Osgood, 1873); Oliver Martin Crosby, *Florida Facts Both Bright and Blue: A Guidebook* (New York: Oliver Martin Crosby, 1887). A Connecticut Yankee who founded the settlement that became Avon Park, Crosby denigrated African Americans and promoted white settlement in south Florida. Crosby, *Florida Facts*, 21–23, 125.

25. John Hope Franklin, "Keeping Tabs on Jim Crow," *New York Times Magazine* (April 23, 1995), http://www.nytimes.com/books/99/08/15/specials/franklin-95mag.html (accessed April 1, 2007); Darlene Clark Hine, "Black Professionals and Race Consciousness: Origins of the Civil Rights Movement, 1890–1950," *The Journal of American History* 89 (March 2003): 1280. For an argument stressing continuities between slavery and post-emancipation labor systems, see Frederick Cooper, *From Slaves to Squatters: Plantation Labor and Agriculture in Zanzibar and Coastal Kenya, 1890–1925* (New Haven: Yale University Press, 1980).

26. Pepper noted that his support of civil rights chagrined power brokers in Florida, and stated, "One of the campaign finance people of Smathers, who defeated me in '50, told me that he personally received $700,000 from the Republicans in the North, that they sent down to Florida to use against me, because I was a friend of labor." Claude Pepper, interview by Jack Bass and Walter De Vries, February 1, 1974, Interview A-0056, Southern Oral History Program, University of North Carolina, Chapel Hill.

27. U.S. Department of Labor Employment Standards, Administration Wage and Hour Division, "State Right-to-Work Laws and Constitutional Amendments in Effect as of January 1, 2007 With Year of Passage," *http://www.dol.gov/esa/programs/whd/state/righttowork.htm* (accessed January 20, 2007). In 1944, Florida became the first state in the nation to pass a "right-to-work" law.

28. See Jane Landers, "Gracia Real de Santa Teresa de Mose: A Free Black Town in Spanish Colonial Florida," *American Historical Review* 95 (Feb. 1990), 9–30; Larry Eugene Rivers, *Slavery in Florida: Territorial Days to Emancipation* (Gainesville: University Press of Florida, 2000), 189–209; Peter H. Wood, *Black Majority: Negroes in Colonial South Carolina From 1670 Through the Stono Rebellion* (New York: Alfred A. Knopf, 1974), 23; Claudio Saunt, "'The English Has Now a Mind To Make Slaves Of Them All': Creeks, Seminoles and the Problem of Slavery," *The American Indian Quarterly* 22 (Winter-Spring 1998): 157; Kenneth Wiggins Porter, *The Black Seminoles: History of a Freedom-Seeking People*, ed. Alcione M. Amos and Thomas P. Senter, (Gainesville: University Press of Florida, 1996); Cantor Brown, "Race Relations in Territorial Florida, 1821–1845," *Florida Historical Quarterly* 73 (1995): 287–307.

29. I am indebted to the great-grandson of the Rev. Albert Sidney James Allen, Alonzo Felder, for correcting the details of this episode that originally appears in *Emancipation Betrayed* (112–13). This story relies in part on new historical documents found on Felder's family web site, including Methodist Church records as well as the "Negro Preacher Killed Near Alachua," *Florida Times-Union* (Jacksonville), April 23, 1904, http://www.duke.edu/~felde001/family/ (accessed April 2, 2007); see "Shaw Not Guilty Said Grand Jury," *Daily Sun* (Gainesville), October 12, 1905.

30. Ortiz, *Emancipation Betrayed*, 70–84; 101–41; Russ Rymer, *American Beach: A Saga of Race, Wealth and Memory* (New York: Harper Collins Publishers, 1998), 123.

31. Cited in Ortiz, *Emancipation Betrayed*, 160–61.

32. Ortiz, *Emancipation Betrayed*, 234–35.

33. Ortiz, *Emancipation Betrayed*, 223–28.

34. See Andrew Kersten, *A. Philip Randolph: A Life in the Vanguard* (Lanham: Rowman & Littlefield, 2007); Paula F. Pfeffer, *A. Philip Randolph: Pioneer of the Civil Rights Movement* (Baton Rouge: Louisiana State University Press, 1990); Jervis Anderson, *The Meaning of Our Numbers* (New York, Harcourt Brace Jovanovich, 1972).

35. *Smith c. Allwright*, 321 U.S. 649 (1944); see Steven F. Lawson, "The View from the Nation," in Steven F. Lawson and Charles Payne, *Debating the Civil Rights Movement, 1945–1968* (Lanham: Rowman & Littlefield, Inc., 1998), 6.

36. Martin A. Dyckman, *Floridian of His Century: The Courage of Governor LeRoy Collins* (Gainesville: University Press of Florida, 2006), 198.

37. Dyckman, *Floridian of His Century*, 2.

38. Cornelius Speed, interview by author, Leon County, Fla., July 27, 1994, "Behind the Veil: Documenting African American Life in the Jim Crow South," Center for Documentary Studies at Duke University, Special Collections Library, Duke University.

39. "Fifty Years in Coming: Our Apology," *Tallahassee Democrat*, May 21, 2006.

40. On Hodges, see William H. Chafe, *Civilities and Civil Rights: Greensboro, North Carolina and the Black Struggle for Freedom* (New York: Oxford University Press, 1980), 49–61.

41. Chafe, *Civilities and Civil Rights*, 53–55.

42. C. Vann Woodward, *The Strange Career of Jim Crow* (New York: Oxford University Press, 1974 [1955]), 162.

43. James Kilpatrick, "A Conservative Prophecy: Peace Below, Tumult Above," in *The South Today*, ed. Willie Morris (New York: Harper & Row, 1965), 87.

44. See Abel A. Bartley, *Keeping the Faith: Race, Politics, and Social Development in Jacksonville, Florida, 1940–1970* (Westport, Conn.: Greenwood, 2000), xv-xvii, 1–24. For pertinent discussions of intergenerational linkages between African American activists, see Charles M. Payne, *I've Got the Light of Freedom: The Organizing Tradition and the Mississippi Freedom Struggle* (Berkeley: University of California Press, 1995); John Dittmer, *Local People: The Struggle for Civil Rights in Mississippi* (Urbana: University of Illinois Press, 1994); William H. Chafe, Raymond Gavins, Robert Korstad, Paul Ortiz, Robert Parrish, Jennifer Ritterhouse, Keisha Roberts, and Nicole Waligora-Davis, *Remembering Jim Crow: African Americans Tell About Life in the Segregated South* (New York: New Press, 2001).

45. Adam Fairclough analyzes this critical question in "The Costs of Brown: Black Teachers and School Integration," *The Journal of American History* 91 (June 2004): 43–53.

46. See, for example, Barbara Ransby, *Ella Baker and the Black Freedom Movement: A Radical Democratic Vision* (Chapel Hill: University of North Carolina Press, 2003); Charles Payne and

Adam Green, eds., *Time Longer Than Rope: A Century of African American Activism* (New York: New York University Press, 2003); Jeanne Theoharis and Komozi Woodard, eds., *Groundwork: Local Black Freedom Movements in America* (New York: New York University Press, 2005).

47. For discussions of the impact of the Cold War on civil rights tactics and ideas, see Carol Anderson, *Eyes Off The Prize: The United Nations and the African American Struggle for Human Rights, 1944–1955* (New York: Cambridge University Press, 2003); Mary L. Dudziak, *Cold War Civil Rights: Race and the Image of American Democracy* (Princeton: Princeton University Press, 2000).

48. Charles Payne, "The View from the Trenches," in *Debating the Civil Rights Movement*, 124.

49. For treatments of the intersection between labor struggles and civil rights organizing, see Robert H. Zieger, ed., *Southern Labor In Transition, 1940–1995* (Knoxville: University of Tennessee Press, 1997); Michael Honey, *Southern Labor And Black Civil Rights: Organizing Memphis Workers* (Chicago: University of Illinois Press, 1993); Robert Rodgers Korstad, *Civil Rights Unionism: Tobacco Workers and the Struggle for Democracy in the Mid-Twentieth-Century South* (Chapel Hill: University of North Carolina Press, 2003).

50. Ransby, *Ella Baker and the Black Freedom Movement*.

51. Vincent Harding, *There is a River: The Black Struggle For Freedom in America* (New York: Harcourt Brace Jovanovich, 1981).

52. Stetson Kennedy, *The Jim Crow Guide: The Way It Was* (Boca Raton: Florida Atlantic University Press, 1990), 177.

53. Martín Espada, *Zapata's Disciple* (Cambridge, Mass.: South End Press), 26; Rebecca Scott, *Degrees of Freedom: Louisiana and Cuba after Slavery* (Cambridge, Mass.: Belknap Press of Harvard University Press, 2005).

54. "Study Labeled Roanoke Most Segregated City," *Roanoke Times*, March 12, 1997; "South Gets to Boast for a Change," *Raleigh News and Observer*, February 9, 1997; "City Ranks High For Segregation," *Sarasota Herald-Tribune*, January 29, 1997.

55. "Slavery? In Florida? In 2003? Yes," *Palm Beach Post*, March 30, 2003; "For Pickers, Slavery Tastes Like Tomatoes," *Palm Beach Post*, February 25, 2004; "Modern-Day Slavery Alive and Well in Florida." CNN.COM, http://us.cnn.com/2004/US/South/02/25/human.trafficking.ap/ (accessed May 1, 2007).

56. "Asthma in Duval a 'Local Epidemic'; Racial Gap," *Florida Times-Union*, February 8, 2008; "Just Breathing Can Be a Problem in Some Poor Neighborhoods," *Florida Times-Union*, February 13, 2008.

57. U.S. Commission on Civil Rights, Voting Irregularities in Florida During the 2000 Presidential Election (Washington, D.C.: Government Printing Office, 2001). For a broader analysis of the erosion of voting rights over the past two decades, see J. Morgan Kousser, *Colorblind Injustice: Minority Voting Rights and the Undoing of the Second Reconstruction* (Chapel Hill: University of North Carolina Press, 1999).

58. The Mexican American Legal Defense and Educational Fund, Diminished Voting Power in the Latino Community: The Impact of Felony Disenfranchisement Laws in Ten Targeted States

(Los Angeles: MALDEF, 2003); Angela Behrens and Christopher Uggen, "Ballot Manipulation and the 'Menace of Negro Domination': Racial Threat and Felon Disenfranchisement in the United States, 1850–2002," *American Journal of Sociology* 109 (November 2003): 559–605.

# CONTRIBUTORS

ABEL A. BARTLEY, a native of Jacksonville, Florida, is the past director of African American Studies at the University of Akron and present director of Pan-African Studies at Clemson University. Among his many studies on the racial heritage of Florida is *Keeping the Faith: Race, Politics, and Social Development in Jacksonville, Florida, 1940–1970.*

GREGORY W. BUSH is associate professor of history at the University of Miami and director of the university's Institute for Public History. He is a leading compiler of oral history in Florida and has published numerous articles and chapters on public/environmental history and the changing facets of African American history in the Sunshine State.

MARVIN DUNN, a specialist on the African American experience in Florida, recently retired from Florida International University. Dunn is the author of a number of works on blacks in Florida and Miami, including *Black Miami in the Twentieth Century.*

LEONARD R. LEMPEL is a professor of history at Daytona Beach State College and a director of the Florida Historical Society. Prior to joining DBSC, Lempel served as a professor of history at Bethune-Cookman College in Daytona Beach. He has authored a number of studies of blacks in Florida, including the well-received "'The Mayor's Henchmen and Henchwomen, Both White and Colored': Edward H. Armstrong and the Politics of Race in Daytona Beach, 1900–1940," in the *Florida Historical Quarterly.*

CONNIE L. LESTER is associate professor of history at the University of Central Florida and editor of the *Florida Historical Quarterly*. Lester has authored *Up from the Mudsills of Hell: The Farmers' Alliance, Populism, and Progressive Agriculture in Tennessee, 1870–1915*, and number of articles on the black agrarian experience in the United States.

PAUL ORTIZ is director of the Samuel Proctor Oral History Program and an associate professor of history at the University of Florida. Ortiz completed his doctorate under William H. Chafe at Duke University and has published numerous works on racial history and the Florida experience, such as his award-winning *Emancipation Betrayed: The Hidden History of Black Organizing and White Violence in Florida from Reconstruction to the Bloody Election of 1920*.

AMY SASSCER graduated from Stetson University with honors and is currently a third-year student at the University of Florida Levin College of Law. While at Stetson, Sasscer completed her honors thesis on legal aspects of the modern civil rights movement in Florida.

LISE M. STEINHAUER focuses on the oral recording, researching, and writing of the history of Florida through her business, History Speaks. She is currently earning a graduate degree at Florida Atlantic University.

IRVIN D. S. WINSBORO is professor of history, African American studies, and Southwest Florida studies at Florida Gulf Coast University. Previously, he taught in the history program of the University of South Florida at Fort Myers. He is the author of *Feminism and Black Activism in Contemporary America: An Ideological Assessment*, and author or editor of six books, nine chapters, and over fifty articles.

# INDEX